REVITALIZATIONS

AND

MAZEWAYS

REVITALIZATIONS

AND

Mazeways

Essays on Culture Change, Volume 1

ANTHONY F. C. WALLACE

EDITED BY

Robert S. Grumet

University of Nebraska Press
Lincoln and London

Acknowledgments for the use of previously published material appear on pages 325–26, which constitute an extension of the copyright page.

∞

Library of Congress Cataloging-in-Publication Data

Wallace, Anthony F. C., 1923–
Revitalizations and mazeways: essays on culture change
/ Anthony F. C. Wallace ; edited by Robert S. Grumet.
p.   cm.
Includes bibliographic references and index.
ISBN 0-8032-4792-3 (cloth : alk. paper)—ISBN 0-8032-9836-6 (pbk. : alk. paper).
1. Social change. 2. Nativistic movements. 3. Personality
and culture. I. Grumet, Robert Steven. II. Title.
GN358 .W35 2003
303.4—dc21   2003004579

Contents

Foreword

ROBERT S. GRUMET

By almost any measure, Anthony F. C. Wallace ranks among the most influential anthropologists of the past half century. Colleagues routinely use this expression and other superlatives such as innovative, authoritative, insightful, provocative, and brilliant to describe his contributions.[1] Others characterize his best-known studies—meticulously documented analyses of innovation among the Iroquois, Rockdale textile mill owners and workers, and St. Clair anthracite miners—as landmarks, classics, models, or exemplars.[2] And, like any influential figure, Wallace also has come in for his share of criticism, variously taken to task for alleged nomenclatural, ideological, or methodological infelicities.[3]

Wallace's numbers are equally impressive. His "Revitalization Movements" (Wallace 1956) ranks among the most frequently cited anthropological articles in several major scholarly citation indexes.[4] A somewhat less authoritative survey of my personal bookshelves reveals that 77 of 79 book-length studies in Iroquois ethnohistory published since 1970 cite his *Death and Rebirth of the Seneca* (Wallace 1970b). A recent search on my Internet browser for Web sites mentioning his name resulted in more than nine hundred hits. To put this into perspective, cultural icons like Margaret Mead and Claude Lévi-Strauss generate thousands of listings; searches for other anthropologists rarely bring up more than a few dozen.

Scholars in fields as diverse as history, psychology, and religion, as well as anthropology, claim Wallace as one of their own. Many further regard him as an elder, lauding him as a founding father of ethnohistory, disaster studies, the history of technology, Iroquois studies, and modern psychological anthropology. His texts in the fields of culture and personality (Wallace 1961; revised 1970) and religion (Wallace 1966) continue to be regarded as standard sourcebooks. He is remembered as an able administrator, serving most prominently as a research director at Eastern Pennsylvania Psychiatric Institute (1958–1961),

as professor and chair of the University of Pennsylvania's Department of Anthropology (1961–1988), and as president of the American Anthropological
Association (1971). He has received numerous honors and awards, most notably the prestigious Bancroft Prize in American History (in 1979 for *Rockdale*
and for which he was the first and, thus far, only anthropologist to be so
honored).

Perhaps his most lasting legacy lies in his vision of culture as an organizer
of diversity rather than as a replication of uniformity. To best appreciate its
revolutionary nature, one must understand the context within which Wallace
developed this insight. Wallace came of age at a time when uniformitarian
and generalizing principles were on the ascendency in anthropology. Anthropologists studied their subjects through the lenses of grand explanatory theories. Culture was variously seen as a unitary phenomenon spreading from
originating places (a central tenet of Fritz Graebner's diffusionism), a reflection of human mental architecture (as in Freudian psychology and various
structuralisms of Émile Durkheim, A. R. Radcliffe-Brown, and Claude Lévi-
Strauss), or of quasi-organic processes in general (as in the functionalism of
Bronislaw Malinowski and his followers). Departures from patterns in these
normative paradigms generally were interpreted as deviant, abnormal, and in
many cases, needful of cure, castigation, or something more drastic.

Largely abandoning the cultural historicism of such founders of the discipline as Sir James Frazer and Franz Boas, anthropologists sought what they
regarded as uncontacted cultures to serve as pristine social laboratories capable of testing new theories. History and historical change were considered
insignificant, unimportant, or, worse, contaminants of pure cultures. Those
who paid attention to history were deplored as particularists ignorant of the
"big picture," armchair dilettantes, or dotty antiquarians.

Anthropology was not alone in this fascination with normative, timeless grand theory. Spurred on by turmoil caused by world wars, a worldwide boom-bust economy, nation-state expansion and collapse, the demise of
classical colonialism and the rise of neocolonial regimes, skyrocketing world
population, and, after the close of World War II, the threats of nuclear annihilation, resurgent epidemic afflictions, and ecological catastrophe, behavioral scientists joined natural scientists in the search for even grander unified
theories capable of freeing mankind from the shackles of geography, time,
culture, and biology itself. Science grew big as big government enlisted scholars to find big solutions for big problems. Scientists searched for regularities
and uniform patterns to develop lawlike generalities considered necessary to

understand (and, it was hoped, increase) human ability to mold and master a dangerously uncertain world.

Born in Toronto in 1923, Wallace first developed his interest in science as a teenager helping his father, noted historian, folklorist, and Lebanon Valley College English professor and department head Paul A. W. Wallace with his research on the history and culture of the Delaware and Iroquois Indians of his adopted state of Pennsylvania.[5] Initially drawn to the study of physics, contact with his father's Iroquois friends in upstate New York and with researchers at places like the Historical Society of Pennsylvania fired his interest in ethnology and history. He carried this interest into combat, where he served as a radioman in the 14th Armored Division during its advance into Germany from southern France between 1944 and 1945. In one of my favorite images of him as a young man, he sits huddled alongside the protecting armor of his half-track somewhere along the Franco-German frontier during a lull in the fighting poring over a dog-eared copy of an abridged edition of Sir James Frazer's *The Golden Bough* brought from home.

After the war, Wallace enrolled at the University of Pennsylvania. There he studied anthropology under Frank G. Speck and A. Irving "Pete" Hallowell. Speck supported his interest in Indians and ethnohistory, supervising a master's degree thesis project on the Delaware leader Teedyuscung.[6] Deeply involved in studies of Ojibwa culture and personality, Hallowell encouraged a growing interest in cognition and the workings of the human mind. Prescribing rigorous classes in psychology, cognition, and psychometry as well as the standard course of study in ethnography and ethnology, Hallowell dispatched Wallace to his father's old haunts in upstate New York to conduct doctoral fieldwork among the Tuscarora people. There Wallace administered Rorschach tests to 70 reservation residents (36 male and 34 female; a sample of nearly one-fifth of the community's entire adult population) during the summers of 1948 and 1949. Expecting to find a majority conforming to a standard modal Tuscarora personality type, he instead discovered that only 26 people, or 37 percent of the sample, conformed to the mode. Another 27 percent clustered nearby, and 40 percent fit neither category.[7] Reviewing a sample of 102 Rorschach protocols collected by Hallowell among the Ojibwas for comparison, Wallace found only 28 percent conforming to the modal Ojibwa personality type.

The result confirmed Wallace's growing awareness that culture was best viewed as providing a diverse range of choices to individuals rather than a single set of rules to which all members must conform. And rather than being a mere antiquarian exercise, charting of change over time instead became the surest way to discover the fullest variety of cultural choices available to individuals and to better understand how people respond to changes in those choices. Wallace has since devoted a lifetime to tracing the ways people organize complexity through a diverse variety of methods, epochs, and settings.

The pages that follow reveal how Wallace has deployed a diverse array of methodological techniques ranging from traditional fieldwork, participant observation, laboratory experimentation, and archival ethnohistory to achieve new insights into culture and the ways people cope with revolutionary developments and sudden change. In the course of these studies, he has sought deeper understandings of life in the 18th-century Northeastern Woodlands of North America; 19th-century mill and mining towns; and in the experiences of late-20th-century people in places such as the upstate New York Tuscarora Reservation; tornado-ravaged Worcester, Massachusetts; the Thule District of Greenland; and the wards of the Eastern Pennsylvania Psychiatric Institute.

The sections of this book contain key examples of Wallace's contributions to studies of culture, change, and personality. Wallace introduces each section with an account detailing how and why he became interested in these study areas. The first section presents seven studies exploring broad processes and particular aspects of culture change written between 1956 and 1983. The section begins with "Revitalization Movements" (Wallace 1956), already noted as his best-known and most widely cited study. In it, he presents a multistage cross-cultural model orchestrating physiological, cultural, and psychological factors involved in the destabilization, reformulation, and revitalization of religious movements in particular and culture change in general. Since its publication, scholars have invoked the revitalization paradigm to explain phenomena as varied as the American Health Food Movement, the Religious Right, Oldtime Fiddling Associations, the Heaven's Gate cult, Queer Religion, the renewal of anthropology as a scholarly discipline, and the rise, as crisis cults, of all organized religions.[8]

The next three articles present examples of Wallace's application of the revitalization movement model to more fully understand Iroquois and Delaware Indian culture change. These are followed by an important but apparently largely overlooked article using Thomas Kuhn's model of paradigmatic change in scientific revolutions (Kuhn 1970) to expand the concept of revitalization into a special case of paradigm development. Exploring the reasons why people adopt new paradigms, Wallace recommends a more nuanced approach seeking change in indirect subtle conjunctions of trivialities and seeming irrelevancies as well as in more widely recognized directly linked causal factors. The final articles in the section draw on case studies from the Aboriginal North America, Mozambique, Australia, 19th-century Pennsylvania, Renaissance Italy, and Victorian England to show how Kuhn's model can be used to explore the role of "cultural fit" in reasons why people accept, reject, or fight over potentially beneficial innovations.

The next section presents significant examples of Wallace's writings on culture and personality. The first of these re-prints the results of Wallace's seminal analysis of personal and community responses to the tornado that devastated the city of Worcester, Massachusetts, in 1952. Commissioned by the National Academy of Sciences–National Research Council to determine potential responses to a nuclear attack on an American city, Wallace interviewed survivors and rescuers to develop multistage models delineating processes of reaction and recovery from the effects of sudden catastrophe. Setting the pattern for time-space models that he would later use to explain revitalization and other phenomena, the Worcester study is today recognized as the first systematic anthropological analysis of the effects of a disaster on a human community (Oliver-Smith and Hoffman 1999).

The next articles describe how individual cognitive maps of self, otherness, and worldview—what Wallace calls a mazeway—disintegrate, resynthesize, and, in "The Psychic Unity of Human Groups," organize diversity. The final articles in the section examine aspects of mental disease and therapy. The first of these, a personal favorite entitled "Dreams and Wishes of the Soul," is an application of Freudian psychoanalytic theory to Iroquois dream-therapy and divination rites that sparked my first appreciation of the therapeutic efficacy of exotic cultural practices. Also included is a report of laboratory observation (coauthored with Raymond D. Fogelson) showing how recognition of the struggle over actual and perceived identities between schizophrenics and their families can be a crucial component of treatment and recovery. Another article in this section shows how a psychotic behavior, an Arctic hysteria known as *pibloktoq* in which the victim runs naked into the snow and collapses into a stupor, may actually be caused by a dietary deficiency of calcium. Disturbed by the suggestion that biological factors played a role in cultural behavior, Margaret Mead termed the calcium hypothesis a "dangerous hypothesis." Expanded to explain widespread occurrences of hysteria treated by Freud with psychoanalytic talking cures in calcium-deprived turn-of-the-century Vienna, the validity of the pibloktoq calcium-deprivation hypothesis was subsequently confirmed by field tests conducted in arctic Alaska (Foulks 1972).

The contributions published in this book and its companion represent some of the more prominent and intellectually innovative examples of a lifetime of research that is nowhere near completion. Absent from these pages are extracts from his recently published and critically acclaimed *Jefferson and the Indians* (Wallace 1999). And, as I write, he is putting the finishing touches on a major analysis of the diverse ways people in different cultures construct, use, and maintain maps of time (Wallace n.d.). As a gathering of his friends and colleagues affirmed at a recent meeting of the American Anthropological Association in Philadelphia, Anthony F. C. Wallace's life is truly a work in progress. Considering the amount of cultural diversity awaiting systematic analysis, it can also be said truly that there is no end in sight for the progress of his work.

NOTES

1. For "influential," see Stevens (1996:1095) and Wise (1975:21); for "innovative," see Spindler and Spindler (1959:40); for "authoritative," see Honigmann (1963:369); for "insightful," see Wolf (1994:224); for "provocative," see Lehmann and Myers (1985:3); and for "brilliant," see Harris (1968:461).

2. Key studies on the Iroquois include his study of Tuscarora modal personality (Wallace 1952) and *Death and Rebirth of the Seneca* (Wallace 1970b). *Rockdale* (Wallace 1978) and *St. Clair* (Wallace 1987) are his best-known studies on the social contexts of innovation during the industrial revolution. See Lessa and Vogt (1979:421) for "landmark"; for "classic," see Brusco 1996:1102), Casson (1983:445), and Kronenfeld (1996:55); sources citing Wallace's work as a model include Eslinger (1999) and Vlahos (1993); Brettell (1998:523), Goodenough (1996:293), Holzberg and Giovanni (1981:340), Marcus and Cushman (1982:63), McElroy and Townsend (1985:304), Murray (1986:265), and Nash (1999:174) cite particular sources as "examples."

3. Nicholas (1973:73–74) criticizes Wallace for ignoring what he regards as important ideological and political determinants in his formulation of revitalization movements; Durbin (1972:389) disagrees with Wallace and Atkins's (1960) contrast of cultural dimensions and values with such linguistic units as phonemes and allophones; Hoffmann (1969:70) lists what he considers methodological weakness in Wallace and Atkins's (1960) analysis of American kinship terminology. In this he is not unique; controversy continues to surround componential analysis of American kin-terms (see, for example, Hollan 2000).

4. Featured as citation classic of the week in the December 17, 1990, issue of *Current Contents* (Wallace 1990:22), the article was noted as cited in 270 major publications in the Social Science (SSCI) and Arts and Humanities (A&HCI) citation indexes.

5. The Wallace family moved to Pennsylvania in 1925. See Davis (1983) for a biographical sketch of Wallace's life. Proceedings of an interview with Wallace detail his career as an ethnohistorian (Grumet 1998).

6. Wallace completed his master's degree requirements in 1947. The thesis, entitled *King of the Delawares: Teedyuscung, 1700–1763,* became Wallace's first book, initially published in 1949 and reprinted by Syracuse University Press in 1990.

7. For a useful account assessing the strengths and weaknesses of Wallace's methodology at Tuscarora, see Price-Williams (1968:327–328).

8. For the American Health Food Movement, see Dubisch (1985:75); Hardisty (1997:3–4) for the Religious Right; Blaustein (1975) for post–World War II American Oldtime Fiddling Associations; Wessinger (2000) for Heaven's Gate and similar movements; Edsell (1998) for Queer Religion; and Clemmer (1974:219–221) for revitalization as a model for understanding Hopi culture change, modern Mohawk activism, and the renewal of anthropology itself. LaBarre (1972:253) recognizes Wallace as the first to suggest that all organized religions begin as revitalization crisis cults.

REFERENCES CITED

Blaustein, Richard. 1975. Traditional Music and Social Change: The Oldtime Fiddlers Association Movement in the United States. Unpublished Ph.D. dissertation. Indiana University, Bloomington.

Brettell, Caroline B. 1998. Fieldwork in the Archives: Methods and Sources in Historical Anthropology. In H. Russell Bernard, ed., *Handbook of Methods in Cultural Anthropology,* pp. 513–546. Walnut Creek CA: AltaMira Press.

Brusco, Elizabeth E. 1996. Religious Conversion. In David Levinson and Melvin Ember, eds., *Encyclopedia of Cultural Anthropology,* Vol. 4, pp. 1100–1104. New York: Henry Holt and Company.

Casson, Ronald W. 1983. Schemata in Cognitive Anthropology. In Bernard J. Siegel, Alan R. Beals, and Stephen A. Tyler, eds., *Annual Review of Anthropology 1983,* pp. 429–462. Stanford CA: Stanford University Press.

Clemmer, Richard O. 1974. Truth, Duty, and the Revitalization of Anthropologists: A New Perspective on Cultural Change and Resistance. In Dell Hymes, ed., *Reinventing Anthropology,* pp. 213–247. New York: Vintage Books.

Davis, Derek S. B. 1983. Studying Mankind Quietly. *Pennsylvania Gazette* 82(2):22–28.

Dubisch, Jill. 1985. You are What You Eat: Religious Aspects of the Health Food

Movement. In Arthur C. Lehmann and James E. Myers, eds., *Magic, Witchcraft, and Religion: An Anthropological Study of the Supernatural*, pp. 69–77. Palo Alto CA: Mayfield Publishing Company.

Durbin, Mridula Adenwala. 1972. Linguistic Models in Anthropology. In Bernard J. Siegel, Alan R. Beals, and Stephen A. Tyler, eds., *Annual Review of Anthropology 1972*, pp. 383–410. Stanford CA: Stanford University Press.

Edsell, Carolyn Lagomasino. 1998. Same Sex Marriage. *http://www.geocities.com/Wellesley/1374/front.html* [retrieved March 30, 1999].

Eslinger, Ellen. 1999. *Citizens of Zion: The Social Origins of Camp Meeting Revivalism.* Salt Lake City: University of Utah Press.

Foulks, Edward F. 1972. *The Arctic Hysterias of the North Alaskan Eskimo.* Anthropological Studies No. 10. Washington, D.C.: American Anthropological Association.

Goodenough, Ward H. 1996. Culture. In David Levinson and Melvin Ember, eds., *Encyclopedia of Cultural Anthropology*, Vol. 1, pp. 291–299. New York: Henry Holt and Company.

Grumet, Robert S. 1998. An Interview with Anthony F. C. Wallace. *Ethnohistory* 45(1):103–127.

Hardisty, Jean V. 1997. The Resurgent Right: Why Now? *The Public Eye Magazine.* *http://www.igc.org/pra/magazine/whynow.html* [retrieved April 13, 1999].

Harris, Marvin. 1968. *The Rise of Anthropological Theory: A History of Theories of Culture.* New York: Harper and Row.

Hoffman, Hans. 1969. Mathematical Anthropology. In Bernard J. Siegel, ed., *Biennial Review of Anthropology 1969*, pp. 41–79. Stanford CA: Stanford University Press.

Hollan, Douglas. 2000. Constructivist Models of Mind, Contemporary Psychoanalysis, and the Development of Culture Theory. *American Anthropologist* 102(3): 538–550.

Holzberg, Carol S., and Maureen J. Giovanni. 1981. Anthropology and Industry: Reappraisal and New Directions. In Bernard J. Siegel, Alan R. Beals, and Stephen A. Tyler, eds., *Annual Review of Anthropology 1981*, pp. 317–360. Stanford CA: Stanford University Press.

Honigmann, John J. 1963. *Understanding Culture.* New York: Harper and Row.

Kronenfeld, David K. 1996. *Plastic Glasses and Church Fathers: Semantic Extension from the Ethnoscience Tradition.* Oxford Studies in Anthropological Linguistics. New York: Oxford University Press.

Kuhn, Thomas S. 1970. *The Structure of Scientific Revolutions.* 2nd edition. Chicago: University of Chicago Press.

LaBarre, Weston. 1972. *The Ghost Dance: The Origins of Religion.* New York: Dell.

Lehmann, Arthur C., and James E. Myers, eds. 1985. *Magic, Witchcraft, and Religion:*

An Anthropological Study of the Supernatural. Palo Alto CA: Mayfield Publishing Company.

Lessa, William A., and Evon Z. Vogt, eds. 1979. *Reader in Comparative Religion.* 4th edition. New York: Harper and Row.

Marcus, George E., and Dick Cushman. 1982. Ethnographies as Texts. In Bernard J. Siegel, Alan R. Beals, and Stephen A. Tyler, eds., *Annual Review of Anthropology 1982,* pp. 25–69. Stanford CA: Stanford University Press.

McElroy, Ann, and Patricia K. Townsend. 1985. *Medical Anthropology in Ecological Perspective.* Boulder CO: Westview Press.

Murray, Stephen O. 1986. Edward Sapir in "The Chicago School" of Sociology. In William Cowan, Michael K. Foster, and Konrad Koerner, eds., *New Perspectives in Language, Culture, and Personality,* pp. 241–292. *Studies in the History of the Language Sciences,* Vol. 41. Philadelphia: John Benjamins Publishing Company.

Nash, Dennison. 1999. *A Little Anthropology.* 3rd edition. Upper Saddle River NJ: Prentice-Hall.

Nicholas, Ralph W. 1973. Social and Political Movements. In Bernard J. Siegel, Alan R. Beals, and Stephen A. Tyler, eds., *Annual Review of Anthropology 1973,* pp. 63–84. Stanford CA: Stanford University Press.

Oliver-Smith, Anthony, and Susanna M. Hoffman, eds. 1999. *The Angry Earth: Disaster in Anthropological Perspective.* New York: Routledge.

Price-Williams, Douglass R. 1968. Ethnopsychology II: Comparative Personality Processes. In James A. Clifton, ed., *Introduction to Cultural Anthropology: Essays in the Scope and Methods of the Science of Man,* pp. 317–335. Boston: Houghton Mifflin.

Spindler, Louise S., and George D. Spindler. 1959. Culture Change. In Bernard J. Siegel, ed., *Biennial Review of Anthropology 1959,* pp. 37–66. Stanford CA: Stanford University Press.

Stevens, Philip, Jr. 1996. Religion. In David Levinson and Melvin Ember, eds., *Encyclopedia of Cultural Anthropology,* Vol. 4, pp. 1089–1100. New York: Henry Holt and Company.

Vlahos, Olivia. 1993. Generic Male, Endangered Gender? *First Things* 30:15–23.

Wallace, Anthony F. C. 1952. *The Modal Personality Structure of the Tuscarora Indians, As Revealed by the Rorschach Test.* Bureau of American Ethnology Bulletin 150. Washington, D.C.: Smithsonian Institution.

———. 1956. Revitalization Movements. *American Anthropologist* 58(2):264–281.

———. 1961. *Culture and Personality.* New York: Random House.

———. 1966. *Religion: An Anthropological View.* New York: Random House.

———. 1970. *Death and Rebirth of the Seneca.* New York: Alfred A. Knopf.

———. 1978. *Rockdale: The Growth of an American Village in the Early Industrial Revolution*. New York: Alfred A. Knopf.

———. 1987. *St. Clair: A Nineteenth-Century Coal Town's Experience with a Disaster-Prone Industry*. New York: Alfred A. Knopf.

———. 1990. Recurrent Patterns in Social Movements. *Current Contents: Social and Behavioral Sciences* 22(51):22.

———. 1999. *Jefferson and the Indians: The Tragic Fate of the First Americans*. Cambridge: Harvard University Press.

———. n.d. *Living in Historical Time*. Cambridge: Harvard University Press [in preparation].

Wallace, Anthony F. C., and John Atkins. 1960. The Meaning of Kinship Terms. *American Anthropologist* 62(1):58–80.

Wessinger, Catherine. 2000. *How the Millennium Comes Violently: From Jonestown to Heaven's Gate*. New York: Seven Bridges Press.

Wise, Gene. 1975. Paradigm Dramas in American Studies: A Cultural and Institutional History of the Movement. Paper first read at the National American Studies Association Convention, San Antonio, Texas, November 8. Online at *http://www.wsrv.clas.Virginia.edu/-tsawyer/DRBR/wise.txt* [retrieved April 20, 1999].

Wolf, Eric R. 1994. Facing Power: Old Insights, New Questions. In Robert Borofsky, ed., *Assessing Cultural Anthropology*, pp. 218–228. New York: McGraw-Hill, Inc.

Preface

As I selected, arranged, and reflected on the writings assembled here, I first had the impression of an extraordinary variety of different topics and methods. But then I realized that there was a common theme, a view of human society not as a tableau of stable, orderly cultures, each dancing to its own tune, but as a scene of diversity, conflict, and change. Some of the change can be seen as relatively slow moving, evolutionary, the world a work in progress, although not necessarily following the measured mark of progress delineated by the early evolutionists; much change is more spasmodic, following the promptings of revitalization movements. The kind of vignettes of cultural systems, exquisitely tuned to click along like a fine watch, that ethnographers like to describe are only small islands of custom, temporarily floating on a stormy sea. Perhaps this view reflects the insight of someone who has lived through most of a century of the most violent, most turbulent, and most changeful times. But in any case, in this view the role of individuals and their motivations and perceptions are crucial for understanding how societies change and cultures develop.

The following collection is divided into sections, each introduced by a brief commentary by the author, unavoidably couched in autobiographical style, intending to explain some of the intellectual and political milieu of the period when the research was being done and the pieces were being written. I have made no effort to follow their fate at the hands of critics or admirers, nor will I pretend to assess their relevance and usefulness to a later generation.

Anthony F. C. Wallace

REVITALIZATIONS
AND
MAZEWAYS

PART 1

PROCESSES OF CULTURE CHANGE

After returning from military service and completing my undergraduate degree, I did graduate work in the anthropology department of the University of Pennsylvania, from 1947 to 1950. The department was then in the throes of the post–World War II academic expansion that was building up anthropology departments all over the country. At Penn, my earliest mentor was Frank G. Speck, a specialist in the cultures and history of Native Americans in the northeast quadrant of the continent. Speck had been a student of Boas and eschewed evolutionary schemata, but nevertheless his view was a deep historical one. When examining the Naskapi of Labrador, for instance, he saw them, down a long vista of time, as essentially an Upper Paleolithic people. The subtitle of his book *Naskapi* was *The Savage Hunters of the Labrador Peninsula,* and his account of their beliefs about the Keeper of the Game, a human figure mounted on a caribou that vanished into some mountain recess in the winter, brought to mind images of shamanic rituals in the caves at Lascaux and Altamira, thousands of years earlier. Speck's former student, A. I. Hallowell, whom he brought back from Northwestern University to the newly enlarged Penn department, had published in a similar vein a monograph on *Bear Ceremonialism in the Northern Hemisphere,* emphasizing the circumboreal distribution and vast antiquity of ritual deference to the bear, apparently having survived into recent times from the Upper Paleolithic and beyond, perhaps even from Neanderthal times. Loren Eiseley, another former student of Speck's, who also joined the department about this time, was an archaeologist and paleontologist then gestating the poetic nostalgias of *The Immense Journey,* which celebrated man's, and indeed all creation's, descent down the river of time.

But my interest in the question of the ultimate origins of Native American cultures was less compelling than issues in the fields of culture change and culture and personality, to which Hallowell was introducing a generation of my fellow students and me. These concerns encouraged me to undertake the biographical study of Native American leaders of the 18th century, records of some of whom I had encountered while traveling and working as a research assistant copying manuscripts longhand (there was no xerox then) for my father, the historian Paul A. W. Wallace. Using notes and copies collected before the war, while my father was doing the research for his biography of the Pennsylvania Indian agent Conrad Weiser, I wrote and published in 1949 a biography of the Delaware political leader Teedyuscung (reprinted by Syracuse University Press in 1990). After receiving my Ph.D. in 1950, I began to collect materials for another biography, this one of the Seneca prophet Handsome

Lake, of whom I had become aware before World War II during a visit with my father to the Iroquois reservation at Grand River, Ontario, in the course of his research on the League of the Iroquois.

The biographical approach was not new in anthropology but contemporary anthropologists were mostly interested in guiding living informants to provide autobiographical accounts that emphasized acculturation and its discontents. I planned to apply this sort of cultural analysis of the individual life to primary documentary, historical materials. (And my historical orientation was being simultaneously reinforced by doing research and testifying as an expert witness in land claims cases brought by Felix Cohen's Joint Efforts Group before the Indian Claims Commission, involving Native American land use in the Northeast and Midwest.) In the course of initial compilation of the Handsome Lake sources, I realized the need for a firmer theoretical structure than a mere chronology of the prophet's career as a reformer. The American Anthropological Association had only recently endorsed studies of "acculturation" and "nativistic movements"; the older Boasian tradition of longtime perspective and reconstruction of unadulterated precontact culture patterns, and the evolutionary schemata before it, had obstructed attention to the microdynamics of culture change. But Hallowell was a vigorous proponent of acculturation studies and this perspective had governed my treatment of Teedyuscung as a doomed culture-broker. Now, for the Handsome Lake study, the model of "nativistic movements" outlined by Ralph Linton in his famous 1943 paper in the *American Anthropologist* provided a theoretical starting point. But it was immediately obvious that Handsome Lake's proposals for social and religious reform were far less nativistic than Linton's examples, such as Wovoka and the 1890s Ghost Dance. The Ghost Dance had been studied in the field by the Smithsonian anthropologist (and Irish nationalist) James Mooney, shortly after the infamous massacre at Wounded Knee, and his monograph on the Ghost Dance movement of 1890, which was prefaced by a valuable collation of sketches of other nativistic movements, had become a classic (which I edited for republication by the University of Chicago Press in 1965). Handsome Lake, however, issued recommendations to adopt, rather than reject, many of the white man's ways. Other anthropologists too were discovering events of revolutionary cultural change in various parts of the world that did not easily conform to the nativistic model, for instance the Paliau movement in the Admiralty Islands then being studied by Margaret Mead and Penn student Theodore Schwartz. Mead learned of my work and visited me at Penn to discuss and compare our cases and I suggested that there ought to be a cargo cult type of movement going on in her area. When she went back into the field, she discovered that there had been in fact a secret cargo cult going on under their noses, unobserved, for at least eight months!

My effort to formulate a more general theory led to the paper "Revitalization Movements," published in the *American Anthropologist* in 1956 under the category "Acculturation," and reprinted in this volume. (I am indebted to my assistant, Sheila C. Steen, for suggesting the term.) Other papers followed on the same subject, but an ambitious project to write a global survey of revitalization movements never got beyond the collection of numerous cases. "Revitalization Movements" has proved to be my most widely read journal article, by 1990 having been cited in more than 270 publications, and reprinted a number of times. The book on Handsome Lake appeared as *The Death and Rebirth of the Seneca* in 1970, long after the theoretical papers, and the textbook *Religion: An Anthropological View,* were published.

Two of the other papers that grew out of the revitalization movement research are reproduced here, "New Religions among the Delaware Indians, 1600–1900," and "The Dekanawideh Myth Analyzed as the Record of a Revitalization Movement," published in 1956 and 1958 respectively. The Delaware paper does not explicitly invoke the revitalization model and includes the efforts of both Christian missionaries and native prophets; its principal thrust was to document the frequency of religious movements, both large and small, and some of them obscure, in a population suffering severe hardship in a deteriorating colonial situation. The Dekanawideh myth — the origin myth of the great Iroquois Confederacy — had been a staple topic for discussion among Iroquoianists for years. The paper itself was presented at one of the early Iroquois conferences at Red House, near the Allegany Seneca Reservation, that were organized by William Fenton, the dean of Iroquoian studies, and a local banker and capable ethnohistorian, Merle Deardorff. The formation of this League, arguably about 1450, as a political device for aborting internecine carnage resulting from endlessly reciprocating blood feuds, is an interesting example of a "neolithic"-level population attempting to limit the damage caused by warfare. It is debatable, however, how effective the League's administrative body, the Onondaga Council, was in controlling war and diplomacy with external tribes and with the encroaching French and British.

Subsequent to the appearance of the "Revitalization Movements" paper in 1956, I should mention that the anthropologist Luther Gerlach, assisted by Virginia Hines, began producing a series of very significant treatments of a complementary type of social movement, less focused and centralized than my revitalization movements, represented by such phenomena as Pentecostalism and Black Power. These movements, characterized by what Gerlach and Hines termed an "acephalous, reticulate" pattern of organization, are composed of many autonomous local cells, and adapt to different social niches by varying details of belief and ritual.

The last three papers, "Paradigmatic Processes in Culture Change," "Technology in Culture: The Meaning of Cultural Fit," and "Paradigms and Revolutions in the Arts," attempt to define the type of culture change characteristic of technology and art.

In the course of writing a historical study of Rockdale, a 19th century cotton manufacturing community experiencing the early Industrial Revolution, it became apparent that the course of technological change in cotton manufacturing—and in other technological domains—seemed to be best described by a model introduced by Thomas Kuhn in his *Structure of Scientific Revolutions,* denominated by him as "paradigmatic." The paradigm, in science, is a set of basic assumptions about some domain of nature, often demonstrable by a famous experiment that is replicable in the classroom. For a more or less extended period of time, scientific research works out the implications and applications of the conventional paradigm, until irreconcilable contradictions with experimental results are discovered that produce a crisis, to be resolved only by the formulation of a new paradigm. Efforts to restrict this model to the rarified intellectual atmosphere of pure science, and to exclude such grubby fields as technology and the capricious schools of fine art, would appear to be overly elitist. In a more catholic spirit, the anthropologist Alfred L. Kroeber had earlier adumbrated the concept of paradigmatic process in his erudite *Configurations of Culture Growth,* which perceived the same kind of internally guided course of development in culture areas over long periods of time, applying it to many domains of behavior.

The paper on the fitness of technology in culture considers the question of the social acceptance, ignoring, or rejection of inventions that appear to the outside observer to be eminently desirable. This paper was presented in 1985 to a faculty seminar at the University of Pennsylvania devoted to encouraging interdisciplinary studies of technology and society. And finally, the paper on paradigmatic processes in the arts looks at the work of the painter Raphael in the context of the growth of Renaissance art. It was read at a 1983 symposium at the University of Notre Dame celebrating the 500th anniversary of the artist's birth.

One of the intellectual problems associated with concepts such as "revitalization movements" and "paradigmatic processes" is indeed to define the optimum scope of their application. If one is a splitter by temperament, one tends to restrict the usage of such terms to a narrow range of phenomena; in the case of revitalization movements, for instance, to religious movements led by a visionary prophet in preliterate societies in colonial situations. To those of us who are lumpers, revitalization can occur in any society, large or small, industrial or preindustrial, be secular or religious, and be led by anyone from a charismatic prophet to a committee of atheistic politicians. Splitters would restrict paradigms to science; lumpers would generously lather the idea over technology, art, theology, and any other field that seems to qualify, under the rule, "If it walks like a duck, and quacks like a duck . . ." Another boundary problem concerns the entity to which reformers address themselves. When the whole society is explicitly intended as the target (as in my formulation), the label revitalization clearly applies. But what are we to call efforts to abruptly reform, or revive, merely an institution like a university or a telephone company, or other small component within the larger society, without pretension to wider goals? Here my own preference would be to recognize the possibility of a similarity of process but not to employ the term "revitalization," lest it be diluted by too liberal usage.

1

Revitalization Movements

Behavioral scientists have described many instances of attempted and sometimes successful innovation of whole cultural systems, or at least substantial portions of such systems. Various rubrics are employed, the rubric depending on the discipline and the theoretical orientation of the researcher, and on salient local characteristics of the cases he has chosen for study. "Nativistic movement," "reform movement," "cargo cult," "religious revival," "messianic movement," "utopian community," "sect formation," "mass movement," "social movement," "revolution," "charismatic movement," are some of the commonly used labels. This paper suggests that all these phenomena of major cultural-system innovation are characterized by a uniform process, for which I propose the term "revitalization." The body of the paper is devoted to two ends: (1) an introductory statement of the concept of revitalization, and (2) an outline of certain uniformly found processual dimensions of revitalization movements.

The formulations are based in major part on documentary data, mostly published. Library research on the project began in 1951 with a study of the new religion initiated by Handsome Lake, the Seneca prophet, among the nineteenth century reservation Iroquois. The Handsome Lake materials being unusually ample (a number of manuscript journals and diaries were found) provided a useful standard with which to compare the various other movements which have since been investigated. Our files now contain references to several hundred religious revitalization movements, among both western and nonwestern peoples, on five continents. These represent only a small portion, gathered in a quick preliminary survey of anthropological literature. An earnest attempt to collect all revitalization movements described in historical, anthropological, and other sorts of documents, would without question gather in thousands. Movements on which we have substantial data include: in North America, the Handsome Lake case (Seneca, 1799–1815), the Delaware

Prophet (associated with Pontiac, 1762–1765), the Shawnee Prophet (associated with Tecumseh, 1805–1814), the Ghost Dance (1888–1896), and Peyote; in Europe, John Wesley and early Methodism (1738–1800); in Africa, Ikhnaton's new religion (ancient Egypt), the Sudanese Mahdi (the Sudan, 1880–1898), and the Xhosa Revival (South Africa, 1856–1857); in Asia, the origin of Christianity, the origin of Mohammedanism (c610–650), the early development of Sikkhism (India, c1500–c1700), and the Taiping Rebellion (China, 1843–1864); in Melanesia, the Vailala Madness (New Guinea, c1919-c1930); in South America, a series of *terre sans mal* movements among the forest tribes, from early contact to recent times.[1]

Accordingly, the formulations presented here are in an intermediate stage: a species has been recognized and certain characteristics (selected, of course, in the light of the author's theoretical interests) described, after the fashion of natural history. More abstract descriptions, in terms of the interaction of analytic variables, can only be suggested here, and other papers will present details of the dynamics of the revitalization process.

THE CONCEPT OF REVITALIZATION

A revitalization movement is defined as a deliberate, organized, conscious effort by members of a society to construct a more satisfying culture. Revitalization is thus, from a cultural standpoint, a special kind of culture change phenomenon: the persons involved in the process of revitalization must perceive their culture, or some major areas of it, as a system (whether accurately or not); they must feel that this cultural system is unsatisfactory; and they must innovate not merely discrete items, but a new cultural system, specifying new relationships as well as, in some cases, new traits. The classic processes of culture change (evolution, drift, diffusion, historical change, acculturation) all produce changes in cultures as systems; however, they do not depend on deliberate intent by members of a society, but rather on a gradual chain-reaction effect: introducing A induces change in B; changing B affects C; when C shifts, A is modified; this involves D . . . and so on *ad infinitum*. This process continues for years, generations, centuries, millennia, and its pervasiveness has led many cultural theorists to regard culture change as essentially a slow, chain-like, self-contained procession of superorganic inevitabilities. In revitalization movements, however, A, B, C, D, E . . . N are shifted into a new *Gestalt* abruptly and simultaneously in intent; and frequently within a few years the new plan is put into effect by the participants in the movement.

We may note in passing that Keesing's assessment of the literature on culture change (1953), while it does not deal explicitly with the theoretical issue of chain-effects versus revitalization, discusses both types. Barnett (1953) frankly confines his discussion to innovations of limited scope in the context of chains of events in acceptance and rejection. As Mead has suggested, cultures *can* change within one generation (Mead 1955); and the process by which such transformations occur is the revitalization process.

The term "revitalization" implies an organismic analogy.[2] This analogy is, in fact, an integral part of the concept of revitalization. A human society is here regarded as a definite kind of organism, and its culture is conceived as those patterns of learned behavior which certain "parts" of the social organism or system (individual persons and groups of persons) characteristically display. A corollary of the organismic analogy is the principle of homeostasis: that a society will work, by means of coordinated actions (including "cultural" actions) by all or some of its parts, to preserve its own integrity by maintaining a minimally fluctuating, life-supporting matrix for its individual members, and will, under stress, take emergency measures to preserve the constancy of this matrix. Stress is defined as a condition in which some part, or the whole, of the social organism is threatened with more or less serious damage. The perception of stress, particularly of increasing stress, can be viewed as the common denominator of the panel of "drives" or "instincts" in every psychological theory.

As I am using the organismic analogy, the total system which constitutes a society includes as significant parts not only persons and groups with their respective patterns of behavior, but also literally the cells and organs of which the persons are composed. Indeed, one can argue that the system includes nonhuman as well as human subsystems. Stress on one level is stress on all levels. For example, lowering of sugar level (hunger) in the fluid matrix of the body cells of one group of persons in a society is a stress in the society as a whole. This holistic view of society as organism integrated from cell to nation depends on the assumption that society, as an organization of living matter, is definable as a network of intercommunication. Events on one subsystem level must affect other subsystems (cellular vis-à-vis institutional, personal vis-à-vis societal) at least as information; in this view, social organization exists to the degree that events in one subsystem are information to other subsystems.

There is one crucial difference between the principles of social organization and that of the individual person: a society's parts are very widely interchangeable, a person's only slightly so. The central nervous system cells, for example, perform many functions of coordinating information and executing adaptive action which other cells cannot do. A society, on the other hand, has a multiple-replacement capacity, such that many persons can perform the analogous information-coordination and executive functions on behalf of society-as-organism. Furthermore, that regularity of patterned behavior which we call culture depends relatively more on the ability of constituent units autonomously to perceive the system of which they are a part, to receive and transmit information, and to act in accordance with the necessities of the system, than on any all-embracing central administration which stimulates specialized parts to perform their function.

It is therefore functionally necessary for every person in society to maintain a mental image of the society and its culture, as well as of his own body and its behavioral regularities, in order to act in ways which reduce stress at all levels of the system. The person does, in fact, maintain such an image. This mental image I have called "the mazeway," since as a model of the cell-body-personality-nature-culture-society system or field, organized by the individual's own experience, it includes perceptions of both the maze of physical objects of the environment (internal and external, human and nonhuman) and also of the ways in which this maze can be manipulated by the self and others in order to minimize stress. The mazeway is nature, society, culture, personality, and body image, as seen by one person. Hallowell (1955a) and Wallace (1955 and 1956a) offer extended discussions of the mazeway and the related concepts of self, world view, and behavioral environment.

We may now see more clearly what "revitalization movements" revitalize. Whenever an individual who is under chronic, physiologically measurable stress, receives repeated information which indicates that his mazeway does not lead to action which reduces the level of stress, he must choose between maintaining his present mazeway and tolerating the stress, or changing the mazeway in an attempt to reduce the stress. Changing the mazeway involves changing the total *Gestalt* of his image of self, society, and culture, of nature and body, and of ways of action. It may also be necessary to make changes in the "real" system in order to bring mazeway and "reality" into congruence. The effort to work a change in mazeway and "real" system together so as to permit more effective stress reduction is the effort at revitalization; and the collaboration of a number of persons in such an effort is called a revitalization movement.

The term revitalization movement thus denotes a very large class of phenomena. Other terms are employed in the existing literature to denote what I would call subclasses, distinguished by a miscellany of criteria. "Nativistic movements," for example, are revitalization movements characterized by strong emphasis on the elimination of alien persons, customs, values, and/or materiel from the mazeway (Linton 1943). "Revivalistic" movements emphasize the institution of customs, values, and even aspects of nature which are thought to have been in the mazeway of previous generations but are not now present (Mooney 1896). "Cargo cults" emphasize the importation of alien values, customs, and materiel into the mazeway, these things being expected to arrive as a ship's cargo as for example in the Vailala Madness (Williams 1923, 1934). "Vitalistic movements" emphasize the importation of alien elements into the mazeway but do not necessarily invoke ship and cargo as the mechanism.[3] "Millenarian movements" emphasize mazeway transformation in an apocalyptic world transformation engineered by the supernatural. "Messianic movements" emphasize the participation of a divine savior in human flesh in the mazeway transformation (Wallis 1918, 1943). These and parallel terms do not denote mutually exclusive categories, for a given revitalization movement may be nativistic, millenarian, messianic, and revivalistic all at once; and it may (in fact, usually does) display ambivalence with respect to nativistic, revivalistic, and importation themes.

Revitalization movements are evidently not unusual phenomena, but are recurrent features in human history. Probably few men have lived who have not been involved in an instance of the revitalization process. They are, furthermore, of profound historical importance. Both Christianity and Mohammedanism, and possibly Buddhism as well, originated in revitalization movements. Most denominational and sectarian groups and orders budded or split off after failure to revitalize a traditional institution. One can ask whether a large proportion of religious phenomena have not originated in personality transformation dreams or visions characteristic of the revitalization process. Myths, legends, and rituals may be relics, either of the manifest content of vision-dreams or of the doctrines and history of revival and import cults, the circumstances of whose origin have been distorted and forgotten, and whose connection with dream states is now ignored. Myths in particular have long been noted to possess a dream-like quality, and have been more or less speculatively interpreted according to the principles of symptomatic dream interpretation. It is tempting to suggest that myths and, often, even legends, read like dreams because they *were* dreams when they were first told. It is tempting to argue further that culture heroes represent a condensation of the figures of the prophet and of the supernatural being of whom he dreamed.

In fact, it can be argued that all organized religions are relics of old revitalization movements, surviving in routinized form in stabilized cultures, and that religious phenomena per se originated (if it is permissible still in this day and age to talk about the "origins" of major elements of culture) in the revitalization process — i.e., in visions of a new way of life by individuals under extreme stress.

THE PROCESSUAL STRUCTURE

A basic methodological principle employed in this study is that of event analysis (Wallace 1953). This approach employs a method of controlled comparison for the study of processes involving longer or shorter diachronic sequences (vide Eggan 1954 and Steward 1953). It is postulated that events or happenings of various types have genotypical structures independent of local cultural differences; for example, that the sequence of happenings following a severe physical disaster in cities in Japan, the United States, and Germany, will display a uniform pattern, colored but not obscured by local differences in culture. These types of events may be called behavioral units. Their uniformity is based on generic human attributes, both physical and psychological, but it requires extensive analytical and comparative study to elucidate the structure of any one. Revitalization movements constitute such a behavioral unit, and so also, on a lower level of abstraction, do various subtypes within the larger class, such as cargo and revival cults. We are therefore concerned with describing the generic structure of revitalization movements considered as a behavioral unit, and also of variation along the dimensions characteristic of the type.

The structure of the revitalization process, in cases where the full course is run, consists of five somewhat overlapping stages: 1. Steady State; 2. Period of Individual Stress; 3. Period of Cultural Distortion; 4. Period of Revitalization (in which occur the functions of mazeway reformulation, communication, organization, adaptation, cultural transformation, and routinization), and finally, 5. New Steady State. These stages are described briefly in the following sections.

I. Steady State

For the vast majority of the population, culturally recognized techniques for satisfying needs operate with such efficiency that chronic stress within the system varies within tolerable limits. Some severe but still tolerable stress may remain general in the population, and a fairly constant incidence of persons under, for them, intolerable stress may employ "deviant" techniques (e.g., psychotics). Gradual modification or even rapid substitution of techniques for satisfying some needs may occur without disturbing the steady state, as long as (1) the techniques for satisfying other needs are not seriously interfered with, and (2) abandonment of a given technique for reducing one need in favor of a more efficient technique does not leave other needs, which the first technique was also instrumental in satisfying, without any prospect of satisfaction.

II. The Period of Increased Individual Stress

Over a number of years, individual members of a population (which may be "primitive" or "civilized," either a whole society or a class, caste, religious, occupational, acculturational, or other definable social group) experience increasingly severe stress as a result of the decreasing efficiency of certain stress-reduction techniques. The culture may remain essentially unchanged or it may undergo considerable changes, but in either case there is continuous diminution in its efficiency in satisfying needs. The agencies responsible for interference with the efficiency of a cultural system are various: climatic, floral, and faunal change; military defeat; political subordination; extreme pressure toward acculturation resulting in internal cultural conflict; economic distress; epidemics; and so on. The situation is often, but not necessarily, one of acculturation, and the acculturating agents may or may not be representatives of Western European cultures. While the individual can tolerate a moderate degree of increased stress and still maintain the habitual way of behavior, a point is reached at which some alternative way must be considered. Initial consideration of a substitute way is likely, however, to increase stress because it arouses anxiety over the possibility that the substitute way will be even less effective than the original, and that it may also actively interfere with the execution of other ways. In other words, it poses the threat of mazeway disintegration. Furthermore, admission that a major technique is worthless is extremely threatening because it implies that the whole mazeway system may be inadequate.

III. The Period of Cultural Distortion

The prolonged experience of stress, produced by failure of need satisfaction techniques and by anxiety over the prospect of changing behavior patterns, is responded to differently by different people. Rigid persons apparently prefer to tolerate high levels of chronic stress rather than make systematic adaptive changes in the mazeway. More flexible persons try out various limited mazeway changes in their personal lives, attempting to reduce stress by addition or substitution of mazeway elements with more or less concern for the *Gestalt* of the system. Some persons turn to psychodynamically regressive innovations; the regressive response empirically exhibits itself in increasing incidences of such things as alcoholism, extreme passivity and indolence, the development of highly ambivalent dependency relationships, intragroup violence, disregard of kinship and sexual mores, irresponsibility in public officials, states of depression and self-reproach, and probably a variety of psychosomatic and neurotic disorders. Some of these regressive action systems become, in effect, new cultural patterns.

In this phase, the culture is internally distorted; the elements are not harmoniously related but are mutually inconsistent and interfering. For this reason alone, stress continues to rise. "Regressive" behavior, as defined by the society, will arouse considerable guilt and hence increase stress level or at least maintain it at a high point; and the general process of piecemeal cultural substitution will multiply situations of mutual conflict and misunderstanding, which in turn increase stress-level again.

Finally, as the inadequacy of existing ways of acting to reduce stress becomes more and more evident, and as the internal incongruities of the mazeway are perceived, symptoms of anxiety over the loss of a meaningful way of life also become evident: disillusionment with the mazeway, and apathy toward problems of adaptation, set in.

IV. The Period of Revitalization

This process of deterioration can, if not checked, lead to the death of the society. Population may fall even to the point of extinction as a result of increasing death rates and decreasing birth rates; the society may be defeated in war, invaded, its population dispersed and its customs suppressed; factional disputes may nibble away areas and segments of the population. But these dire events are not infrequently forestalled, or at least postponed, by a revitalization movement. Many such movements are religious in character, and such religious revitalization movements must perform at least six major tasks:

1. *Mazeway reformulation.* Whether the movement is religious or secular, the reformulation of the mazeway generally seems to depend on a restructuring of elements and subsystems which have already attained currency in the

society and may even be in use, and which are known to the person who is to become the prophet or leader. The occasion of their combination in a form which constitutes an internally consistent structure, and of their acceptance by the prophet as a guide to action, is abrupt and dramatic, usually occurring as a moment of insight, a brief period of realization of relationships and opportunities. These moments are often called inspiration or revelation. The reformulation also seems normally to occur in its initial form in the mind of a single person rather than to grow directly out of group deliberations.

With a few exceptions, every religious revitalization movement with which I am acquainted has been originally conceived in one or several hallucinatory visions by a single individual. A supernatural being appears to the prophet-to-be, explains his own and his society's troubles as being entirely or partly a result of the violation of certain rules, and promises individual and social revitalization if the injunctions are followed and the rituals practiced, but personal and social catastrophe if they are not. These dreams express: 1. the dreamer's wish for a satisfying parental figure (the supernatural, guardian-spirit content), 2. world-destruction fantasies (the apocalyptic, millennial content), 3. feelings of guilt and anxiety (the moral content), and 4. longings for the establishment of an ideal state of stable and satisfying human and supernatural relations (the restitution fantasy or Utopian content). In a sense, such a dream also functions almost as a funeral ritual: the "dead" way of life is recognized as dead; interest shifts to a god, the community, and a new way. A new mazeway *Gestalt* is presented, with more or less innovation in details of content. The prophet feels a need to tell others of his experience, and may have definite feelings of missionary or messianic obligation. Generally he shows evidence of a radical inner change in personality soon after the vision experience: a remission of old and chronic physical complaints, a more active and purposeful way of life, greater confidence in interpersonal relations, the dropping of deep-seated habits like alcoholism. Hence we may call these visions "personality transformation dreams." Where there is no vision (as with John Wesley), there occurs a similarly brief and dramatic moment of insight, revelation, or inspiration, which functions in most respects like the vision in being the occasion of a new synthesis of values and meanings.

My initial approach to the understanding of these visions was by way of psychoanalytic dream theory. This proved to be of some use in elucidating the meaning of the vision. From an analysis of its manifest content and from the circumstances of the dreamer's history and life situation, it is possible to make more or less plausible interpretations of the nature of the prophet's personal preoccupations and conflicts. But conventional dream theory was designed to explain the conflicts represented in ordinary night dreams. Prophetic visions, while essentially dream formations, differ in several respects from ordinary symptomatic dreams: they often occur during a waking state as hallucinatory experiences, or in an ecstatic trance rather than in normal sleep; they impress the dreamer immediately as being meaningful and important; the manifest content is often in large part rational and well considered intellectual argument and cogent moral exhortation; and recollection of them is in unusually rich detail. This brings to mind Fromm's position (1951), that many dreams are not so much symptomatic of unconscious neurotic conflict as insightful in a positive and creative sense. But this additional consideration did not seem adequately to account for the most remarkable feature of all: the transformation of personality, often in a positive therapeutic sense, which these dreams produced. Prophetic and ecstatic visions do express unconscious conflict; they sometimes reveal considerable insight, but they also work startling cures.

We therefore became interested in pursuing the dynamics of personality transformation dreams. As a type of event, they would seem to belong to a general clinical category of sudden and radical changes in personality, along with transformations occurring in psychotic breaks, spontaneous remissions, narcosynthesis, some occasions in psychotherapy, "brainwashing," and shock treatments. There are, incidentally, some interesting similarities between the physical state of prophets and converts in the vision-trance, and patients undergoing shock (Sargant 1949, 1951). Physical stress and exhaustion often seem to precede the vision-trance type of transformation, and it seems probable that chemical substances produced in the body under stress may be important in rendering a person capable of this type of experience (Hoffer, Osmond, and Smythies, 1954). The relationship of this sort of sudden personality change to slower maturational processes, on the one hand, and to what happens in rites of passage, on the other, should be points of interest to social scientists generally.

Nonclinical analogues of the prophet's personality transformation vision appear in several contexts: in accounts of individual ecstatic conversions and experiences of religious enthusiasm; in the guardian spirit quest among American Indians and elsewhere; and in the process of becoming a shaman, which is similar in many cultures all over the world. Conversion, shamanism, and the guardian-spirit vision seem to be phenomena very similar in pattern. All three of these processes are distributed globally; in many cultures all three are normal phenomena; all involve persons who are faced with the opportunity (if not necessity) of assuming a new cultural role and of abandoning an earlier role in order to reduce stress which they will not be able to resolve if they stand pat. A precipitating factor in many cases is some sort of severe physical stress, such as illness, starvation, sleeplessness, or fatigue. After the vision experience, the individual is often able to assume a new role requiring increased or differently phrased emotional independence. In the vision experience, he has invented a fictitious, nurturing, parent-like supernatural figure who satisfies much of his need for authority and protection; thus he is presumably able to loosen emotional ties to certain cultural objects, roles, and persons, and to act without undue inhibition and anxiety. Inconvenient wishes are displaced onto a fictitious but culturally sanctioned supernatural pseudo-community, leaving the personality free for relatively healthy relationships to the real world. An essential function of the vision is that the demands for energy made by transference wishes are minimized by displacement onto supernatural objects which can in fantasy be perceived as uniformly supporting and protective.

Inasmuch as many prophets were suffering from recognizable and admitted mental disorders before their transformation, which they achieved by means of a type of experience (hallucination) that our culture generally regards as pathological, the relevance of psychopathology to the vision experience needs to be explored. We have under way some observations on the case histories of a series of persons in a state mental institution who have been known to attendants for their excessive religiosity.[4] This survey, which we hope to extend to include interview materials, is not complete, but I can summarize our initial impressions. Chronic schizophrenics with religious paranoia tend to believe that they are God, Jesus, the Virgin Mary, the Great Earth Mother, or some other supernatural being. Successful prophets, on the other hand, usually do not believe that they are the supernatural, only that they have communicated with him (although their followers may freely deify them). Prophets do not lose their sense of personal identity but psychotics tend to become the object of their spiritual longing.

There are in this institution several persons who were hospitalized during the course of an experience which resembles in many respects the process of becoming a prophet. A man, burdened with a sense of guilt and inadequacy, and sensible of the need to reform his life, has a religious conversion in which he sees God or hears his voice; thereafter he displays a changed and in some ways healthier (or at least less rapidly deteriorating) personality; he undertakes an evangelistic or prophetic enterprise which is socially inconvenient to spouse, relatives, employer, warden, or other closely associated persons; he is thereupon certified as insane and hospitalized. Such frustrated prophets, being unable any longer to satisfy important human needs and suffering the obvious disapproval of the community, may also lose confidence in their relationship to the supernatural pseudo-community. They cannot return to their preconversion state because the hospital situation makes anything remotely approaching normal cultural and social participation impossible. Many therefore take the emotionally logical but unfortunate next step, and become the guardian spirit.

At this time, then, we would tentatively conclude that the religious vision experience per se is not psychopathological but rather the reverse, being a synthesizing and often therapeutic process performed under extreme stress by individuals already sick.

2. *Communication.* The dreamer undertakes to preach his revelations to people, in an evangelistic or messianic spirit; he becomes a prophet. The doctrinal and behavioral injunctions which he preaches carry two fundamental motifs: that the convert will come under the care and protection of certain supernatural beings; and that both he and his society will benefit materially from an identification with some definable new cultural system (whether a revived culture or a cargo culture, or a syncretism of both, as is usually the case). The preaching may take many forms (e.g., mass exhortation vs. quiet individual persuasion) and may be directed at various sorts of audiences (e.g., the elite vs. the down-trodden). As he gathers disciples, these assume much of the responsibility for communicating the "good word," and communication remains one of the primary activities of the movement during later phases of organization.

3. *Organization.* Converts are made by the prophet. Some undergo hysterical seizures induced by suggestion in a crowd situation; some experience an ecstatic vision in private circumstances; some are convinced by more or less rational arguments, some by considerations of expediency and opportunity. A small clique of special disciples (often including a few already influential men) clusters about the prophet and an embryonic campaign organization develops with three orders of personnel: the prophet; the disciples; and the followers. Frequently the action program from here on is effectively administered in large part by a political rather than a religious leadership. Like the prophet, many of the converts undergo a revitalizing personality transformation.

Max Weber's concept of "charismatic leadership" well describes the type

of leader-follower relationship characteristic of revitalization movement organizations (1947). The fundamental element of the vision, as I have indicated
above, is the entrance of the visionary into an intense relationship with a supernatural being. This relationship, furthermore, is one in which the prophet
accepts the leadership, succor, and dominance of the supernatural. Many followers of a prophet, especially the disciples, also have ecstatic revelatory experiences; but they and all sincere followers who have not had a personal revelation
also enter into a parallel relationship to the prophet: as God is to the prophet,
so (almost) is the prophet to his followers. The relationship of the follower to
the prophet is in all probability determined by the displacement of transference dependency wishes onto his image; he is regarded as an uncanny person,
of unquestionable authority in one or more spheres of leadership, sanctioned
by the supernatural. Max Weber denotes this quality of uncanny authority and
moral ascendancy in a leader as charisma. Followers defer to the charismatic
leader not because of his status in an existing authority structure but because
of a fascinating personal "power," often ascribed to supernatural sources and
validated in successful performance, akin to the "mana" or "orenda" of ethnological literature. The charismatic leader thus is not merely permitted but
expected to phrase his call for adherents as a demand to perform a duty to
a power higher than human. Weber correctly points out that the "routinization" of charisma is a critical issue in movement organization, since unless this
"power" is distributed to other personnel in a stable institutional structure, the
movement itself is liable to die with the death or failure of individual prophet,
king, or war lord.

Weber, however, is essentially discussing a quality of leadership, and one
which is found in contexts other than that of revitalization movements. In
consequence, his generalizations do not deal with the revitalization formula
itself, but rather with the nature of the relationship of the early adherents
to their prophet. Furthermore, there is a serious ambiguity in Weber's use of
the charisma concept. Weber seems to have been uncertain whether to regard
it as an unusual quality in the leader which is recognized and rationalized
by his adherents, or whether to regard it as a quality ascribed to the leader by
followers and hence as being a quality of their relationship to him, determined
both by the observed and the observer in the perceptual transaction. We have
used it to denote the libidinal relationship which Freud described in *Group
Psychology and the Analysis of the Ego* (1922).

It would appear that the emotional appeal of the new doctrine to both
the prophet and his followers is in considerable part based on its immediate

satisfaction of a need to find a supremely powerful and potentially benevolent leader. For both the prophet and his followers, this wish is gratified in fantasy (subjectively real, of course); but the follower's fantasy is directed toward the person of the prophet, to whom are attributed charismatic properties of leadership (Weber 1946, 1947).

4. *Adaptation.* The movement is a revolutionary organization and almost inevitably will encounter some resistance. Resistance may in some cases be slight and fleeting but more commonly is determined and resourceful, and is held either by a powerful faction within the society or by agents of a dominant foreign society. The movement may therefore have to use various strategies of adaptation: doctrinal modification; political and diplomatic maneuver; and force. These strategies are not mutually exclusive nor, once chosen, are they necessarily maintained through the life of the movement. In most instances the original doctrine is continuously modified by the prophet, who responds to various criticisms and affirmations by adding to, emphasizing, playing down, and eliminating selected elements of the original visions. This reworking makes the new doctrine more acceptable to special interest groups, may give it a better "fit" to the population's cultural and personality patterns, and may take account of the changes occurring in the general milieu. In instances where organized hostility to the movement develops, a crystallization of counter-hostility against unbelievers frequently occurs, and emphasis shifts from cultivation of the ideal to combat against the unbeliever.

5. *Cultural Transformation.* As the whole or a controlling portion of the population comes to accept the new religion with its various injunctions, a noticeable social revitalization occurs, signalized by the reduction of the personal deterioration symptoms of individuals, by extensive cultural changes, and by an enthusiastic embarkation on some organized program of group action. This group program may, however, be more or less realistic and more or less adaptive: some programs are literally suicidal; others represent well conceived and successful projects of further social, political, or economic reform; some fail, not through any deficiency in conception and execution, but because circumstances made defeat inevitable.

6. *Routinization.* If the group action program in nonritual spheres is effective in reducing stress-generating situations, it becomes established as normal in various economic, social, and political institutions and customs. Rarely

does the movement organization assert or maintain a totalitarian control over all aspects of the transformed culture; more usually, once the desired transformation has occurred, the organization contracts and maintains responsibility only for the preservation of doctrine and the performance of ritual (i.e., it becomes a church). With the mere passage of time, this poses the problems of "routinization" which Max Weber discusses at length (Weber 1946, 1947).

V. The New Steady State

Once cultural transformation has been accomplished and the new cultural system has proved itself viable, and once the movement organization has solved its problems of routinization, a new steady state may be said to exist. The culture of this state will probably be different in pattern, organization or *Gestalt,* as well as in traits, from the earlier steady state; it will be different from that of the period of cultural distortion.

VARIETIES AND DIMENSIONS OF VARIATION

I will discuss four of the many possible variations: the choice of identification; the choice of secular and religious means; nativism; and the success-failure continuum.

I. Choice of Identification

Three varieties have been distinguished already on the basis of differences in choice of identification: movements which profess to *revive* a traditional culture now fallen into desuetude; movements which profess to *import* a foreign cultural system; and movements which profess neither revival nor importation, but conceive that the desired cultural end-state, which has never been enjoyed by ancestors or foreigners, will be realized for the first time in a future *Utopia.* The Ghost Dance, the Xhosa Revival, and the Boxer Rebellion are examples of professedly revivalistic movements; the Vailala Madness (and other cargo cults) and the Taiping Rebellion are examples of professedly importation movements. Some formulations like Ikhnaton's monotheistic cult in old Egypt and many Utopian programs, deny any substantial debt to the past or to the foreigner, but conceive their ideology to be something new under the sun, and its culture to belong to the future.

These varieties, however, are ideal types. A few movements do correspond rather closely to one type or another but many are obvious mixtures. Handsome Lake, for instance, consciously recognized both revival and importation themes in his doctrine. It is easy to demonstrate that avowedly revival movements are never entirely what they claim to be, for the image of the ancient culture to be revived is distorted by historical ignorance and by the presence of imported and innovative elements. Importation movements, with professed intentions to abandon the ancestral ways, manage to leave elements of the ancestral culture intact, if unrecognized, in large areas of experience. And movements which claim to present an absolutely new conception of culture are obviously blinding themselves to the fact that almost everything in the new system has been modeled after traditional or imported elements or both. Although almost every revitalization movement embodies in its proposed new cultural system large quantities of both traditional and imported cultural material, for some reason each movement tends to profess either no identification at all, a traditional orientation, or foreign orientation. This suggests that the choice of identification is the solution of a problem of double ambivalence: both the traditional and the foreign model are regarded both positively and negatively.

Culture areas seem to have characteristic ways of handling the identification problem. The cargo fantasy, although it can be found outside the Melanesian area, seems to be particularly at home there; South American Indian prophets frequently preached of a migration to a heaven-on-earth free of Spaniards and other evils, but the promised-land fantasy is known elsewhere; North American Indian prophets most commonly emphasized the revival of the old culture by ritual and moral purification, but pure revival ideas exist in other regions too. Structural "necessity" or situational factors associated with culture area may be responsible. The contrast between native-white relationships in North America (a "revival" area) and Melanesia (an "importation" area) may be associated with the fact that American Indians north of Mexico were never enslaved on a large scale, forced to work on plantations, or levied for labor in lieu of taxes, whereas Melanesians were often subjected to more direct coercion by foreign police power. The Melanesian response has been an identification with the aggressor (vide Bettelheim 1947). On the other hand, the American Indians have been less dominated as individuals by whites, even under defeat and injustice. Their response to this different situation has by and large been an identification with a happier past. This would suggest that an important variable in choice of identification is the degree of domination exerted by a foreign society, and that import-oriented revitalization movements will not develop until an extremely high degree of domination is reached.

II. The Choice of Secular and Religious Means

There are two variables involved here: the amount of secular action which takes place in a movement, and the amount of religious action. Secular action is here defined as the manipulation of human relationships; religious action as the manipulation of relationships between human and supernatural beings. No revitalization movement can, by definition, be truly nonsecular, but some can be relatively less religious than others, and movements can change in emphasis depending on changing circumstances. There is a tendency, which is implicit in the earlier discussion of stages, for movements to become more political in emphasis, and to act through secular rather than religious institutions, as problems of organization, adaptation, and routinization become more pressing. The Taiping Rebellion, for instance, began as a religious preoccupied movement; opposition by the Manchu dynasty and by foreign powers forced it to become more and more political and military in orientation.

A few "purely" political movements like the Hebertist faction during the French Revolution, and the Russian communist movement and its derivatives, have been officially atheistic, but the quality of doctrine and of leader-follower relationships is so similar, at least on superficial inspection, to religious doctrine and human-supernatural relations, that one wonders whether it is not a distinction without a difference. Communist movements are commonly asserted to have the quality of religious movements, despite their failure to appeal to a supernatural community, and such things as the development of a Marxist gospel with elaborate exegesis, the embalming of Lenin, and the concern with conversion, confession, and moral purity (as defined by the movement) have the earmarks of religion. The Communist Revolution of 1917 in Russia was almost typical in structure of religious revitalization movements: there was a very sick society, prophets appealed to a revered authority (Marx), apocalyptic and Utopian fantasies were preached, and missionary fervor animated the leaders. Furthermore, many social and political reform movements, while not atheistic, act through secular rather than religious media and invoke religious sanction only in a perfunctory way. I do not wish to elaborate the discussion at this time, however, beyond the point of suggesting again that the obvious distinctions between religious and secular movements may conceal fundamental similarities of socio-cultural process and of psychodynamics, and that while all secular prophets have not had personality transformation visions, some probably have, and others have had a similar experience in ideological conversion.

Human affairs around the world seem more and more commonly to be decided without reference to supernatural powers. It is an interesting question whether mankind can profitably dispense with the essential element of the religious revitalization process before reaching a Utopia without stress or strain. While religious movements may involve crude and powerful emotions and irrational fantasies of interaction with nonexistent beings, and can occasionally lead to unfortunate practical consequences in human relations, the same fantasies and emotions could lead to even more unfortunate practical consequences for world peace and human welfare when directed toward people improperly perceived and toward organs of political action and cultural ideologies. The answer would seem to be that as fewer and fewer men make use of the religious displacement process, there will have to be a corresponding reduction of the incidence and severity of transference neuroses, or human relationships will be increasingly contaminated by character disorders, neurotic acting out, and paranoid deification of political leaders and ideologies.

III. Nativism

Because a major part of the program of many revitalization movements has been to expel the persons or customs of foreign invaders or overlords, they have been widely called "nativistic movements." However, the amount of nativistic activity in movements is variable. Some movements—the cargo cults, for instance—are antinativistic from a cultural standpoint but nativistic from a personnel standpoint. Handsome Lake was only mildly nativistic; he sought for an accommodation of cultures and personalities rather than expulsion, and favored entry of certain types of white persons and culture-content. Still, many of the classic revivalistic movements have been vigorously nativistic, in the ambivalent way discussed earlier. Thus nativism is a dimension of variation rather than an elemental property of revitalization movements.

A further complication is introduced by the fact that the nativistic component of a revitalization movement not uncommonly is very low at the time of conception, but increases sharply after the movement enters the adaptation stage. Initial doctrinal formulations emphasize love, cooperation, understanding, and the prophet and his disciples expect the powers-that-be to be reasonable and accepting. When these powers interfere with the movement, the response is apt to take the form of an increased nativistic component in the doctrine. Here again, situational factors are important for an understanding of the course and character of the movement.

IV. Success and Failure

The outline of stages as given earlier is properly applicable to a revitalization movement which is completely successful. Many movements are abortive; their progress is arrested at some intermediate point. This raises a taxonomic question: how many stages should the movement achieve in order to qualify for inclusion in the category? Logically, as long as the original conception is a doctrine of revitalization by culture change, there should be no requisite number of stages. Practically, we have selected only movements which passed the first three stages (conception, communication, and organization) and entered the fourth (adaptation). This means that the bulk of our information on success and failure will deal with circumstances of relatively late adaptation, rather than with such matters as initial blockage of communication and interference with organization.

Two major but not unrelated variables seem to be very important in determining the fate of any given movement: the relative "realism" of the doctrine; and the amount of force exerted against the organization by its opponents. "Realism" is a difficult concept to define without invoking the concept of success or failure, and unless it can be so defined, is of no use as a variable explanatory of success or failure. Nor can one use the criterion of conventionality of perception, since revitalization movements are by definition unconventional. While a great deal of doctrine in every movement (and, indeed, in every person's mazeway) is extremely unrealistic in that predictions of events made on the basis of its assumptions will prove to be more or less in error, there is only one sphere of behavior in which such error is fatal to the success of a revitalization movement: prediction of the outcome of conflict situations. If the organization cannot predict successfully the consequences of its own moves and of its opponents' moves in a power struggle, its demise is very likely. If, on the other hand, it is canny about conflict, or if the amount of resistance is low, it can be extremely "unrealistic" and extremely unconventional in other matters without running much risk of early collapse. In other words, probability of failure would seem to be negatively correlated with degree of realism in conflict situations, and directly correlated with amount of resistance. Where conflict-realism is high and resistance is low, the movement is bound to achieve the phase of routinization. Whether its culture will be viable for long beyond this point, however, will depend on whether its mazeway formulations lead to actions which maintain a low level of stress.

SUMMARY

This programmatic paper outlines the concepts, assumptions, and initial findings of a comparative study of religious revitalization movements. Revitalization movements are defined as deliberate, conscious, organized efforts by members of a society to create a more satisfying culture. The revitalization movement as a general type of event occurs under two conditions: high stress for individual members of the society, and disillusionment with a distorted cultural *Gestalt.* The movement follows a series of functional stages: mazeway reformulation, communication, organization, adaptation, cultural transformation, and routinization. Movements vary along several dimensions, of which choice of identification, relative degree of religious and secular emphasis, nativism, and success or failures are discussed here. The movement is usually conceived in a prophet's revelatory visions, which provide for him a satisfying relationship to the supernatural and outline a new way of life under divine sanction. Followers achieve similar satisfaction of dependency needs in the charismatic relationship. It is suggested that the historical origin of a great proportion of religious phenomena has been in revitalization movements.

NOTES

1. The Handsome Lake project, supported largely by a Faculty Research Fellowship of the Social Science Research Council, with supplemental funds from the Behavioral Research Council and Committee for the Advancement of Research of the University of Pennsylvania, has served as a pilot study, and the larger investigation is now largely financed by the National Institute of Mental Health (U.S. Public Health Service), Grant M-883, with supplemental funds from the American Philosophical Society and the Eastern Pennsylvania Psychiatric Institute. I should like to express my appreciation to Sheila C. Steen (who has been the "field director" of the project, responsible for much of the empirical research and participant in conceptual formulation), and to research and clerical assistants Josephine H. Dixon, Herbert S. Williams, and Ruth Goodenough. Persons whose comments and suggestions on the first draft of this paper have been of value in its revision include Margaret Mead,

Theodore Schwartz, Walter Goldschmidt, A. I. Hallowell, David F. Aberle, Betty S. Wallace and Ward Goodenough. The Handsome Lake movement will be described in detail in a book the writer is now preparing. [Published in 1970 as *Death and Rebirth of the Seneca.*] For other treatments now in print, see Parker, 1913; Deardorff, 1951; Voget, 1954; and Wallace, 1952a and 1952b.

2. This article is not the place to present a general discussion of the notions of order and field, function and equilibrium, the organismic analogy, the concept of homeostasis, and certain ideas from cybernetics, learning and perception, and the physiology of stress, which would be necessary to justify and fully elucidate the assumptions on which the revitalization hypothesis is based. See however, Wallace 1953, 1955, and 1956a for further development of the holistic view and more extended discussions of the mazeway concept.

3. After we had coined the term "revitalization movement," we discovered that Marian Smith in an article on the Indian Shakers (Smith 1954) uses the closely related term "vitalistic movements" ("a vitalistic movement may be defined as 'any conscious, organized attempt on the part of a society's members to incorporate in its culture selected aspects of another culture in contact with it' "). However, she uses this term for what I would call nonnativistic revitalization movements with importation (rather than revivalistic) emphasis.

4. I should like to express my appreciation to Dr. Arthur P. Noyes, Superintendent, and Drs. Warren Hampe and Kenneth Kool of the staff of Norristown (Pa.) State Hospital, for their assistance in making this survey possible.

2

The Dekanawideh Myth Analyzed as the Record of a Revitalization Movement

Several historians and ethnologists have preserved versions of the Dekanaw-ideh myth of the founding of the Iroquois Confederacy.[1] This myth presents the usual theoretical problem: Is myth a reflection, however distorted, of historic events; is it an expression and rationalization of the values (religious, political, moral, personality, etc.) of a society; is it a "disease of language"; is it a "program" for a ritual? In this paper I propose to treat the current Dekanawideh myth as if it were an orally transmitted, and considerably distorted, record of a reasonably ancient revitalization movement, and under this assumption, to reconstruct in outline, from the elements of the myth, the main events of the movement itself. This proceeding will in another paper be generalized into a theory of the processes of origin and development of myths and rituals. Such a theory, insofar as it invokes historically unrecorded events, cannot appeal to more than internal consistency and general plausibility for measures of its validity; but this weakness is shared by any theory of myth which invokes ancient events, which cannot be verified by reference to contemporary literary and archaeological remains, to explain the existence of texts recently recorded by historians and ethnologists.

REVITALIZATION MOVEMENTS

In another publication (Wallace 1956b; chapter 1, this volume) I have detailed the components of an ideal-type model of the revitalization process. A revitalization movement may be defined as a deliberate, organized effort by members of a society to produce a more satisfying culture. In brief, the process consists of five stages:

   I. Steady state
  II. Period of increased individual stress
 III. Period of cultural distortion
 IV. Period of revitalization
       1. Revelation ("Mazeway Reformulation")
       2. Communication
       3. Organization
       4. Adaptation
       5. Cultural Transformation
       6. Routinization
  V. New steady state

In many instances, the event of revelation is inaugurated with the experiencing of a vision by an individual who has been suffering severe stress, brought
on by a combination of psychological conflicts, personal misfortunes, and
awareness of disruption of the socio-cultural system. We need not here enter
into discussion of the theoretical constructs necessary to describe this event
of revelation. The central element of the experience is the vision, in which
typically a supernatural being appears in a vision, and/or addresses the visionary, explaining to him the sources of his misery and of the troubles of
his society, and formulating, often in great detail, a new code of behavior.
This code generally prescribes elements of ritual, cosmological belief, moral
doctrine, and kinship, political, and economic practices which will ensure
salvation both for the individual and for his society. The visionary is often
charged with the mission of preaching this new gospel as well as following
its injunctions himself; and if he does undertake the mission, he becomes in
effect a prophet. Thus he communicates, gathers and organizes a following
of disciples, converts, and interested listeners, formulates new and modified
portions of the code. The movement often encounters opposition, and if it is
to succeed, reduces it in ideological or physical combat. If all goes well, the
code is finally institutionalized by the society as a part of its culture.

     The formulation thus outlined has been successful in describing a wide va-
riety of nativistic movements, cargo cults, millenarian sects, and similar social
events. Let us see whether we may not discern, in the Dekanawideh myth, the
shadowy outlines of just such a revitalization movement, partially obscured by
a particular distortion which has intervened in the course of retellings of the
history of the movement and of the code.

RELEVANT CONSTANT ELEMENTS OF THE MYTH

Despite the differences of the versions available, certain elements which are constant may be selected because they are exemplars of the components of the revitalization model. They may be listed as follows:

1. The existence of an Iroquoian village culture distorted by the functional consequences of the institution of the blood-feud, which leads to war and murder among the Iroquois themselves, as well as between Iroquois and other tribes.
2. The presence of a natural man named Hiawatha.
3. The experiencing by Hiawatha of an episode of severe agitated depression following bereavement.
4. The presence of a supernatural personage named Dekanawideh. (His supernatural status is indicated by his virgin birth, the mission to which he is appointed, his miracles, and his disappearance.)
5. A dramatic meeting between Hiawatha and Dekanawideh, following which Hiawatha undertakes to assist Dekanawideh in his appointed mission to bring peace to the Iroquois.
6. A dramatic "cure" of an important shaman named Atotarho who is relieved of his hostility and his cannibalistic appetite.
7. The formulation by Dekanawideh of the code (the so-called "Constitution of the Five Nations").
8. A concern by Hiawatha over the sorrow and social disorganization attendant upon unrestricted application among families, clans, villages, tribes, and groups of tribes, of the blood feud.
9. The actual mission by Hiawatha and Dekanawideh to convert the Iroquois, the gradual development of an organization, the continuous amplification and tactical reformulation of the code to render it acceptable, and the final general acceptance, institutionalization, and routinization of the code.

RECONSTRUCTION OF HIAWATHA'S REVITALIZATION MOVEMENT

The nine elements of the myth may be readily arranged, with only minor modifications, to form the portrait of a classic typical revitalization movement. Let us follow the outline of stages of a revitalization movement, as given above.

I. Steady State

We assume a group of Iroquoian-speaking tribes resident in what is now New York State. They are village-dwellers, the men hunters and the women gardeners; the villages are loosely organized into an "ethnic-confederacy" according to the conventional pattern of the northeast (Wallace 1947). Their population is small however, and rather widely scattered, as is also the case with their neighbors. The blood-feud (of which chronic inter-group violence or war is merely an extension) does not involve a large proportion of people at any one time because the diffuseness of the population permits only a low rate of social interaction.

II. Period of Increased Individual Stress

Population increases, possibly as a result of the increasing effectiveness of the horticultural enterprise and possibly as a result of a general increase in the effectiveness of the village-with-horticulture pattern; villages become larger, new settlements are formed, and hunting territories are more intensively used. The increase in the number and density of the population increases the frequency of the incidents which lead to blood-feud. In consequence, the number rises of persons involved in this process at any given time. Direct involvement in blood-feud itself may be as personal victim, as friend or relative of victim, or as one obligated to go on the warpath to obtain revenge. Indirectly, psychological involvement, through fear of provoking attack, of being injured, or killed, or of seeing loved ones injured or killed, affects almost everyone. The woods are no longer safe.

III. Period of Cultural Distortion

Direct or indirect involvement in blood-feud reduces social cohesion, inhibits effective hunting and horticulture, promotes increased suspicion of witchcraft. War and killing preoccupy the attention of the males; villages have to be palisaded. The need for reduction of the anxiety elicited by the high probability of attack leads to the extolling of an increasingly spartan ideal of personal conduct.[2]

IV. Period of Revitalization

1. *Revelation.* A Mohawk (or Onondaga) sachem named Hiawatha is bereaved of some favorite female relative or relatives.[3] He then experiences an episode of agitated depression, wandering alone in the woods, suffering from the delusion of being a cannibal monster named Atotarho, with a crooked body, snakes in his hair,[4] and great and destructive shamanistic powers. (There may also have been a real shaman named Atotarho.) The first partial remission of the psychosis occurs when he sees his face reflected in water in a kettle; it seems to him that it is not really the face of a monster.[5] Thereafter he has a vision in which a supernatural being named Dekanawideh reveals himself and appoints Hiawatha to be his messenger. The first message relates primarily to devices for relieving the minds of those burdened by sorrow.

2. *Communication.* Hiawatha wanders about from village to village, constructing poles on which he hangs strings of wampum, and recites the first eight items of the requickening address of the condolence ritual. He preaches the code as revealed by Dekanawideh.

3. *Organization.* He obtains some disciples and followers who regard him as a prophet and believe his accounts of the nature, powers, and sayings of Dekanawideh.

4. *Adaptation.* Hiawatha continues to experience visions, in the course of which much new matter is added to the original condolence address, and the principle is generalized into a code for a revitalized ethnic confederacy. The strategic innovation is the prohibition of blood-revenge by members of one of the five tribes against members of their own tribe or of any of the other four. The ritual details of the condolence ceremony, and the formal institutionalization of the council of forty-nine chiefs at Onondaga (of whom Dekanawideh is, of course, not one), are designed to produce a politically acceptable structure which will maintain intra-Iroquois peace and will make possible the inclusion of other tribes into this peace.

5, 6. *Cultural Transformation and Routinization.* The proposals of Hiawatha, with their authorship ascribed to the divine Dekanawideh, are accepted by the Seneca, Cayuga, Onondoga, Oneida, and Mohawk. This effectively transforms the Iroquois ethnic confederacy into a political confederacy.

V. Steady State

The institutionalization of the prohibition on intra-Iroquois blood-feud makes it possible for the village culture to develop in more stable fashion.

A true steady state of Iroquoian culture is not, of course, achieved, if for no other reason than that the arrival of Europeans created new stresses and distortions. But the political machinery thus devised to solve the internal feud problem gives the Iroquois a sufficient degree of unity (in spite of the League's essentially non-military character) to promote the efficiency of external war, to permit the peaceful joint use of large hunting territories to the north, south, and west, to allow an extremely effective policy of admitting "dependent" tribes to settle on their territory, and to facilitate the development of a fairly well-coordinated policy of playing off contending European powers against each other for nearly a century.

SUBSEQUENT DISTORTIONS OF THE MYTH

The date of the founding of the confederacy (the Hiawatha movement) has been variously estimated, most suggested dates falling between about 1400 and 1600. The early date would probably provide sufficient time, about 500 years, for distortions and variations to have befallen the myth prior to its recording by such ethnologists as Parker, Goldenweiser, Fenton, and Hewitt.

Two processes might, on *a priori* grounds, be expected to produce *some* change in the form of any myth which is being passed on by word of mouth during 500 years or at least fifteen generations. (These processes are, of course, considerably slowed when external symbols more permanent than sound patterns are used, but they may be expected to operate even then.) The first is the accumulation of changes of content in any given lineage of speakers (i.e., any specific sequence of the form hearing-repeating-hearing-repeating . . .). The second is the development of divergent forms in different speakers' lineages. The working of these processes renders it meaningless for an ethnologist to attempt to find the most nearly "authentic" text by such criteria as Hewitt (1917) invoked in his review of Parker's and Scott's texts.[6] The only "authentic" text, in Hewitt's sense, was the one first spoken, 300 to 500 or more years ago. Our reconstruction of the Hiawatha movement is an outline of what this first text must have contained; the statements of a man, Hiawatha, about a number of visions in which a supernatural being named Dekanawideh appeared to him and dictated a code for the revitalization of Iroquois society; the statements of Hiawatha (and no doubt others) of other circumstances surrounding this vision, such as Hiawatha's bereavement and illness; and the statements of Hiawatha and others about the history of the mission and its success.

The most significant probable distortions of the original text are three:

1. Failure to continue to specify that the words and behavior of Dekanaw-ideh are invariably dream or vision revelations by Hiawatha (and even-tually, perhaps, by others). This leads to statements about Dekanaw-ideh which employ linguistic forms appropriate to actors in nonvision contexts. Dekanawideh thus becomes, in the myth, a real man with supernatural powers.
2. The ascription (in most versions) of Hiawatha's cannibalistic symp-toms to another individual, Atotarho, who is independently cured by the (now-reified) Dekanawideh.
3. The blurring of the distinctions between the historical role of Hiawatha (visible to other people) and the role which Dekanawideh played in Hiawatha's visions ("visible" to others only in Hiawatha's accounts).

When to these distortions are added omissions of detail, minor misrenderings of names, reversals of order, and similar errors, the departures from the original text approximate the ethnologically known version of the myth. The most important distortion, however, is the first—the ascription of historical reality to the envisioned supernatural; and this, in a society which assumed that this being was indeed a real being, even though his behavior was observed only by Hiawatha, is precisely the easiest distortion to make, since in such a cultural context it is trivial.

CONCLUSION

We have analyzed the Dekanawideh myth of the Iroquois as a distorted record of the events, and code, of a revitalization movement led by Hiawatha some 300 to 500 years before the currently available texts were first written down. The versions of myth yield certain constant features which can be readily ar-ranged as exemplars of components of the ideal-type model of the revital-ization movement. Certain specific distortions, particularly a failure to label the actions and words of the supernatural Dekanawideh as the substance of the visions of the prophet, are postulated as leading to a form of the myth in which Dekanawideh appears as an historical figure with supernatural powers, and as the leader of the movement.

NOTES

1. In the preparation of this paper I have consulted the following translated versions and syntheses: Parker 1916, Scott 1912, P. A. W. Wallace 1946. Scott's text is a minor variant of the second of the three texts printed by Parker. Wallace's treatment, not a text in itself but a literary synthesis of several texts, includes material from the unpublished "Gibson version" recorded by Hewitt and translated by Fenton, but never published. Other variants have been recorded and still others exist. Since I am not concerned with the particular texts as linguistic productions but only as the loci of the major themes of a myth, I have not been concerned to make detailed comparisons or evaluations.

2. It need not be supposed that because warfare was common in Iroquois experience that therefore it was not attended by anxiety. The Jesuit priests record many examples of warriors, and women as well, wakening in panic from nightmares of war, captivity, and torture. See Wallace 1958 (chapter 11, this volume).

3. It is noteworthy that in the historically documented case of Handsome Lake, a later Iroquois prophet, the death of a favorite niece immediately preceded his vision (and was part of its subject matter).

4. Handsome Lake's code describes the case of a Seneca psychotic who wandered off and was found by his horrified relatives playing with a nest of snakes. See Parker 1913.

5. This reconstruction of the kettle incident, although it may appear to be arbitrary, is supported by at least two versions of the myth in which the cannibal sees a face in the kettle which is (in the myth) said to be actually the face of Dekanawideh, looking down through the smoke-hole from the roof. A curiously similar case of partial remission from psychosis, with consequent mildly messianic religious conversion, has been described by a psychotherapist. The (white) patient in this case also experienced a change of self-image while looking at his face in a mirror (in this instance while shaving). See Bergman 1953.

6. Hewitt's assault on Parker has echoed for years in the halls of Iroquoianists, and seriously damaged Parker's reputation. The relevance of Hewitt's critique is based on the assumption that the main object of ethnology is to procure authentic, accurate texts, free of "errors," "blunders," and so forth made by ill-qualified informants, from which the unadulterated native culture might be reconstructed. Most of the errors for which Hewitt castigates Parker were "errors" made by Parker's informants, not by Parker, who was simply reprinting matter furnished by his informants. Hewitt, indeed, admittedly helped his informants to give "accurate" information! If Parker had published the "correct" Hewitt version, the review would doubtless have been more complimentary.

3

New Religions among the Delaware Indians, 1600–1900

Sequential analysis of the successive religious movements which members of one society may support during an extended period of time can, even in fragmentary data, reveal some regular associations between type of belief and social circumstance.[1] Such intra-societal associations may be useful in the search for the "origin" of religious movements, which is normally made difficult by the uncertainty of the identification of comparable variables in cross-cultural research.[2] Although the search for "origins" is sometimes deplored as an antiquarian avocation, when the phenomenon is not conceived to have originated once but many times, the search for origins is equivalent to the search for "laws" describing the conditions under which the phenomenon occurs. "New religions" are a type of phenomenon which is recurrent, and about which many hypotheses have been spawned. In this study we shall be particularly concerned with three aspects of the problem: the frequency, on an order-of-magnitude basis, with which new religions are accepted by some members of a given society; the association, if any, between social acceptance of a new religion and what his been termed, rather vaguely, "social deprivation" of the acceptors; and the logical fitness of the new belief to the circumstances of the acceptors, as they are seen by an historically informed anthropologist.

The Delaware religious history illustrates also the importance of what may be called "non-acculturative adaptive change": the development of new cultural forms, in response to situational demands, which are neither acculturative nor contra-acculturative, but simply adaptive innovations which do not result in any approximation of a foreign culture. The Big House ceremony, frequently and incorrectly attributed to the Delaware aboriginal culture, is the best example of this in the Delaware religious series. Herein we may see the danger of attributing an ethnographically observed "native" or non-acculturative form or pattern to an aboriginal past, when it fact it may have been developed only a few years before the arrival of the field worker, and centuries after contact. (The reverse danger of assuming that any formal similarity to foreign custom, observed after contact, must be the result of acculturation—is less easy to demonstrate, because for most sorts of data the historical record stops at the contact date.)

The Algonkian-speaking Delaware, aboriginally of the Middle Atlantic states, and currently placed on several reservations in Kansas, Oklahoma, and Ontario, offer themselves as a laboratory for a study in what might be called the epidemiology of religious movements. The Delaware have been the subject of periodic description by good observers for about three hundred years, and in particular have attracted the interest of missionary authors and ethnologists interested in primitive religion. In the relative completeness and relevance of the materials, therefore, they are well suited for the type of sequential analysis which is desired. In this paper the Canadian bands (which split off from the group who migrated west across the Mississippi, around 1800) will be excluded from analysis so that one continuous line of cultural heredity will run back from Oklahoma, to Indiana, to Ohio, to Pennsylvania, New Jersey, and Delaware.

THE CHRONICLE OF DELAWARE RELIGIOUS MOVEMENTS

The Delaware were a people whose culture combined hunting and horticultural systems. There were family hunting territories, as in the circumboreal north; and the politically autonomous community was small, consisting of the several dozen to several hundred people who summered in the same village. Sib and lineage affiliation were matrilineal, and the women cared for the corn plots. The Delaware "tribe," at contact, was an ethnic group rather than a political unit (Wallace 1949). Traditional Delaware religion was in part a private matter; favored individuals experienced a vision of a guardian spirit ("manito"), sometimes at adolescence, occasionally earlier, and sometimes in later life. The Green Corn ceremony, in the early fall, was the high point of the annual festival calendar.[3] The cosmology was elaborate and philosophical; but the relationship between the visionary and his guardian spirit seems to have been the preeminent theme to laymen and shamans alike.[4]

Dutch fur traders established permanent commercial settlements on the Hudson River in 1609 and on the Delaware Bay in 1623, after several years of exploratory (and profitable) trading ventures up the local rivers. Thereafter the 8,000 or so Delaware Indians then resident in what are now the states of Delaware, New Jersey, and Pennsylvania remained in close and continually intensifying contact with Europeans (Dutch, Swedes, and English). These Europeans were, at first, chiefly interested in bartering goods for skins and furs; later they also became interested in exchanging goods and money for land.

Before the end of the seventeenth century Europeans (particularly the Swedes) had begun more or less active missionary work among the Delaware. Between 1642 and 1648, the Swedish Lutheran evangelist, John Campanius Holm, learned the local native language, preached to the Indians on Delaware Bay, and translated the Lutheran catechism into Delaware. He made a few converts among the natives settled in the neighborhood of the White settlements, and his later successors (after an interval of nearly fifty years) made other Lutheran converts between 1696 and 1723. The net effect of the Lutheran evangelism was slight, however, and the venerable John Campanius' grandson, evaluating the religious status of the Delaware, remarked that they were not easy to convert and were generally "unacquainted with the true worship of God" (Holm 1834 [1702]:63–75, 139–141; Fisher 1935)." These early Lutheran converts seem to have been few in number, and to have included only those who had already developed a personal attachment (for economic or other reasons) to Europeans. It is noteworthy also that up to about 1700, the relations between the Delaware and the Europeans had by and large been friendly. Land cessions had been relatively orderly and limited in area, and trade relations had been mutually profitable. The wholesale massacres and territorial dispossessions which were so salient a feature of Puritan New England's Indian history had no counterpart in the bulk of the Delaware country.

Spiritual concern for the Delaware was, in the case of the Quakers, expressed less in evangelical preaching than in generally honest and friendly dealings. Although a few Quakers were moved to carry the word of God to the natives of Pennsylvania and New Jersey, the visits of Quaker preachers were sporadic and such preaching as there was most frequently was a matter of individual impulse. George Fox had preached to a number of Indians, possibly including the Delaware, during the seventeenth century; Penn had a brief message interpreted to the Indians at the treaty in 1701. It is reported that an Indian friend of Penn's was once inclined toward Christianity (Fisher 1935:135). John Richardson, possibly addressing Delawares, early in the eighteenth century, excoriated a crowd of natives for their propensity to drunkenness, adultery, murder, brawling, theft, and divorce; " . . . they wept, and

Tears ran down their naked Bodies, and they smote their Hands upon their Breasts . . ." Quaker philanthropy, later in the century and during the nineteenth led Friends to perform many good offices, and to exhort the Indians to a more Christian-like spiritual life. But Quakerism never was offered to the Delaware as an organized religion, with a definite ritual and dogma, and with opportunity of organizational affiliation for Indians; very few if any Indians ever became Friends in the sense of membership in a Meeting. Evangelism was so diffused in practices of diplomacy, commerce, and philanthropy that Quakerism never became a "new religion" to more than a few individuals, even in later times when the Delaware were flocking to new standards.[5]

The full impact of the White invasion struck the Delaware Indians in the decade 1730–1740. The Delaware of southern New Jersey had by then lost their lands and for the most part were refugees west of the river of their name; a few hung on in New Jersey as beggars among their White neighbors. In Pennsylvania, the 1730's saw the cession of the Schuylkill lands and the execution of the hotly resented Walking Purchase. By 1740, the Delaware had lost most of their own territory, and were forced to live on the lands of their haughty uncles, the Six Nations, or on the lands of equally haughty Europeans. Their condition was pitiful: drunken, disillusioned, dependent, and hostile, they were a people in limbo.

Presbyterian David Brainerd seems to have been the first missionary to devote himself wholly to the spiritual improvement of the demoralized Delaware. He was active at Crosswicks and Cranberry, in New Jersey, and in the Forks of Delaware, from June 1744 until his death in October 1747. Brainerd, a somber, intensely devoted man who suffered under an almost continuous sense of melancholy and guilt, preached passionately to the Indians of sin and redemption. He worked remarkable conversions. At Crosswicks, in July 1745, after a year in the field, he had made only about eleven converts, but, preaching to sixty-five Indians on the afternoon of August 8th, on a text (Luke 14:16–23) dealing with those who refuse to heed the call, he produced a state of mass hysteria very similar to what Whitefield and Wesley were effecting among the White folks. Men, women, and children broke down, wept, and prayed for mercy; many could neither walk nor stand. Even a few White people, who had come to scoff, were caught up by the "swelling deluge," as Brainerd described the phenomenon of religious passion which seized the assembly. And in the same month he made a convert, in the Forks of Delaware, of one Moses Tattamy (who was to have a long career as an interpreter to the province of Pennsylvania). Tattamy for a time had suffered under a miserable sense of sin, believing that he had "never done one good thing," and that both he and the world around him were in danger of perishing. But at last, and suddenly, the word came to him, "There is hope; there is hope." He was hereafter, according to Brainerd, a "new man." Some of these conversions, apparently, were deep enough to maintain an effect on belief and behavior for years, if not for life.

Not all Indian religious enthusiasts were inspired by Christian sermons, however. In May of 1745, Brainerd met an Indian prophet, probably a Delaware (to judge from his ritual garb) some distance up the Susquehanna. This man, far from attempting to imitate Christianity, sought to revive what he supposed was the ancient religion of the Indians. Brainerd was terrified by the appearance of this reformer, who appeared in a

> coat of bear skins, dressed with the hair on, and hanging down to his toes; a pair of bear skin stockings; and a great wooden face painted, the one half black, the other half tawny, about the colour of an Indian's skin, with an extravagant mouth, cut very much awry; the face fastened to a bear skin cap, which was drawn over his head. He advanced towards me with the instrument in his hand, which he used for music in his idolatrous worship; which was a dry tortoise shell with some corn in it, and the neck of it drawn on to a piece of wood, which made a very convenient handle. As he came forward, he beat his tune with the rattle, and danced with all his might, but did not suffer any part of his body, not so much as his fingers, to be seen. . . . He had a house consecrated to religious uses, with divers images cut upon the several parts of it. I went in, and found the ground beat almost as hard as a rock, with their frequent dancing upon it.

But Brainerd was very much impressed by his discourse, and sympathized with him as much as he could with a pagan.

> He told me that God had taught him his religion, and that he never would turn from it; but wanted to find some who would join heartily with him in it; for the Indians, he said, were grown very degenerate and corrupt. He had thoughts, he said, of leaving all his friends, and travelling abroad, in order to find some who would join with him; for he believed that God had some good people some where, who felt as he did. He had not always, he said, felt as he now did; but had formerly been like the rest of the Indians, until about four or five years before that time. Then, he said, his heart was very much distressed, so that he could not live among the Indians, but got

away into the woods, and lived alone for some months. At length, he says, God comforted his heart, and showed him what he should do; and since that time he had known God, and tried to serve him; and loved all men, be they who they would, so as he never did before. He treated me with uncommon courtesy, and seemed to be hearty in it. I was told by the Indians, that he opposed their drinking strong liquor with all his power; and that, if at any time he could not dissuade them from it by all he could say, he would leave them, and go crying into the woods. It was manifest that he had a set of religious notions which he had examined for himself, and not taken for granted, upon bare tradition; and he relished or disrelished whatever was spoken of a religious nature, as it either agreed or disagreed with his standard. While I was discoursing, he would sometimes say, "Now that I like; so God has taught me;" etc., and some of his sentiments seemed very just. Yet he utterly denied the existence of a devil, and declared there was no such creature known among the Indians of old times, whose religion he supposed he was attempting to revive. He likewise told me, that departed souls all went southward, and that the difference between the good and the bad, was this: that the former were admitted into a beautiful town with spiritual walls; and that the latter would forever hover around these walls, in vain attempts to get in. He seemed to be sincere, honest, and conscientious in his own religious notions; which was more than I ever saw in any other Pagan. I perceived that he was looked upon and derided among most of the Indians, as a precise zealot, who made a needless noise about religious matters; but I must say that there was something in his temper and disposition, which looked more like true religion, than anything I ever observed amongst other heathens (Brainerd 1822:210–215, 218–220, 237–239).

Brainerd's missionary activities were ended by his death in 1747; but the Moravians took up the mission to the Delaware, and carried it forward vigorously for the next three generations, until the bulk of the Delaware had migrated west of the Mississippi and north of the Great Lakes. The story of Moravian evangelism among the Delaware, so dramatic and so tragic, has been often told and is one of the more familiar chapters of American frontier history. I shall only briefly recite its outline here. In 1744, the mission of the Brethren among the Mahican at Shekomeko, in New York, was abandoned because of persecution by hostile Whites. In 1745 the missionaries and many of their Mahican converts came down to found Gnadenhuetten, a new mission settlement a few miles north of Bethlehem. A number of Delaware converts, including the famous Teedyuscung, joined the *Unitas Fratrum* in the period 1745 to 1755. But the successful little community was burned by French Indians in November, 1755, ten of the missionaries killed, and the several hundred Indian converts dispersed.

After the war, in 1765 David Zeisberger reestablished the mission at Friedenshuetten, far up the Susquehanna, at the mouth of the Wyalusing. Many more converts were made at this place, but land disputes among the White people made the location untenable. In response to the invitation of the council of the Delaware in the Ohio, therefore, in 1772 several hundred Moravian Delaware converts moved with their missionaries again, this time to the Tuscarawas branch of the Muskingum. Their three settlements here were called Schoenbrunn, Gnadenhuetten, and Lichtenau. But the Revolutionary War ruined this work too: after some moving of towns and the apostasy of many converts, there occurred the notorious massacre at Gnadenhuetten of over ninety Christian Indians by White frontiersmen.

After the war, the Moravians tried again. In 1792 the settlement at Fairfield was established in Canada on the Thames River, and in 1798 the town of Goshen on the Tuscarawas. But the vigor of the convert faction among the Delaware had been weakened; many had left the faith, and others looked askance at the Christians, accusing them of trying to "tame" the Indians so as to make them easier to kill. Zeisberger planned a mission on the White River in Indiana, where the great council was situated; but this mission failed. By this time the Delaware had turned to native prophets for guidance.

The Moravian missions were a successful experiment in cross-cultural education. Although the Brethren sought to make converts, they also sought to teach a new way of life. The mission settlements were apparently small communal enterprises, on the utopian plan popular in that day, with the Brethren supplying capital goods and teaching the Indians European methods of farming and animal husbandry, spinning and weaving, carpentry, smithwork, and other necessary technical knowledge. Economically valuable ethics—sobriety, punctuality, performance of contract—and the provision of European *materiel* and know-how made these Moravian Indian settlements objects of admiration (and of suspicion) among frontier Whites and Indians alike. Their ultimate failure was the result of outside hostility rather than of internal deficiency; and even if, in the end, few Delaware remained Christians, many of the ideas, values, and skills so sedulously taught by the *Unitas Fratrum* came to be shared at the last by pagan Indians who consciously professed only contempt for Christianity.

The first successful nativistic revivals of the old time religion, with auxiliary promulgations of new doctrine, did not come until fifteen years after the missionaries had begun to work. (Brainerd's "reformer" was not a popularly accepted leader.) During the decade 1760–1770, no less than four, and perhaps more, new prophets arose among the Delaware along the Susquehanna and on the branches of the Ohio, and they continued to preach and to make converts (and to subvert the efforts of the *Unitas Fratrum*) until almost the end of the century.

The prophets, in Delaware custom (and also in conformity with the manner of prophets of other times and places), achieved their revelations by means of a vision which came to them in a period of hardship. Papoonan, for instance, held a long conversation with a Quaker during a trip to Philadelphia.

> He was formerly a Drunken man [recorded the Quaker] but the Death of his Father bringing sorrow over his Mind, he fell into a thoughtfull Melancholy State, in which state his Eyes, were turned to behold the Earth, and to consider and to consider [sic] the things that are thereon, and Seeing the folly and wickedness that prevailed his Sorrows increased. But it was given to him to believe that there was a great Power that had Created all those things. After this his Mind was turned from beholding this Lower world to look towards him who had Created it; and strong Desires were begot in his heart for a further Knowledge of his Creator: nevertheless the Almighty was not pleased to be found of him, but his Desires increasing he forsook the town and went to the Woods in great Bitterness of Spirit: the other Indians missing him and fearing Evil had befallen him went from the town in Search of him but could not find him. But at the end of five days it pleased God to appear to him to his Comfort and to give him a sight of his own inward State, and also an acquaintance into the Works of Nature—for he apprehended a sence was given him of the Virtues, and Natures, of Several herbs, Roots, Plants, and trees, and the Differant, Relation they had one to another, and he was made Sensible that Man stood in the nearest relation to God of any Part of the Creation. It was also at this time he was made Sensible of his Duty to God and he came home Rejoicing and Endeavoured to Put in Practice what he apprehended was required of him.[6]

Papoonan's town on the upper Susquehanna, after the prophet began to preach in 1758, was an orderly place, with well-constructed communal houses, and ample supplies of corn. The Indians at this town did not drink, disbelieved in war, and in quarrelsomeness, and sought earnestly "the way" to the "Place of Happiness." Although they were not Christian and did not wish to be Europeanized, they were not hostile to Christianity itself, because they believed that good was found in many revelations; and so they listened attentively to Quaker and Moravian teachings. Papoonan became a friend of the Quaker evangelist John Woolman and visited Friends in Philadelphia. In fact, they listened so attentively that in 1763 the village council decided to jettison Papoonan and to accept the first Christian missionary who came to the place. David Zeisberger, the Moravian, arrived first and got the job, and established the Friedenshuetten mission, which survived until the emigration of 1772.

Meanwhile at Assinisink another prophet was promoting another, more ecstatic religious revival. "The old Preast" who was the author of this new religion "hase A Book of Pickters whish he Maid him Self and there is Heaven and Hell and Rum and Swan hak (White men] and Indians and Ride Strokes for Rum. . . ." The old man read from his book "Like Mad" every morning and would sing to the rising sun. He, like Papoonan, preached against liquor. He apparently was making elaborate ritual innovations, and the rituals which he promoted included a dream-recitation rite at a spring thanksgiving festival by spectacularly painted and flower-bedecked men and women, night-long dances (at the conclusion of which many Indians wept), prayers to the Sun at dawn, and first-fruits offerings. The fate of this revitalization at Assinisink is not known (Post 1942 [1760]; Hays 1760).

About the same time on the Cuyahoga River south of Lake Erie, a third Delaware was preaching the Indians to repentance. This was the celebrated "Delaware Prophet," or Neolin, "The Enlightened." Like Papoonan and the unnamed "old priest" at Assinisink, he was against rum. He was also opposed to European ways, and urged the Indians in the Ohio country to return to the simple, pure manners of their ancestors. Neolin was taken into the presence of God, the Master of Life, and from Him obtained instructions on the proper course of the Indian life, and on the mode of worship most acceptable to him. If the Indians would abandon guns, powder, and all other White appurtenances, He would send back the vanishing game. The Indians were to drive off the Whites who were encroaching on their lands; they were to recite, morning and evening, a written prayer, and were to live chaste and friendly lives. The Prophet made a chart of the path to heaven, showing obstacles placed by White men, by their rum, and by the Indians' own forsaking of primitive virtue, in the way of entry. He made many converts, not only among the Delaware, but also among the Shawnee, Ottawa, and other tribal populations in the Ohio valley. Among those impressed by his words was Pontiac, who rationalized his assault on Detroit by reference to the Prophet's message.[7]

After the collapse of the Indians in the series of wars initiated by Pontiac, still another Delaware prophet, Wangomend by name, rose among the Ohio bands. This Munsee pagan preacher began his evangelical career in 1766. When a Moravian mission town was built in 1768 along the Allegheny River, he sought edification from the Brethren; but after a time he broke with them. Wangomend claimed that he had been chosen of God to reveal the true way of salvation to the Indians, and he was critical and suspicious of many White customs, condemning for instance the enslavement of Negroes, and prohibiting the drinking of the rum brought to them from the White settlements. He was very much exercised over a supposed conspiracy of witches, and in 1775 proposed a general witch-hunt, which at the last moment the Delaware council declined, for fear of the social disorganization it would entail. Wangomend continued to preach — to the great annoyance of David Zeisberger, who regarded him as a professional rival — into the 1790's (Heckewelder 1876:293–295; Zeisberger 1910:133–136).

The next wave of religious enthusiasm broke over the Delaware in the decade 1800–1810. A major part of the tribe, together with some Nanticoke and Mahican, had been settled along the White River in Indiana since the 1790's, as co-owners with the Miami, the original proprietors; here was their chiefs' council; here was the heart of the nation. Although the Delaware now had a central tribal council which was attempting to collect the scattered population and reorganize their collective life, the condition of these emigrants from, successively, New Jersey, Pennsylvania, and Ohio, was deplorable: they were half-drowned in whiskey, swept by plagues, and chronically hungry. During the hard months from February to early summer, 1805, a Munsee Indian woman, an apostate from Friedenshuetten, had a series of visions, in which angels enjoined her to tell the Indians many things: that at the ceremonies there was too much juggling and not enough sacrifice and prayer; that they would have to live as in the olden times, and love one another sincerely, or a terrible storm would come to kill them all. The words of the female prophet created a "state of revolution" which appalled the unhappy Moravian missionaries who witnessed it In accordance with her revelation, a "large house [was] newly built for the sacrifice," and in it was performed the ritual which Speck has described in detail in his study of the Delaware Indian Big House ceremony. It is difficult to learn how much of innovation there was in the Munsee woman's ritual prescriptions. The focus of the ceremony prescribed by the female prophet was the recitation of guardian spirit visions; this was the main thing in the Big House ceremony as Speck described it, and was also the point emphasized by the "old priest" at Assinisink; and the guardian spirit theme has been important in Delaware religion from aboriginal times to the present day. There already existed a Green Corn ceremony incorporating some of the Big House elements; this ceremony was performed in the early fall. It would seem, however, that the Munsee prophetess revealed the final and organized form of the Big House ceremony which has been preserved until recent times.[8]

For a time, however, the Big House movement was eclipsed by the rise of the notorious Shawnee Prophet, Tenskwatawa, Tecumseh's brother. He began to gain Delaware converts along the White River in December of 1805. His doctrine, like that of the other prophets, was a blend of moral injunction, cultural reform, and ritual innovation, based on direct revelation from God. The moral doctrine was hardly one that the Christian missionaries could criticize: no alcohol, sexual chastity, love thy neighbor, and similar injunctions. The cultural reforms, like those of the Delaware prophets of forty years before, centered about rejection of European customs and a return to the ancestral Indian ways. What made the Shawnee Prophet a terror to the missionaries was his preoccupation with witchcraft. In the spring of 1806, he visited the White River Towns and had two civil chiefs, Brother Joshua (the Moravian convert), and several others tomahawked and burned, on suspicion of being witches. One of the chiefs was burned in the Moravian mission village. The missionaries, who had with them wives and children, were so horrified that they abandoned the mission a few months later (Gipson 1938:392–422).

The War of 1812 ended the widespread influence of the Shawnee Prophet, and with the sale of the White River lands in Indiana in 1817, and of the remaining reservations in Ohio in 1829, the bulk of the Delaware removed west of the Mississippi where they continued the Big House ritual, while the Green Corn Dance—before 1805 the major traditional ritual—fell into abeyance.

The decade 1830–1840 saw a wave of Christian missionary efforts among the Delaware newly placed in the trans-Mississippi country. In addition to the Moravians, who followed their remaining charges westward, Mormons, Methodists, and Baptists all sought to bring Christian enlightenment to the tribe. Mormon emissaries in 1830, only six months after the organization of the Mormon Church, aroused much interest; the Delaware even agreed to build a council house for Mormon use. But the local Indian agent ordered the Latter Day Saints out of the territory (Foreman 1946:58fn.27). The Methodists and

Baptists were more successful, both entering the field in 1832; the Methodists went on to establish a manual training school for Indian children, and the Baptists printed religious and elementary school books in the Delaware language (Wright 1951:149). The pressure of Christian evangelism was thus maintained, and no doubt has been ever since; but to what degree of success it attained during the nineteenth century, we do not know.

About 1880, the Delaware received peyote. The prophet in this event was John Wilson, an Oklahoma Indian, part Caddo and part Delaware. Wilson learned about peyote from the Comanche, and during two or three weeks of seclusion, when he was experimenting with the drug, he experienced a series of visions in which a complete system of belief, ritual, and ethics was revealed to him. Peyotism, in Wilson's system, was a syncretism of Christianity (Christ was a major divinity) and traditional Delaware religion (the Big House ceremony was endorsed, and other elements of the old ceremonial calendar), united under the agency of the peyote. The ethical recommendations were standard: sobriety, chastity, marital fidelity, peacefulness, honesty; he abhorred and attacked witchcraft. Peyotism has remained a living religion among the Delaware: there has even been a major splinter-cult, led by Elk Hair, and a variety of minor variant rituals have developed.[9]

The Ghost Dance temporarily interrupted the development of the peyote movement, however, as the Shawnee Prophet had interrupted the development of the Big House. Beginning with the vision of Wovoka, about 1887 or 1888, this ecstatic new religion — also a blend of Christian and Indian beliefs, with some interesting affinities to Mormon teachings, but with emphasis on an apocalyptic world's end in which the Whites would be destroyed and the spirits of the dead would return — reached the Delaware in Oklahoma and was for a time accepted by part of them. Apparently the same John Wilson, who had earlier brought peyote to the Delaware, was now the leader of the Ghost Dance among them. Mooney visited him in 1893, and found him then chiefly identified as a Caddo and as the local Ghost Dance prophet; but he noted that he was half-Delaware, and "also prominent in the mescal rite, which has recently come to his tribe from the Kiowa and Comanche" (Mooney 1896: 903–905).

Although the Ghost Dance has faded away, peyotism remains among many Oklahoma Delaware today, and other "pagan" rituals among many Canadian Delaware, despite the continuing efforts of Christian missionaries. There is no reason to suppose that there is any final end-point for the evolution of Delaware religion, for even should peyotism and every vestige of the "traditional" Delaware religions disappear, new Christian denominations and revivals will constantly present themselves, as well perhaps as other, secular, social movements which have a religious spirit.

ANALYTICAL CONSIDERATIONS

The foregoing outline of data on Delaware religious movements lends itself to analysis from several points of view.

Frequency. Over a period of three hundred years, some Delaware Indians in the Oklahoma line participated, as converts or innovators, in varying numbers and with varying enthusiasm, in no less than fifteen separate *new* religious movements. This is a minimum number; there were almost certainly other movements which I have failed to include. Even with the minimum number, however, the *average* rate of new-religion-acceptance by a noticeable part of the population was once every twenty years.

There is, however, a clustering of the inception-times of the movements into five decades: 1740–1749 (3 cases), 1760–1769 (4 cases), 1800–1809 (2 cases), 1830–1839 (3 cases), and 1880–1890 (2 cases). Fourteen out of the fifteen are first reported during these fifty years. This suggests (if one accepts the data as a representative time series) that the rate of inception of religious movements is neither constant, nor randomly variant about a normal rate, but rather sharply clustered. Two possible general explanations offer themselves: (1) that variation in external circumstances affecting the society as a whole controls the rate (e.g., the higher the degree of situationally determined stress, the higher the rate of acceptance of new religions); (2) that the occurrence of one movement in itself is a stimulus for the occurrence of others (e.g., a process of suggestion or intra-societal stimulus diffusion is at work). Both explanations may be valid, since both processes could operate simultaneously (environmentally produced stress could stimulate several independent religious inventions, and also generally increase the degree of suggestibility of the population, allowing both direct conversion and stimulus diffusion within the society to operate more easily).

The Adaptive Nature of Religious Change. The sequence of historical situations of Delaware society can be conveniently divided into five stages, each of them marked by a characteristic style of religious innovation, and by a characteristic situational problem faced by the tribe. The data can be conveniently presented in tabular form (table 3.1).

Reviewing the series of modes of religious adaptation, it becomes apparent that, over a period of three hundred years, new religions among the Delaware represent successively different patterns of reaction to situational pressures. The first new religion is Christianity, accepted in friendly fashion by a few Delaware, closely associated with Whites, who probably did not abandon native beliefs at all; the bulk of the society remained undisturbed in their faith. This was the period of maximum good-feeling between Whites and Indians, and of mutual and profitable acculturation without cultural distortion. The aboriginal lands were lost in the second period, during which little religious change occurred. In the third period, as the economic situation deteriorated, and the culture began to disintegrate, two opposed tendencies in new religions developed: a panic-stricken attempt to identify with the Whites in religion; and an equally panic-stricken effort to revive the traditional religious culture, but without any particularly nativistic attitudes. In the fourth period, when wars with the Whites occurred, interest in a new White-oriented religious identification continued for some, but more and more the emphasis lay on nativism and revival of the old-time religion, with various modifications. In the fifth period, faith in the Whites was completely broken, and the Christian converts began to backslide, few new converts were made, and the new religions were violently nativistic. In the sixth period, after an initial flurry of interest in Christianity, there followed two generations of resentful but peaceful relations with Whites. The reservation system was accepted, and the new religions toward the end of the period deliberately combined a mild nativism with appeals to a Christian God, either putting off violence and noncooperation with Whites to a day of judgment, or else rejecting violence and noncooperation entirely.

It is worth noting that the nativistic, violently anti-White type of response is neither the initial, nor the prevailing, nor the last mode of adaptation, but rather occurs only during a transitional phase between acceptance of and trust in the Whites as friends, and acceptance of them as the fundamentally hostile powers that be. The most enduring tendency is that of identification with the Whites, which is notably present to some degree under all circumstances except those of the most extreme provocation and disillusionment (and, if one examines the data closely, it is present even then in details of doctrine).

Table 3.1   Stages of Delaware Religious Innovation

Stage	Period	New Religions	Historical Situation	Nature of Religious Adaptation
I	1600–1670	Mildly Evangelistic Dutch (Lutheran), Swedish (Lutheran), and English (Quaker) missionaries make a few converts among natives domiciled near White settlements. Conversions are made individually rather than in the mass.	The Delaware are for the most part undisplaced geographically, and their political sovereignty is unimpaired. Acculturation is selective and controlled by Delaware society. Intercultural contacts are largely amicable and symbiotic. Delaware morale remains high except in neighborhood of White settlements toward the end of the period.	The individual converts are (probably) motivated by personal friendships, politeness, and desire for closer commercial ties. Conversion may be a matter of lip service, or of the maintenance of two separate religious systems. There is no felt need to reconcile logical conflicts between the two religions. Most Delaware follow traditional religious forms.
II	1670–1740	None are recorded, beyond a few possible individual conversions of the tepid variety characteristic of the previous period.	Although intercultural relations remain superficially peaceful and friendly, the Delaware by 1740 have sold almost all their lands and are mostly living as displaced persons on Iroquois territory north of the Alleghenies, along the Susquehanna and Ohio rivers. A few reservations and remnant groups remain behind. White material culture extensively replaces the aboriginal. "Race prejudice" against Indians develops among the Whites. Delaware morale disintegrates rapidly, and hunting for the trade tends to become more, and agriculture less, important.	Traditional religious forms are maintained, but (probably) with declining confidence as morale generally declines.
III	1740–1760	Brainerd (Presbyterian) and Moravian missionaries make mass conversions, Brainerd producing "camp-meeting" hysterias. The Moravians develop utopian interracial communities. A revivalistic prophet arises but has little success.	The cold war between France and England over the control of the Ohio valley develops, and there are two hot wars (1744–1748 and 1754–1760), interrupting the trade and forcing the Delaware to choose sides (choice depending largely on locality). Migrations are necessary; horticulture and hunting are disrupted; relations with Whites become confused and sharply ambivalent.	Whole Delaware communities are converted to Christianity, particularly remnant groups resident near Whites. A few Delaware in the Indian country become concerned to revivify the ancient religion.

Table 3.1   Continued

Stage	Period	New Religions	Historical Situation	Nature of Religious Adaptation
IV	1760–1800	Moravian convert communities maintain themselves for a time but largely die out by 1800, except for a Canadian band. Four more or less revivalistic cults develop in the 1760s and one at least continues up to 1800.	Relations with Whites deteriorate rapidly. British Indian policy becomes punitive and restrictive, trade languishes. Delaware participate in the disastrous Pontiac Wars. During the Revolution, they are divided into American and British factions. During and after the Revolution, they are displaced from Pennsylvania and much of Ohio. The Battle of Fallen Timbers (1794) and the Treaty of Greeneville (1795) mean the collapse of Indian resistance to White encroachment west of the Ohio. Delaware are losing confidence in themselves and in all White people.	Two distinct tendencies of religious adaptation emerge during this crisis: (1) to identify with White Christianity; (2) to revitalize, with some innovations, an "Indian" type of religion, often with strong nativistic elements. The nativistic, revivalistic tendency becomes more prevalent, and Christian identification peters out, particularly after Americans massacre the peaceable Moravian Indian community in 1782. Both Christian and revivalistic movements (including the severely nativistic) are much concerned with moral codes, particularly opposing alcoholic indulgence, witchcraft, and sexual promiscuity.
V	1800–1820	The Big House movement and the Shawnee Prophet.	The Ohio Indians (including the Delaware), following the collapse of their resistance to the United States's expansion west of the Ohio River, find themselves confined to large reservations. The Delaware chiefs' council attempts to unite the tribe and to initiate cultural reforms, but drunkenness and other disorderly behavior interfere. Pressure (religious, political, territorial) from Whites is severe; faith in Whites is gone almost completely. The Shawnee Prophet's movement is associated with the second Indian effort to reestablish the Ohio River Line during the War of 1812; this too fails.	Both the Big House movement, and the Shawnee Prophet's doctrine that temporarily interrupts it, are revivalistic and extremely nativistic. Christian missionaries, for the first time, meet with open hostility from almost everyone except old converts, and many of these "slide back" into the new paganisms.

Table 3.1, *continued*

Table 3.1   Continued

Stage	Period	New Religions	Historical Situation	Nature of Religious Adaptation
VI	1820–1900	Mormon, Methodist, and Baptist missions; peyotism and the Ghost Dance.	The reservation period. Following the collapse of the Indian confederacy after the War of 1812, the United States intensifies its efforts to acquire Indian lands. The Delaware by 1840 are all on reservations west of the Mississippi, in Kansas and in the Indian Territory in Oklahoma. Relations with Whites are generally peaceful but not cordial, and the reservation system becomes stabilized as a way of life.	The Christian missions apparently achieve a measure of success in the period immediately after removal. Later the Ghost Dance and peyotism attempt to synthesize certain elements of Christian and traditional native belief. Although the apocalyptic and revivalistic aspects of the Ghost Dance emphasize its nativistic component, other elements of the Ghost Dance emphasize compliance with White culture until the millennium, and Jesus is invoked as the Indian Messiah. The philosophy of peyotism is one of passivity and withdrawal, and it too appeals to the divinity of Jesus. The Ghost Dance (short-lived) and peyote thus are a syncretism of nativistic and accommodation tendencies, with peyote, the less nativistic and more passive faith, surviving.

The Deprivation Hypothesis. Although this is not the place to examine at length the deprivation hypothesis, advanced frequently as the explanation for religious and other revitalization movements,[10] it is apparent that "deprivation" of one kind or another seems to have some association with the Delaware series. As a matter of fact, however, the decades during which the Delaware experienced the onset of their new religions were not the decades of maximum "objective" deprivation at all. The periods of maximum hardship for groups who ultimately accepted new religions were 1730–1740 (loss of lands and geographical displacement), 1754–1760 (the French and Indian Wars), 1775–1795 (the Revolution and the war for the Northwest Territory), and 1810–1830 (the War of 1812, the loss of reservations in Ohio and Indiana, and displacement west of the Mississippi). The five decades of new religious acceptance followed some years after the years of impact of disaster, and they were not so much adaptations to the disaster itself as to the derivative, long-term cultural distortions which the disaster revealed and induced. Thus the

1740–50 religions aimed not at restoring or rationalizing the loss of the land, but at restoring moral order and defining group identity (as either "White" or "Indian"). The 1760–70 religions were concerned less with the issues of the war and the economic hardship it brought than, again, with morality, morale, and group identification. The 1800–1810 religions, among the Delaware, emphasized a policy of nativism which, in the Shawnee Prophet's case, envisaged the recovery of lost lands, but again much of the concern was over morality (particularly witchcraft), morale, and a re-acceptance of an Indian way of life. The re-acceptance of Christian missions in 1830–40 followed the wars, land sales, and migrations of the preceding two decades. The final decade of religious innovation (1880–1890) came along after the reservation system had for the Delaware pretty well stabilized itself economically and militarily.

In other words, if one wishes to speak of deprivations, it is loss of confidence in a familiar and expectedly reliable pattern of social relations, rather than deprivation of food, shelter, and other economic wants, that stimulates the innovation or acceptance of new religions. Although economic or military stresses may precipitate the social disorder, the social disorder itself develops slowly and does not achieve impact until some years after the economic or other situational stress has been applied.

This formulation of the concept of deprivation is similar to Nash's reformulation of the material dealing with differential responses to the Ghost Dance on the Klamath reservation. Nash remarked: "Participants in the revival were people who in some measure had failed to derive the satisfactions they anticipated in following a particular course of action. In this sense they were deprived . . ." (Nash 1955). Barber likewise employs a somewhat generalized concept, similar to the Durkheim-Merton concept of anomie (Barber 1941; Merton 1949). The only essential modification of these concepts suggested on the basis of the Delaware material here recited is the postulation that it is the awareness of specifically *social* disappointments that constitutes the psychologically determinant deprivation, and that these are apt to achieve impact some years after the economic and military disasters which appear as the more "objective" indices of deprivation.

NOTES

1. This paper is based on research performed under Research Grants M-883 and M-1106 of the National Institute of Mental Health, United States Public Health

Service. An abbreviated version was read at a meeting of the Archaeological Society of Delaware, 22 June 1955.

2. Cf. the discussion of the difficulty of identifying cross-culturally reliable variables in the report of the Social Science Research Council's Conference on Cross-Cultural Studies of Personality Development, by M. Brewster Smith (*Items,* vol. 9, pp. 27–31, 1955). It might also be asked whether, in effect, the "same" society at two different times is really the "same" society at all; if it is not (and often it is demonstrably different in almost every respect save name), then the cross-cultural problem applies not only to spatial but also to temporal comparisons.

3. See Witthoft 1949. Witthoft in his study of Green Corn ceremonialism in the eastern woodlands found that the Green Corn dance, rather than the Big House ceremony, was the ritual described by observers of the Delaware in early contact times. This view agrees with my own opinion, as developed later in this paper, that the Big House was a "new religion" dating from 1805. Speck (1941) and Harrington (1921), however, seem to imply that the Big House as it is seen on twentieth-century reservations is identical with the earlier reported versions of the Green Corn. As a later section of this paper argues, the Big House ceremony probably was a reorganized form of the Green Corn, with innovations both in ritual detail and in over-all pattern.

4. See particularly Lindestrom [1656] 1925.

5. See Kelsey 1917, for a general account of Friends and Indians.

6. *Papoonan's Revelation* in Friends Historical Society collection.

7. Heckewelder 1876, pp. 291–293; Peckham 1947, pp. 98–100; Schoolcraft 1839, pp. 239–248.

8. Gipson 1938, pp. 333–335; Speck 1941. See fn. 4.

9. For studies of Delaware peyotism, see Petrullo 1934 and Speck 1933.

10. See Barber 1941, Mooney 1896, and Nash 1955 for varying statements of the deprivation hypothesis.

4

Handsome Lake and the Decline of the Iroquois Matriarchate

During the seventeenth and eighteenth centuries, Iroquois Indian men earned a reputation among the French and English colonists for being the most astute diplomatically and most dangerous militarily of all the Indians of the northeast. Yet at the same time the Iroquois were famous for the "matriarchal" nature of their economic and social institutions. After the colonial era came to an end with the victory of the United States in the Revolutionary War, the traditional diplomatic and military role of the Iroquois men was sharply limited by the circumstances of reservation life. Simultaneously, the "matriarchal" character of certain of their economic, kinship, and political institutions was drastically diminished. These changes were codified by the prophet Handsome Lake.

Handsome Lake, the Seneca prophet, founded a new religion in the early years of the nineteenth century. His religion was enthusiastically adopted by many of the Seneca and other Iroquois Indians then living on small reservations in the eastern United States and Canada. Its code emphasized sobriety, the practice of agriculture by males in the white man's style, the abandonment of witchcraft, and certain changes in kinship behavior. The changes in kinship behavior which he recommended, and which to a considerable degree were carried out by his followers, amounted in Hsu's terms (1965) to a shift in dominance in kin relationships from mother-daughter to husband-wife. Handsome Lake's reforms thus were a sentence of doom upon the traditional quasi-matriarchal system of the Iroquois. An examination of the conditions under which this event occurred may throw light on the problem of change implicit in Hsu's theory of dominant kin relationships.

THE CLASSICAL IROQUOIS PATTERN

In ethnographic tradition, the Iroquois have sometimes been regarded as a quasi-matriarchal society because of the important role women played in the formal political organization. An Iroquois tribe, of several thousand persons, was typically divided into several sibs, each of which in turn was divided into lineages. Inheritance of lineage, and therefore of sib, membership was matrilineal. A town was usually composed of members of a number of lineages, from several different sibs, each lineage owning a house (the so-called "longhouse"). The occupants of a longhouse were (theoretically) all of the living female members of the lineage in that locality, plus their unmarried sons and their husbands of the moment. Marriage was monogamous, but a woman might have a number of husbands in the course of her life. Residence after marriage was in the wife's longhouse. The women of a lineage are believed collectively to have worked their own cornfields near the village. The men of the village were responsible for hunting, for trading peltries, for warfare, and for diplomacy, all of which kept them away from their households for long periods of time, and all of which were essential to the survival of Iroquois society. An expedition of any kind was apt to take months or even years, for the 15,000 or so Iroquois in the seventeenth and eighteenth centuries ranged over an area of great size, on the order of a million square miles (literally, from the Hudson and Delaware rivers on the east to the Mississippi on the west, and from Hudson's Bay on the north to the Carolinas on the south). It is not an exaggeration to say that the full-time business of an Iroquois man was travel in order to hunt, trade, fight, or talk in council.

The women exercised political power in three main circumstances. First, whenever one of the forty-nine chiefs of the great inter-tribal League of the Iroquois died, the senior woman of the lineage he represented nominated his successor (although the nominee could in principle be rejected by the council itself). Second, when tribal or village decisions had to be made, both men and women attended at a kind of town meeting, and while men normally did the public speaking, the women caucused behind the scenes and lobbied with the spokesmen. Third, a woman was entitled to demand publicly that a murdered kinsman or kinswoman be avenged by *lex talionis* or be replaced by a captive from a non-Iroquois tribe, and her male relatives, particularly lineage kinsmen, were morally obligated to go out in a war party to secure scalps and/or captives, whom the bereaved woman might either adopt or consign to torture and death. Adoption was so frequent during the bloody decades of the beaver wars and the early colonial wars that some Iroquois villages were preponderantly composed of formally adopted war captives. Thus Iroquois women were entitled *formally* to start war, to nominate chiefs, and to participate in consensual politics.

Such a quasi-matriarchy, of course, had a certain face validity in a situation where the division of labor between the sexes required that men be geographically peripheral to the households which they helped to support and did defend. Thus, an Iroquois village over time might be regarded as a collection of infinitely long strings of successive generations of women, domiciled in their longhouses by their cornfields in a clearing while their sons and husbands traveled in the forest on supportive errands of hunting and trapping, of trade, of war, and of diplomacy. The Iroquois population was, in effect, divided into two parts: sedentary females and nomadic males. Given the technological, economic, and military circumstances of the time, such an arrangement was a practical one. But it did have an incidental consequence: It made the relationship between husband and wife an extremely precarious one, for the husband, away from the household for long periods of time, was apt in his travels to establish a liaison with an unmarried girl or a woman whose husband was also away. Since such liaisons were, in effect, in the interest of everyone in the longhouse, they readily tended to become recognized as marriages. The emotional complications introduced by these serial marriages were supposed to be resolved peacefully by the people concerned. The traveling husband who returned to find his wife living with someone else might try to recover her; if she preferred to remain with her new husband, however, he was not entitled to punish her or her new lover, but instead was encouraged to find another wife among the unmarried girls or wives with currently absent husbands. She was expected to keep the children.

THE REVISED IROQUOIS PATTERN

Handsome Lake was deeply concerned with the fragility of the classic Iroquois nuclear family. Under the quasi-matriarchal system, marriages were dependent upon the mutual satisfaction of the spouses. Couples chose one another for personal reasons; free choice was limited, in effect, only by the prohibition of intra-sib marriage. Marriages were apt to fray when a husband traveled too far, too frequently, for too long; on his return, drunken quarreling, spiteful gossip, parental irresponsibility, and infidelity led rapidly to the end of the relationship. Handsome Lake deplored this process and devoted much of his preaching to homilies on domestic tranquility. His "Great Message" contains, in Parker's published version of the Code, about 130 sections (Parker 1913). The first four sections define the four cardinal sins: drinking whiskey, practicing lethal witchcraft, using magical charms, and using medicines to sterilize a woman. Three of these four contributed directly to the instability of the nuclear family, for drunkenness led to quarrels between husband and wife, the magical charms included love charms which facilitated promiscuity, and sterility unnaturally limited not only the number of a woman's descendants but also the number of children in the household. In the latter case, Handsome Lake singled out the mother-daughter relationship as centrally responsible for the problem:

> Now the Creator ordained that women should bear children.
>
> Now a certain young married woman had children and suffered much. Now she is with child again and her mother wishing to prevent further sufferings designs to administer a medicine to cut off the child and to prevent forever other children from coming. So the mother makes the medicine and gives it. Now when she does this she forever cuts away her daughter's string of children. Now it is because of such things that the Creator is sad. He created life to live and he wishes such evils to cease. He wishes those who employ such medicines to cease such practices forevermore. Now they must stop when they hear this message. Go and tell your people.

Following his discussion of the four evil words (whiskey, witchcraft, magic, and abortion), the prophet in the next twelve sections delineates his conception (attributed, of course, to the heavenly messengers of the Creator) of how the members of the nuclear family should and should not behave. He condemns the mother who urges her daughter to leave her husband:

> Tell your people that the Creator has ordered regular marriage customs. When the young people are old enough to marry, tell them so. When they marry they will live pleasantly. Now it may happen that the girl's mother discovers that she is very happy with her husband. Then she endeavors to make her daughter angry with her husband when he returns from a journey. But when the husband returns the young wife forgets the evil advice and greets him lovingly. Now the older woman, the mother, seeing this, speaks again hoping to stir up an ill feeling. Says the old woman, "My daughter,

your spirits are dull, you are not bright. When I was young I was not so agreeable. I was harsh with my husband." Now the Creator is sad because of the tendency of old women to breed mischief. Such work must stop. Tell your people it must stop.

He condemns quarreling between husband and wife:

> The married often live well together for a while. Then a man becomes ugly in temper and abuses his wife. It seems to afford him pleasure. Now because of such things the Creator is very sad. So he bids us to tell you that such evils must stop. Neither man nor woman must strike each other. . . . Love one another and do not strive for another's undoing. Even as you desire good treatment so render it. Treat your wife well and she will treat you well.

He condemns scandalous gossip about the misbehavior of wives while their husbands are away hunting:

> Now some live together peaceably and keep the family as should be. Then after a time the man resolves to go off on a hunting excursion in the woods for a number of days. So he goes, having agreed with his wife about it. All is well and he returns with a load of game. He feels well and thinks he is doing well in thus providing for his family. On his way homeward he meets some one who tells him that in his absence his wife has been living with another man. When he hears this report he feels sad and angry. He refuses to go to his home and turns from his path and goes to his relatives. Now whoever makes mischief of this kind does a great wrong before the Creator. So he bids his people to forever stop such evil practices.

He praises the wife who forgives her husband who strays, but condemns the erring husband:

> Now this concerns both husband and wife. Now it may happen that a man and wife live together happily. At length the man thinks that he will go to another settlement to visit relatives there. His wife agrees and he goes. Now when he gets to the village he induces some agreeable woman to live with him saying he is single. Then after some time the man goes back to his own family. His wife treats him cordially as if no trouble had occurred. Now we, the messengers, say that the woman is good in the eyes of her Creator and has a place reserved for her in the heaven-world. Now the woman knew all

that had been done in the other settlement but she thought it best to be peaceful and remain silent. And the Creator says that she is right and has her path toward the heaven-world, but he, the man, is on his way to the house of the Wicked One.

He condemns philandering men:

This concerns a certain thing that human creatures follow. It is concerning *gakno'we'haat*. Some men desire constant new experience, that is some men are always following *yē'o^n'*. Now it is a great evil for men to have such desires. This is a thing that the so sinful must confess. A man who desires to know *gagwēgo^n yeē'o^n'sho'* will never be satisfied, for *yē'o^n'* will arise whom he cannot know and he will fall flat. Now we, the messengers, say that all this is sinful and men must not follow such desires.

He condemns the punitive mother:

An old woman punished her children unjustly. The Creator is sad because of such things and bids us tell you that such practices must cease.

He urges the mother to heed her daughter's admonitions against wrongdoing:

Parents disregard the warnings of their children. When a child says, "Mother, I want you to stop wrongdoing," the child speaks straight words and the Creator says that the child speaks right and the mother must obey. Furthermore the Creator proclaims that such words from a child are wonderful and that the mother who disregards them takes the wicked part. The mother may reply, "Daughter, stop your noise. I know better than you. I am the older and you are but a child. Think not that you can influence me by your speaking." Now when you tell this message to your people say that it is wrong to speak to children in such words.

He condemns the drunken father:

Some people live together well as man and wife and family, but the man of the family uses strong drink. Then when he comes home he lifts up his child to fondle it and he is drunk. Now we the messengers of the Creator, say that this is not right for if a man filled with strong drink touches his child he burns its blood. Tell your people to heed this warning.

He urges the childless couple to adopt children of the wife's sister (rather than separate):

> Some people live together righteously as man and wife according as the Creator ordained, but they have no child. When this is so let this be the way: If the wife's sister has children, of these let the wife without issue take from one to three and rear them and thereby fulfill her duty to the Creator. Moreover when a woman takes children she must rear them well as if born of herself. We, the messengers, say that you must tell this to your people.

He condemns gossiping women who spread rumors that a woman's husband is not the father of her child:

> Tell your people that ofttimes when a woman hears that a child is born and goes to see it, she returns and says in many houses where she stops that its mother's husband is not its father. Now we say that is exceedingly wrong to speak such evil of children. The Creator formed the children as they are; therefore, let the people stop their evil sayings.

And he urges grandchildren to care for aged and helpless grandparents.

The remainder of the code contains a number of admonitions concerning the proper social and economic roles of men and women. A woman should be a good housewife: generous, serving food to visitors and neighbor's children, never a petty thief, always helping the orphans of the community, and avoiding gossip. A man should "Harvest food for his family," build a good house, and keep horses and cattle; he should not be boastful and vain of his appearance or strength; he should be respectful of his father.

And those who disobeyed these various injunctions, the prophet said, were punished in the next world in a special house reserved for the unending torment of the wicked. Here the drunkard was compelled to swallow molten metal, the loose woman had red hot penises inserted into her vagina, quarreling spouses were forced to dispute until their eyes bulged from their heads, their tongues lolled out, and flames spurted from their genitals. Punishments of similar severity were designed to fit other crimes.

In review of Handsome Lake's moral admonitions, it is plain that he was concerned to stabilize the nuclear family by protecting the husband-wife relationship against abrasive events. A principal abrasive, in his view, was the hierarchical relationship between a mother and her daughter. Mothers, he believed, were all too prone to urge their daughters toward sin, by administering abortifacients and sterilizing medicines, by drunkenness, by practicing witchcraft, and by providing love magic. They set their daughters' minds against their husbands, condoned mother's severity to their children, and were above accepting advice from their own offspring. Thus, in order to stabilize the nuclear family, it was necessary to loosen the tie between mother and daughter. Furthermore, men were supposed now to assume the role of heads of families, being economically responsible for their wives and children, and not frittering away their energies on strong drink, gambling, dancing, and philandering, nor in mother-in-law trouble. Although he did not directly challenge the matrilineal principle in regard to sib membership, or the customs of nominating sachems, he made it plain that the nuclear family, rather than the maternal lineage, was henceforward to be both the moral and the economic center of the behavioral universe.

EXPLANATIONS: MOTIVATIONAL AND FUNCTIONAL

Just why should Handsome Lake have developed and expressed such views as these at this time? And why did the Iroquois so wholeheartedly endorse and follow his injunctions?

Handsome Lake himself was, in some respects, a classic Iroquois: that is to say, he had been a hunter and warrior, had himself undertaken many times the long hunting, warring, and diplomatic journeys characteristic of the colonial period; he had become, by the nomination of a clan matron, one of the forty-nine chiefs of the great Council of the Six Nations. He and his famous brother Cornplanter were sons by different fathers, Cornplanter reputedly having been sired by a wandering Dutch peddler, and Handsome Lake by a Seneca warrior. He had seen the death of his wife and some of his children and nieces, and at the time of his visions was living as a drunken invalid in the house of his brother, along with his own daughter and her husband—unsustained, in other words, by the classic matrilineal system but dependent instead upon his brother and the remains of his own nuclear family. And his visions occurred only after the reservations had come into being and he was no longer a notable hunter, warrior, and forest diplomat, and was cooped up in a little slum in the wilderness, exposed to precept and example from various pushing white people, including Quaker missionaries then living in the same village.

But most Iroquois men found themselves in similar circumstances, no longer able, or needed, to range over thousands of miles to hunt, to fight, and to negotiate at treaties and councils. In these new circumstances, the irritations inherent in the classic matriarchal system became intolerable. The classic system, with its pattern of sedentary females and nomadic males had been workable only with a combination of belief in romantic love and easy divorce; now, with the small reservations perennially crowded with unemployed and demoralized males, the old pattern of sexual freedom simply aroused endless jealousy, bickering, quarreling, drunkenness, mayhem, and murder.

The European system of agriculture offered both a motivational and functional solution to the dilemma. By adopting the family-farm system, with private property, fenced fields, frame houses, horses and cattle, and the plow, the Iroquois male would be given a new role and, potentially, a new self-respecting identity, both tribally and vis-à-vis white men. But for the family farm system to work, the continuous economic cooperation of a husband and wife was necessary; it required dispensing with the open cornfields tilled by the women of a lineage, the loosening of the tie between mother and daughter, and the stabilization of the nuclear family.

These functional prerequisites Handsome Lake undertook to define. Just how aware he was of the combination of emotional and functional advantages of the new system, it is impossible now to say. But his proposals were, by and large, accepted by most Iroquois and the reservations were parceled out into family farms owned, worked, and inherited, as long as they were in use, by men as heads of families. To be sure, the system was not, and is not, perfectly followed. Many men continued to travel, as circus entertainers, high steel workers, soldiers, and so on; but the old matriarchy was never restored.

ON THE CONDITIONS OF CHANGE IN KINSHIP DOMINANCE

As we have seen, the Iroquois during the classic two centuries of the colonial period were a population of sedentary females and nomadic males. The men, frequently absent in small or large groups for prolonged periods of time on hunting, trading, war, and diplomatic expeditions, simultaneously protected the women from foreign attack and produced a cash crop of skins, furs, and scalps which they exchanged for hardware and dry goods. These activities, peripheral in a geographical sense, were central to the economic and political welfare of the Six Nations. The preoccupation of Iroquois men with these tasks, and the pride they took in their successful pursuit, cannot be overestimated. But the system depended on a complementary role for women, who had to be economically self-sufficient, through horticulture, during prolonged absences of men, and who maintained genealogical and political continuity in a matrilineal system in which the primary kin relationship (not necessarily the primary social relationship) was that between mother and daughter. Under these conditions, a marital system based on virtually free sexual choice, the mutual satisfaction of spouses, and easy separation was a necessity.

When the Iroquois were confined to reservations, between 1783 and 1797, the system changed. No longer were females sedentary and males nomadic; both males and females were sedentary. The system—under encouragement from whites—shifted to a family farm economy, with the man as the major farm worker, with the nuclear family replacing the matrilineage as the effective socioeconomic unit for the sedentary population, and with the husband-wife replacing the mother-daughter relationship in kinship primacy.

The Iroquois system was, to a significant degree, pre-adapted to this change. The existing marital pattern, although characterized by domestic instability, already emphasized the importance of emotional attachment between spouses and permitted virtually free mate selection, based on mutual attraction, satisfaction, and compatibility. Modifications in the social context of this marital pattern could be made so as to adapt it to the family farm system. The system that emerged was not yet a peasantry, and was neither patrilineal nor patriarchal, in any sense comparable to European, Asian, or African traditions; the sib system was unchallenged, polygyny was not endorsed, and the contracting of marriages for reasons of family alliance or economic convenience was not practiced. In a sense, the pattern that emerged was more similar to that of America of the twentieth century than that of the nineteenth.

This sequence suggests that, far from copying Europeans, the Iroquois were creatively developing potentialities inherent in their own kinship system to their new technological and political circumstances. And this in turn suggests that, in societies of sedentary females and nomadic males, one functional adaptation will be matriliny with relatively free marital choice; and that, when for any reason both sexes become sedentary, the next adaptation will involve de-emphasizing the mother-daughter relationship and developing and stabilizing the husband-wife relationship in a nuclear family system, rather than shifting to patriliny.

Indeed, one may speculate that a nice, rhythmic, unilinear evolutionary sequence exists in kinship dominance, associated with technological and economic development (table 4.1).

In this scheme (and in the preceding discussion of the Iroquois) dominance in kin relationships is estimated not so much in terms of emotional closeness but in terms of legal and economic importance. It is an interesting question whether dominance in this legal-economic sense corresponds well with emotional closeness. In the case of India, as analyzed by Hsu (1963) in *Clan, Caste, and Club*, it would appear that the closest emotional relationship is mother-son even though father-son is more important in a legal and economic sense. Such discordance may not be rare and, where it occurs, may give rise to strain in social relationships and personality structure and perhaps ultimately to culture change.

Table 4.1   Unilinear Evolutionary Sequence of Kinship Dominance

Dominant Kin Relationship	Economy
Husband-wife	Hunting and gathering requiring mobility of both sexes
Mother-daughter	Horticulture for women and hunting, war, trade, and diplomacy for men; females sedentary, males nomadic
Husband-wife	Farms managed by nuclear families; males and females sedentary
Father-son	Rural-urban civilization with capital accumulations managed by males and inherited patrilineally among both peasantry and urban dwellers; males and females largely sedentary
Husband-wife	Industrial urban civilization with capital accumulations managed by bureaucratic organizations; mobility of both sexes

5

Paradigmatic Processes in Culture Change

The purpose of this paper is to direct attention to, and to delineate more thoroughly, a type of process in culture change which of late has been relatively neglected by anthropologists. Kroeber and his contemporaries a generation ago (*vide* Kroeber 1939, 1944) emphasized the importance of paradigmatic regularities in historical process in their studies of the growth of culture areas and civilizations. A historian of science, Thomas Kuhn, more recently has formulated in greater detail some of the essential features of the paradigmatic process in his well-known essay on the nature of scientific progress, *The Structure of Scientific Revolutions* (1962, 1970). I propose here to amplify their statements, to generalize them still further into a model of a type of culture change (which I shall call "paradigmatic"), and to outline some of the many applications of the model to the study of culture change in domains other than science itself. Finally, I shall illustrate the use of the model in brief case studies of the Industrial Revolution in England and in America.

KUHN'S MODEL OF CULTURE CHANGE

Kuhn argued that contrary to the belief of most scientists and of many historians of science, scientific evolution has not been a steady, continuous accumulation of data and modification of theory. It has proceeded, rather, in alternating phases of normal and revolutionary science. During the course of "normal science," an unchanging paradigm governs the work of most investigators in any given field or discipline. These paradigms are the "recurrent and quasi-standard illustrations of various theories in their conceptual, observational, and instrumental applications" (Kuhn 1962:43). Explicit rules, theories, and assumptions may accompany paradigms but are not necessary for the guidance of research. The student learns the paradigm primarily by repeating as training exercises the very "illustrations" which constitute the paradigm itself, i.e., by re-doing the laboratory experiments, deriving the equations, intuiting the concepts and findings which are described in the textbooks as classic and fundamental achievements. Later his professional work as a normal scientist is to discover new applications of the same paradigm, to resolve ambiguities and apparent contradictions in the rules and theories, and to work out the as-yet-undiscovered theorems implicit in its logic. His work is problem-solving within the continuously developing domain of interpretations of the paradigm itself. Thus the Greek geometers before Euclid established a paradigm for the study of plane and solid forms based upon constructions which could be accomplished by ruler and compass, by the sectioning of spheres, cones, and cylinders, and by the use of syllogistic reasoning. The formulation of axioms and theorems, and the application of Euclidean geometry to science and technology, was a problem-solving enterprise that occupied the Greek mathematical community for hundreds of years.

In the case of the Greek geometers, no new geometrical paradigm supplanted the old in their own time; truly non-Euclidean geometries did not appear until the nineteenth century. But inevitably, sooner or later, new paradigms directly confront and replace older ones. This confrontation occurs when the number of nagging, insoluble problems and internal inconsistencies associated with an existing paradigm has accumulated to the point where a whole new way of approaching the problem is seen as necessary by some irritated members of the scientific community. In response to the crisis, a new paradigm is devised which is able to account for most of the phenomena explicable under the old but which is also able to solve the crucial problems refractory to it. If, after some intellectual conflict, the new paradigm is accepted, and with it a redefinition of the worldview of the discipline, a "scientific revolution" may be said to have occurred. Examples of such scientific revolutions are the replacement of Ptolemaic by Galilean astronomy and the overthrow of the phlogiston theory of combustion by the oxygen theory. The development of the oxidation paradigm led directly to the complex set of principles and procedures which constituted the new atomic chemistry.

Both paradigmatic processes—normal science and revolutionary science—involve the activity of a scientific community. Such a community (or discipline, or school, or tradition, or what have you) is not usually a community in the ordinary sociological sense, of course, but rather a group of intercommunicating specialists, unrestricted in time or space, who jointly develop the applications of the paradigm. Kuhn does not elaborate on the nature of this community but its existence is explicitly recognized in his argument.

THE GENERAL MODEL OF PARADIGMATIC PROCESSES

The paradigmatic process has five essential components: innovation, paradigmatic core development, exploitation, functional consequences, and rationalization. It is possible to think of them as overlapping stages in which each comes to the forefront of attention in the aforementioned order, but the latter four "tasks" are actually continuous during the life of the paradigm.

This model attempts to embrace a far wider range of culture change processes than Kuhn's, first because Kuhn is centrally concerned with the history of science, and second because he is not attempting to deal at all with exploitation, functional consequences, or rationalization. But my model does not claim to describe *all* sequences of innovations and their consequences. *It applies only to those change sequences in which a paradigmatic core development process occurs.* This restriction is essential to the application of the model.

Innovation of a new paradigm may (as Kuhn emphasizes) entail a conflict with an older one, which it must replace; in this case one may speak of a "revolution," such as the scientific revolutions of which Kuhn writes, or the cultural "revolutions" associated with the development of agriculture, urban life, and industrial technology. Whether the innovation of a new paradigm is always a revolutionary event, in the sense that it immediately challenges the adequacy of existing practice, is debatable; not all innovations basic to a new paradigm necessarily contradict an earlier paradigm, for some may initiate an entirely new line of development. But it is difficult to think of clear-cut examples of this sort of event, and for practical purposes it is probably useful to assume paradigmatic conflict to be the best evidence of fundamental innovation. A more important consideration is that not all innovations are paradigm-forming. Many can best be considered under other headings (core development, functional consequences, and rationalization). And some, perhaps, are simply not relevant to any paradigm process at all.

To qualify as paradigm-forming, an innovation need not be a complete and adequate theory or model; rather, it is an event which solves a limited problem but does so in a way which opens up a whole new line of development. It is a major "break-through." Furthermore, the paradigmatic innovation has a symbolic and charismatic quality. It is often associated with the name of a culture hero (human or divine) and it can be simply represented by some visual image or phrase or manual procedure.

In the history of American anthropology, for instance, one can find a convenient illustration in the origin of the "fieldwork" paradigm. Whether accurately or not, one thinks of Franz Boas stepping off the boat in an Eskimo village with his suitcase in hand, preparing for a long stay in residence. This image *is* the paradigm: the subsequent development of field techniques, standards of ethnographic description, ethnological theory, and training requirements for the Ph.D. stem from, and are implied by, the symbol of Boas as lone fieldworker taking up prolonged residence in a small community. This symbol is opposed in a revolutionary way to a nineteenth century tradition of library scholarship and of uncritical use of the comparative method to derive models of cultural evolution. Of course Boas was not actually the first to do fieldwork; he did not in all respects do adequate fieldwork by the standards of his own paradigm, and he did not really deny the value of library work or of studies of cultural evolution. But all that is beside the point: he did effectively establish the fieldwork paradigm for American academic anthropology.

Paradigmatic core development is the continuous elaboration of the ideas which constitute the original paradigm, according to the rules of the paradigm itself. In science, Kuhn calls this the process of "normal science." Generations of trained workers make "contributions" to the perfection of the paradigm by resolving any surviving internal ambiguities or contradictions and by demonstrating its utility in solving newly discovered problems. Doctoral dissertations, for instance, are expected to be paradigmatic contributions in their own fields. People who are working on the same paradigm tend to be visible as a profession, or a school of thought, or a tradition, and to function as a community whose reference objects are other members of the community rather than the world outside. Such paradigmatic communities in our own culture history are readily recognizable not only in science but outside of science as well, in such fields as philosophy, theology, music, art and literature, and technology, and Kuhn (1970) has already recognized that humanistic scholarship traditionally assumes a paradigmatic scheme in its approaches to intellectual history and criticism.

Let us briefly consider theology, art, and literature (we shall return to the technology application later in more detail). In the case of religion, almost as soon as the prophet of a revitalization movement has begun to lay down the new paradigm in the form of a code based on his revelations, his disciples begin to discuss, interpret, and apply it. Even within non-literate or marginally literate cultures, this process of editing, interpreting, and applying the text goes on incessantly, and a body of auxiliary belief and commentary rapidly builds up within the paradigmatic community of disciples, preachers, priests, and other followers. There is a continuing process of defining and redefining the standard symbols and formulas as new historical circumstances arise. Similarly in art, once a new idea or approach has been successfully broached, a "school" is likely to develop, perhaps at first consisting of only a few disciples, who work busily at amplifying and developing their master's paradigm. And again in literature, once a classic work has been created, it provides the format for dozens or hundreds of followers who play with and explore the possibilities implicit in the original.

There is a peculiar arbitrariness in the core development process. It is often remarkably independent in its direction (though not in velocity), once launched, from surrounding events, although it influences them. It is as though, once defined, the paradigm must be developed according to its own inner law; like a gyroscope, its attitude remains stable in a shifting historical frame. It is notoriously difficult to censor, suppress, or destroy a process of core development by economic, religious, or political pressures. Furthermore, within the paradigmatic community, new developments are in a sense unpredictable, for to predict the event in any detail is to have anticipated it; the event predicted occurs in the course of its own prediction. Thus, even though core development follows its own inner logic and works to realize latent implications, its course is also accompanied by a constant sense of surprised discovery.

By *exploitation* is meant the recognition and embracing of the paradigm, at some stage in its evolution, by an economic, military, religious, or political organization which sees in its application an opportunity for the protection or advancement of its own interests. The paradigmatic community can, theoretically, exploit its own paradigm, but this in all likelihood rarely happens. More commonly the exploitation is carried out by others, very often in as monopolistic a fashion as possible. The exploiting group may not only wish to apply the paradigm, and be the only applier of it; they may wish to direct in some measure the further development of the core itself, both as to direction and rate. It is in the relationship of the paradigmatic and exploitive community that some of the most interesting features of the process lie, and we shall return to them later in this paper.

By *functional consequences* are meant the new, specific problems which the exploitation of the core development process creates for society and the way in which society responds, at first by expedients, and eventually by cultural change. Recent examples in science are all too obvious: the applications of core development in normal science to the creation of new physical, chemical, and biological weaponry has threatened the survival of mankind, created new industries, developed new patterns of international relations, and so on. Ecological damage from indiscriminate waste disposal, from the incautious use of DDT and other insecticides, and from over-use of natural resources is almost as serious a threat. A result of medical research and improved methods of food production has been a vast increase in the world's population; this increase has entailed further pressure on the ecosystem; and so on *ad infinitum*. It is easy to discover examples of catastrophic problems presented by the innocent development of a core by an oblivious paradigmatic community and an ambitious exploiting group. Typically, core development will create opportunity for some; and if that opportunity is seized, functional consequences will include advantages for some and new problems for others, and perhaps even eventually for the opportunist himself. And the solutions to any one problem will produce other problems and the solutions to these problems still more problems. This peculiar Pandora's box quality of the offerings of continuing core development and exploitation almost invariably generates an ambivalence, sometimes even a taboo toward the paradigmatic community by the rest of the society, with some parties interested in exploiting the new developments, others in suppressing them, and many feeling both ways at the same time.

But whether or not there is ambivalence, the problems produced by paradigmatic development are real ones and the policies which political and economic communities concoct to deal with them are an interesting field for cultural analysis, for experimental procedures tend to become policy and, when successful, to harden into conventional practice—*ad hoc* procedure becomes policy and policy becomes culture.

By *rationalization* is intended the ethical, philosophical, religious, and political justifications which the paradigmatic community members offer for their participation in the core development process and which general community members offer for their relationship to the paradigm. As Garfinkel (1967) and other ethnomethodologists have pointed out, people tend to act in such a way as to validate their theory of the world; but when new actions are made necessary by the challenges of functional consequences of exploiting a paradigm, a new theory must be constructed. The para-community is generally rather monotonous in its rationalizations, saying in effect that working on the paradigm is doing God's work, or that it will lead to a better world, or that basic research is a good thing in itself and will always pay off eventually. The general community has a more interesting problem. In its initial "seizure" of the paradigm for the first application, the exploiting community group may account for its action with familiar and established explanations. Indeed, as Smelser (1959) and my student Kasserman (1971) point out, the exploiter may be an essentially conservative person who is simply trying to maintain his footing in a changing world. Later on, however, as more and more expedients must be contrived to cope with spin-off problems, the rationalization must change to take account of the functional changes in the society and in their own lives. Thus, for example, commercial exploiters of the rock music paradigm may in order to establish their bona fides with officialdom find it necessary to invest in centers for the treatment and rehabilitation of drug users, and to accept other social entailments of their role, and eventually to define themselves as brokers between the movement and the establishment rather than merely as entrepreneurs.

RELATIONS BETWEEN THE PARADIGMATIC
COMMUNITY AND THE REST OF SOCIETY

To the historian and sociologist of science, it has long been an appealing hypothesis that the language, the customs, and the values of the general society subtly determine the ideas of supposedly objective fields. The paradigmatic notion looks at the process in another way, concentrating on the evolution of the irrelevant to the point where relevance is discovered. The discovery of relevance is the moment of exploitation. At once the paradigmatic community is confronted by organizations, up to and at times including the sovereign institutions, which make claims upon them. The interaction between these two interest groups is the subject of high drama in our own time—and even in our own profession, where the exploitation of the fieldwork paradigm by government agencies entails serious probable functional consequences and thus generates intense discussion of ethical issues. There are a number of dimensions along which the relations may vary and for the sake of introductory discussion let us enumerate some of them. With respect to *support*, the policy of the general community may range from across-the-board support of an entire para-community (e.g., of a discipline like physics) by granting unrestricted research funds and fellowships, by favorable patent and copyright laws, by establishing new research and development communities; or it may restrict support to selected aspects of the field (such as weapons research) and other purely applied projects; or it may make deliberate efforts to destroy the entire para-community (e.g., by accusing them of treason, of being witches, or whatever). With regard to *communication,* the general community may favor open channels (by avoiding censorship, endorsing freedom of speech, and the like) or it may impose censorship, place embargoes on immigration or emigration or even travel, or restrict foreign trade. With respect to *power,* the general community may eagerly include the para-community in the power structure, or exclude it from certain sorts of decision-making forums (by requiring a nonpolitical position as a condition of support), or even generally wall off the para-community into a caste-like minority group or ghetto population. With respect to *control of applications,* the general community may take the initiative and attempt to seduce, hire, or coerce members of the para-community into providing service, or the responsibility for exploitation may be handled jointly, or the para-community may attempt to control the nature, timing, and degree of exploitation of its paradigm, in some cases urging applications, and in others attempting to restrict or control them. And, of course, the *reward* system for paradigmatic work may vary from material goods, money, and power through symbolic rewards (medals, prizes, and so on) to rewards in the form of status or prestige in the para-community alone.

The development of the relationships between paradigmatic and lay communities is, in a sense, a side play, separate from the immediate paradigm development, functional consequence, and rationalization problems. It is, however, an important political process whose course will affect the course of the whole society.

THE MILLS ON CHESTER CREEK: A CASE STUDY

The idea of formulating the theory of paradigmatic process in culture change was originally prompted by the need to develop a frame of thought for an ethno-historical study. During the past two years the writer and some of his colleagues and students have been investigating in some detail the rise and fall of the early textile mills, and their associated industrial villages, along the streams in southeastern Pennsylvania. In the period from about 1810 to 1850, dozens of cotton and woolen spinning mills, with weaving sheds attached, were established along the small streams which cut down across a fall line toward the Delaware River, from Philadelphia on the north (where "The Manchester of North America" existed for a time in Manayunk on the banks of the Schuylkill River) to Wilmington on the South (where the du Pont family eventually established their vast powder and other chemical works). One of these streams was Chester Creek, which is the geographic focus of the empirical study.

The mills along this fall line were pre-adapted to the Industrial Revolution. During the hundred and twenty-five years or so of settlement after William Penn's arrival in 1682, the region had been combed for mill sites. Literally hundreds of dams and races and small stone mills (over forty on Chester Creek alone, in a distance of fifteen miles) had been built. They were powered by breast and overshot water wheels and maintained such diverse enterprises as iron forges, paper factories, fulling mills, saw-mills, grist-mills, and oil-mills. The iron-masters, papermakers, and millers were the rural elite, possessed of more capital and more education than even the most prosperous farmers, and already in effective control of the community, for they often served as the local magistrates and election supervisors, and were lay leaders in the local churches. As Kasserman (1971) points out, as forests and wheat fields exhausted their potentialities, mill owners in what was then an underdeveloped country invested in textile machinery, along with their other interests, as soon as it became available either from the memories of illegal emigrants from England before the War of 1812 or by direct purchase after 1815. Perforce they had to keep up with the continuous improvements in spinning machinery, turbines, and power looms as the technology accelerated. Soon Philadelphia was the center for a machine tool industry, and the lower Delaware Valley became for a time one of the major textile-producing centers of the world.

After the middle of the nineteenth century, efficient Corliss steam engines were made available to manufacturers, who generally found it to their advantage thereafter to concentrate their production in cities with their much better commercial, engineering, and transportation facilities; but even after the obsolescence of the water wheel and water turbine as transmitters of power, the old mills remained active along the little creeks and rivers because a trained labor force, attached to their homes, remained there in the old hamlets. The last of the old textile mills are only now ceasing to operate on Chester Creek and other fall line streams. But long ago the little rural mill villages lost their economic advantage, and only a dim folk memory persists of a past age of industrial glory. The hamlets still survive amid the ruins of an obsolete technology. The ancient mansions and whitewashed stone tenements are crumbling, and the old mill buildings one by one are collapsing into rubble; but the old families stay, and probably much of the old political and economic structure which the mills produced, in all-White communities which are remarkable not only for their poverty and conservatism but also for an astonishing degree of freedom from drugs, crime in the streets, and other more familiar urban symptoms of the social tensions of the time. One's impression, in surveying the ruins of these towns, is of a community which gave birth to a whole new way of life, and now lies exhausted after the labor of creation.

It is obvious enough that the driving motive in the process of industrialization was financial security and profit; but directional control was given by the technology of dams and races, water wheels and turbines, masonry and carpentry, gears and belts, and spinning and weaving machinery. The mechanics, inventors, and engineers who made the mills inevitably determined, not that capital would be invested by men seeking profit, but precisely how that capital would be embodied. Factory social organization depended on the technical requirements of the machines; and the factory system in turn affected domestic life and family social structure. For instance: the great danger to the early textile mills was fire and flood; soon the volunteer fire company replaced the militia as the place where men paraded their manhood in socially responsible fashion. Mill owners had to develop small communities of tenement-housed worker families around their mills because local farmers could not provide room and board for so many people. The churches and their Sunday Schools were financially endowed by the mill-owners because the churches were the mill-owners' allies in opposing drunkenness and other vices which reduced a worker's productivity. Some owners and some churchmen even enjoyed Utopian fantasies and looked upon factory life as an opportunity to build Jerusalem anew. A sharp awareness of a difference in the interests of the operatives as a class and the manufacturers as a class emerged in the class-conscious Jacksonian era of the 1830s and 1840s in the wake of strikes, riots, conspiracy trials, child labor legislation, and the development of unions, workmen's educational associations, and manufacturers and businessmen's associations. Mill owners, compelled at certain times (or so they thought) by financial pressures to lay off workers or reduce wages, agonized over the breakdown of the old solidarity between management and labor. At least one whose autobiography survives, previously an agnostic, turned to religion and philosophy for assurances that what he had to do for business reasons was the right thing for moral ones. And the resurgence of religion and the rise of the businessmen's fraternal orders (the reconstituted Masons, the Red Men, etc.) contributed to a new industrial ethic (or at least rationalization) of hard work, religious faith, denial of the reality of social classes, and community leadership rather than of class exploitation. But all of these changes were responsive to a process of continuously developing technology and each local mill was anchored to the sophisticated rigors of the engineers who, associated in regional and national societies like the Franklin Institute in nearby Philadelphia, were slowly perfecting the art of spinning and weaving by machine.

How can one best comprehend a process of industrialization visible in eight or ten little water-powered textile mills huddled together along one stream, the population of whose associated hamlets totaled only a few thousand—a community on the traditional ethnographer's scale, but a community which is tied into the regional, state, and national organizations of the mill-owners and managers and, beyond them, the international guild of inventors? In an attempt to formulate a plan for the study, I was led to consider the paradigmatic process along the lines which have just been described.

THE INDUSTRIAL REVOLUTION IN GREAT BRITAIN AS A PARADIGMATIC PROCESS

Although the model which we have just outlined is immediately useful in guiding the research strategy for such projects as the Chester Creek study, it can be illustrated on a grander scale, by one of the major saltations in cultural evolution: the origin of the Industrial Revolution itself. The English Industrial Revolution exemplified the paradigmatic process very well. Let us consider it according to the five stages which are outlined above: innovation, core development, exploitation, functional consequences, and rationalization.

Innovation and Paradigmatic Core Development

Although many factors combined to create the milieu in which the Industrial Revolution occurred, the most spectacular and symbolically important innovations, by all accounts, were the inventions in the decade of the 1760s of spinning machinery by James Hargreaves and Richard Arkwright in England and of the modern steam engine by James Watt in Scotland. But it is certainly not the case that these gadgets burst unexpectedly upon a surprised world; rather, they—and a number of other innovations in pottery-making, metalworking, agriculture and transportation—represented the first exploitable products of a technological paradigm which had been established at least a century before. Thus Thomas Savery in 1698 had made a workable steam engine for the purpose of pumping ground water from Cornish mines; and Thomas Newcomen in 1708 had developed another type of steam engine for pumping out collieries. Silk-throwing machinery had been introduced from Italy in 1717, and a true factory was developed for its use; the flying shuttle had been invented by John Kay to improve weaving in 1733; and a primitive roller spinning device was produced in 1738. All of this interest in the improvement of mechanical gadgetry had roots in the efforts of mill-wrights, clockmakers, instrument makers, clergymen, poets, physicians, barbers, and even scientists, to solve various technical problems which had already been conventionally isolated and defined. The notion that mathematical thinking, applied to naturalistic observation and experiment, and expressed in clock-work-like machines, could lead to the solution of practical problems, had so thoroughly taken hold that by 1754— *before* the critical inventions had been made—there had been founded a Society for the Encouragement of Arts, Manufactures, and Commerce, which offered prizes to inventors.

It is evident then that the inventions of the 1760s, which constituted the classic expressions of the industrial paradigm, were nonetheless the product of several generations of optimistic work by scientists and mechanics. Hargreaves, the mill-wright; Arkwright, the barber; Watt, the instrument maker, in a sense did for mechanical invention what Euclid did for Greek geometry—they codified and put in a conspicuously applicable form a body of skills and knowledge which had been accumulating for decades. The latent paradigm on which the scientists and engineers had been working was the clock, an intricate system of carefully made and mathematically articulated wheels, gears, and shafts which accepted a source of power at one end and applied it to the performance of a useful and precisely quantifiable task at the other.

Exploitation

What made the machine paradigm into an industrial revolution was its combination with an old concept: the factory. There had been factories since Roman times where large numbers of skilled artisans plied their trade under one roof and under some sort of supervision. The new factory was occupied by large numbers of clock-work-like machines, powered by an external source of energy, that performed precise manual tasks under the supervision of a group of trained operatives. This application of the paradigm, it is said, was achieved first in 1717 by Thomas Lambe in his water-driven silk works in Derby, where 300 workmen were employed; and Lambe's model was copied by Arkwright in a water-driven cotton factory at Cranford which by about 1772 employed about 600. About the same time Josiah Wedgewood—without major mechanical innovations—introduced the factory method into pottery making when in 1769 he set up the Etruria works.

But before this application could be accomplished, a process of exploitation had to occur. Scientists and mechanics for generations had been producing all kinds of finely made devices which—except for the clocks themselves—were of restricted practical value. The first spinning jennies were made and sold without even the taking of a patent by their inventor, and they were adopted primarily in domestic industries, where they simply amplified the income of household spinning-and-weaving enterprises. Richard Arkwright realized the potential profitability of assembling numbers of improved spinning machines, attaching them to a water-wheel as power source, and training and employing factory hands ("operatives") to guide the machines.

The initial conditions for profitable exploitation of the new machinery in England included a capitalist commercial ethic, expanding markets, demand for a higher rate of production than conventional technology could accomplish, and the availability of large sums of money which could be borrowed at relatively low interest rates or which could be attracted as investment in corporate ventures. Thus an economic milieu existed in mid-eighteenth century England which made possible the assembling of capital required for the exploitation of technical innovations. The industrial exploiter used his capital to perform a complex task; first, to buy, or rent, or develop a mill-site, including dam, races, wheel, and mill-machinery, a building housing the mill, some associated housing for manager and workers, and transportation facilities; second, to buy, or have made, the desired machines, and to install them in the mill; third, to hire, train, supervise, and pay the operatives.

Functional Consequences

With the securing of capital, the commissioning of machinery, and the employment of operatives, there was defined a triad of communities whose mutual confrontations launched a still-continuing process of social and cultural change. The exploiting community consisted of the owner or owners of the mill, the banks and other lending institutions, the suppliers of raw materials, and the distributors of finished goods. They jointly risked financial loss and jointly hoped for financial gain, and their efforts to make their investment more secure and their profits higher and more certain eventually required society-wide cultural innovations in insurance, in banking, in credit relations, in measures against periodic "panics," in fire and flood control, in labor legislation, local government, and so on.

An interesting analysis of spin-off from the cotton industry's changes during the Industrial Revolution in Great Britain has been provided by the sociologist Neil J. Smelser in his study, *Social Change in the Industrial Revolution* [1959]. He approaches the question with a Parsonian scheme that views culture change as a response to the perception that some technique or institution is not functioning adequately or that there is a bottleneck in a process (e.g., the flying shuttle enabled household weavers to supply more cloth to satisfy foreign markets; this placed a demand on spinners which was eventually met only by the adoption of the jenny). Most of his attention is directed to the families of cotton spinners. Initially the technical innovations and the early factories merely strengthened the traditional spinner households. Their real income increased, and factory-operative spinners were able to hire and supervise their own children and other kinfolk much as they had earlier in the days of the cottage industries. Thus despite the massive increase in the production of cotton products resulting from the development of the new machinery and the building of factories, the initial effect on the English cottage family was to confirm its traditional structure. The problem for the spinner family really began in the 1820s (fully two generations after the critical innovations), when spinning machines became so complex that a spinner had to supervise more helpers than his own family could provide and when the availability of efficient steam engines made it possible to locate factories in large towns and cities rather than at the country mill-sites. Under these conditions, the authority of the father in many a family was threatened, because his children were able to enter the "free" labor market to work as spinner's helpers for other spinners and also to work as factory-employed hands in machine weaving rooms. The dissatisfaction with the differentiation of labor within the family was in part responsible for the rise of labor unions, the introduction of factory-hour legislation, the rise of cooperative stores and savings banks, and the rapid spread of state or industry-supported schools for factory children who could no longer be educated and socialized by their parents.

Rationalization

The initial understanding of what the new machinery and the new factories meant tended to be somewhat Utopian. There was an anticipation of wealth to be gained by merchant adventurers, inventors, and investors; there was an increase in real income among the cottage spinners and weavers; and there was an expectation that the factory system, which required high standards of punctuality and efficiency, would teach the Protestant ethic to the shiftless poor. But these interpretations of the event were made from an optimistic eighteenth-century perspective. By the 1820's the English had had enough experience with the new system to realize what some of the functional consequences of industrialization were. And so, about this time, serious efforts to rationalize the process were begun. Some sought to justify a depersonalization of man (which was implied by a national labor market responding to the prod of starvation) by anticipations of improvement in the general welfare. The utopian scientists quickly saw both the human costs and benefits; this line of thought received a classic expression in the somewhat romantic, even nostalgic analysis by Karl Marx in *Das Kapital* in 1867. Thinking along somewhat different lines were the *laissez-faire* theorists, including Adam Smith, Thomas Malthus, Ricardo, and later the Social Darwinists. Such writers as these, as Polanyi (1944) has pointed out, served to make the Industrial Revolution understandable not in simple eighteenth-century "enlightenment" terms but in terms of the kinds of decisions that industrialists, bankers, government officials and legislators, the clergy, and working people had to make in coping with the deluge of machinery suddenly let loose upon the world. Each of these lines of rationalization, furthermore, became a paradigm for further intellectual work, much as a theological tradition grows up after a new messiah formulates a religious code.

OTHER APPLICATIONS OF THE MODEL

The paradigmatic model is obviously closely related to the revitalization movement model; indeed, one could conceive of revitalization movements as being a special case of paradigm development. In both cases one is dealing with deliberate efforts to innovate continuously over a substantial period of time. Evidently also some of the major saltations in general evolution can be regarded as paradigmatic — not merely the Industrial Revolution, but, if we had the data, probably also the Neolithic and Urban revolutions, and conceivably even earlier processes, such as the development of stone tool traditions. The paradigm model would not, however, be useful in all acculturation studies, for in many situations one suspects that the paradigm is precisely what is not communicated across the interface between two cultures. The difficulty of communicating paradigms may have something to do with the problems of development in recently colonial societies and in minority communities. And finally, the paradigm model fits well with such concepts as Kroeber's culture climax and the pattern-fulfillment concepts embodied in most philosophies of history. Culture-historical analysis might be able to use such concepts too, even though the problems usually addressed are those of survival and distribution.

The examples so far cited have tended to lay emphasis largely on scientific and technological cores, with occasional reference to theology and the arts. Perhaps such "hard" domains attract attention because problems can here be phrased in relatively formal, and therefore finite and solvable, terms. It may be that the aesthetic urge which in part prompts the process of core development is best satisfied in working with systems that permit highly structured, cumulative thinking. But paradigmatic thinking itself does not necessarily address itself to the practical problems of the world; it may appear, to those outside the paradigmatic community, that it is a domain of trivialities, a menagerie of hair-splitting pedants, cranks, and ivory-tower types whose preoccupations are irrelevant to the "real" world. Irrelevant, that is, until the paradigm has been developed to a point where one of its aspects presents a means for solving someone's practical problem. The "practical" problem, of course, may in fact be equally trivial, in comparison with the giant and enduring social and emotional problems of mankind. But it seems to be the case that the world has repeatedly been transformed by the conjunction of trivialities: specifically, by the application of new navigational gadgets to the problem of securing spices for dining tables and beaver pelts for felt hats, by the application of mechanical rollers to the problem of making enough cotton thread to satisfy the demand for cotton cloth created by the importation of Indian cottons from recently conquered India—and so on. It remains to be seen whether paradigmatic development proceeds in as effective a way in the field of political and economic organization. Indeed, the conditions under which domains of culture become susceptible to paradigmatic change would be an interesting subject for research.

CONCLUSION

The purpose of this paper has been to draw attention to a pervasive, but not adequately conceptualized, process of culture change which, after Thomas Kuhn, we shall call *paradigmatic*. A tentative general model of such processes has been presented, delineating as stages or functions the processes of *innovation* and *paradigmatic core development, exploitation, functional consequences,* and *rationalization*. The English Industrial Revolution was considered as a prime example of the process, and finally some general questions were raised about the conditions under which such processes occur, and the relation of the paradigmatic process to other processes in culture change.

6

Technology in Culture

The Meaning of Cultural Fit

It can be argued that efforts to introduce newly invented or newly imported technology into a society almost always generate some degree of social conflict. The new technology is perceived by some as advantageous, by some as disadvantageous. Thus there is likely to follow a more or less protracted process of "fitting in," in which modifications are made in the technology and its manner of use in order to win the cooperation of those initially threatened by it. One of the classic illustrations of this point is provided in Manning Nash's study of the introduction of modern cotton manufacturing to a Maya Indian community in nineteenth-century Guatemala. Peasant women were traditionally the makers of textiles, but neither they nor the men would at first work in the mills, despite the advantages of the cash income they could earn there. Then the Spanish mill owners and British managers discovered the source of the problem: they were scheduling an unbroken day's work in the mill, as they were used to doing in Europe. By simply permitting the workers to split the day, allowing a four-hour midday break—during which wives could cook, care for their children, and do necessary household chores, and the men could work in their fields—the objections were overcome. The traditional time off for fiestas was made up by Saturday afternoon work. But it took more than fifty years—from the construction of the mill in 1876 to the early 1930s—for these and other mutual accommodations to build the successful enterprise that the mill became in the twentieth century (Nash 1958:17).[1]

However, the problem of how new technology fits or does not fit or is gradually fitted into a culture is complex. The scenarios range from simple preadaptation to elaborate processes of conflict and compromise. To illuminate these processes, I shall turn to three societies that have been studied by anthropologists to look into the question. In one case, the Thonga miners of Mozambique, a new technology at first served old institutions perfectly. In a second, among a group of Australian aborigines, the introduction of admittedly more efficient steel axes upset the status system and confounded the belief system; steel axes did not fit Yir Yoront culture. And in a third case, that of the Iroquois, a formerly rejected technology—the European-style family farm—was finally fitted in by a judicious redesign of social relations. Having stated in general terms what we can learn from these three "primitive" societies about the fit of technology in culture, I shall examine the case of the anthracite industry, where violent social conflict accompanied industrialization. I shall then conclude with an attempt to describe how in complex societies where its social and ideological implications are different for different groups, new technology is "fitted in."

VARIOUS ANTHROPOLOGICAL USES OF THE WORD "CULTURE"

The older, traditional use of the word "culture" has been the *holistic* one, as defined by E. B. Tylor in his early textbook *Anthropology:* "Culture . . . is that complex whole which includes knowledge, belief, art, morals, law, custom, and any other capabilities and habits acquired by man as a member of society" (Tylor 1874, 1:1). This holistic conception of culture as a collection of learned habits is expressed in its most systematic form in the *Outline of Cultural Materials* (Murdock et al. 1950), which serves as the coding and indexing guide for the Human Relations Area Files. That guide recognizes, exclusive of background and methodological information, seventy-four major categories of behavior that are "cultural," including the language of the society and other communication devices (3 categories), technology (at least 20 categories, ranging from the "food quest" to "military technology"), economic organization (at least 7 categories from "property" through "marketing" to "labor"), kinship and other forms of social organization (12 categories, from "social stratification" through "in-groups" to "political behavior"), law and justice (3 categories), life cycle (8 categories), religion (3 categories), and miscellaneous others, including some that the symbols-and-meanings anthropologists would recognize under their definition of culture: "behavior processes and personality," "total culture," and "ideas about nature and man" (Murdock et al. 1950). No ethnographer, of course, actually writes a descriptive monograph following these encyclopedia outlines in detail, but some ethnographers do index and file their field notes according to the outline to aid information retrieval.

But philosophically, this holistic concept of culture has an important corollary. It says, in effect, that culture is man's means of evolutionary adaptation. Our species no longer depends on genetic change and natural selection to adapt to new or changed circumstances. Men and women learn to make tools and to arrange their social relations in a fashion that facilitates survival; and children learn from their parents. Culture then is the transgenerational learning of *all* those categories of behavior that contribute to human adaptation. (I leave aside the important qualification that some aspects of the culture of a particular community may in fact be maladaptive.) Culture is what makes us different from the "lower" animals (although they too may display elements of cultural behavior, at least with respect to tool fabrication and use).

Putting to one side the question of the broader evolutionary significance of culture, the ethnologist is confronted by the great cultural diversity of present (and recent) human societies. One approach to this panorama—an approach that inspired Tylor and the other cultural evolutionists of his time, including the American Lewis Henry Morgan—was to arrange the cultures of the world on a scale of cultural evolution. Morgan was even able to recognize culture as an adaptive mechanism in the dam-construction behavior of the beaver. And his broad, comparative vision struck a sympathetic chord in the mind of Friedrich Engels, who helped to establish cultural evolution as a scientific principle in Marxist thinking. Explicit in the cultural evolutionary view, whether advanced by Marxist or non-Marxist scholars, was a conception of technology as the prime mover in culture change. Culture in the holistic paradigm may be divided essentially into three parts: the basic technology, consisting of various materials, tools and machines, and the mechanical and social skills involved in their use in production and distribution; social organization, particularly the kinship system, community, and (eventually) the state; and religion, ideology, world-view, and other aspects of expressive culture. Major changes in technology alter work organization; alterations in work organization require compensatory changes in other areas of social organization; and changes in social organization demand appropriate changes in ritual, myth, and ideology.

Such a holistic view of technology-*in*-culture is particularly convenient when one is studying the great transformations in human life that go by such names as the Upper Paleolithic to Mesolithic transition, the Neolithic revolution, the urban revolution, and even the recent and currently unfolding industrial revolution. For the more remote eras, and for the preliterate societies of the world—where little or nothing in the way of written documents exists—much of the work of ethnographic reconstruction depends on inferring social organization from the mute evidence of artifacts: stone tools, hearths, pottery, grave goods, settlement patterns, and the evidence of tool use provided by fragments of human and animal bones. A similar line of logic applies also to those civilizations, beginning with the Near East, where written records are to be found together with archaeological remains. And similar procedures are currently in use by historical and industrial archaeologists investigating our own recent past. The whole process of interpreting culture change using a holistic concept of culture has been popularized in a non-dialectical, marginally Marxist manner by anthropologist Marvin Harris. In books like *Cultural Materialism* he advances a more or less conventional tripartite outline of cultural materials: "infrastructure" (the technology and practices employed in production and reproduction), "structure" (the domestic and political economies), and "superstructure" (religion, art, science, recreation, and other aspects of higher-order expressive and cognitive systems). Citing Marx as the original promulgator of the idea, Harris advances as the basis of cultural dynamics the principle of infrastructural (i.e., economic) determinism: infrastructure determines structure and superstructure (Harris 1979).

We need not review here the various criticisms of the evolutionary and cultural materialist position; they are directed not so much at the holistic conception of culture or economic determinism, as at the inability of the broad comparative and theoretical evolutionary perspective to focus on the historical and ethnographic uniqueness and complexity of individual societies. In America, Franz Boas and his students established a tradition of field work that required prolonged residence with the community under study—learning the native language, extensively recording texts, and collecting objects of "material culture" for study and comparison in museums. A tribal community's unique history of migrations, trade, and social contact was deemed to have determined its present culture; and tribes were compared trait by trait and then arranged by culture area rather than by evolutionary position. In Europe, by a somewhat different route, the intensive study of colonial native cultures was begun by British and French anthropologists, and it led not to the American style of historicism but rather to a kind of timeless functionalism. The problem was to discover how that complex whole called "culture" functioned like a homeostatic organism, each part delicately adjusted to the rest, and each contributing to the integrity of the whole. In this holistic scheme, the mode of production need have no priority in the causal chain because the focus of interest is not change; rather, the system's manner of operation in a state of equilibrium is the object of study. Thus Malinowski in two celebrated works, *Argonauts of the Western Pacific* and *Coral Gardens and Their Magic,* began his treatises with detailed descriptions of, respectively, the building of an ocean-going canoe and the preparation of a garden for planting. But here the primacy of technology was merely a convenient literary device, providing the reader with an understandable visual image, to which would be attached prolonged accounts of social organization and magical belief. Again, the conception is of technology-*in*-culture, intimately fitted to the other elements in a timeless embrace, rather than technology acting as an independent variable, a changing or intrusive influence, brutally compelling adjustment by social organization and religion.

The structural-functionalist tradition, however, as it developed in Britain under the magisterial guidance of A. R. Radcliffe-Brown, introduced a terminological innovation that reflected a clear break with the economic determinism of the evolutionists. Radcliffe-Brown took the familiar tripartite divisions of culture and rearranged them. Social structure became the prime mover and principal focus of attention (hence the term "social anthropology"), and the maintenance of social equilibrium or solidarity became the ruling dynamic principle: for this emphasis Radcliffe-Brown acknowledged his intellectual debt to Durkheim. The term "culture" was restricted to the sphere of sentiments and values, especially those that animated and directed persons to do what the social structure required for its maintenance. This, for example, is Radcliffe-Brown on religious ritual: "Thus, if it is a valid generalization to say that the chief function of ritual or ceremonial is to express and thereby maintain in existence sentiments that are necessary for social cohesion, we can 'explain' any given ritual or ceremonial by showing what are the sentiments expressed in it and how these sentiments are related to the cohesion of the society" (Quoted in Harris 1968:532). The techno-economic was thus relegated to the role of a necessary but not particularly interesting material basis for social structure. Radcliffe-Brown considered the task of social anthropology to be the discovery of the scientific laws of social structure, particularly as embodied in kinship; and he and his students formulated a number of putative universal principles—such as "the equivalence of brothers"—that together formed the bare bones of human social structure. Society, he asserted, had to be explained in terms of society, not of biology or psychology. To some of us, interested in understanding cross-cultural differences and culture change (in the holistic sense), these principles, being advanced as universal constants, did not appear to be very useful. Time was cyclical for the orthodox follower of Radcliffe-Brown, whose object was to see what made the social system function in perfect equilibrium.

We are now ready to consider the second major and contrasting concept of culture, that associated with the analysis of *symbols-and-meanings*. Not to be confused with the Lévi-Straussian tradition of symbol analysis, the symbols-and-meanings school of thought derives from both the British social anthropological tradition, at least as it was represented by Radcliffe-Brown, and the American culture-and-personality movement, with its concern for a society's concepts of self, identity, and world view. In symbols-and-meanings usage, the term "culture" refers to a pattern of ideas, a cognitive system, consisting of a relatively small set of abstract propositions, of both descriptive and normative kinds, about the nature of the human self and society, and about how people should feel and behave. This "culture" is shared, and shared uniquely, by the competent adult members of the community; it forms a template for all behavior. These cultural propositions are collective representations, encoded in such public symbols as literary texts, graphic art, dance, drama, and religious ritual. Thus both the symbols and their meanings are readily accessible to anthropological observation and inquiry. These high-order generalizations about how members of a community see themselves and each other help the anthropologist to understand the social structure and the economic system, as the writings of the best-known representatives of the symbols-and-meanings school—Clifford Geertz, Victor Turner, and Mary Douglas—have demonstrated to a wide public.

With the maturation of the symbols-and-meanings school, a certain symmetry has been reached among the various usages of the term "culture." Ancestral to all the usages, and one still observed by many self-styled cultural anthropologists (including myself), is the old Tylorean holistic view of culture as a complex whole, the functions and the manner of integration of whose parts is the object of ethnographic analysis. Conventional wisdom divides this complex whole into three sections: the techno-economic, the social-structural, and the expressive-ideological. Three specialized approaches to this tripartite concept have endured that emphasize one or other of the three as the prime mover or at least as the essential glue. The cultural evolutionist or cultural materialist tradition gives priority in the analysis of change to events in the techno-economic sphere. Social anthropology regards the social structure as the central object of inquiry, with the techno-economic and the expressive-ideological (the latter constituting Radcliffe-Brown's "culture") serving in auxiliary roles. And the symbols-and-meanings school concentrates on the expressive-ideological sphere, interpreting its "texts" in terms of the set of fundamental propositions (which they call "culture") about self, society, and human nature.

THE THONGA MINERS OF MOZAMBIQUE: A CASE OF ETHNIC LABOR SPECIALIZATION

To bring this discussion of concepts down to earth, let us turn to some ethnographic data that have been variously interpreted by anthropologists holding different views of culture. It is a case of ethnic labor specialization, a commonly observed phenomenon in complex societies, wherein a specific ethnic subgroup, distinguished by religion, language, race, or national origin, commits a large proportion of its labor force to a particular occupation. Familiar examples include the Mohawk workers in high steel construction, Gypsy tin smiths in Europe, Chinese shopkeepers in southeast Asia. The explanations for such specialization presumably lie in cultural and historical factors. Here we are considering the Thonga miners of southern Africa.

The Thonga are one of the Bantu-speaking peoples of southeast Africa and number on the order of a million souls. For the past century they have supplied a principal part of the labor force working in the gold mines in the neighborhood of Johannesburg and in the diamond mines at Kimberley. They probably mined most of the gold produced in South Africa for decades after 1897, when an agreement was reached between the Chamber of Mines and the Portuguese colony of Mozambique permitting the Chamber to recruit Thonga miners in Mozambique to work in the diggings in the Transvaal (one of the republics that eventually formed the Union of South Africa in 1910). Mozambique, in return, received assurances that South Africa would use Mozambique's port at Lourenço Marques, on Delagoa Bay, to service the mining regions. By the 1920s, their principal ethnographer (and resident Protestant missionary), Henri Junod, was able to write: "The fashion of going to the *Transvaal mines,* to earn money, has become so universal that a Thonga would think he had in some sort failed if he had not made a stay in town" (Junod 1962 [1927], 2:147).

He estimated that 70,000 Thonga worked in the Transvaal mines at any one time. Cultural materialist Marvin Harris, who did field work among the

Thonga in Mozambique in the 1950s, estimated that 93 percent of Thonga men were migrant laborers, with 40 percent of them—over 157,000—working in the Union of South Africa at any one time, about 100,000 in the mines. Far fewer of the more numerous and less distant Zulu, Swazi, Sotho, and other Bantu tribesmen came to the mines. And the Thonga were preferred, in any case, because they stayed for longer periods, a year or more at a time, and because their employment pattern was steady all year round, not seasonal.

European discovery of diamonds in commercial quantity in the late 1860s set in motion the pattern of migrant labor for the Thonga and other black tribesmen. At first diamond mining was carried out in great open pits or quarries, small sections of which (on the order of 31 feet by 25 feet) were leased by the landowner to private miners. At Kimberley Pipe, for instance, there were 430 such plots. Digging the soft diamond-bearing stone, hauling it to the surface, and separating the diamonds from the matrix were all labor-intensive jobs and during the 1870s migrant labor was brought in. The demand for labor increased when open-pit mining ended in the late 1880s and vertical shaft mining was begun. Laborers were housed in closed compounds for the term of their contracts (3 to 6 months).[2] The pattern established at the diamond mines was immediately applied at the gold mines after the discovery of the great Witwatersrand reef, the long seam of gold-bearing rock that outcropped around Johannesburg. As at Kimberley, after a brief orgy of small-plot surface quarrying along the outcrop, large corporations took over in the early 1890s and began to sink deep shafts and import migrant laborers, who were housed in compounds for the term of their contracts.

What these migrants—including the Thonga—actually learned of European mining technology was limited. In the gold mines, where the vast majority were employed, about 40 percent worked underground with pick and shovel, filling tram cars with ore and steadying the cars as they moved on tracks, pulled by an endless rope. About 20 percent were busy placing roof support timbers and masonry. About 20 percent were trained to do the semiskilled job of drilling holes in the working chambers to receive the explosives placed there by white experts. (At first this task involved a hammer and hand drill; after 1898, heavy compressed air drills were used.) And about 20 percent worked on the surface, where the ore was crushed and the gold separated, at first in mercury amalgam and after 1894 by the cyanide process. But in addition to learning the manual tasks assigned them, the workers obviously also learned a great deal more—about railroad travel, compound housing and equipment, mine elevators, signs of danger, and methods of mining in general.[3]

It is important to note that the commitment of the Thonga to migrant labor actually preceded the imposition of effective colonial control by the Portuguese. The Portuguese were not able to impose their administration anywhere in southern Mozambique, except around the port cities, until they had defeated the Ngoni kingdom of Gaza (of which most Thonga were subjects) in 1898. Similarly in South Africa, wars and uprisings continued until the 1880s. The system of apartheid in South Africa, with its pass laws and native homelands, was only gradually established in the twentieth century as a procedure for supplying cheap labor for expensive mines that produced only low-grade ore. As early as 1897, an ordinary deep mine (3,000 feet) cost on the order of $650,000. Only by employing migrant contract labor—from native reserves in South Africa, from native homelands, and from Mozambique, with the miners' families continuing to engage in marginal subsistence farming—could the mining companies see themselves as earning a profit. Indeed, the Mozambique miners may have unwittingly contributed to the establishment of the apartheid system, by providing the model of migrant laborers from another country who were allowed to claim only the limited and temporary rights in South Africa specified in the contract. The fiction of "Bantu homelands" as separate nations providing foreign migrant labor was prefigured by the importation of Thonga miners from Mozambique.[4]

From the Thonga point of view, the prime motive for going to work in the mines may eventually—well on in the twentieth century—have been the need to avoid virtually unpaid forced labor, to which "unemployed" Africans were subject by law in Mozambique. But in the early days, before the Portuguese conquest of the Gaza kingdom, *chiballo* (forced labor) was not a serious threat.[5] What "caused" this occupational specialization on the part of the Thonga—with its necessary accompaniment, the learning of some aspects of European mining technology and work habits—was certainly not proximity to the mines either, for the Mozambique border is a good 250 miles from Johannesburg, as the crow flies—and the crow would fly over intervening Swazi and Zulu country. Therefore there had to be something about Thonga culture that is, or was, different from the culture of other Bantu tribes in the region that made for a better fit with the occupation of migrant mine laborers. The answer is not hard to find. Among the agricultural Bantu, the men traditionally have been responsible for herding cattle, and the women, with seasonal help from the men, have been responsible for raising grain and vegetables. Among the Thonga, however, there have been—for reasons to be given shortly—virtually no cattle at all for the past 165 years. With no cattle to care for and manage, the men had become full-time migrant laborers and of necessity had turned over their few agricultural tasks to the women.

But let us explore this matter a little more fully. According to Junod, who relied on native tradition, up to 165 years ago the Thonga shared fully in the traditional southern Bantu way of life, including the cattle complex. If one had wandered through Thonga country at the beginning of the nineteenth century, one would have found a landscape of mixed forest and field. Here and there were isolated settlements, each consisting of a cattle enclosure at the center surrounded by a ring of from three or four to twenty or thirty conical thatched huts, the whole ringed by a low fence of thorn bushes (intended only to keep out witches). Chickens and goats roamed about in profusion. The women worked the fields nearby, tilling with iron hoes (shaped like the ace of spades and hafted onto short wooden staves), thereby raising the community's basic subsistence crop of millet, as well as maize and miscellaneous vegetables. Little boys tended the settlement's herd of cattle, mostly oxen, and the men fished and hunted in and about the forests and on the plains. Each settlement was virtually self-sufficient, although there was some traffic with Portuguese (earlier Arab) traders on the coast, of which more later.

Each of these little settlements was occupied by a single extended family, a lineage linked by patrilineal descent, consisting of a senior male and his brothers, if any, their sons, and grandsons, and all their wives (who came from other hamlets and were members of other lineages), together with their unmarried daughters and granddaughters. Some men had two or more wives, and since each wife occupied a hut of her own with her children, the number of huts in a compound tended to grow with time. The male social ideal was to accumulate as many wives and children as possible and to help his junior lineage mates to acquire wives too. But such accumulations depended on cattle, for each bride had to be "paid for" with a "bride price" (*lobola*) consisting of a number of oxen—on the order of fifteen—paid to her lineage. The cattle, in fact, were important not so much as a source of meat (only ritually slaughtered oxen were eaten) but rather as a currency that circulated among the villages permitting marriages to occur. Each time a village surrendered *lobola* cattle to legitimate a marriage (and thus to legitimate a man's children), the cattle-acquiring village had *lobola* for one of its unmarried sons. Theoretically, without *lobola* patrilocal marriage would cease and the patrilineage system would no longer work; for a woman who married without *lobola* (and there were occasionally such unions) had to bring her husband to live with her mother's lineage, most likely in the compound of her mother's brother. The offspring of such a marriage were rejected by the patrilineages of both bride and groom and became members of the mother's lineage. If such marriages occurred on a large scale for any length of time, the effect would be a transformation of the social structure from patrilineal to matrilineal descent and from patrilocal to matrilocal residence—a shift rarely if ever observed in human history.

But early in the nineteenth century—before the onset of Boer, British, and Portuguese economic domination—the Thonga were confronted with precisely this dilemma. They lost virtually all their cattle and were left with the choice of abandoning the *lobola* system or finding a new *lobola* currency. They did not hesitate for a moment in opting for a new currency. The circumstances through which the Thonga lost their cattle were traumatic. To the north and east were the Zulu, and under the prompting of Dingiswayo and Chaka, a new military system was being devised. The young men were drafted from their family compounds, housed in barracks, and trained for battle; it has been suggested that the system was developed after the Zulu observed the effective discipline of British troops. The army assumed responsibility of providing *lobola* for its men after their period of service. Furthermore, a royal lineage was established that, by a combination of marital alliances and military threat, effectively united the hitherto autonomous Zulu lineages into something close to a nation-state. Then Chaka and his Ngoni allies proceeded to conquer neighboring tribes and in turn to militarize and organize them along Zulu lines. The Thonga in the 1820s were subdued by an Ngoni army and forced to accept the sovereignty of a Ngoni lineage. But in the process, the Ngoni stole and slaughtered most of the Thonga cattle, and the surviving remnant were further thinned during internal wars of succession, raids from Swazi country, and the final war with the Portuguese in 1894–98. As late as 1950 the herds had not been restored and cattle keeping was still a rare Thonga occupation, with only 1 percent of the men owning herds of fifty head or more.

With the disappearance of the cattle, a new *lobola* took the place of oxen—the iron hoes traditionally used by the women in cultivation. They were metaphorically referred to as "oxen," and ten or so of them were handed over by the groom's lineage to that of the bride in the marriage ceremony. The hoes were apparently acquired as a profit skimmed from a new but growing Thonga occupation. Men of Thonga lineages formed small trading companies that served as middlemen between the gold- and iron-producing tribes of the Transvaal and the Arab and Portuguese traders on the coast. It was a dangerous trade, subject to attack and pillage by the warriors of unfriendly tribes, but it provided enough hoes to sustain the *lobola* system from about 1840 to 1870.

In the late 1860s the Boers began to develop the diamond mines at Kimberley on a substantial scale and after 1886 the gold mines of the Witwatersrand around Johannesburg. Thonga traders were already accustomed to travel to these areas and they quickly brought back word of the new opportunities. Thonga men were only too glad to give up the dangerous business of itinerant trader for the apparently safer and better-paying jobs as migrant laborers in and about the gold and diamond mines. Thonga society had already adapted to the prolonged absences of Thonga men. Now cash was substituted for iron hoes, and an inflation of sorts took place—an average bride price rose to £10, enough to purchase 100 hoes, and the price continued to climb. But the old cattle metaphors were still used; a young unmarried man who went to work in the mines for a year or two was said to be "starting a herd for himself." As we have seen, the mining specialization absorbed the efforts of virtually the entire male population and it has continued to do so until serious anti-apartheid protests led to modifications of the migrant labor scheme.[6]

So we have here a case in which a preliterate, preindustrial society—as a result of internal war and foreign colonization—in the course of about sixty years (about 1830 to about 1890) shifted the labor specialization of its males from cattle herding to itinerant trading to migrant mine labor, and in the process adopted a cash economy with respect to bride price. Furthermore, the shift was prompted by the conscious desire to preserve and stabilize the traditional social structure—the patrilineage system—by continuing the bride-price system. In effect, we see here a major technological change with virtually no change in social structure or ideology—at least not until the development of the anti-colonialist resistance movement in Mozambique after 1945. The initial function of technological change, for the Thonga, was to preserve the traditional social order.

Interestingly enough, the only anthropologists to recognize the process I have just described were evolutionary-oriented and employed an explicitly holistic concept of culture that not merely permitted but required the investigator to ask how technology was related to the rest of the system. Henri Junod's two-volume monograph on the Thonga was first published in 1912 and in a revised and expanded second edition in 1927 was entitled *The Life of a South African Tribe*. The first volume, subtitled *Social Life,* was organized into sections devoted to the successive stages of the life cycle of men and women, to the customs of the family and of the village, and to the national political structure. The second volume, ambiguously subtitled *Mental Life,* included a section on Thonga traditional technology (not including the technology of mining and other occupations supported by whites), literary and artistic activities, and religion, magic, and witchcraft. He thus covered the three main divisions of the holistic concept of culture. And being influenced by Sir James Frazer and other British cultural evolutionists, he tried to interpret certain Thonga customs as survivals of a presumed earlier stage of matriarchy. His approach in general, as was commonly the case in his time, was to reconstruct the traditional way of life as it had existed apart from European influence; but he did include enough historical information scattered throughout the work to provide the basic data about ethnic labor specialization and the shift in *lobola* currency. Marvin Harris, the only other anthropologist known to me to have done original research and writing on the Thonga, published a paper entitled "Labour Emigration among the Mozambique Thonga: Cultural and Political Factors" in 1959. The paper reviewed the basic pattern first noted by Junod and brought it up to date with statistics from the 1950s. Harris also linked the relatively prolonged and nonseasonal nature of Thonga migrant labor to the exclusively female pattern of agriculture and to the need to secure a *lobola* fund adequate to the needs of the patrilineage system.

One might of course expect the proponents of "cultural materialism," with its tripartite holistic conception of culture, to search automatically for economic and technological bases for social organization and ideology. But what has made the Thonga famous among anthropologists is a scholarly dispute over what, from the perspective of this paper, is a side issue: the interpretation of the joking relationship between a young man and his mother's brother. The young man is expected to treat his mother's brother with extraordinary arrogance and disrespect, demanding food, making lewd propositions to his uncle's wife, making off with his property, and even, when the older man dies, stealing the sacrificial chicken from the funeral site. The maternal uncle, on the other hand, is required to treat his nephew with affection, respect, and indulgence and to come to his aid in case of distress.

Junod interpreted this apparent anomaly in the ordinarily patriarchal social scheme of the Thonga as a survival from the former matriarchal era. But in 1925 A. R. Radcliffe-Brown—the social anthropologist who, the reader will recall, proposed to restrict the study of "culture" to sentiments and values—set out to refute Junod's evolutionary notion in a famous paper in the South *African Journal of Science* entitled "The Mother's Brother in South Africa." Radcliffe-Brown introduced supposedly universal sociological principles— such as the equivalence of siblings and the nonequivalence of parents (mother is loved, father is respected)—to explain not only the Thonga case but similar mother's brother customs in other societies around the world. In effect, these sociological principles dictated that the mother's brother be treated as a male mother (expected to be indulgent and forgiving), while the father's sister was treated as a female father (respected and obeyed) (Radcliffe-Brown 1965 [1925]).

Radcliffe-Brown's arguments deepened the analysis of the lineage systems of the Thonga and other tribes but did not satisfy Junod, who wrote a brief rejoinder in the 1927 edition of his book. In fact, a small literature has grown up in the wake of Radcliffe-Brown's paper. Africanist Igor Kopytoff, for instance, took Radcliffe-Brown to task in 1964 in a short paper in the *American Anthropologist,* showing that Radcliffe-Brown had confused two different mother's brothers — that of the child and that of the child's mother (Kopytoff 1964). And in his history of anthropological theory, Marvin Harris offered his own alternative, economic interpretation. The nephew takes advantage of his mother's brother because he has an economic claim on that man's wife and children, since the *lobola* cattle with which his mother's brother paid for his wife first came to him from the nephew's father. Mother's lineage "owes" something to her son's lineage. By emphasizing the importance of cattle in a partly pastoral society, "the function of the mother's brother-sister's son relationship is to maintain the population's techno-economic adaptation" (Harris 1968:529–530). But the culture-and-personality viewpoint has not really gotten into the act. In *Cooperation and Competition among Primitive Peoples,* edited by Margaret Mead, the Thonga (described in a chapter by Irving Goldman) were characterized as extremely cooperative and remarkably secure as individuals. The joking relationship is ignored, and no hint is given of Thonga migrant labor (Goldman 1937). As far as I know, no one in the symbols-and-meanings school has given an interpretation of Thonga culture (in the narrower sense), although Robert LeVine, a culture-and-personality expert as well as a symbols-and-meanings specialist, has interpreted a similar joking relationship in another African tribe where the young man jokes obscenely with his father's mother. LeVine suggests that what is communicated in these little joking-relationship "dramas" are rather abstract propositions: first, that incestuous sexuality and aggression are not to be "excluded from attention" but used (along with complementary avoidance relationships) as symbols of "contrasts in kin relationships"; second, that "what matters most in relationships is the specific type of genealogical linkage" (LeVine 1984:75).

But the reader will note that by now the discourse in the hands of non-holistic ethnographers has left far behind the real Thonga world of mines, migrant labor, no cattle, and cash for *lobola,* and has retreated to an era of Thonga social life as it is presumed to have been two centuries ago, long before any anthropologist had visited the tribe. This shift of the focus of attention from the technological and economic aspects of culture to social structure, national character, and "culture" in the symbols-and-meanings sense has gone furthest among social and symbolic anthropologists. These scholars are of course perfectly capable of dealing with technology and the economic system. But with interest invested primarily in fascinating sociological and semantic issues like the role of the mother's brother and the meaning of joking relationships, the day-by-day work experience of migrant laborers appears to be not only rather dull but essentially irrelevant.

Presumably Thonga men in the nineteenth century would have entered en masse into *any* occupation that provided a reliable source of money (or other exchangeable objects) for *lobola.* They could have become seamen, agricultural laborers, factory operatives, or mercenary soldiers, and the effects on the social structure and symbol system would probably have been the same—the preservation of the patrilineage system—provided the place of work was physically distant from the homeland. But this analysis does not pretend to describe conditions after World War II and probably for some time before that. The "fit" of migrant mine labor to Thonga culture has become skewed: the prolonged absence of males has allegedly contributed to high rates of divorce and desertion: and widespread intertribal violence in the compounds has supposedly reduced the solidarity of labor. Since 1975 Mozambique has been an independent Marxist state, and the government has declared its intention to end migrant labor as soon as per capita payments to the government by the mining companies can be replaced by some other form of national income.

Thus the Thonga represent a kind of limiting type of technology and culture relationship, where at least for a time *any* technology will fit into an existing and unchanging social and symbol system, provided it produces a sufficient flow of *some* acceptable commodity whose exchange is necessary and sufficient for the perpetuation of the system—whether it be oxen, or iron hoes, or money, or whatever. But the Thonga case is not representative of many of the situations of culture change to be observed in both preindustrial and industrial societies, where the "fit" of a new technology to the rest of the culture must be much more nicely tuned. So before returning our attention to the modern (post 1700) industrial world, let us examine another ethnographic example.

STEEL AXES FOR STONE-AGE AUSTRALIANS: A CASE OF NEW TECHNOLOGY THREATENING THE SOCIAL AND SYMBOLIC SYSTEM

One of the most intriguing accounts of the tragic consequences of a new technology that did not "fit" — at least not for some time — the social and symbolic system is cultural anthropologist Lauriston Sharp's paper "Steel Axes for Stone Age Australians." The paper was published in 1952 in a case book entitled *Human Problems in Technological Change,* edited by Edward H. Spicer and published by the Russell Sage Foundation. Sharp's field work with the Yir Yoront along the Coleman River in York Peninsula, in the extreme northern part of Australia, was done in the years 1933–35; he spent one stretch of thirteen months alone in the bush with his hosts without seeing another white man. Actually, the Yir Yoront had been in regular if infrequent contact since about 1915 both with a mission station and with cattle ranches on the southern borders of their territory; and they had been receiving European goods through native channels of trade for some time before this. But most of the year the Yir Yoront supported themselves in their traditional native territories by hunting, fishing, and foraging and carried out the full range of totemic ceremonies, spear fighting and feuding, and stealing of women, with little apparent change in their essentially Paleolithic culture. The missions prevented the introduction of firearms, liquor, and narcotics but did distribute, among other approved items of technology, short-handled steel axes (Sharp referred to them as "tomahawks" in his notes).

These axes, or hatchets, were somewhat more efficient than the stone axes traditionally used. Stone ax heads were not made in Yir Yoront territory but came from quarries four hundred miles to the south. They reached the Yir Yoront via a network of trade that connected the southern quarries with the Yir Yoront and other tribes to the north. Ax heads were exchanged for spears tipped with sting-ray spines, which are particularly destructive because they shatter as they enter flesh. The price of an ax head increased from about a dozen spears per ax head at Cape York to one spear for one ax head 150 miles south, and no doubt at the quarries still farther south one spear could buy a number of ax heads. Trade was conducted in the dry season, when hundreds of natives congregated at initiation ceremonies and a man could expect to meet his personal trading partners from groups to the north or south.

Once in the hands of a Yir Yoront man, the ax was easily hafted with local withes and glue. Axes belonged to men but were often used by women, children, and other people related to the owner. The loan of an ax, however, always required a formal request, and the ax was always referred to as "his ax" or "so-and-so's ax." The ax was used for breaking firewood, making huts and shelters, gathering honey, and in ceremonies (from which women were excluded). The steel ax could be used in all these contexts except the ceremonies and was preferred because it kept an edge longer and was easier to sharpen.

To understand the impact of the steel ax in Yir Yoront culture, it is necessary first to know something about the tribe's social and symbolic systems. The Yir Yoront—all six hundred or so of them—were divided into about twenty patrilineal clans, each of which owned a number of tracts of land and also "owned" for ceremonial purposes a number of "totems." Totems are classes of things—including animal species, localities, and personal names—that are associated with the clan's ancestors and can be represented by carvings, paintings, or instances of the thing itself. The stone ax was a totem of the Sunlit Cloud Iguana clan. The clans exchanged women in a prescriptive order, A providing wives to B, B to C, and so on, to the clan that provided wives to A, in a regular system not unlike the trading partner pattern. And (shades of the Thonga!) a man had a very special relationship with his mother's brother—not a joking relationship but one of respect by the nephew and nurturance by the uncle—because this man's daughter was the preferred choice for marriage (i.e., it was a society practicing matrilateral cross-cousin marriage).

In addition to the details of kinship, all Yir Yoront relationships were explicitly characterized in terms of higher and lower status. All men were superior to all women; all elders were superior to their juniors. These relationships were embodied in countless transactions in daily life (such as the wife of a son having to ask her husband or her husband's father for permission to use "his" ax) and also in ceremonials from which women were excluded, whose symbolism expressed the value placed on gender and age. But these ceremonials also conveyed a certain cosmological idea that made technological change peculiarly unpleasant to the Yir Yoront. The Yir Yoront believed that long ago, when the world began, the ancestors of the various clans (in animal form) interacted in certain ways now perpetuated in the ceremonies. But they also believed that the present world was a mirror of the ancestors' world, reflecting the same landscape, the same species, the same names, the same man-made objects, the same culture. Everything that exists has always existed and is the totem of a certain clan.

The steel ax was an exception to the symmetry of past and present. On the level of social organization it interfered with the status hierarchy that had always defined all human relationships. For the missionaries, as a reward for "good" behavior and as an encouragement to learn the white man's superior culture, handed out axes indiscriminately to men, women, and children. A woman with a steel ax could say, "my ax," and did not have to ask her husband for permission to use it. A child at a Christmas party at the Mission might receive as a present a steel ax, sharper and more durable than his father's stone ax, for which the father had waited and worked for months. Nor were the men entitled to expropriate the steel axes, for there was no prescription in the mythology defining the social relationship symbolized by the steel ax. Stone axes belonged to the Sunlit Cloud Iguana clan. But steel axes were relegated to the Head-to-the-East Corpse clan, along with ghosts, white people, and things associated with white people. And unlike native things, European goods—including the steel ax—had no distinctive origin myth, no association with ancestors, no ritual.

The problem thus existed overtly on the level of changes in status relationships that, Sharp felt, were making the men feel very uncomfortable. Malevolent magic was being directed by older men at mission personnel and younger men. But the presence of so much cultural material that was not rationalized in the origin myths was beginning to raise a question in Yir Yoront minds about the validity of the myths themselves. Farther south, where the natives had already been "engulfed by European culture" at missions and cattle stations, there had been a social catastrophe. As faith in the old myths—i.e., faith in the meaningfulness of the symbol system—was destroyed and rituals crumbled, "there follows an appallingly sudden and complete cultural disintegration and a demoralization of the individual such as has seldom been recorded for areas other than Australia. Without the support of a system of ideas well devised to provide cultural stability in a stable environment but admittedly too rigid for the new realities pressing in from outside, native behavior and native sentiments and ideas are simply dead. Apathy reigns" (Sharp 1952:89). Symptoms of the approaching *Götterdämmerung* were present, Sharp felt, in the collection of 149 dreams he collected from 43 men and 8 women. A sense of frustration with the status system is suggested by the fact that in dreams of aggression the most common situation is the dreamer being attacked by a member of an out-group (17 cases); and the next-most-common (12 cases) is the dreamer being attacked by his mother's brother (!). Even more telling is the frequency of dreams of death (49 deaths in 37 dreams), usually as a result of violent assault, often with butchery of the body into small pieces. (But also intriguing is the theme of the corpse coming back to life that occurs in a number of dreams. Were the Yir Yoront dreaming of the death and rebirth of their society?) (Schneider and Sharp 1969)

The Yir Yoront case differs from the Thonga in two major respects: technological change had different desirability for different groups in their society; and both the new technology and the social changes it produced put in question the adequacy of the traditional world view. Accustomed to societies in which social change normally prompts the modification of ideology, Sharp was puzzled by the failure of the Yir Yoront to resolve the confusion created by the steel ax. "Can anyone," he asked, "sitting of an afternoon in the shade of a ti tree, create a myth to resolve this confusion? No one has. . . ." Indeed, the only creative response to the decline of senior male status was the organization of a witchcraft cult. The old men were stealing Sharp's toothpaste and using it in newly invented magical rites intended to restore their status by injuring missionaries and some of the younger men, turning the white man's magic back on himself, so to speak.

THE VISIONARY RESPONSE TO SOCIAL DISORDER

But Sharp was not naive in expecting the Yir Yoront to create new myths to account for new realities in a society ripped apart by a new technology that did not "fit." Perhaps in time the new steel axes would have been "fitted in." In many cultures, industrial and preindustrial, imperial and colonial, efforts are made to make the society and the new technology fit better, to reduce conflict; and an important part of these efforts is carried on either by missionaries introducing a different faith or by indigenous religious prophets envisioning a new heaven and a new earth—creating, as Sharp put it, "The constitution of a new cultural universe." An example of this process occurred among the Iroquois Indians of New York and Pennsylvania, in the period from the end of the American Revolution to the year 1815.[7]

The 25,000 or so Iroquois Indians first encountered Europeans in the sixteenth century. They were village farmers, living in palisaded towns and subsisting largely on the corn, squash, and beans raised by the women in communal gardens. The Iroquois were matrilineal, descent in clan and lineage being reckoned strictly in the female line, and they were also matrilocal with respect to marriage, the husband ordinarily coming to live in the longhouse of his wife's lineage. But because of the husband's frequent and prolonged absences, husbands (and wives) tended to be replaced rather frequently. Each longhouse bore the emblem of the clan to which it belonged. Thus the stable inner core of an Iroquois village was the set of longhouses, each occupied by several generations of women who owned and worked the fields surrounding the village. The men were, in a sense, peripheral to the village and the clearing, constantly coming and going on hunting trips, on raids to avenge the killing of a woman's kin, and on diplomatic missions to arrange intertribal affairs. The chiefs represented the matrilineal clans and lineages and were nominated by the senior women. To European eyes, it appeared that the Iroquois system was a matriarchy, but to Iroquois males, who thought of themselves as good hunters, fierce warriors, and wise counselors, the self-reliance of the women simply meant that the men were free to play their own supremely important role. In this respect the situation resembles that of the Thonga.

The European presence brought about practically no change in this pattern for some two hundred and fifty years. The Iroquois took to hunting and trading fur-bearing animals in order to secure European hardware and dry goods—steel axes ("tomahawks"), steel traps, guns, knives, copper vessels, glass bottles (originally containing whiskey), cloth, glass beads (to substitute for the rarer native wampum), cosmetics, musical instruments, and much more—even cannon to defend their villages. They selected only those items that replaced and improved on native wares point to point. Aspects of European culture that did not fit, like the horse or Christianity, were left aside. And they were supremely indifferent to white men's impertinent suggestions that the lazy warriors ought to get to work in the summertime, relieving their women of the labor of farming, and regularize their somewhat casual attitude toward the marital bond.

This traditional world was destroyed at the end of the American Revolution when Great Britain in 1783 signed a peace treaty with the colonies that granted them independence but failed to mention the Indian warriors resident in the new nation, who for the most part—including most of the Iroquois—had fought effectively on the British side. With many of their villages burned down by American troops, their population decimated by combat casualties, starvation, and epidemics of infectious diseases in refugee camps, the Iroquois were persuaded by threats and bribes to sell most of their lands to various land companies. By 1797, all their land in New York and

Pennsylvania was gone except for tiny "reservations" at the sites of the principal old villages. Abandoned by their allies, outflanked and outgunned by the American army, the once proud warriors had to lay down their arms; the ambitious hunters and fur traders hardly dared to leave the reservation lest they be ambushed; and their chiefs, no longer able to extort goods and privileges from rival colonial governments by threats of force, had nothing much to do but drink, while their wives continued their usual agricultural tasks.

"Chief" Cornplanter, a village leader among the Seneca (the largest of the Iroquois tribes), believed that the Indians had to imitate the white man's customs, including farming, and sent his son to the Philadelphia area for a couple of years to be educated in the white man's ways. On his son's return, Cornplanter invited the Quakers to send some of their own people to teach the Seneca the techniques of the white man's farming. In response, some Quakers from Delaware County, with federal encouragement, set up a mission among the Seneca and settled on the upper Allegheny River on both sides of the New York–Pennsylvania border. They came not to evangelize the Indians but to instruct them in rural technology. To this end they brought ploughs, oxen, sawmill irons, spinning wheels, looms, blacksmithing and carpentry tools, and the rest of the apparatus needed to establish a rural community just like that in Delaware County. Along with showing the men and women how to operate their equipment, they set up a school to teach a few of the children the three R's (in English, of course) and set about formally telling the Indians through an interpreter (Cornplanter's son) what social arrangements were necessary to make it all work. First of all, the men had to take care of the animals, build fences, and plow the land; the women were to spin, weave, and make soap. And since they were to be family farms, the marital unit had to be stabilized; serial marriages were not conducive to efficient farm management and the proper upbringing of children.

These proposals aroused considerable controversy. Despite the rational encouragement of the chief and his interpreter son, many men and women objected to the reversal of the male role from warrior to cultivator. Raising corn was women's work, and some men who started to plough the fields with Quaker guidance were jeered at by the more traditional. Education of the young in the white man's school was also objectionable to many. The issue remained in doubt for two years until a religious prophet emerged who put it all together in a series of visions that became the gospel of a new religion.

The prophet, Cornplanter's half-brother, a Seneca chief named Handsome Lake, was instructed by four angels, who represented the Great Spirit, in matters concerning the survival of the Indian people. Much of the message was apocalyptic: unless the Indians confessed their sins and stopped drinking, practicing witchcraft, dancing to fiddle music, and attending the increasingly orgiastic meetings of the secret medicine societies, they would be destroyed in a fiery holocaust. There was a social gospel as well that spelled out in some detail a new code of social relations and a new world view that fitted the circumstances of reservation life. Handsome Lake explicitly recommended the Quaker model of a farming community and urged his people "to pursue the course of life . . . and . . . habits of industry" that the Quakers were promulgating. This "course of life" included the construction of detached houses to be occupied by a man, his wife, and their children; and this meant that the old tradition of serial marriages had to be replaced by the pattern of stable, enduring unions needed to operate family farms. With clear ethnographic insight, he detailed the trouble caused by gossiping mothers-in-law, in whose interest it was to break up their daughters' attachments to absent husbands by relating malicious gossip. This amounted to challenging the primacy of the maternal lineage as the focus of communal solidarity. Instead of the maternal lineage, he proposed the nuclear family as the central institution of kinship. He was equally emphatic in his attacks on the evils implicit in the traditional belief that the unconscious wishes of the soul had to be fulfilled in order to avoid disease (a theory of the emotions and of the mind remarkably similar in many respects to psychoanalytic dream theory). He urged instead self-control and confession of sin, and announced that there was a hell for Indians who were guilty of such sins as greediness, gossip, fornication, gambling at cards, and playing the fiddle.

The result of Handsome Lake's preaching was the development of a social movement that swept through the Iroquois villages with much the same fervor that attended the simultaneous Great Awakening among frontier whites. The movement was consolidated after his death in 1815, and by the time anthropologist Lewis Henry Morgan began to investigate it in the late 1840s, Handsome Lake's new gospel of acculturation had been institutionalized as the "Old Way of Handsome Lake" and preachers were being trained to repeat an orthodox version of his visions and sayings. The Iroquois men had become farmers.

What is notable in the Handsome Lake case is the amount of mental work the prophet and his followers had to do in order to accept and use a new technology. Male farming appeared to be necessary if the reservation communities were to survive, but a prejudice against men taking up the tools of agriculture and a fear that some would become rich at the expense of their fellows prevented full implementation of the technological program presented by the Quakers until a compatible social organization and conception of self had been articulated and presented with all the authority of the Great Spirit himself. The Iroquois radically redesigned their social and ideological culture to fit a new technology.

WHEN DOES TECHNOLOGY FIT?

Three ethnographic examples drawn from preindustrial societies may not be a very large sample, but at least it suggests some tentative propositions about what we mean when we say that a particular technology does or does not fit in with the rest of a culture. So I shall try, in this section, to articulate what seems to me a useful conceptual apparatus for observing and analyzing fit.

First of all, a tripartite conception of culture has proven to be generally useful, the parts being technology (including both implements, tools, and machines and the learned skills and work organization necessary for their use), social organization (including the more remote social structure, such as kinship and community administration), and ideology (including here the more abstract values, world view, and conceptions of self and society of the sort that symbols-and-meanings scholars refer to as "culture"). Saying that a particular technology fits does not imply that it will not ultimately prove to be, in an outside scientific observer's opinion, too costly to continue without modification, or that its costs may not at some time in the future lead to unanticipated stresses and strains. We are not talking about environmental pollution or the danger of accidents. We are saying something about how members of the society in question at a certain moment in time perceive themselves to be advantaged or disadvantaged by the presence of a particular technology. The issue generally is raised about technology newly introduced, either by internal invention or by cultural borrowing, but it is certainly applicable even when the technology has been around for a long time. Our cases all involve newly introduced foreign technologies, but insofar as internal sponsors of imported innovation are active, the processes of acceptance or rejection are probably the same as in the case of internal innovation.

Our first case, the Thonga, displays the quick acceptance of new tools and learning of new skills by the men and the continued use of traditional tools and skills by the women, with minimal resistance or complaint. Apparently no one was disadvantaged when Thonga men initially took up gold mining, because their earnings made possible—at least in the first decades—the continued existence of the system of social relations centering in the patrilineage and bride price, and the same values, sentiments, and sense of self. Later, of course, mine work was pressed on the Thonga by the economic need to avoid lower-paying forced labor. The Thonga case exemplifies what is probably a very large category of events wherein new technology is essentially compatible with, or even helps to maintain, the status quo. In a word, it fits by conserving an existing system.

The opposite case, where no one sees any particular advantage in a new technology and some would suffer acutely from its introduction, is exemplified by the prereservation resistance of the Iroquois to male agriculture. For at least a hundred and fifty years the Iroquois had opportunity to observe white farming methods and were repeatedly advised, by missionaries and others, to lift the burden of toil from their womenfolks' backs and assume it themselves. But they steadfastly avoided emulating the white man in this regard. It was not until confinement to small reservations left the men with virtually no significant role, unable to hunt extensively, make war or engage in the traditional forest diplomacy, that male agriculture became acceptable.

But there is a third class of situations where it is not generally perceived that everyone will benefit or suffer equally from the adoption of a new technology, and both the Yir Yoront and the post-reservation Iroquois belong in this category. Here, acceptance of the new damages the status of some group. In both our cases it was the men, particularly the senior males among the Yir Yoront and the younger males among the Iroquois. Among the Yir Yoront, social conflict broke out (the "toothpaste cult"), and a proper myth incorporating the steel ax into the traditional social system (or sanctioning a change in the system) had not been formulated by the time the anthropologist departed. Among the Iroquois, in contrast, the change in the status of men and in the role of the nuclear family, and the issue created by potential economic inequality, were all addressed in the newly envisioned code of Handsome Lake. A certain amount of conflict had already developed over the sawmill, which had been expropriated by "Chief" Cornplanter along with its profits because it had been set up on some land granted to him personally by the state legislature. In response to this, Cornplanter was ostracized socially and Handsome Lake reiterated the old egalitarian principles in preaching against "greed." His code recognized the possible accumulation of some profit by a hard-working farm family but sanctioned it only if it was motivated by a man's desire to care for his family; those who disposed of communal property for private gain (as in corrupt land sales) were bitterly condemned.

But our three cases come from essentially nonliterate, nonurban, preindustrial tribal populations in colonial situations, living on the fringes of the industrial world. European societies experiencing the introduction of the technology of the Industrial Revolution were larger in population, contained urban centers, were centrally administered states, and—of particular importance to our argument—were socially more complex. As we have seen, even in small, relatively homogeneous, egalitarian societies, the cleavage lines of age and sex provide the potential for conflicts of interest. In state-societies, and particularly industrial states, in addition to age and sex there are hierarchical structures of caste and class, a number of ethnic groups, an intricate network of economic roles (artisans of many kinds, traders, bankers, priests, soldiers, bureaucrats), a market system of distribution. Almost inevitably, any proposed innovation will simultaneously promise advantage to some group and disadvantage to another. Such perceived conflicts of interest must therefore be addressed by proposals for social and ideological change, or by assurances that anticipated disadvantages are not really so serious. And even these measures may not abort a brewing struggle; for different groups are likely to put forth very different proposals, and compromise may not be easy to reach. Furthermore, in industrial societies, major innovations are introduced so frequently that rational estimation of their costs and benefits to all groups concerned can hardly be achieved in advance of experience in the field and in the marketplace. It is small wonder that a new intellectual discipline—the philosophy of technology—has emerged to formulate what are hoped to be appropriate changes in world view and to suggest sensible adjustment in the social system.

The typical situation, then, for industrial societies since about the year 1800 is one of unequal losses and benefits for different parts of the population. Typically, a sponsoring group (an industry, the military, or government, for example) anticipates benefits for itself or some target population from the introduction of new technology, while at least one other group (or even a target group) perceives its interests as being threatened. Each group produces communications that attack or defend the new technology on the basis of its implications for social structure and the values of the society. A principal task for the student of technology and culture is to investigate how these political and ideological responses are formulated, how they are communicated, and how they affect public policy.

We might, as an example, turn to the introduction of the electronic computer and the various views of its social and ideological implications. For my own case material, however, I think I will do better to return to the nineteenth century and take a look at the social and intellectual maelstrom that surrounded the newly introduced and technologically changing anthracite industry in Pennsylvania. There we can see, with the advantage of hindsight, the changes in group interaction, the process of myth making, and the formation of a new public policy.

THE MINERS OF SCHUYLKILL COUNTY: WHO IS TO BE RESPONSIBLE FOR THE VICTIMS OF INDUSTRIAL ACCIDENTS?

When hard coal, or anthracite, was first mined in Schuylkill County in the 1820s and 1830s, it was simply quarried from the surface or reached by long, nearly horizontal tunnels. These shallow mines did not descend below water level and consequently did not require pumps; and with a short air hole at the end of the gangway, they could be ventilated by the natural movement of air. But the supply of coal above water level began to shrink noticeably in the 1830s and 1840s, and most mine owners had no choice but to turn to long-practiced British methods of mining below water level. Where the landowner had located an outcrop on his land, the preferred technique was to sink a "slope." A slope was an inclined tunnel driven down through the slanting vein of coal; the gangways were run off on both sides at levels about 100 yards apart, and the coal was then mined from chambers (called "breasts" in Schuylkill) that extended uphill, so that the broken coal fell down to the gangway by force of gravity. Breasts were separated by "pillars" of unbroken coal that supported the roof. It was not until 1854 that the first vertical shaft was sunk in the county. In this method, the coal was lifted directly to the surface by elevators but the inside work was done via gangways and breasts, just as in slope mines.

The introduction of British deep mining technology was hailed by spokesmen for landowners and colliery operators, who expected increased profits from the enlarged scale of operations. But this increase in scale brought coal mining into the same economic sphere as the other smokestack industries of the time, including the railroads and iron manufacturing. In the old days, an individual miner could save a few dollars, lease an outcrop from a landowner, drive his own drift, and become a colliery operator. Now, a few years later, to open a colliery required on the order of a hundred thousand dollars to sink a slope or shaft several hundred feet, install steam engines and pumps, erect a breaker, and pay for all the other preliminary labor and equipment necessary to the opening of a mine. And once opened, an average colliery had to employ between two hundred and five hundred men and boys.

Furthermore, as experience soon demonstrated, deep-shaft and slope mines were far more dangerous than the former quarries and drifts. Not only did the workers have to cope with machinery—pumps, steam engines, elevators, rail cars, breaker rolls—but with vastly increased underground dangers, particularly from falls of coal or rock from roofs weakened by gunpowder blasting, and also from explosions of the fire damp (methane gas, CH_4) that was constantly exuded from the coal and could be ignited by miners' lamps, the process of blasting, or the incautious use of metal tools. In the mid-1850s a correspondent of the *Miner's Journal,* an influential Pottsville newspaper that specialized in collecting statistical information about the coal trade, estimated that each year in Schuylkill County 6 percent of all colliery employees were killed at work, 6 percent were so severely crippled as to be unable to work again, and 6 percent were injured but not so severely as to prevent an eventual return to work (*Miners Journal* (Pottsville), 18 December 1858). Casualty figures collected by the inspector of mines from 1869 on do not rise as high as this; but they were collected *after* the passage of the first mine safety law and even so reveal that anthracite miners in Schuylkill county were experiencing a death rate nearly four times as high as English miners (*Inspector of Mines, Annual Report,* 1869–). Official casualty rates for anthracite miners were comparable to average casualty rates in the Civil War.

The social and cultural situation in the anthracite district was of course complex; here I wish only to trace the major social and ideological consequences of the introduction of a new system of mining technology that was characterized, as in other major industries, by a large number of employees working for each employer and by a gross escalation of danger. The course of events in Schuylkill was by no means independent of similar changes occurring in Britain and the rest of the United States; but for America, the Schuylkill mining industry served as a pace setter.

In Schuylkill, the industry was governed at the beginning by what in England was called the "butty" system. It was essentially a system of subcontracting. The owner of the mineral rights to a tract—the "landowner"—leased (in writing couched in legal jargon) the right to mine coal in a particular vein to an "operator," who agreed to pay a rent of so many cents for every ton of coal mined, with a minimum annual tonnage required. The operator in turn leased (by verbal agreement) the right to extract the coal physically from a particular breast—specified by lift, gangway, and breast number—to a "contract miner." To mine the coal out of a breast might take a miner a year or more. The miner hired his own laborers to help him, purchased his own tools, fuses, gunpowder, and lamp oil, and was paid by the ton or wagon; in fact, the contract miner was styled as a company in some "operators" books, John Smith appearing in the ledger as "John Smith & Co." The operator also contracted with specialty miners to sink shafts, drive gangways and headings, and perform other necessary but non-coal-producing services. [8]

The miner thus served the mine operator in much the same relationship as a carpenter, a mason, or a painter might serve a gentleman farmer or a mill owner. For the contract miner to maintain the status of artisan was a crucially important matter, for it differentiated him from the laborers who loaded the cars, the boys who sorted coal in the breakers, and the miners who worked by the day. The contract miner was a man of superior experience, skill, and judgment who handled dangerous materials under extremely risky conditions. He decided for himself on matters of ventilation, timbering, and the use of the safety lamp; he refused to work in the presence of bosses, simply sitting down when anyone in authority appeared. And if the operator made decisions that in his miners' opinion made the mine riskier than it need be (such as providing them with inadequate ventilation), they "turned out," refusing to work except at a premium wage. If the miner was injured or killed, the miner or his widow, following ancient British rules of common law, could sue the operator if he had failed to provide a safe workplace or to warn his employee of dangers lurking in it.

But the realities of the new high-energy, high-employment, high-risk industries characteristic of the industrial revolution did not fit well with the principle of "employer's liability." That had worked well enough where it was a matter of a prosperous gentleman occasionally hiring a painter or carpenter or mason from the village. But the mining business in Schuylkill, like mining, the railroads, and iron and steel—both in Great Britain and elsewhere in America—was causing casualties at a far greater rate than did traditional industries. And the operators—certainly those in Schuylkill—were poorly capitalized, victimized by the absentee landowners, and forced to economize on safety measures; and they usually went bankrupt within a few years.

Thus both sides in the relationship sought to make changes. The operators and their champions in the legal profession did everything possible to deny responsibility for the wave of deaths and injuries in their collieries. Both the colliery operator and the railroads serving the collieries refused, for instance, year after year to support public proposals to build a special "miners' hospital" to provide expert medical and nursing care for the hundreds of blinded, burned, and maimed victims of colliery accidents that the industry produced each year. Residents of coal towns still recount with bitterness the callousness of company officials who brought the dead and wounded in wagons to their cottages and dumped them on the front porch, with no medical attention, for the families to care for as best they could. (Those able to walk—for example, boys with broken arms—were sent home on their own.) But these acts of seemingly casual cruelty were expressions of a larger pattern of denial of responsibility for accidents by industrialists who (presumably) feared they could be inundated by personal injury lawsuits and by demands for greater safety expenditures if the employer's liability principle were not curtailed. And in fact it was curtailed. Beginning in the 1840s in both England and the United States, courts hearing personal injury suits began to introduce new grounds for holding employers blameless. From time immemorial, of course, negligence by the injured employee that contributed significantly to causing the accident had exculpated the employer. But now two new principles of common law were articulated for the first time (in the United States particularly by Massachusetts Judge Lemuel Shaw, a former consultant to railroads and other new industrial concerns) that suited the defensive needs of dangerous and labor-intensive industries: the "fellow-servant" rule and "assumption of risk." The first held that a worker injured as a result of the negligence of a fellow employee could not sue their common employer. The second decreed that if a worker knew in advance that certain risks were inherent in an occupation, he assumed responsibility for his own injuries thereafter. These "three wicked sisters" made it virtually impossible for an injured employee to sue his employer successfully, no matter how gross the neglect by the employer of even the most elementary safety measures.[9]

Along with a reduction in the scope of the employer's liability, a complementary public image of the miner as a habitually careless daredevil was being zealously promulgated. In the pages of the Pottsville *Miner's Journal,* for instance, gas explosions were routinely blamed on careless miners who refused to use their safety lamps; that the presence of gas in high enough concentrations to support an explosion indicated an inadequate ventilation system was never mentioned. And the economic problems that chronically plagued the industry (in part the result of high disaster rates) were uniformly blamed on the government's failure to enact an adequately protective tariff. The foremost advocate of this position was the influential political economist Henry Carey, erstwhile Philadelphia publisher, who was one of the principal owners of coal lands in the Pottsville district, including the town of St. Clair. One of Carey's followers was Benjamin Bannan, editor of the *Miner's Journal;* another was industrialist Joseph Wharton, founder of the Wharton School, whose insistence that the business school provide instruction in the social sciences was prompted by his conviction that Carey's *Principles of Social Science* and other writings had proved that national prosperity depended on a protective tariff on various products including iron, much of which in America was smelted in anthracite-fired furnaces. Carey's views on the tariff, and the necessity for a system of free labor and free capital, were influential in shaping the platform of the Republican party from its very inception in the 1850s. And on welfare issues Carey was staunchly opposed even to private charity, let alone public, on the grounds that it amounted to unwise intervention in the workings of socioeconomic laws of the marketplace, which in Carey's mind operated with the same sublime precision as the laws of physics. The protective tariff, however, was justified by the fact that it was British neocolonial economic imperialism that was interfering with the operation of universal laws of human behavior, including economic laws, in the developing countries, particularly the United States.

The view that all that was wrong with the coal trade (including, by implication, its accident rate) was caused by outside interference was given its most dramatic expression in the course of the Molly Maguire trials in 1875 and 1876. Led by Irish-American lawyer Franklin B. Gowen, a former mine operator and now president of the Philadelphia and Reading Railroad (whose principal haulage was coal from Schuylkill County), prosecuting attorneys charged that the Ancient Order of Hibernians, ostensibly an Irish benevolent society, was in reality the tool of the Molly Maguires, a secret international Irish terrorist organization. The Molly Maguires were accused of conspiring to rule, or to destroy, the coal trade in Schuylkill and its neighboring counties by a campaign of assassination and sabotage, and eventually twenty Mollies were convicted of murder and hung. (One of the twenty was posthumously pardoned a few years ago by the governor of Pennsylvania.) The Molly Maguire trials—whatever the guilt or innocence of the accused—were a public ceremony symbolizing the position that the troubles of the coal trade and of the coal country were caused not by the operators and landowners but by the miners, especially the Irish miners.[10]

The miners for their part were finding themselves in increasingly precarious economic and safety circumstances as the mines got deeper and the financial difficulties of their employers increased. They were increasingly regarded as socially inferior, not only to the traditional middle class, but also to other respectable tradesmen. For instance, by the 1880s they were excluded from the Odd Fellows lodge in Pottsville. They were regarded as violent and drunken; and if they were Irish and Catholic, they were suspected of involvement in popish plots. Since an increasing proportion of miners were Irish, the Irish stereotype tended to apply to all miners. Furthermore, the old welfare safety net for the working class, the extended family that could take in and support the crippled, the widowed, and the orphaned, was being stretched to its limit by a rate of casualties from the mines that far exceeded rural, preindustrial levels.

The result, of course, was the formation of unions. The first county-wide, permanent union, the Working Men's Benevolent Association, was founded in St. Clair in 1868 (just before unions were made legal in Pennsylvania), and it survived until 1875, when it was broken in the "long strike" of that year. One of the principal goals of the WBA was industrial safety. Union lobbyists in the state capitol at Harrisburg presented petitions demanding a mine safety law and the establishment of a miners' hospital supported by the state. In 1869 and 1870 mine safety laws were indeed passed. The first applied only to Schuylkill County because the senator from Luzerne claimed, falsely, that there was no danger from gas in his county. After a mine fire in his own district killed over one hundred men a few months later, a second, stiffer law was passed that applied to all the anthracite counties. And, after much delay, a state-run Miners' Hospital was built, partly as a result of the efforts of a WBA leader elected to the state legislature on the Labor Reform party ticket.

The Mine Safety Acts of 1869 and 1870 contained provisions that significantly changed the nature of colliery management and along with it the role of miners. The union gave up certain traditional privileges of the contract miner. Safety lamps now became the property of the colliery; the colliery maintained them, serviced them, and issued them to workers; and a company man, the fire boss, was required to order their use when he, not the miner, deemed it to be necessary. Ventilation, too, was now to be entirely the responsibility of the colliery; a colliery could be closed down if the air was bad. The office of state inspector of mines was created, and the inspector and his deputies were required to visit all mines regularly, to hear workers' complaints, and to fine, or close down, collieries not in compliance. All injuries were to be reported to him; he was to investigate every accident; and all accidents were to be described in the annual published report, which also contained essays on the state of the industry and descriptions of every operating colliery.

In effect, both labor and management—the former willingly, the latter reluctantly—gave up a degree of freedom in decisions affecting safety and placed authority in the hands of a third party. The state had entered the coal industry as a regulatory agency. And within five years, nearly all the landowners in Schuylkill County had sold their mineral rights to a newly created corporation, the Philadelphia and Reading Coal and Iron Company—a subsidiary of the Philadelphia and Reading Railroad—which replaced many of the old-time operators with its own employees. In 1875 the company crushed the WBA and in the next year assumed credit for destroying the Molly Maguires. In effect, Schuylkill County's coal region became a state within a state, with one corporation owning nearly all of its industry, running nearly all its railroads, protecting its interests with its own state-commissioned Coal and Iron Police, and exerting much political clout in the state capitol.

Let us now recapitulate the process. The introduction of slope mining in the 1830s and deep-shaft mining in the 1850s resulted in a large and unanticipated increase in human casualties and colliery failures. The desire to reduce the rate of accidents contributed to the founding of the first large, permanent unions in the coal field and the development of an articulate, militant consciousness of class. Union lobbying led to the passage of mine safety acts that, in effect, reduced the miner's control of the workplace but also laid on management's shoulders the burden and expense of responsibility for safety. The butty system of small landowners and small operators collapsed, and the Reading Coal and Iron Company took over. Now a big labor union and a big corporation confronted one another over an industrial battlefield.

The safety issue was not finally resolved in 1869 and 1870. Spokesmen for the coal trade complained in 1870 that the only fair way to regulate industrial safety was by means of national safety legislation that covered all parts of the economy. The country did not see such legislation, however, until the establishment of the Occupational Safety and Health Administration (OSHA) in 1970—one hundred years later! Federal safety legislation for coal mines did not pass until 1952. But in addition to state and federal regulation, subsequent years have seen the development of a system of insurance that in effect compensates victims of industrial accidents and rewards companies with good safety records. (Of course unions like the WBA also maintained funds to help the injured and their families.) During the decades after 1910 most states established no-fault workmen's compensation insurance. Social security now protects the disabled. Moreover, private life insurance and medical insurance eventually became affordable for most workers, and insurance against personal injury suits became available to most employers.

What has happened is that in consequence of the reinterpretation of the old common-law principle of employer's liability, a whole new system of relations between employer and employee has developed in the matter of safety. The state has intervened with regulatory agencies; the employee has to some degree lost control of the workplace as the state placed more responsibility in the hands of management; and a huge health and accident insurance fund—a patchwork of lesser funds, to be sure—has replaced the employer as the principal source of relief in case of work-related illness or injury.

The shift in the symbol system can best be represented, perhaps, by contrasting a century in which the "employer's liability" for his "careless employees'" safety was the concept in dispute and a century in which the "employee's entitlement" to benefits from the state is the salient issue. Just as the employers' refusal to honor traditional norms of *noblesse oblige* elicited bitter recriminations then, so proposals to "change Social Security" now arouse storms of protest. "Social Security" now symbolizes a whole world view about what the individual is entitled to expect from the community in the way of safety and recompense for injury or ill health. In this new moral environment, deep-shaft mining for anthracite fits the culture better than it did a hundred and fifty years ago. But ironically, deep-shaft mining for anthracite is no more, itself a victim of competition from other fuels more cheaply, safely, and reliably produced.[11]

CONCLUSION

In this excursion into the realm of culture theory, we have been considering how a technology "fits" in a culture; and if at first it does not, how it is "fitted in." We have been using a traditional concept of culture as a domain divided into three parts, which for convenience may be dubbed technology, social organization, and ideology. To illuminate the issues, we looked at four societies as case studies: the Thonga tribesmen of Mozambique, whose occupation as gold and diamond miners at first fitted perfectly the needs of the Thonga lineage and marriage system; the Yir Yoront of Australia, an aboriginal group who found that the steel ax introduced by whites disrupted the patriarchal status system and confounded their mythology; the Iroquois, an American

Indian tribe who for generations rejected male plow agriculture because their whole way of life was organized around female horticulture, but who took up male agriculture under the urging of a prophet when traditional male roles disintegrated on the reservation; and the miners and mine operators of nineteenth-century Schuylkill County, who discovered that fundamental changes in both social organization and ideology had to be made in order to cope with catastrophically high rates of industrial accidents unexpectedly attendant on the new system of deep-shaft mining.

Cultures are very complex systems, and it is difficult to predict the consequences of a particular change in any one component. Our four cases may suggest some simple generalizations; but explanation or prediction require close study of the particular culture in question and of the specific historical situation. In exploring the unique as well as the general features of individual cases, I believe that it is useful to keep in mind the tripartite, holistic concept, which explicitly directs attention to the wide range of behaviors, groups, and institutions that a technology fits or does not fit.

Of these simple generalizations I can offer only three, each concerning a type of historical situation. First, there are cases where all the interested subgroups are satisfied with a traditional technology and reject apparently superior new technology because it would force changes in social organization and ideology (e.g., prereservation Iroquois and stable cultures in general). Second, there are cases where a new technology is embraced by all because it appears to serve the same social and ideological functions as a prior technology recently rendered inoperative by historical events (e.g., the Thonga). A third category is probably more common in complex pluralistic and hierarchical states and in industrial nations, but it applies even in simple societies. Here a technological innovation introduced by a subgroup in its own interest or for the sake of what it considers to be the public good (e.g., by an aristocracy, a business firm, a government agency, the military, a group of reformers) is found, after longer or shorter experience, to be discommoding to some other group or groups. One should look in such cases for evidence of social and ideological conflict, as the groups in question seek to formulate, along more or less different paths, changes in the technological, social, and ideological aspects of the culture that will render the new technology mutually advantageous. The successful integration of radically new technology into culture may even require the services of a utopian social movement.

NOTES

1. For a more general discussion of some aspects of these consequences of innovations, see Wallace 1978, Appendix.

2. For accounts of the early days of the diamond industry, see Lenzen 1970, Levy 1982, and Williams 1905.

3. Gold-mining technology and labor practices in the first few decades along the Witwatersrand are described in Letcher 1974 [1936]. See also Van Onselen 1982 and Wilson 1972.

4. An anthropologist's analysis of the role of Thonga male labor in South African mines is provided in Harris 1959; the increasingly important and innovative agricultural work of Thonga women is described in Young 1977. The cooperative policies of South Africa and Mozambique are analyzed in Katzenellenbogen 1982.

5. The circumstances of post–World War II Thonga miners are described in First 1983, Mayer 1980, Murray 1980, and Winters 1977.

6. Junod 1962 [1927] is the main source for the account of traditional Thonga culture and its transformations in the nineteenth century; see also Smith 1973 for Thonga-Ngoni relationships. For a critique of Junod, see Harries 1981. Native African mining and metal-working technology are described in Cline 1937 and Austen and Headrick 1983.

7. The Iroquois case is derived from my earlier study, Wallace 1970b, which was based on primary documents and field work.

8. For contemporary manuals of the technology and work practices in nineteenth-century anthracite collieries, see Daddow and Bannan 1866 and Chance 1883.

9. For an analysis of the impact of Judge Shaw's decision and of the implications of the "three wicked sisters," see Gersuny 1981 and Levy 1957:166–182 ("The Fellow Servant Rule").

10. The most scholarly account of the Molly Maguire affair is that of Broehl 1964.

11. The interpretation here of the nineteenth-century coal industry in Schuylkill County is based on Wallace 1987. Brief accounts of the technology and safety problems of the industry may be found in Wallace 1982, 1983.

7

Paradigms and Revolutions in the Arts

If a cat may look at a king, an anthropologist may be pardoned for treading on the turf of art historians and taking a peek at the sublime Raphael. But in fact I am peeking from behind the coat sleeve of one of my ethnological mentors—Alfred Louis Kroeber (1876–1960)—whose erudition was equal to almost any task, and who did take an interest in the history of Western art, seen in the perspective of the laws of the growth and decline of civilizations.

When I was a graduate student in the late 1940s, the dean of American anthropologists was Alfred Louis Kroeber. Unlike most of the following generation of ethnographers, Kroeber considered all human history to be our discipline's province, and he wrote extensively on the rise and fall of the great civilizations as well as of what he called the "minor civilizations" of the North American Indians and other nonliterate, nonurban populations. In this sense he belonged to the 19th century with such men as Lewis Henry Morgan, Edward Tylor, and Sir James Frazer who wrote as much about the Egyptians, Greeks, and Romans as about the Iroquois, the Hawaiians, and the Zulu. And, in common with such men as these he considered the history of art as central to an understanding of the configurations of culture growth.

Kroeber was—if you will excuse the metaphor—a "Renaissance man." Privately educated as a youth in the classical languages, he studied history and natural history at Columbia, and earned an M.A. there in English literature before he came under the sway of Boas and anthropology. He switched fields and wrote his doctoral dissertation on the art of the Hupa Indians of California. For a while he earned part of his living as a psychoanalyst in San Francisco while he organized the anthropology department at Berkeley. Eventually he became the acknowledged leader among students of the American Indian.

What makes Kroeber relevant to the purposes of a conference on Raphael, however, is his concern with the historical development of art styles as an aspect of the rise and fall of cultures and civilizations. In his book *The Con-figurations of Culture Growth* (1944) he does mention Raphael as one of the "geniuses" who produced the Italian Renaissance. But it is Kroeber's general ideas about the way in which whole cultures evolve, reach a culmination, and decline that are of interest to us here. He approached this problem initially in a book entitled *Cultural and Natural Areas of Native North America* (1947), which is devoted largely to relating the topographic and climatic regions of the continent to "culture areas." Culture areas were large zones occupied by tribes that shared many features of culture—art and decoration, technology, social organization, religion, and so forth—that were not shared with adjacent zones. Each culture area was examined historically (with the aid of archaeology, primarily) and assigned a center or climax, from which Kroeber argued, innovations flowed out toward loosely defined boundaries. But, taking the developmental view, and influenced by Sir W. M. Flinders Petrie's influential little book *The Revolutions of Civilization* (1911) he also recognized a process of growth, culmination (which he also termed "climax"), and decline in the history of each area. In his general discussion of the process, he explicitly compared the American Indian cases with the Mediterranean civilizations. And he agreed that the American Indian cases, insofar as they were known, seemed to confirm Petrie's argument that "climax attainment" in the arts precedes that in literature, science, and technology.

Kroeber had no use for many of the "peremptory" and "drastic" opinions of Petrie, such as his insistence that all progress depended on "strife," and that man's future progress depended on racial segregation and eugenics (intermittently interrupted by judicious hybridization to plant new civilizations). But he did pursue Petrie's idea that, methodologically, the study of the development of an artistic style was a key to unlocking the secret of civilizations. In his enormously influential textbook, simply titled *Anthropology*, he set forth an expanded depiction of the concept of *style* that anticipates Thomas Kuhn's later notion of *paradigm*. It is worth quoting: "The basic reason for the concentrations of productivity seems to be that for things to be done well they must be done definitely, and definite results can be achieved only through some specific method, technique, manner, or plan of operations. Such a particular method or manner is called a *style* in all the arts, as we have seen. And 'style' is perhaps the best available word that will cover also the corresponding methods or plans in other activities" (Kroeber 1948:329–320). Kuhn's definition of *paradigm* is restricted (by Kuhn) to science and is relatively brief: "Some accepted examples of actual scientific practice—examples which include law, theory, application, and instrumentation together—provide models from which spring coherent traditions of scientific research. These are the traditions which the historian describes under such rubrics as 'Ptolemaic astronomy' (or 'Copernican'), 'Aristotelian dynamics' (or 'Newtonian'), 'corpuscular optics' (or 'wave optics'), and so on" (Kuhn 1970 [1962]:10). Kuhn, however, adds a corollary to his definition that is missing from Kroeber's version—and this addition makes a crucial difference in the usefulness of the two approaches to the history of art (or of science, or technology). Kuhn immediately refers the paradigm to a particular network of people who apply it (and ultimately change it in "revolutions"):

> The study of paradigms, including many that are far more specialized than those named illustratively above, is what mainly prepares the student for membership in the particular scientific community with which he will later practice. Because he there joins men who learned the bases of their field from the same concrete models, his subsequent practice will seldom evoke overt disagreement over fundamentals. Men whose research is based on shared paradigms are committed to the same rules and standards for scientific practice. That commitment and the apparent consensus it produces are prerequisites for normal science, i.e., for the genesis and continuation of a particular research tradition. [Kuhn 1970 [1962]:10–11]

The difference is apparent in the empirical studies of the two scholars. Kroeber in his major effort to test, and revise, Petrie's model, undertook an encyclopedic survey of the clusterings of "genius" (i.e., of great productivity) in time and space. But no attention is paid to the actual associations, the networks, the social organization of scientists, or painters, or sculptors. The view is "super-organic" (to use Kroeber's own term) and essentially similar to the vision of culture climax elaborated earlier, and now applied to culture areas and periods like Renaissance Italy. Kuhn, by contrast, constantly writes about the community of scientists that shares the paradigm, or, when serious difficulties arise with it, goes through the period of criticism and revolution when a new paradigm is achieved. He discovers the relationships among the members of this community, he refers to them by name, and quotes from their correspondence.

This approach has proved serviceable to me in studies of the Industrial Revolution in Europe and America, where it is technology—the technology of cotton manufacture, of iron smelting, of refining of the steam engine, and of coal mining—to which the term style or paradigm is applied. In the period from about 1700 to 1900 an extraordinary number of mechanical inventions were produced whose use in large numbers has transformed the world in many ways. In order to understand how this torrent of inventions was released, it is not enough to cite some sort of *Zeitgeist,* like the Protestant ethic or capital accumulation or population increase, or even the frequency distribution of certain social or psychological characteristics of the individual inventors, such as their religious preference or facility in ritual thinking or enjoyment of bringing order out of Chaos. (The latter attribute has even been cited by Kuhn, following the work of psychologists on the test behavior of artists and other creative people, as one that especially productive scientists and artists share [Kuhn 1970 [1962]:79; Barron 1958].) It is necessary to recognize, first, the paradigmatic nature of the invention sequences, and second, the way in which the community of mechanicians was organized. Let us spend a little time examining the Industrial Revolution in this frame, because it is a frame that I propose to apply to the development of humanism, and particularly the arts, in the Italian Renaissance.

The most familiar symbol of the new industrial age is the steam engine. There were actually two paradigms for the steam engine. The first, developed during the 17th century, was a plan for a pump that could remove water from coal mines, raise water into cisterns and reservoirs, and drain swamps. The pump worked in two phases: first, sucking water up out of a swamp into a receiver in which a partial vacuum had been created by cooling and condensing steam; and second, driving this water out of the receiver into an ascending pipe by the power of expanding steam. Valves were the only moving parts required. There were several shortcomings in the device, however. First of all, the receiver and the furnace and boiler had to be located less than 32 feet above the surface of the swamp, because the pressure of the atmosphere could not raise water higher even into a perfect vacuum. And second, the pump could not produce a reciprocal or rotary mechanical motion to provide power for either force pumps or other machinery driven by belts, gears, or cams. The second paradigm, which replaced the first early in the 18th century, was a plan for a piston moving back and forth in a cylinder, driven by either the pressure of the atmosphere working against a partial vacuum produced by the condensation of steam, or by the force of expanding steam, or both. The latter paradigm represents many of the steam engines in use today. (But not all. Another paradigm, the steam turbine, evolved out of the earlier water turbine that replaced the water wheel in hydraulic power plants.)

The first thing one can say about the community of mechanicians that by, say, the year 1850, had produced the steam engine is that it was a true "invisible college." The three hundred or so mechanicians who created the major technology of the Industrial Revolution up to 1850 were mostly residents of western Europe and North America; they knew one another by name and reputation, if not personally, and traveled and corresponded widely in order to keep up-to-date; they read one another's works and examined one another's machinery. In the case of the steam engine, the major figures were drawn from several countries and they were well aware of what their forebears and contemporaries were doing. Della Porta in Italy in 1601, and Salomon de Caus in France in 1615, both published a clear description and diagram of a pump that drove water up a pipe by the expansion of steam in a closed, heated vessel; Cornelius Drebble, a Dutchman, illustrated water being driven by atmospheric pressure into a vessel from which the air, or steam, had been driven out by heat. The English Marquis of Worcester (who had traveled extensively on the continent) and his assistant, the Dutch mechanic Kaspar Kalthoff, were experimenting with a steam pump based on the above-mentioned principles in the middle of the 17th century. And Captain Thomas Savery, who finally produced and sold such an engine based on the first paradigm, was a member of the Royal Society well acquainted with progress in the mechanical arts throughout Europe. With respect to the piston paradigm, there was Sir Samuel Morland, who in 1661—anticipating Huygens by more than a decade—patented an atmospheric piston engine in which the vacuum was produced by exploding gunpowder. Huygens's assistant, the French physicist Denis Papin, in 1690 published a scientific paper proposing an atmospheric piston engine in which the vacuum was produced by the condensation of steam. This paper was abstracted in English and published in the *Philosophical Transactions* of the British Royal Society in 1697. By 1700, Thomas Savery (who, we recall, was a member of the Royal Society) was experimenting with a piston engine utilizing high pressure steam). And, about 1712, Thomas Newcomen and Savery were jointly marketing the successful second-paradigm engine, operated by atmospheric pressure driving a piston into a cylinder in which steam was condensed by a spray of cold water. Slow, ponderous, inefficient "fire engines" were vastly successful at pumping water out of English coal mines and were manufactured by the hundreds. But the "Newcomen engine," because of its excessive coal consumption, was soon being improved, most notably by John Smeaton and James Watt. And early in the 19th century—over Watt's objections—high pressure steam was finally substituted for atmospheric pressure (and the low steam pressures that Watt's engines employed) in order to adapt the steam engine to railroads and marine transportation. In this effort, dozens of engineers took part.[1]

We have spoken of these mechanicians as constituting an "invisible college," a true paradigmatic community that worked to perfect and apply first one, and then another paradigm of the steam engine, after the fashion of what Kuhn has called "normal science." It was a community of several hundred that survived for several generations, spread over two continents, and maintained always a steady, rich flow of communication about the state of the art. But let us look at this community a little more closely. Let us examine the actual context in which the mechanicians produced their inventions, the shops where they worked, the organization of support services, even the sources of the money that provided the infrastructure. For knowing about this institutional infrastructure may tell us something about the conditions under which such paradigmatic processes can take place at all.

In the case of steam we can at once identify two of the institutions that made development possible. One was England's Royal Office of Ordnance. In the 16th and 17th centuries, the ordnance department commanded the largest share of the royal budget. It was responsible for all arsenals, fortifications, and military bridges, for the naval dockyards that outfitted the navy with the cast-iron guns, for setting the specifications for weapons of all kinds and for testing them, for maintaining and operating the Tower of London, and for transporting and operating all artillery. In order to improve its capacity to carry out its mission, the Ordnance also, in the 17th century, set up a special section for experimental weaponry, at first in the Tower of London, and then at Vauxhall estate in the Lambeth suburb of London. Virtually every 17th-century figure who contributed to the development of steam did so in Lambeth under the auspices of the ordnance department or at least in its quarters. Drebbel and Kalthoff worked in the Tower or in adjacent quarters, Worcester and Morland occupied Vauxhall and used its laboratories and workshops, and Savery completed his own steam engine in Lambeth. One may say that it was the Royal Office of Ordnance over a period from about 1630 to 1700 that financed and equipped the research and development process that led to the first successful steam engine.

Other large and enduring organizations provided the context in which the Newcomen engine developed and was improved. Newcomen's own ironmongery works may not have been extensive, but he had the backing of Savery and his Lambeth works, and large and enduring foundries, like that of the Darby's at Coalbrookdale, made the essential castings. And Watt's improvements on Newcomen's engine, culminating in the double-acting rotary engine operating by steam pressure rather than atmospheric pressure, were all supported by large and enduring organizations, first the University of Glasgow, and finally, the large Soho Iron Works of Matthew Boulton in Birmingham.

Watt's contributions to the steam engine were so extensive that he has been popularly credited with being its "inventor." This error, however, points to another feature of Kuhn's model of the paradigmatic process that is relevant to technology (and, we shall argue, the arts as well). In the history of science, Kuhn pointed out that new paradigms do not emerge as the result of continuing progress of normal science. To the contrary, it is commonly the case that the new paradigm is introduced at a time of intellectual, and emotional, crisis in the scientific community. Normal science finds itself unable to solve internal contradictions or awkward experimental disconfirmations in terms of the old paradigm. When a new paradigm appears that solves the new problems and the old, a scientific "revolution" occurs, a period of intellectual strife that ends with most of the scientific community converting to the new paradigm.

In the case of technology, it is not always possible to demonstrate the origins of a new paradigm in a revolutionary phase. Thus the development of the Savery and Newcomen engines at the end of the 17th century was the culmination of a slow and gradual process akin to normal science. Savery engines were not immediately discarded when the atmospheric piston engine appeared; they were still being manufactured as late as 1850. And the atmospheric engine was not immediately displaced by the Watt's rotary double acting machine; they too found use on into the middle of the 19th century. But there was a moment, within the development of the double-acting rotary engine—which may be thought of as a sub-paradigm—when something akin to a scientific revolution, in Kuhn's sense, took place. This issue had to do with high pressure steam.

The original Newcomen engine worked at atmospheric pressure, depending on a partial vacuum in the cylinder to provide a pressure differential of about six pounds per square inch, sufficient to move the piston down into the cylinder against the resistance of the force-pump apparatus. The cylinders were massive, as much as five or six feet in diameter and nine feet in length, and the movement was very slow, no more than 14 strokes per minute at best. In 1769, Watt added a separate condenser to the Newcomen engine, which cut its coal consumption in half. In 1782, Watt converted the motive force to the pressure of expanding steam, which was let alternately into one end of the cylinder at about 20 pounds per square inch, while the steam at the other end was exhausted into the cooled condenser. This further reduced coal consumption and simultaneously increased the horsepower. Further increases in horsepower and fuel efficiency were clearly possible at *really* high steam pressures—say 150 pounds per square inch—and were allowed in the double-acting engine. But Watt, impressed by the danger of working with high pressure steam, vehemently refused to build such engines, regarding their employment as tantamount to "murder."

There was, however, a vast potential market, not only for efficient stationary engines to pump water and drive cotton mills, but also for compact, powerful, fuel efficient engines to move ships, carriages, and trains of railroad wagons. Watt's assistant, Murdock, developed high pressure engines, but their sale was blocked by Watt, who held the patent. About the time that Watt's patent ran out, Richard Trevithick in England and Oliver Evans in the United States constructed and demonstrated high pressure engines on the road. By 1816, steamboats were in common use in the United States, and in 1830 Robert Stephenson's first practical steam locomotive was tested on the Liverpool and Manchester Railway. Thereafter, high pressure steam became the prevalent sub-paradigm.[2]

One of the interesting things about the crisis over steam pressure is that it was not generated by intellectual argument. The demand for compact, powerful, fuel efficient engines came from industry; the argument against it—a valid one, considering the toll of human lives in steam boiler explosions—was based on a concern for public safety. Another interesting feature is that the individual popularly credited with inventing the steam engine was actually the person who, after a hundred years of development, brought the atmospheric piston engine to the peak of its development. He fulfilled the potentialities of that paradigm. With respect to the subsequent paradigm—the high-steam-pressure piston engine—he recognized it, he took a brief and timid step into its development, and then pulled back, leaving it to others to bring it to perfection on behalf of patrons in industry and government, outside the community of mechanicians itself.

Before going on to compare the paradigmatic processes of the Renaissance with those of the Industrial Revolution, let us try to state what we have been describing in more general terms. In an earlier paper (Wallace 1972, chapter 5, this volume) I proposed a generalization of Kuhn's model to cover not only science but also technology, theology, and the arts. In this formulation, the paradigmatic process was considered to have five essential components:

innovation, paradigmatic core development, exploitation, functional consequences, and rationalization. It is possible to think of them as overlapping
stages in which each comes to the forefront of attention in the aforementioned
order, but the latter four "tasks" are actually continuous during the life of the
paradigm.

This model attempts to embrace a far wider range of culture change processes than Kuhn's: first because Kuhn is centrally concerned with the history
of science, and second because he is not attempting to deal at all with exploitation, functional consequences, or rationalization. My model does not claim to
describe *all* sequences of innovations and their consequences. *It applies only to
those change sequences in which a paradigmatic core development process occurs.*
This restriction is essential to the application of the model.

Innovation of a new paradigm may (as Kuhn emphasizes) entail a conflict with an older one, which it must replace; in this case one may speak
of a "revolution," such as the scientific revolutions of which Kuhn writes,
or the cultural "revolutions" associated with the development of agriculture,
urban life, and industrial technology. In individual societies, also, one may
think of "revitalization movements" led by religious prophets or charismatic
political leaders as efforts to establish a new cultural paradigm. Whether the
innovation of a new paradigm is always a revolutionary event, in the sense
that it immediately challenges the adequacy of existing practice, is debatable;
not all innovations basic to a new paradigm necessarily contradict an earlier
paradigm for some may initiate an entirely new line of development. The development of the 17th-century paradigms for the steam engine is an example.
And this brings up the point that paradigms, as ideas and procedures, may
come into existence as innovations *before* they are accepted and shared by a
community. A more important consideration is that not all innovations are
paradigm-forming. Many can best be considered under other headings such as
core development, functional consequences, and rationalization. And some,
perhaps, are simply not relevant to any paradigm process at all.

To qualify as paradigm-forming, an innovation need not be a complete
and adequate theory or model; rather, it is an event that solves a limited problem but does so in a way that opens up a whole new line of development.
It is a major "break-through." Furthermore, the paradigmatic innovation has
a symbolic and charismatic quality. It is often associated with the name of
a culture hero (human or divine) and it can be simply represented by some
visual image or phrase or manual procedure.

Paradigmatic core development is the continuous elaboration of the ideas that constitute the original paradigm, according to the rules of the paradigm itself. In science, Kuhn calls this the process of "normal science." Generations of trained workers make "contributions" to the perfection of the paradigm by resolving any surviving internal ambiguities or contradictions and by demonstrating its utility in solving newly discovered problems. Doctoral dissertations, for instance, are expected to be paradigmatic contributions in their own fields. People who are working on the same paradigm tend to be visible as a profession, or a school of thought, or a tradition, and to function as a community whose reference objects are other members of the community rather than the world outside. Such paradigmatic communities in our own culture history are readily recognizable not only in science but also in such fields as philosophy, theology, music, art and literature, and technology, and Kuhn has already recognized that humanistic scholarship traditionally assumes a paradigmatic scheme in its approaches to intellectual history and criticism.

Let us briefly consider theology, art, and literature (we shall return to the technology application later in more detail). In the case of religion, almost as soon as the prophet of a revitalization movement has begun to lay down the new paradigm in the form of a code based on his revelations, his disciples begin to discuss, interpret, and apply it. Even within nonliterate or marginally literate cultures, this process of editing, interpreting, and applying the text goes on incessantly, and a body of auxiliary beliefs and commentary rapidly builds up within the paradigmatic community of disciples, preachers, priests, and other followers. There is a continuing process of defining and redefining the standard symbols and formulas as new historical circumstances arise. Similarly in art, once a new idea or approach has been successfully broached, a "school" is likely to develop, perhaps at first consisting of only a few disciples, who work busily at amplifying and developing their master's paradigm. And again in literature, once a classic work has been created, it provides the format for dozens or hundreds of followers who play with and explore the possibilities implicit in the original.

There is a peculiar arbitrariness in the core development process. Once launched it is often remarkably independent in its direction (though not in velocity), from surrounding events, although it influences them. It is as though, once defined, the paradigm must be developed according to its own inner law; like a gyroscope, its attitude remains stable in a shifting historical frame. It is notoriously difficult to censor, suppress, or destroy a process of core development by economic, religious, or political pressures. Furthermore, within the paradigmatic community, new developments are in a sense unpredictable, for to predict the event in any detail is to have anticipated it; the event predicted occurs in the course of its own prediction. Thus, even though core development follows its own inner logic and works to realize latent implications, its course is also accompanied by a constant sense of surprised discovery.

Nonetheless, the process of core development does not occur in a vacuum. There is always a supportive infrastructure of money, personnel, and physical plant whose presence is a necessary condition for normal development of the paradigm. Such an institutional infrastructure must be transgenerational, as in a government agency like the office of ordnance or the extended families that supported innovation in iron during the Industrial Revolution.

By *exploitation* is meant the recognition and embracing of the paradigm, at some stage in its evolution, by an economic, military, religious, or political organization that sees in its application an opportunity for the protection or advancement of its own interests. The paradigmatic community can, theoretically, exploit its own paradigm, but this in all likelihood rarely happens. More commonly the exploitation is carried out by others, very often in as monopolistic a fashion as possible. The exploiting group may not only wish to apply the paradigm, and be the only applier of it; they may also wish to direct in some measure the further development of the core itself, both as to direction and rate. It is in the relationship of the paradigmatic and exploitive community that some of the most interesting features of the process lie, and we shall return to them later in this paper, for in the effort to apply the new paradigm to the practical ambitions of exploiters, conflicts within the paradigm may be exacerbated or even created. The conflict over high pressure steam is a case in point.

By *functional consequences* are meant the new, specific problems that the exploitation of the core development process creates for society and the way in which society responds, at first by expedients and eventually by cultural change. Recent examples in science are all too obvious: the applications of core development in normal science to the creation of new physical, chemical, and biological weaponry has threatened the survival of mankind, created new industries, developed new patterns of international relations, and so on. Ecological damage from indiscriminate waste disposal, from the incautious use of DDT and other insecticides, and from overuse of natural resources is almost as serious a threat. A result of medical research and improved methods of food production has been a vast increase in the world's population; this increase has entailed further pressure on the ecosystem and so on ad infinitum. It is easy to discover examples of catastrophic problems presented by the innocent development of a core by an oblivious paradigmatic community and an ambitious exploiting group. Typically, core development will create opportunity for some; and if that opportunity is seized, functional consequences will include advantages for some and new problems for others, and perhaps even eventually for the opportunist himself. And the solutions to any one problem will produce other problems and the solutions to these problems still more problems. This peculiar Pandora's box quality of the offerings of continuing core development and exploitation almost invariably generates an ambivalence and sometimes even a taboo toward the paradigmatic community by the rest of the society, with some parties interested in exploiting the new developments, others in suppressing them, and many feeling both ways at the same time.

But whether or not there is ambivalence, the problems produced by paradigmatic development are real and the policies that political and economic communities concoct to deal with them are an interesting field for cultural analysis, for experimental procedures tend to become policy and, when successful, to harden into conventional practice—ad hoc procedure becomes policy and policy becomes culture.

By *rationalization* is intended the ethical, philosophical, religious, and political justifications that the paradigmatic community members offer for their participation in the core development process, and that general community members offer for their relationship to the paradigm. As Garfinkel (1967) and other ethnomethodologists have pointed out, people tend to act in such a way as to validate their theory of the world, but when new actions are made necessary by the challenges of functional consequences of exploiting a paradigm, a new theory must be constructed. The para-community is generally rather monotonous in its rationalizations, saying in effect that working on the paradigm is doing God's work, or that it will lead to a better world, or that basic research is a good thing in itself and will always pay off eventually. The general community has a more interesting problem. In its initial "seizure" of the paradigm for the first application, the exploiting community group may account for its action with familiar and established explanations. Indeed, as Smelser (1959) and Kasserman (1971) point out, the exploiter may be an essentially conservative person who is simply trying to maintain his footing in a changing world. Later on, however, as more and more expedients must be contrived to cope with spin-off problems, the rationalization must change to take account of the functional changes in the society and in their own lives.

To the historian and sociologist of science, it has long been an appealing hypothesis that the language, the customs, and the values of the general society subtly determine the ideas of supposedly objective fields. The paradigmatic notion looks at the process in another way, concentrating on the evolution of the irrelevant to the point where relevance is discovered. The discovery of relevance is the moment of exploitation. At once the paradigmatic community is confronted by organizations, up to and at times including the sovereign institutions, which make claims on them. The interaction between these two interest groups is the subject of high drama in our own time, and even in our own profession, where the exploitation of the fieldwork paradigm by government agencies entails serious probable functional consequences and thus generates intense discussion of ethical issues. There are a number of dimensions along which the relations may vary, and for the sake of introductory discussion let us enumerate some of them: With respect to *support,* the policy of the general community (e.g., of a discipline like physics) by granting unrestricted research funds and fellowships, by favorable patent and copyright laws, by establishing new research and development communities; or it may restrict support to selected aspects of the field (such as weapons research) and other purely applied projects; or it may deliberate efforts to destroy the entire para-community (e.g., by accusing them of treason, of being witches, or whatever). With regard to *communication,* the general community may favor open channels (by avoiding censorship, endorsing freedom of speech, and the like), or it may impose censorship, place embargoes on immigration or emigration or even travel, or restrict foreign trade. With respect to *power,* the general community may eagerly include the para-community in the power structure, or exclude it from certain sorts of decision-making forums (by requiring a nonpolitical position as a condition of support), or even generally wall off the para-community into a castelike minority group or ghetto population. With respect to *control of applications,* the general community may take the initiative and attempt to seduce, hire, or coerce members of the para-community into providing service, or the responsibility for exploitation may be handled jointly, or the para-community may attempt to control the nature, timing, and degree of exploitation of its paradigm, in some cases using applications, and in others attempting to restrict or control them. And, of course, the *reward* system for paradigmatic work may vary from material goods, money, and power through symbolic rewards (medals, prizes, and so on) to rewards in the form of status or prestige in the para-community alone.[3]

An attempt to apply the notion of the paradigmatic community to both the Renaissance and the Industrial Revolution implies that they are comparable phenomena. And, indeed, it is not difficult to discover grounds for comparison. There is, for one thing, a direct continuity of concerns in science and technology. It is not merely Leonardo da Vinci's anticipation of later concepts in his famous, but long unpublished, *Notebooks*. Much of the knowledge of the Renaissance engineers with fortifications, weaponry, and industrial machinery was published in the well-known picture books that served to communicate and explain the principles of technology in an age when visual and verbal thinking were equally respectable.[4] Renaissance courts, like later royal establishments, actively encouraged experiment and innovation in such aspects of technology as clockwork mechanisms, printing, and mathematical instrument making (Moran 1981). And Galileo in a well-known passage paid tribute to the contributions of the centuries-old paradigmatic community of mechanicians maintained at the Arsenal of Venice: "The constant activity which you Venetians display in your famous arsenal suggests to the studious mind a large field for investigation, especially that part of the work which involves mechanics, for in this department, all types of instruments and machines are constantly being constructed by many artisans, among whom there must be some who, partly by inherited experience and partly by their own observations have become highly expert and clever in explanation" (Quoted in Wallace 1982:29).

Thus there would seem to be no doubt that in the High Renaissance of the 16th and 17th centuries science and technology were being driven forward by paradigmatic communities similar to those of the 18th and 19th. In a sense, one may view the Industrial Revolution as a direct continuation and intensification of paradigmatic processes in technological change that began during the Renaissance.

But what of the arts, and particularly of Raphael and his world in the late sixteenth and early seventeenth centuries? This is not the occasion for a thorough examination of the arts in the Renaissance within the framework of the paradigm model. But we may ask some of the general questions, and suggest the kind of further, more specific queries that even a superficial acquaintance with the history of the period suggests, in the hope that others better qualified will pursue the subject more thoroughly.

Perhaps the easiest general question to ask, and to answer, is: *was there a paradigmatic community?* and, if so, *who belonged to it? how was it organized?* Certainly for Raphael's lifetime, and for generations before and after, the answer to the general question must be *yes, there was a paradigmatic community.* Its most conspicuous Italian members, including Leonardo, Raphael, and Michelangelo, are household words. Some of the other members of the network in Raphael's time are almost equally well known: the writer Castiglione

Ariosto, the architect Bramante, the linguist Bembo. . . . The list would grow, I suspect, to include a hundred or more creative men and women who constituted a network of persons who knew each other personally, either by face-to-face visitation or by correspondence and the inspection of their works. The group differs somewhat from that of the Industrial Revolution's mechanicians, however, in embracing not only literary and artistic Humanists but also mathematicians, engineers, and scientists. And many of the community were themselves polymaths, more so than the later engineers, who might be both artist and mechanic, like Samuel F. B. Morse and Robert Fulton, but rarely also had literary pretensions (like Raphael's father and even Raphael himself). It has been observed that the literary members of this network were usually members of the nobility (including the church) and that the artists came from artisan backgrounds.[5] But the interesting question is, then, how did Renaissance society manage to tolerate a union of those who thought in words and those who thought in pictures, a union reflected by the classical world that they professed to emulate? How was this community of scholars, artists, and engineers held together? What were its patterns of communication both within and beyond Italy? What were the qualifications for membership in this "invisible college?" How did the "schools" of the major artists function? Apparently in some cases, like Raphael's, such organizations went far beyond a simple master and apprentice relationship and were virtually art factories, employing dozens of artists and artisans, in which not only production but also education and research and development were carried on. Were these schools a mechanism by which rapid communication of new techniques and new achievements throughout the paradigmatic community was effected *via* peripatetic "students," some of them mature artists, who traveled about Italy and perhaps to the north as well, like bees carrying pollen from flower to flower?

The second broad question is, *what was the paradigm* to whose development and application this community was dedicated? In an equally broad way, we can give the answer that the community itself gave. The paradigm was, ostensibly, the literature and art of classical antiquity. I emphasize the word "ostensibly." Although for sculpture the models may indeed have been the actual remnants of Greek sculpture, this cannot have been the case for painting. Renaissance painting was not based on imitation of a classical tradition but grew from western European roots. The paradigm after Leonardo, Raphael, and Michelangelo may have indeed been their works, but *their* paradigm was, presumably, a collection of earlier examples of primarily Christian religious art. The feature of this paradigm that connects it most directly with classical models is, perhaps, perspective, which permits the artist to represent on a flat or domed surface the three-dimensional architecture and sculpture and human figures of the classical era, as well as structures and people and animals of the contemporary world. But perspective was only one technique for creating the impression of three-dimensionality on two-dimensional surfaces. Careful attention had also to be paid to rendering light values on figures and to creating the effect of distance by rendering distant objects in a hazy light. But the definition of the early Renaissance paradigm in painting is a topic that I leave to art historians. Much technical innovation was going on and it must be dealt with as an autochthonous development that, once launched, evolves according to its own inner logic.

The third broad question concerns *the larger social context of innovation.* Beyond the paradigmatic community there exists a larger world, a supportive infrastructure that provides the buildings, the materials, the menial labor, the early encouragement, and the commission without which the paradigmatic community cannot do its work. What were the social institutions that supported the artists of Renaissance Italy in Raphael's time (and before and after)? Did the Renaissance happen when and where it did because social conditions, these institutions, had reached an appropriate stage of development? An examination of similar issues in regard to the early Industrial Revolution revealed that two of the major innovations, the steam engine and the substitution of coal (coke) for charcoal in the smelting and refining of iron, took place in a state-supported research-and-development institute and a single large extended-family business, respectively. Both institutions were able to provide multigenerational support for a cadre of specialists working on the problem; both had redundant resources; both maintained a policy of investing some part of their capital in new men with new ideas.

A similar situation existed in Italy with respect to innovation in the arts and the humanities. State institutions, such as the court of Urbino, where Raphael got his start and where Castiglione pursued a career, and the Vatican itself, where at one time or another Leonardo da Vinci, Raphael, Michelangelo, and a host of others lived and worked, provided long-term support in commissions and facilities and even in appointments to courtly or clerical office. And from all over the country, from merchants and councils in large and small towns, from provincial churches and monastic orders, came commissions for artwork. These evolved, it would seem, a cultural compulsion to invest public, church, and private funds in original art work, to an extent that far exceeds contemporary American standards and may have represented a substantial part of the gross national product. How did the new wealth of Renaissance merchants and bankers, princes and prelates, come to be diverted into the support of the liberal arts?

Another similarity between the Industrial Revolution and the Renaissance is the important role played by the extended family. I have elsewhere noted the importance of the bilateral extended family (more technically referred to by my fellows in the anthropological trade as the "cognatic descent group," ["Families of Iron" in the next volume]) in providing the mechanism for capital formation and insurance against financial disaster in early iron and textile industries in England and America before the widespread use of the limited liability corporation. In the Renaissance period, a similar type of cognatic descent group seems, in the absence of a single powerful sovereignty, to have provided the glue that held together larger political entities than individual towns and duchies could provide. The Sforzas, the della Roveres, the Borgias, the Medicis, by means of judicious marital alliances and procreations—the two not necessarily connected—were able to concentrate power, even to assume the papacy. And this power was used, among other things, to support scholars, artists, and engineers. Furthermore, the extended family provided security, at least for some, even at a far humbler level. We need only recall the situation of the youthful Raphael himself, at first the protégé of a maternal uncle who encouraged his artistic education, later the friend of a distant kinsman Bramante, who urged the pope to bring him to Rome, and near the end of his life the fiancé of a match-making Cardinal's niece. Attention to this genealogical detail raises such questions as the importance of the cognatic descent group in Italian society in general in this period and its importance to introducing artists as clients to important patrons. Certainly Sir Francis Bacon, a century later, was impressed by the importance of cognatic or nonunilinear descent groups in Italy, observing: "The Italians make little difference between children and nephews or near kinfolks; but so they may be of the lump, they care not though they pass not through their own body" (Quoted in Wallace 1982:71).

The comparison of the Industrial Revolution and the Renaissance leads us to a third, and even more general, issue concerning the social contexts favorable to innovation. In answering the question, why the Industrial Revolution occurred in poor, disorganized England rather than in wealthy, centralized France, the historian John U. Nef found the key in the very looseness of the English state apparatus. Instead of a centralized royal bureaucracy that stifled initiative and preempted the middle class, England's loose administrative style encouraged immigration, tolerated religious nonconformity, and encouraged an innovative middle class; it even permitted social contacts between persons interested in science and technology irrespective of class. Perhaps the looseness of Italy's political structure, despite its cost in the endless warfare among popes, emperors, kings, princes, and towns, provided similar encouragement to innovation in science and the arts.

Finally, I should like to raise a fourth general issue, and one that applies, perhaps, particularly to the role of Raphael himself in the paradigmatic process we have been discussing. *What was the relationship between the paradigmatic community and its supportive (and exploitative) infrastructure?* And specifically, between Raphael and the papacy?

The place of Raphael in the development of Renaissance art is ambiguous. Historians and critics from Vasari on have applauded his supreme skill but have also observed that his special talent lay in learning from and improving on the techniques of others. In perfecting the synthesis of his predecessors' and contemporaries' skills, he became, as it were, the paradigmatic painter for the High Renaissance. But this was by no means a revolutionary achievement; rather, it is a central feature of the "normal" evolution of a paradigm. The more revolutionary contribution of Raphael would seem to have been his development of ideological art, that is to say, art that expresses not merely the conventional symbolism of a culture, but that asserts a set of values, a worldview, as part of a political argument. Raphael was known as the "philosophical painter" but his philosophy was political; his works depict an ideal system of social relationships. Working on commissions for popes and cardinals, on intimate terms with the high clergy of the Vatican, he seems to have identified with the struggle of Julius II and Leo X to revitalize the papacy and make it the central political and cultural, as well as spiritual, institution of Christendom. One wonders, indeed, whether the papacy co-opted Raphael or whether Raphael's vision of the city of God on earth in fact inspired the popes. But the papacy was not re-establishing its authority without opposition from important quarters: the French crown, the Holy Roman Empire, dissident councils within the Church, and—just three years before Raphael's death—the challenging Martin Luther. The papacy in the 15th century had lost both spiritual and political authority. Now, as Julius and Leo attempted to recoup these losses, Raphael presented a utopian vision of a world of order and harmony, where the worldly art and wisdom of the ancients would be combined with the spiritual knowledge of Christianity in a great church-state. All eyes turn inward; the body of Christ, in the form of the church itself, personified by the popes, is the implicit spirit and flesh. It is a world of perfect harmony, where opposites—ancient and modern, church and state, the ideal and the real—are joined in centripetal compositions that say, "All we are united and made whole in the body of Christ."

And in his last painting, *The Transfiguration,* we see the other half of this political message, which is, in effect, "And only in Christ can we be united and made whole." This painting, in a sense, inverts the harmonious, centripetal compositions that decorated the papal apartments. It is divided into two levels, Christ and three awed apostles above, a crazed youth and his desperate family, arguing with incompetent doctors, below. The eyes of the real world find no cynosure and gaze wildly in all directions. And only one hand points up toward the shining body of the transfigured Christ, soaring toward heaven. If we read the chapter of the New Testament in which the events of transfiguration are described (Mark 9:1–29), we find that Raphael has chosen to illustrate two events that, in Mark, have no explicit connection: the transfiguration itself and the miraculous casting out of a "dumb spirit" that possessed a youth and made him insane. In the transfiguration Christ takes three disciples—Peter, James, and John—up onto a high mountain. There he was transfigured, i.e., "his raiment became shining, even white as snow," and the prophets Elias and Moses appeared, and God's voice spoke from a cloud, saying, "This is my Son: hear him." Christ also revealed that he would die and rise from the dead. The three disciples were, however, to say nothing about the incident until the Resurrection. Then the group came down from the mountain, to find a multitude surrounding the other disciples, angrily questioning them about their inability to exorcise the spirit that possessed a young man and afflicted him with fits (which sound like epileptic seizures). The father asked Jesus to cure the boy and so he did, casting out the spirit and making him whole. Then Jesus explained that faith in Him, and prayer and fasting, would cure such conditions.

The painting does not show the child being cured but rather the presumably simultaneous transformation on the mountain and failure of the disciples to cure the boy in front of an angry and disorganized crowd. In contrast to the utopian paintings, this one says, in effect, the only hope for a sick world is the Christ, and inasmuch as the Church is the mystical body of Christ on earth, the only hope for suffering humanity is the Church itself, which alone can unite mankind and make men whole.

But this is not an essay about Raphael but rather about the application of the idea of paradigmatic processes to the arts. We have seen, I think, that the notion of normal art, drawn from the concept of normal science and normal technological development, may generate useful questions. We are on less certain ground with the notion of revolution. It is not so easy to discern a stage of self-conscious crisis in Renaissance art comparable to what one would, I suspect, find in the 15th and 20th centuries. We have already noted the importance of three-dimensional representation, which seems to me to be a revolutionary development, but I am not aware of a self-conscious crisis in the Western art world that gave birth suddenly to the new paradigm. Although Piero della Francesca attributed the knowledge of geometrical perspective to ancient Greek painters, it would appear to have been rediscovered in early Renaissance times. Cennino Cennini, who worked in the tradition of Giotto di Bondone, emphasized its importance early in the 15th century; and by Leonardo's time, it was combined with other techniques—the rendering of light and shade, and diminution in distinctness of form, in size, and in color—to simulate three dimensionality. As Leonardo put it, "The first requisite of painting is that the bodies which it represents should appear in relief, and that the scenes which surround them with effects of distance should seem to enter into the plane in which the picture is produced by the means of the three parts of perspective" (Goldwater and Treves 1945:50). Gradual, incremental improvement seems rather to have been the way of change until the 18th or 19th century and the confrontation of the impressionists with traditional painting.

This suggests that the paradigmatic model of "normal" incremental progress works well in many periods of artistic and technological development and that it also accounts for gradual change in paradigms, contrary to the Kuhnian model of scientific change. The case of Raphael and the arts of the Renaissance may have taught us something about paradigmatic processes in general.

NOTES

1. This account of the development of steam power is drawn from Wallace 1982, chapter 1.

2. See Ferguson 1967.

3. See Wallace 1972 (chapter 5, this volume), for an earlier version of this discussion.

4. For discussions of visual thinking, see Ferguson 1977, Hindle 1981, and Wallace 1978.

5. See Partridge and Starn 1980:36–41.

PART 2

CULTURE AND PERSONALITY

When he arrived at Penn, A. I. Hallowell was already well known as an expert on northeastern Algonkian peoples and as a pioneer in the field of culture and personality. He had used the Rorschach test—one of a class of so-called projective techniques for assessing personality that were then widely employed in clinical settings—among the acculturated Ojibwa in Wisconsin and the less acculturated bands east of Lake Winnipeg. He was interested in comparing his Ojibwa profiles with Rorschachs obtained from Iroquois. To that end he assigned Iroquois Rorschach studies as dissertation projects to three graduate students. I was trained in giving and interpreting the Rorschach test at Bruno Klopfer's summer workshop (where Hallowell had learned the technique), and in addition I took a course in descriptive statistics in the psychology department. The result was a dissertation on the Rorschachs provided by a sample of subjects on one Iroquois reservation. A statistical analysis of the results showed that only about a third of the respondents could be described, even in the most generous way, as displaying the same modal personality structure. This finding seemed to fly in the face of the conventional assumption, promoted by Margaret Mead, Ruth Benedict, and other leaders in the field of culture and personality, that supposedly uniform child-rearing practices in a homogeneous society would produce a commonly shared basic personality structure or national character, and that those who did not share this personality structure were "deviants" or even mentally ill. This doctrine had gained currency during World War II as Americans strove to understand the behavioral propensities of allies like the Russians and enemies like the Germans and Japanese. In the passage reproduced here from *Culture and Personality* (1961), and in other writings, I argued that rather than a monolithic sharing of cognitions and personality traits there was an inevitably large spectrum of diversity even in small, apparently homogeneous cultures, let alone large, culturally pluralistic societies, and that the process necessary to the formation of community was not a replication of uniformity but the organization of diversity.

During the early 1950s, despite the surge in interest in anthropology, there still were few openings available to newly minted Ph.D.'s in anthropology departments across the country, and my position as instructor in the sociology department at Penn was insecure. In 1955 when I was offered a job as a research specialist at the newly created Eastern Pennsylvania Psychiatric Institute in Philadelphia, I eagerly accepted. EPPI was one of two such institutions in the state; the other was established in Pittsburgh before the war. Similar psychiatric research institutes were being built in a number of states at this time, inspired by the belief that scientific research into human behavior would soon provide means for the prevention and cure of the whole Pandora's box of mental illness. My own interest in psychiatric research was strong, based on my training in clinical psychology and projective techniques at Penn, participation in the program in educative analysis of the Philadelphia Psychoanalytic Association, and experience in the National Research Council's program of disaster studies (which was prompted by the National Security Council's concern over such matters as the feasibility of mass evacuation of American cities in anticipation of atomic attack, or mass panic after such an attack had occurred). The NRC program in disaster studies, administered by William N. Fenton as executive secretary of the Division of Anthropology and Psychology, focused on assembling the literature on past natural and human-made disasters, the field study of fresh disasters, and the formulation of models of human behavior in extreme situations. My own field study was of the tornado in Worcester, Massachusetts, in 1954, and an excerpt from this study, describing a response pattern, the "disaster syndrome," commonly found among disaster victims, is included in this section.

The approach to research at EPPI was based on a university model, with a wide spectrum of separate and generally independent departments, ranging from the most orthodox psychoanalytic on the ground floor, claiming that mental illness is totally generated by social experience, to the most dogmatically organic on the ninth floor, insisting that mental illness in all its varieties is solely a matter of chemistry. In addition to my own little anthropology department, which included graduate student assistants from time to time, such as Raymond Fogelson and Robert Ackerman, another, major, anthropological presence was a team of investigators led by Margaret Mead, who commuted from New York, and Ray Birdwhistell, devoted to studying communication processes, both verbal and nonverbal, in the development of mental disorders and their psychotherapy. The unseen presence of another anthropologist, Gregory Bateson, was also strongly felt, in the form of his celebrated "double-bind" hypothesis, which attributed some forms of psychotic thinking and feeling to the victim having been subjected, by such significant others as the mother, to contradictory commands on two different logical levels, such as saying, "Do this or I will punish you" and then saying, "Don't pay attention to anything I say." It is worth noting that at this time it was estimated that about one out of every six anthropologists in the United States was supported by psychiatric research grants and fellowships. Some administrators in the National Institute of Mental Health (which was funding my revitalization movements project) expected that soon every graduate student in the behavioral sciences in the United States would be the recipient of an NIMH fellowship.

In this loosely structured setting, it was possible for me to pursue a variety of research paths, including completing the biography of Handsome Lake, continuing studies of revitalization movements and the visionary experience, observing clinical experiments with group therapy, and applying the findings of disaster studies to theory about mental dynamics. The paper "Dreams and the Wishes of the Soul" grew out of work in psychoanalysis and the reading of Iroquois ethnography and ethnohistory while writing the Handsome Lake biography. The paper "The Psychic Unity of Human Groups" developed some of the implications of the "non-sharing" thesis that had been inspired by the earlier analysis of projective technique results. The concept of mazeway as the individual's unique system of cognitive maps was central to the view of culture as not requiring cognitive homogeneity; out of disaster studies came the consideration of mazeway disintegration; speculation about what went on in the prophet's head as he experienced the revelation of his code prompted the paper "Mazeway Resynthesis."

But the principal impact on my thinking at EPPI was made by the awareness of the important role of organic factors in mental and emotional function. The world of clinical and basic research was bubbling with new ideas, new treatments, and new research avenues. In 1955, when I arrived at EPPI, research was just starting on the treatment of chronic psychotic patients with thorazine, one of the first of the tranquilizers, and one of my colleagues in Clinical Research, Dr. Harold Rashkis, took me out to the notorious state hospital at Byberry (a.k.a. Phildelphia State Hospital) where he was comparing the patients he was treating with thorazine with those receiving old-fashioned custodial care. The difference was dramatic: in custodial back wards one saw patients, many of whom had been incarcerated for ten, 20, or 30 years, wallowing in their own excrement, babbling incoherently in unknown languages, endlessly twisting wads of paper. The patients on tranquilizers might still display behavior deemed inappropriate by the staff, but they were relatively quiet and easy to manage. Other researchers were exploring the role of diet, the mechanisms of electric and insulin shock, and even experimenting with so-called psychotomimetic drugs, including mescaline, LSD, and atropine in large doses; anthropologists from other institutions were reporting on their experiences with other exotic drugs, such as South American *ayahuasca*. The basic research program in its laboratories on the ninth floor, inhabited by scientists who wore white lab coats, was devoted to the study of the chemistry and physics of nerve impulse transmission. The core of the group had come from the Army Chemical Center at Aberdeen, Maryland, where the physiology of nerve gas was being studied; some of the men had been brought over from German laboratories at the end of World War II. These scientists walked around followed by assistants with hypodermic syringes in hand filled with antidote, lest a test tube bearing the deadly gas be dropped, and there were little overhead shower fixtures in the halls to wash down anyone accidentally exposed. Others were reviewing twin studies and other kinship data for clues to possible genetic factors. And similar research programs were being pursued at comparable institutions in New Jersey, New York, and other states.

This milieu of research in what could broadly be called the neuro-physiology of mental illness inspired me to think closely about the process of prophetic visions, guardian spirit visions, trance, and possession, all traditional subjects of anthropological interest. These altered states of consciousness, while considered normal and even desirable in their own cultural settings, were regarded as symptoms of mental illness if they occurred within the purview of the typical Western clinical psychologist or psychiatrist. Seeking to understand the prophet's revelation, I came across the then-influential work of Hans Selye on stress and the "general adaptation syndrome." I had used the concept of stress, in a metaphoric sense, in presenting the theory of revitalization movements in the paper reprinted in this volume, but this new application of the term was to strictly physiological processes, as described by Selye and those in psychiatric research who were using his ideas (for instance, in understanding combat fatigue as displayed by troops returning from Guadalcanal). The papers "Mazeway Disintegration" and "Mazeway Resynthesis" were products of this line of thought. Another set of research questions, prompted by this physiological research setting, had to do with the possible role of physiological factors in the etiology of the so-called ethnic psychoses reported in the ethnographic literature—seemingly exotic forms of mental illness occurring in non-Western cultural settings, like "arctic hysteria," "running amok" in Malaysia, or "voodoo death" in Australia. The paper "Mental Illness, Biology, and Culture" addresses this theme. It focuses particularly on a condition commonly observed, particularly among the Thule Eskimo, and denominated by the term *pibloktoq*, which I interpreted as an effect of extremely low intake of calcium in the Eskimo diet during certain seasons. This hypothesis, which I went on to apply to the cases of "grand hysteria" on which Freud based his early formulations of psychoanalytic theory, was repudiated by Margaret Mead in a review as a "destructive hypothesis." With several colleagues at EPPI, I made ambitious plans to visit Thule to observe the syndrome and collect blood samples but alas (but understandably) the hunters' council refused permission and the project had to be abandoned. One of my doctoral students, however, an M.D. psychiatrist, Edward Foulks, was able to partially confirm the theory in several cases of hysteria among Alaskan Eskimos. An equally ambitious attempt to tie together the biochemical and psychosocial approaches to the theory of mental disorder was inserted into a chapter on "Culture and Mental Illness" in the textbook *Culture and Personality* (1970). Speaking of schizophrenia, I wrote, "It is the writer's opinion that this psychosis is precipitated and maintained by a biochemical disorder or disorders for which hereditary predisposition is common. Biochemical disorder reduces the 'semantic capacity' of the individual below the level necessary for adequate cultural participation" (1970b:217).

At this time it was still legal to conduct experiments with hallucinogenic substances, like mescaline, atropine, and LSD, in the expectation of producing "model" transient psychoses for clinical study. Such experiments were being conducted at a number of research institutions across the country. As an anthropologist, I felt that inadequate attention was being made to the way in which the subject's cultural background influenced not only the content of the primary hallucinatory experience but also his response to it. This line of thought stimulated several papers, including one reprinted here, "The Trip," which explores the long tradition of spiritual interpretation of "psychotic" experiences in Western culture. Also in a clinical context Raymond Fogelson and I, and others including our unit's secretary, Josephine Dixon, watched family therapy sessions from behind a one-way mirror and recorded the proceedings. Some of our resulting impressions were published as a chapter in a text prepared by the codirectors of this innovative therapy program. That chapter, entitled "The Identity Struggle," is included here.

In these early days of experimentation with psychotropic drugs on patients committed involuntarily to psychiatric hospitals, legal and ethical issues came to be matters of concern to administrators, and particularly to me as Director of Clinical Research. The Nuremberg trials had brought to public notice the cruel experiments of Nazi doctors with helpless prisoners in concentration camps, and out of the trials came a code of ethics for medical research. The Nuremberg Code was the basis for recommendations by the National Institutes of Health of rules to govern the practice of clinical research. But efforts to formulate and implement such rules, and particularly the requirement that the patient or his guardians give "informed consent" before being subjected to research procedures and experimental treatments, such as untried drugs whose efficacy and safety were imperfectly understood, for a time encountered determined resistance. At EPPI, clinicians felt that their medical judgments would be subject to bureaucratic interference, and researchers, both medical and nonmedical, objected to any infringement on the sacred domain of science, where unimpeded intellectual freedom was traditionally regarded as essential to the advancement of knowledge and the benefit of mankind. Disgusted by what appeared to me (as administrator) to be self-interest cloaked in protestations of principle, I resigned as Director of Clinical Research and at Loren Eiseley's invitation returned to teaching in the anthropology department at the University of Pennsylvania.

The salad days of hospital-based psychiatric research were coming to an end, anyway. In Pennsylvania and other states, government officials and legislators were increasingly dismayed at the huge cost of maintaining large hospitals filled with chronically ill mental patients; and the research institutes, like EPPI, that once were expected to create new treatments that would rapidly reduce these patient populations, were producing no major breakthroughs. It began to appear to state administrators that the state hospital systems, rife with corruption, were doing no good, and that the best way to handle the chronically ill was to release them from the sickening confines of the back wards and return them to the community. There they could get by, it was believed, with the aid of tranquilizers and other psychotropic drugs doled out by community mental health centers. But many failed to enter the mainstream and joined instead the ranks of the homeless on the streets. Research could be left to pharmaceutical companies and universities. Philadelphia State Hospital was emptied; and in 1980 the state gave EPPI to a nearby medical school, to be used primarily as a clinical and teaching facility.

Meanwhile, within anthropology, the field of culture and personality was attracting less attention and fewer followers. Some of its interests were being absorbed into the "symbols and meanings" tradition, and into the newer studies of culture and cognition. Psychoanalytically informed approaches suffered from the wholesale assault on Freud and Freudian concepts by the biochemically oriented wing of psychology and psychiatry, and the validity of projective techniques, like the Rorschach, was severely challenged. My own interests in the psychology and culture domain shifted toward the cognitive side.

8

The Disaster Syndrome

In my initial field memorandum on the Worcester tornado, and in the later memorandum on the literature on human behavior in extreme situations, I drew attention to what appeared to be a very common behavioral reaction, which had rather definite stages. I called this the "disaster syndrome."

The disaster syndrome is a psychologically determined defensive reaction pattern. During the first stage, the person displaying it appears to the observer to be "dazed," "stunned," "apathetic," "passive," "immobile, or "aimlessly puttering around." This stage presumably varies in duration from person to person, depending on circumstances and individual character, from a few minutes to hours; apparently severely injured people remain "dazed" longer than the uninjured, although this emotionally dazed condition is no doubt often overlaid by wound shock. The second stage is one of extreme suggestibility, altruism, gratitude for help, and anxiousness to perceive that known persons and places have been preserved; personal loss is minimized, concern is for the welfare of family and community. This stage may last for days. In the third stage, there is a mildly euphoric identification with the damaged community, and enthusiastic participation in repair and rehabilitation enterprises; it sometimes appears to observers as if a revival of neighborhood spirit has occurred. In the final stage, the euphoria wears off, and "normally" ambivalent attitudes return, with the expression of criticism and complaints, and awareness of the annoyance of the long-term effects of the disaster. The full course of the syndrome may take several weeks to run.

The frequency of this syndrome, and particularly of its first stage, is difficult to learn. If one used the data presented in Chapter 3 [of the original study], one would conclude that in Worcester, at about impact-plus-fifteen minutes (on the average) approximately 33 per cent of uninjured or slightly injured persons were displaying stage one. Probably the incidence of stage one declines in proportion to time elapsed after impact, so that the earliest observers would have seen it more commonly than later observers. The conditions under which this syndrome occurs seem to be four: an impact which destroys or damages much of the visible cultural environment and kills or injures, or threatens to kill or injure, many people; an impact which is unexpected; an impact which is sudden; and an impact with whose consequences the individual is not trained to cope. General cultural differences seem not to be a major determinant, since such a "dazed" reaction is reported from widely scattered disaster-struck communities. I would speculate that the more sudden the impact, the more unexpected, the more destructive and the less trained the population is to act in its wake, the more severe and the more widespread will be the "dazed" reaction.

In this section of the report, I shall try to delineate further some of the characteristics of the syndrome and the conditions under which it occurs. . . .

A large number of the persons in the impact area during the isolation period (i.e., up to about half an hour after impact) were incapable of more than minimal (and often inadequate) care for themselves and their families. Many of these uninjured apparently were unable or unwilling even to walk out of the area. Far from panic, there was a dissociated state variously alluded to as "daze," "shock," "apathy," in which the normal cognitive structure was severely limited and affect was limited except for occasional emergences of irrational dependency, hostility, or "hysteria." One has the feeling that the dazed, helpless, floundering state represents a partial regression to a level of behavioral organization in which the individual is limited in his ability to perceive the actual physical environment and cannot act coherently with regard to the objects and dangers around him. We shall discuss later possible determinants of this regression.

The first rescuers from the community aid area found the survivors in a random movement state. . . . After recognition that help had arrived, however, the dazed and apathetic stage disappeared, and survivors participated more extensively in rescue, first aid, and evacuation activities. . . .

The pastor at St. Michael's on the Heights Episcopalian church was away from the impact area at impact, and was able to return by 6:30, during the height of the rescue period. By this time, it would seem, a common modality of behavior was mutual reassurance. Finding his family unhurt (the house was in the fringe impact area), he donned his cassock and made the rounds of his parishioners' homes asking, "Are you all right?" "People would cry when

I asked. . . . I feel they knew I represented God as well as my own personal concern for their safety. . . . People wanted more than anything else to know people cared about them. . . . If they knew me, they would give me a hug. They wanted to be reminded that they were all right. . . . They wanted comfort rather than physical help." Another minister who was also making the rounds of his parish about the same time remarked, "Almost everyone wanted to go beyond a handshake, wanted an embrace; wanted to lean on you. Some want to kiss and be kissed in reassurance." Both ministers referred to the cooperativeness, politeness, and willingness to help which the people showed to each other in the impact area during the rescue period.

Among those being evacuated to the hospitals, a similar type of complaisant, helpful, and grateful attitude was observed. . . . These observations on victims in the impact area and in the hospitals during the rescue period show a partial continuation of the dazed state, with relatively flat affect, but an improved capacity for action if organized community aid personnel (physicians, nurses, firemen, police, *et al.*) were present to give directions. In the presence of such personnel, with equipment, giving instructions, the victims were markedly obedient. They also indicated intense gratitude and pleasure at receiving any help or verbal expressions of concern or interest. Injured victims seem usually not to have gone into wound shock until after evacuation; but the incidence of wound shock after evacuation was apparently high. The interplay of physical and emotional trauma in producing the "disaster syndrome" should be investigated.

The next stage, the early rehabilitation period, saw a further development of the syndrome. In this stage, a cardinal feature was altruism. The dazed component and the extreme passivity had passed. In the words of the Bakst report [p. 28 of the report], quoting Bishop Wright: "The general impression of observers is that the injured and uninjured alike were more concerned for others than for themselves and were so awed by the enormity of the disaster that 'each person became a saint for about ten days.' " One Protestant pastor whom I interviewed also testified to the prevalence of the altruistic component among the residents of his part of the impact area up to June 19. This pastor noted that among his parishioners, in the Burncoat area, there was a real "revival" of community and church spirit; there was much freer personal contact; manners were more "natural;" everyone pitched in to help clean up the church property; old feuds were forgotten, and persons with mental disease symptomatology or histories of hospitalization showed a notable remission of symptoms or at least no relapse. Another pastor commented on the continuous desire victims felt for people to come to them, their anxiety and fear at having to go to apply (e.g., to the Red Cross). Perhaps the altruistic component has a demanding and dependent side as well as a generous one.

Consolidating the data given above, one can describe the overt behavior of the disaster syndrome as displaying three stages, corresponding roughly to the isolation, rescue, and early rehabilitation periods:

1. *Isolation period:* many survivors in the impact area, injured and un-injured, are "dazed," "apathetic," "stunned"; awareness of the extent and intensity of destruction, to person, family, and community, is in-adequate; efforts at first aid, rescue, and evacuation are perfunctory, frequently inadequate, and often entirely absent; many people simply stare, wander aimlessly, "putter about"; expressions of strong emotion (grief, fear, pain, anger, etc.) are missing or sporadic and inappropriate.

2. *Rescue period:* with the arrival of organized protective personnel, with equipment (firemen, police, Civil Defense, Red Cross, etc.), survivors remaining in the impact area are able to perform routine tasks in res-cue, fire-fighting, etc., operations, under orders; survivors evacuated to hospitals, aid stations, and other mass care centers are also able to follow orders and are extremely docile and obedient, but they tend to remain "dazed" longer, or, if injured, to go into severe wound shock; both groups are better oriented than during the isolation period and can usually tell an interviewer what happened to them; both groups are extremely grateful for care and concern; both groups are also self-sacrificing and willing to let others be cared for first.

3. *Rehabilitation period* (first ten days at least): both injured and unin-jured, in hospitals and in the impact area (but perhaps not to the same degree if they are no longer receiving evidences of mass care, as in cases where evacuees have gone to live with relatives) show a mild euphoria, marked by intense altruism and willingness to work for the community welfare, readiness to give up old grudges, to ignore barriers of social dis-tance, and to merge the self in a kind of neighborhood revival spirit, to participate in a strong "we-feeling" shared by impact-area survivors but not by others; at the same time, in spite of professions of thankfulness and gratitude, there is also a tendency, inconsistent with the foregoing, to complain of the coldness and efficiency of mass care organizations, to become very sensitive over applying for aid in any form, and to be willing to accept assistance only if it is brought to them. The three

stages of the syndrome might be labeled, for purposes of reference, the random movement stage, the suggestible stage, and the euphoric stage.

This syndrome describes the behavioral modality of an unknown proportion of the survivors in the impact area. Some persons—notably those with pre-defined roles to play in a disaster—do not succumb to the syndrome, although they probably have tendencies toward it; some few persons seem to escape it by immediate and direct "hysterical" outbursts; some, of course, are so severely injured that physiological trauma governs behavior. (The incidence and nature of the "hysteria" occasionally but vaguely described is another point worthy of investigation.) I would hypothesize that this syndrome will invariably occur following a disaster characterized by a sudden impact involving physical destruction and injury affecting a large part of the survivors' visible community environment, and that cultural differences will not affect it appreciably.[1]

The determinants of the syndrome are, in my opinion, not primarily physical injuries, physical shock, physical upset by buffeting and being "pushed around by a lot of air;" they are psychological. This is evidenced by the fact that the disaster victim can display this syndrome whether or not he has been injured; it is also evidenced by the fact that injured disaster victims display the syndrome more frequently than do accident cases (the latter being said usually to be noisier, more demanding, more sensitive to pain, more susceptible to the physician's bedside manner, etc.). The precipitating factor in the disaster syndrome seems to be a perception: the perception that not only the person himself, his relatives, and his immediate property (house, car, clothing, etc.) have been threatened or injured, but that practically the entire visible community is in ruins. The sight of a ruined community, with houses, churches, trees, stores, and everything wrecked, is apparently often consciously or unconsciously interpreted as a destruction of the whole world. Many persons indeed, actually, were conscious of, and reported, this perception in interviews, remarking that the thought had crossed their minds that "this was the end of the world," "an atom bomb had dropped," "the universe had been destroyed," "the whole city of Worcester may have been destroyed," etc. The objects with which he has identification, and to which his behavior is normally tuned, have been removed. He has been suddenly shorn of much of the support and assistance of a culture and a society upon which he depends and from which he draws sustenance; he has been deprived of the instrumentalities by which he has manipulated his environment; he has been, in effect, castrated, rendered impotent, separated from all sources of support, and left naked and alone, without a sense of his own identity, in a terrifying wilderness of ruins.

The response to the assault of this realization is withdrawal from perceptual contact with this grim reality and regression to an almost infantile level of adaptive behavior characterized by random movement, relative incapacity to evaluate danger or to institute protective action, inability to concentrate attention, to remember, or to follow instructions. Such individuals appear to be "dazed," "shocked," "stunned," "apathetic." Actually they are far from being indifferent; it is the intensity of the previously felt anxiety which has prompted this blocking of perception and this regression.

The remainder of the syndrome represents the gradual restitution of the pre-impact behavioral organization. The individual first seems to emerge from the cocoon of apathy at the appearance of rescue personnel from the outside; he becomes very dependent on these people, identifies with them, is extremely suggestible and obedient, idealizes the care they give, rejoices in embracing and touching them. This is the suggestible stage. Following this comes a stage in which there is a joyful resurgence of identification with the community, a re-acceptance of the adult role, although the reassurance of unsolicited aid and assurance is constantly demanded. Finally, there is the development of complaints and blame. This is an ambivalent stage. Eventually, no doubt, most individuals return approximately to their pre-disaster state, after perhaps two weeks or a month. The various phases of the syndrome, after the initial plummeting regression, appear like a telescoped passage through the familiar stages of behavioral maturation.

In the evolution of the disaster syndrome in a middle-aged small-business man, who was uninjured or only slightly injured (he does not mention any injury), one can see the syndrome from the inside. Although it [is] apparent . . . that virtually everything in sight around him was severely damaged or completely destroyed, he thought for half an hour that only he and his property had been damaged (thus blocking out awareness of the community's destruction). At the same time that he said he thought consciously the storm had affected him alone, however, he was expressing concern over the welfare of his family in other parts of the city. It was half an hour before he was capable of recognizing consciously that this was a community disaster. Days afterward he is dreaming that nothing has happened to anyone but him, and that his teacher (mother) is going to come to his rescue promptly: at the same time, in

[a] dream he is a passive, helpless little boy again. His altruistic identification with other victims makes him come close to bursting into tears. His behavior seems inexplicable to himself. And he admits that other people thought he was "stunned." His memory for personal experience during impact is very clear, but as far as the record goes, there is partial amnesia for the first half hour after impact with the exception of recollections of trying to locate his family. He did not make any effort to engage in rescue or first aid. During this time, apparently he was quite literally unaware of the extent of the disaster, in spite of the fact that buildings were visibly in ruins and one of them on fire all around him; and he was puttering about aimlessly trying to sweep up twenty-three truck loads of debris with a broom.

THE COUNTER-DISASTER SYNDROME

Persons in the community outside of the impact area at the time of impact, but with close emotional ties to persons and places struck, suffered from a complementary behavioral and emotional syndrome. If the essential behavioral characteristic in the first phase of the disaster syndrome was passivity and (after a first awareness of the extent of damage) ignoring of community trauma, and the responsible mechanism denial and regression, the essential characteristic in the counter-disaster syndrome is over-conscientiousness and hyper-activity, and the responsible mechanism is a defense against feelings of guilt. Fewer observations have been made on the counter-disaster syndrome, partly because many of those who are in a position to describe it are suffering from it and hence are rather defensive in the presence of interviewers or readers.

In its initial stages, the counter-disaster syndrome seems to be characterized by extremely vigorous activity oriented toward rescue, first aid, the making of a contribution of some kind. Certainly there is nothing pathological in activity aimed at helping victims of a disaster; the quasi-pathological quality appears when this activity is, despite the enthusiasm of the helper, relatively low in efficiency and is unduly "panicky." It is interesting that at Worcester, the only two groups whom I have seen described as being "panicky" after impact were absent parents and other relatives returning to the impact area and finding that it had been devastated in their absence, and hospital personnel. "Panic" is not technically the proper word to use: "hyperactive and less rational than normal" might describe it better. Trained personnel, such as firemen and police and local relief personnel, are affected, as well as untrained volunteers.

The first stage, which prevails chiefly during the period of rescue, evacuation, and emergency medical care, is characterized by extreme anxiety, with a profusion of automatic symptoms: tachycardia, shortness of breath, sweating, muscular cramps, etc. The rescue worker is likely to over-exert himself physically, sometimes to the point of collapse; perhaps some of the exhaustion should be ascribed to the large quantity of energy consumed in maintaining internal tension. Far from being passive and dependent, the sufferer is likely to prefer working on his own, or to take a position of responsibility. He does a great deal of work, and its value is considerable, but it is apt to be hastily done and it may require checking and possibly redoing by less emotionally involved personnel. An example of this in Worcester was the suturing of contaminated wounds by doctors on the night of impact.

There are a few descriptions of the counter-disaster syndrome in the interviews. One observer, a psychiatrist, commented on a rescue worker who got into the Great Brook Valley very early:

> . . . He happened to be driving past and got out and went into the wrecked area that I'm talking about. It was the worst area in terms of destruction, I don't know about the wind, how fast the wind was blowing or where the storm was worst, but this was the worst place. I think they eventually took about fifty dead people out. I didn't think there were that many. I had no idea. But he was overwhelmed by what he saw, as I interpret his behavior, and he just ran around over the tops of the rooms, just running around and I don't know what he thought he was doing, that is, I don't know what he did. I'm sure he thought he was doing the best he could but he didn't do anything, at least at that time.

There were also various descriptions of the behavior of returning parents: men running up the hill to their homes, and virtually collapsing with exhaustion when they got home; a hysterical woman screaming when a neighbor tried to comfort her; a pastor who spoke of his feeling of "guilt and frustration" at having been away from home when he was needed. To a minor extent, even trained crews of firemen seem to have suffered from this syndrome:

> . . . it was very hot, we had rubber goods on anyway, you know all our rubber goods, and it made it awfully hot; and the way we were running around there like mad, trying to do what we could . . . Sweating, oh yes.

We were exhausted. We were exhausted, that's what it was. Exhaustion was coming on, because we were rushing, trying to do everything we could, it was really exhaustion that was coming on, see.

And I myself was panic stricken. I was panic stricken all the time. I didn't know what had happened to my family.

I believe the captain felt the same way; now, I didn't speak to the other fellows about it, but they probably felt the same way . . . (The captain) was excited. He really was because he . . . But he was working like mad, and directing us here and ordering us there, you know, and he was carrying out his duty and in the meantime you could see that worried look on his face.

It should be emphasized that it is the *reaction* to concern for family, friends, and community that is referred to as the counter-disaster syndrome, not the concern itself. Certainly it is not implied that a sense of responsibility for the welfare of others is undesirable.

Within a few hours, the impact area was swarming with people who had come in from the community outside to help; hospitals had long lines of blood donors, and finally had to turn people away; people called up the Red Cross, Civil Defense, and other agencies, and offered their services. Much of this urge to help simply resulted in obstructing the efforts of trained personnel, or required the detailing of such personnel essentially to combat the counter-disaster syndrome in the community. Hospital corridors and entrances had to be guarded; road blocks had to be established and traffic police assigned; the National Guard had to be assigned to keep out "sight seers" (many of whom undoubtedly were people anxious to help in some way).

In succeeding days, the continued pressure of the need to demonstrate conclusively the adequacy of one's charity and conscientiousness contributed directly (in my opinion, at least) to the peculiar inter-agency squabbles. These squabbles took two forms: squabbles over the justification for "red tape" (e.g., in Red Cross registration and inquiry practices); and squabbles over the "possession of the disaster" (to use John Powell's happy phrase). The former type of squabble tended to divide local agencies and popular opinion from regional, state, or national offices: thus the National Red Cross was accused of "seeking publicity," was bitterly criticized for trying to register evacuees, for inquiring into financial status of those being assisted, and even for expecting candidates for assistance to apply. And Federal Civil Defense, who requested a housing survey before ordering five hundred trailers sent in from Missouri, were similarly attacked for stalling, heartlessness, etc. One suspects that the relatively unemotional, uninvolved, professional competence of the outsider simply aggravates guilt feelings of the local action-people, who see someone who obviously can't be blamed for what happened, coming in to help and advise (thereby implying the local agencies aren't able to cope with it themselves). Local personnel tend to feel threatened by outside experts, anticipating (not too rationally) criticism of their efforts, and loss of opportunity to make good before the world.

Squabbles, however, between local agencies—e.g., between the Red Cross and Civil Defense over welfare administration—also grow out of this competition for the privilege of giving help. In situations where supply is so ample that everyone who wants to help can be given a slice of the material to distribute, it does not matter, but the consequences of competition for short supply could be a disastrous waste of manpower, time, or materials.

The only two cases of severe mental breakdown as a result of the tornado (in my records, at least) occurred among people who had shown the counter-disaster syndrome. Traumatic hysterical symptoms (e.g., phobias for thunderstorms) were common among victims from the impact area, but several observers testified that some notoriously unstable personalities seemed to be undisturbed. This is possibly because, in the disaster-syndrome, there is minimal conflict, minimal guilt, simply regression and later restitution. The core of the counter-disaster syndrome, however, is guilt, and this means conflict, and this means the possibility of conflict-induced mental breakdown.

The desire to be of assistance and to receive recognition for having been a competent actor in the emergency is a powerful one, and if it is not satisfied, disturbed behavior can result (presumably, in presensitized persons particularly) as resentment and guilt build up. Survivors from outside the impact area need to "get into the act" and interference with their efforts to play a satisfying relief role may precipitate emotional conflicts which reduce efficiency in rescue and relief operations.

THE LENGTH OF THE ISOLATION PERIOD

It may be contended that one of the most crucial factors governing the incidence of casualties and property damage is the length of the isolation period.

The logic behind this statement is as follows. If two tornadoes (or any other impact agent) strike two inhabited areas, occupied by the same number and sorts of people and structures, but if a given quantity of protective personnel and equipment moves into the impact area after half an hour in the first case, while they move in within five minutes in the second: there will inevitably be a larger number of casualties and more property damage in the first case than in the second. In symbolic form,

$$D = f(\text{I.P})$$

where D is the quantity of damage in some category of phenomena (e.g., number of deaths), I is the length of the isolation period in hours, P is the pre-impact quantity of the phenomenon. This relationship should be valid because within the impact area, during the isolation period after a sudden impact, a continuous process of secondary impact will increase damage: fires, exposure, sepsis in wounds, shock, and the continuation of lethal processes (like bleeding, asphyxiation, etc.) set in motion by the primary impact. The chief function of the rescue force is to terminate secondary impact before it increases casualties and damage above the amount left by primary impact. Anything which lengthens the isolation period for an impact area, or a part of an impact area, will thereby increase the incidence of injury or damage. An added fifteen minutes of isolation in Worcester would certainly have substantially increased both property damage and casualty lists; one recalls that the fire engines were barely in time to prevent a major conflagration in the Greenhill-Burncoat areas (the three-house fire had almost passed beyond the reach of hose lines from the few still-functioning hydrants). If, instead of a warm June evening, it had been windy, subzero weather and night-time, exposure would have been an important factor, and time here would have been of critical importance. One would venture to predict that, in the absence of aid from outside the impact area, damage would increase somewhat as follows in Figure 8.1. The reason for the acceleration-point in the isolation period is that certain types of secondary impact (bleeding, asphyxiation, lethal wound shock, and fires) should, if unimpeded, combine to produce a second wave of injuries several minutes after impact. The reason for the leveling of the curve is that the dazed state will eventually "wear off" by itself, and after this point an increasing number of victims will be able to care for themselves, while many of the most serious consequences of secondary impact will already have run their course.

Various factors affect the length of the isolation period at any particular point in an impact area. One of these is the distance from that point to the edge of the impact area—in other words, the larger an impact area, the longer

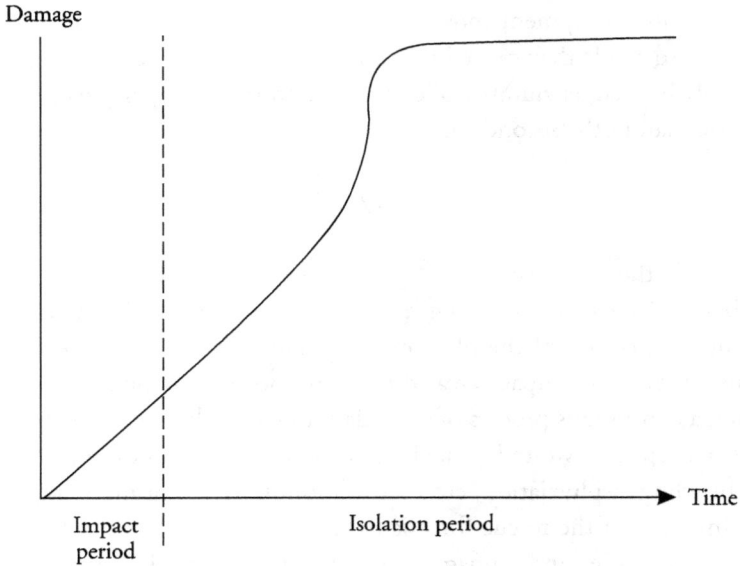

Figure 8.1   Extent of Damage Correlated with Length of Isolation

the average isolation period for all points in the impact area. Another factor, of course, is the extent to which the impact has interfered with communication and transportation. A third factor is the distance from the edge of the impact area to the protective units. A fourth is the quickness with which the protective units are notified; a fifth, the quickness with which they mobilize; a sixth, the completeness of the reconnaissance and inventorying by the protective units, both before and after reaching the impact area. The list can obviously be extended to include a great many other factors which affect the length of time which passes before a given unit of impact area space is reached by outside aid.

It is evident also that many other things, having no relation to the length of the isolation period, also affect the amount of damage: the nature of the impact agent, the kind of structures in the impact area, composition of the population in the impact area, the efficiency of protective personnel and equipment, and the quantity of protective personnel and equipment brought to bear, at any given point, are particularly important. I have emphasized the time factor in the relationship between the protective agencies and the secondary impact: here there is, as it were, a race between rescue agencies and secondary impact agents to reach potential targets.

THE "CORNUCOPIA THEORY"

The rescue and rehabilitation operations at Worcester were considered to have been relatively successful. The isolation period was short, rescue and evacuation was fast, medical care was quickly made available to all victims requiring it, and the rehabilitation procedures of every kind were furnished with lavishness. While specific instances of inefficiency were pointed out, very few instances of failure could be. The principles of "wave supply" and "mana from heaven," pointed out by Rosow, meant that even when efficiency was low, the sheer mass of services and materiel were able to satisfy needs as they came up. Comparison might be made with military firepower: a good marksman with a finely tooled and sighted rifle may be more efficient, but a machine gun gets better results in holding down an enemy position—provided there is more ammunition available than is needed to account for each enemy soldier. In disaster operations, when materiel and personnel are pouring out of a cornucopia, deluging the impact area, the results in rescue and rehabilitation are almost inevitably impressive.

This is what happened at Worcester. The impact area was blanketed with protective agencies: hundreds of police, firemen, National Guards, public works people, CD volunteers, and miscellaneous helpers invaded it during the rescue period; hospitals had more blood donors than they could handle; the Red Cross mobilized hundreds of nurses; equipment and supplies of all kinds were funneled into Worcester from all over the northeast, and four hundred twenty-five trailers came from Missouri. While the results of this sort of provision are so good that post-mortem studies have little to criticize except relatively minor matters and little to recommend except more efficient utilization of what was already available, they take for granted the fact that the cornucopia principle's successful application at Worcester depended on the fortunate (and not at all inevitable) co-existence of two conditions: a complete lack of damage to Worcester's own protective agencies and to those of any other source of regional aid; and the absence of any competition from anywhere nearer than Ohio for emergency supplies and personnel.

A glance at the map of the city, showing the path of the tornado and the location of protective agencies, will show that this impact could, however, have wiped out or severely crippled most of the police stations (including ambulances), fire stations, hospitals, Red Cross and CD headquarters, and government centers, if it had passed through Worcester on a different course. If it had taken such a course, also, the number of primary-impact casualties (to say nothing of the results of secondary impact) would probably have been much greater. Furthermore, if the tornado had proceeded another thirty miles, into the Boston area, considerable quantities of supplies, personnel, and equipment which in reality found their way to Worcester, would probably have stayed in (or gone in) to Boston.

The cornucopia theory thus rests on the two assumptions that any given disaster will not destroy the cornucopia itself, and that any given disaster or combination of disasters will be unable to exhaust the cornucopia before adequate relief and rehabilitation can be provided. I have the feeling that this theory is widely held if rarely formally stated. In all probability, these assumptions are valid for most natural disasters (fires, floods, earthquakes, tornadoes, hurricanes, tidal waves, epidemics, etc.). It is a question, however, whether the assumption does apply to disasters which might be produced by atomic or hydrogen explosions. In such events, it might well be that the cornucopia would be itself largely smashed and its supplies exhausted long before the secondary impact was under control.

Now pointing out the potential inadequacy of the cornucopia does not imply that there is anything wrong with having a cornucopia. The questions which I should like to raise, however, are: (1) Does the faith in the cornucopia, as experienced in natural disasters, produce a tendency to think in terms of repair rather than prevention? (2) Does the faith in the cornucopia tend to produce organizations which are better adapted to excess supply than to inadequate supply? In other words, there is a basic question whether the type of organization and planning which gets results where there is more than enough of personnel and supply will be most effective when everything is short.

I don't have ready answers to these questions. But it is striking, in the case of the Worcester tornado—a severe natural disaster, but minor in comparison with what a military disaster would be—that for most rescue and rehabilitation functions, there were several responsible agencies with overlapping jurisdictions, and usually more than enough personnel and supplies to go around. Indeed, many people were kept busy simply acting as organizational traffic policemen, to keep people and agencies off each other's toes. Everything seemed to move in an atmosphere of, "There's plenty to go around, and if I run short, I'll call Joe on the phone and he'll send some over." The cornucopia nourishes a sort of autonomy and duplication of organizations in the midst of plenty. If Red Cross and Civil Defense dispute over the supervision of welfare activities, the solution can wait for thirty-six hours, and finally both can be given some responsibility in this area. This is fine when supply exceeds necessity. But if there weren't enough food or clothing, or shelter in the area, and two autonomous agencies squabbled over what little there was, not only would the utilization of that little be inefficient, but the personnel of one of the organizations would be wasting their time while they could be doing something else.

Furthermore (referring to the first question above), a profusion of rescue and relief agencies seems to be conducive to an atmosphere or waiting till it happens before doing anything about it. Reams have been written about the behavior of organizations after the tornado; but only passing attention has been paid to analyzing the factors which allowed a tornado to march for an hour through central Massachusetts without any part of the general population ever being warned to take cover. A combination of radio announcements and telephone calls from central exchange points could have had perhaps 90 per cent of the population in cellars within minutes. Such a warning would have saved more lives than any conceivable improvement of procedures in the rescue and rehabilitation phases. In other words, I wonder whether we ought not to put more stress on "stop it from happening," even while we keep "repair and replace" procedures at the highest possible peak of effectiveness. And this would apply with even greater force to anticipations of military impacts, following which the "repair and replace" cornucopia may not be there any more.

NOTES

1. Descriptions of "typical" behavior at Hiroshima and Nagasaki and in severely bombed German cities, after earthquakes, and after sudden floods, while not organized as here, seem to be referring to the essential elements of the disaster syndrome.

9

Mazeway Resynthesis

A Biocultural Theory of Religious Inspiration

The scientific student of human behavior must be struck by the importance of the phenomenon of religious inspiration.[1] Provided he does not permit his professional bias against "superstition" to make the subject distasteful, he quickly discovers that religious inspiration, far from being a matter of individual psychopathology, is essentially a therapeutic process. He further discovers that many major cultural mutations have been formulated by the religiously inspired. As his interest in the subject deepens, he becomes aware that these religiously inspired movements belong to a large class of events, called revitalization movements, that may be defined as deliberate, organized efforts by members of a society to create a more satisfying culture (Wallace, 1956b). The study of the process of religious inspiration, particularly of the inspiration that emphasizes the need for social or cultural as well as individual reform, is thus of central importance in the analysis both of processes of socio-cultural change and of individual therapeutic reorganization.

Let us examine a case of religious inspiration in the context of a revitalization movement, namely, the rise of the new religion initiated by an Indian named Handsome Lake among the Seneca tribe of the Iroquois confederacy of New York State. Here we may observe a typical example of the process of religious inspiration and its role in the larger process revitalization. In 1799, the 1,000 to 1,500 Seneca Indians had reached the nadir of their fortunes. Since 1775, things had been going badly for them: they had joined the British in attempting to suppress the American revolutionaries; General Sullivan's hit-and-run invaders in 1779 had devastated many of their villages and burned their cornfields and orchards; in 1783, although they had not laid down their own arms, they had found themselves abandoned by the British, who made a separate peace to close the Revolutionary War; in 1784, their delegates at Fort Stanwix, N.Y., with others of the Six Nations, had signed away the confederacy's interests in land in Ohio and western Pennsylvania; their own councils soon split into squabbling factions, pro-British versus pro-American, pro-acculturation versus conservative; their confederates to the east were selling off their lands, and their dependents to the west were contemptuous of their policy of cooperation with Washington; they saw, in 1794 and 1795, American military victory over the Ohio tribes; and, finally, in 1797, their chief men succumbed to rum, bribes, and blandishments, and sold the tribe's entire remaining domain west of the Genesee River, reserving to the Seneca nation only a series of tight little reservations, soon to be separately islanded by the tide of white settlement. The survivors of this generation of disaster were a pathetic people: they were unable to take the traditional way to self-respect as hunters, warriors, and wise counselors; they had less than enough to eat; they no longer had the comfortable houses and mellow orchards that Sullivan had sacked; they were the objects of mingled hatred, contempt, and pity from their white neighbors. Many of them drank to excess, families brawled among themselves, and mutual suspicions of witchcraft and double-dealing made orderly community life difficult. Minor prophets arose to recount their visions and exhort the people to virtue and virility, only to subside into obscurity like bubbles on the surface of boiling water. What made the agony of the Seneca the more complete was the contrast between their present condition and the glory of past tradition. Only a generation before, they had been the most powerful nation within the famed League of the Iroquois, which had destroyed in war, or made dependents of, most of the tribes of the present states of Ohio, New York, Pennsylvania, and New Jersey, and for nearly 60 years had been able, by pursuing a policy of armed neutrality, to hold the balance of power between England and France in North America. Now, however, the dignity of their nation was destroyed, and they found themselves the survivors of a disaster that had almost annihilated their way of life.

A man named Handsome Lake (Ganiodaiio) lived in the Seneca village of Jenuchshadago, on the Allegheny River just south of the Pennsylvania state line. He was about 54 years old, had served as a warrior during the campaigns of the Revolutionary War, and was one of the 49 chiefs who constituted the Great Council of the League of the Iroquois. His younger half brother was Cornplanter, the famous leader of a pro-American faction. Cornplanter, as a reward for his services, had been given, by Pennsylvania, title in fee simple to the tract of land on which Jenuchshadago was located. Handsome Lake, however, was himself neither famous nor powerful, in spite of his title. He was a confirmed drunkard who, by the spring of 1799, had almost drunk himself to death, and now spent his days bedridden, brooding over the loss of his wife, the death of his favorite son, his abandonment by another son, and the death of a favorite niece (Cornplanter's daughter). He felt that the community was being undermined by witches; he feared his own imminent death; in his drunken days he recklessly sang sacred songs such as the *Ohgiwe,* which was supposed to be sung only by Chanters for the Dead and, when he was sober, he worried over his impiety and his sinful life. He was a very sick man.

In June 1799, Handsome Lake experienced the first of a series of visions that were to transform not only his own life but the lives of the Seneca people and, indeed, of the Iroquois generally. During a deathlike trance he dreamt that three angels came down from heaven to talk to him. After explaining that his illness was owing to the sin of drinking liquor, and that the trouble with the Seneca as a nation was that too many of them drank too much and practiced witchcraft, the angels assured him that if he gave up drink and behaved well he would not die that summer. Handsome Lake came out of the trance while his relatives were preparing him for burial. He told them what he had seen (by fortunate chance, a Quaker missionary happened to be living close by and recorded a translation of his words) and, at Handsome Lake's direction, Cornplanter assembled the people and reported the vision. Handsome Lake felt better and, after a few more visions, was able to leave his bed and take up the mission to which he felt he had been appointed. He had many subsequent visions, preached vigorously to the Seneca and the other Iroquois tribes on their several reservations, and was appointed the spiritual and moral censor of the Seneca nation. His disciples carried the "good word" to other nations, and delegations came from many westerly tribes to gain his counsel. Not long after his death in 1815, his disciples gathered at Tonawanda, N.Y., and put together what they remembered of his visions, sayings, and actions. This "Code of Handsome Lake," the "Gaiwiio" or Good Message, became the gospel of the Old Way of Handsome Lake, as the new religion was called.

Handsome Lake's message was detailed and systematic. There were extensive moral recommendations: he was against liquor, dancing, card playing, and witchcraft; he advised against adultery, wife beating, malicious gossip, the sale of land, the mistreatment of children, especially orphans, and he deprecated greed and stinginess. He foresaw the coming destruction of the world in a holocaust. The wicked were destined for hell, where they would be tortured by a devil (using techniques reminiscent of the ancient ritual tortures by fire), and the good were destined for heaven. No white men could get to heaven, and the best of all white men, George Washington, hung suspended at a halfway house between heaven and hell. Handsome Lake recommended that some Seneca learn to read and write the English language, and that the men take up the plow, build fences, erect frame houses, and raise horses and cattle. Some of the ancient religious rituals were to be dropped or modified, others were to be retained and strictly performed.

The sources of Handsome Lake's notions were undoubtedly various. Some, like the ban on liquor, represent both a traditional Indian recognition of the socially disintegrating effects of alcohol and the current preachments of the three Quaker missionaries who established themselves along the Allegheny in 1798 and were trying, not to convert the Seneca to Christianity, but to teach them the "Protestant ethic" (sobriety, industry, and dependability), to give the children schooling, and to demonstrate to the adults the uses and techniques of plow-farming, spinning and weaving, and the care of livestock. Handsome Lake's recommendations toward literacy and male agriculture (women being the traditional corn gardeners) were no doubt inspired both by white example and by reflection on the practical necessity of cultural change. Other recommendations were revivalistic, hence the name "Old Way" for his religion. The ceremonies, the exclusion of cards and fiddles, the moral admonitions and injunctions to generosity, loyalty, and indulgence of children all hark back to the past-as-Utopia. Witches were never social favorites among the Seneca, but the extreme concern with them at this time resulted in a number of bloody executions of suspected women. The apocalyptic, hell-fire, end-of-the-world prognostications would seem to reflect Seneca anxiety over the possible further disintegration of their sociocultural system.

The effect on the Seneca of these preachments astounded white observers. Traders, accustomed to use rum as a lubricant for commercial transactions, remarked in amazement that these Indians would no longer touch liquor. They insisted on sugar water instead. Almost the whole nation went dry. Men, who hitherto had despised farming as women's work, took to the plow, fenced fields, amassed herds of cattle and pigs, and built substantial frame houses. Indian children went to school by the dozens. Within ten years, with economic help from Quaker and federal funds, the Seneca transformed themselves from a frontier slum society to a vigorous and enterprising nation.

About a generation after Handsome Lake's death, the Old Way of Handsome Lake was institutionalized as a "pagan" church. The gospel was codified, and a formal ecclesiastical organization was established, with preachers, the equivalents of deacons (the male and female Faith-Keepers), a sort of college at Tonawanda that licensed itinerant preachers, definable congregations, and church property that consisted of a longhouse and its appurtenances. Handsome Lake still has many followers today on the Iroquois reservations in New York and Ontario (see Parker 1913; Deardorff 1951; Wallace 1952a and 1952b; and Voget 1954 for accounts of the Handsome Lake religion).

THE PROBLEM OF CHANGES IN INDIVIDUAL PERCEPTION OF SOCIOCULTURAL SYSTEMS

The major event of religious inspiration in the case of Handsome Lake was his second vision, on August 8, 1799. Handsome Lake fell into a trance at about seven o'clock in the morning and did not wake until about three in the afternoon. Perceptible respiration had stopped, and his extremities were cold as far as his knees and elbows. During the eight-hour trance he saw himself guided on a tour of heaven and hell. He met his departed son and niece, and they discussed the rights and wrongs of familial relations, particularly the sin of disrespect of parents shown by their children. Handsome Lake's supernatural Guide enjoined him against the drinking of liquor and against attendance at any social "frolicks and dancing" at which liquor was used, and he revealed that the Evil Spirit was the promoter of the liquor traffic among the Seneca. The Indians, he said, must abstain. On the subject of acculturation, the Guide said that "White people were come into their Towns to instruct their Children, and that is right if they can all agree to it, but many of them are not willing, but will keep to their old habits of living, well that may be right too, but if they do they must not drink Wisky [*sic*] for that belongs to White people, and was not made for Indians." The people must make some religious reforms: the concept of the Great Spirit had to include the notion that He "sees & knows all things and nothing is hid from Him"; the White Dog had to be burned to forestall pestilence; dreams had to be analyzed more carefully to make sure they were not inspired by the Evil Spirit; and the Worship Dance was to be the most sacred of ceremonies. As for Handsome Lake himself, if he behaved well, he would live until one half of the hairs of his head had turned gray. Next day the local Quaker missionary visited Handsome Lake to record his visions, and he noted incidentally that he "had then much recover'd of his sickness." Handsome Lake thereafter went on vigorously to preach these revelations as part of his gospel (Wallace 1952b).

Three characteristics of this event of religious inspiration (which is, in my judgment, typical of the prophetic revelation) are noteworthy: (1) the change it produced in the visionary's perception of the world; (2) its suddenness and briefness in time; and (3) the unusual physiological status of the individual experiencing it.

Let us examine first the change in perception (perception may be defined for our purposes as the process by which the coded messages from receptor organs are translated into statements about the condition of self and environment). The more closely one examines this vision and the others that preceded and followed it, the more apparent it becomes that the perceptual changes that occurred during the hours of inspiration constituted a reorganization of the system of translation of sensory data. Some new objects were perceived, such as the angels in his first vision and, later, the Guide. The major shift lay, however, in the divestment from some familiar objects of previously associated characteristics, and the addition of characteristics to other familiar objects. These divestments and additions were expressed in terms of associated good or bad consequences, that is, in terms of the functional relation conceived to exist between and among objects. Actually, two distinct sociocultural systems were represented in the postrevelation scheme: a good system, consisting of the Great Spirit and other benevolent supernaturals and of people who did not drink, practice witchcraft, or commit various other sins, and a bad system, consisting of the Evil Spirit, drunkards, witches, and persons who do various sinful acts. Objects were perceived and acted toward in accordance with their membership in one or the other system. Handsome Lake's mission in life was to destroy or modify objects belonging to the bad system, and to bring into dominance the good system.

How can such systematic changes in perception of a sociocultural system have come to pass? We are accustomed to recognize perceptual reorganization as a result of accumulating new data, that is, by learning. In the case of Handsome Lake, however, we can be reasonably certain that Seneca society did not change during his eight-hour trance and, even if it had, he could not have been aware of it. Hence we must postulate some process as having occurred within his brain, a process that produced fundamental changes in his system of perceptual organization during the space of eight hours.

THE MAZEWAY

In the act of perception, not only the stimulus but also the perceiver determine the perception itself. Consequently, different perceivers, in the presence of the same stimulus, report different perceptions. Introspectively, we can identify at any point in time what may be called cognitive residues of previous perceptions that determine what we are able to perceive in any following instance. I am not referring to specific memory traces but to those assemblages of memories that summarize, rather like statistical distribution charts, the frequencies of perception of discriminable patterns (including patterns of association) in the sensory data, and define normal values. These cognitive residues of perception are thus really generalizations about the ways in which sensory data distribute themselves, and these generalizations are interrelated in a complex but systematic way.

Since every individual's course of experience is unique, every human brain contains, at a given point of time, as a product of this experience, a unique organization of generalizations. The total complex of generalizations about the body in which the brain is housed, various other surrounding things, and sometimes even the brain itself, is the "mazeway." Its content consists of an extremely large number of assemblages, or cognitive residues of perception. It is used by its holder as a true and more or less complete representation of the operating characteristics of a "real" world.

The mazeway may be compared to a map of a gigantic maze. On this map are represented three types of assemblage: (1) goals and pitfalls (values, or desirable and undesirable end states); (2) the "self" and other objects (people, other organisms, and things); and (3) ways (processes, techniques, and relations) that may be circumvented or used, according to their characteristics, to facilitate the self's attainment or avoidance of values. These elements can be combined in an almost infinite variety of imagined action sequences.

The concept of mazeway thus embraces, in one field, several phenomena already generally recognized in the literature: the "body image" (Schilder 1935), "role," "self," "the other," "generalized other" (Mead 1934), "behavioral environment" (Hallowell 1955b), "world view" (Redfield 1953). It is reminiscent of Tolman's "cognitive maps" (Tolman 1949) and of the topological concept of "life space." Within this field, self and nonself interact according to predictable, if more or less idiosyncratic, "laws."

ORGANIZATION AND FUNCTION OF THE MAZEWAY

The basic function of the mazeway is to give meaning to messages, to relate incoming sensory data to the whole complex of objects, values, and techniques that is the mazeway, so that action may be taken that can be expected to reduce stress or maximize pleasure not merely in the presenting situation but within the great maze of situations that the mazeway represents.

The mazeway must therefore have fairly high levels of internal communication, of internal consistency, and of correspondence with reality.

In regard to communication, the representation of any given sequence of action should lead to the representation of the effects of implementing this sequence on other possible sequences. In other words, the mazeway must answer the question, "What effect will pursuit of sequence A have on sequences B, C, D . . . N?" Variation in adequacy of communication is evidently possible, and the larger the proportion of possible sequences predictably related to any contemplated sequence, the higher the level of communication Failures of communication would seem to lead to the phenomena of dissociation and the unconscious.

A mazeway may be more or less internally consistent. Implementation of sequence A, in imagination, may evoke representations of consequent facilitation or blockage of sequences B, C, D, . . . N. Blockage is normally avoided by some sort of priority system that arranges a hierarchy of values and provides for substitute values, techniques, and objects. In the absence of an adequate priority and substitution system, the internal contradictions of the mazeway make decision making difficult or impossible in many areas. Consistency is also variable, and the lower the probability that sequence A will contradict possible sequences B, C, D, . . . N, the higher the degree of consistency.

The third desideratum is correspondence with reality. This, too, is variable. Any mazeway will make wrong predictions on occasion. To judge from the reluctance of individuals to change their "ideas" even when they are demonstrably "wrong," individuals tend to prefer to maintain an intact mazeway in spite of a certain amount of negative feedback, that is, failure to achieve values, rather than to make changes. A possible explanation is that a local change in the mazeway, even though it promises in some situations to reduce negative feedback, could reduce the level of communication and consistency by introducing new and contradictory assemblages, thus making the process of prediction more difficult and the likelihood of conflict and blockage more serious.

It is implicit in the foregoing remarks, and should now be argued explicitly, that the higher the degree of order in the mazeway system, as it was defined basically by communication and consistency levels, the lower the level of chronic stress, because the rate of experience of uncertainty, conflict, or error, as the response to stimuli, will be correspondingly lower. Noncorrespondence with reality, however, will lead to stress, immediately by way of error in some matters, and eventually by the introduction of inconsistent cognitive residues.

PATHOLOGICAL DISORDER OF THE MAZEWAY

The normal process of individual maturation and extension of experience requires that every organism's mazeway undergo gradual and intermittent change in order to maintain sufficient correspondence with reality to make useful predictions. True "extinction" of mazeway elements seems to occur only with difficulty, however, so the individual tends to accumulate an increasing quantity of mutually inconsistent mazeway elements and areas, some of which must be bypassed in the communication processes, or be "repressed," to use the psychoanalytic term, in order to reduce the probability of conflict. Most normal individuals, as the mazeway becomes more complex, develop increasingly general protocols ("religious belief" and "philosophy of life" are such protocols) to enable them to handle the dilemma of repression versus inconsistency.

Sometimes, however, mazeway development remains or becomes inadequate. Inadequacy is possible in three dimensions: (1) internal lack of communication, (2) internal inconsistency, and (3) lack of correspondence with reality. Although the conventional diagnostic categories are fuzzy of definition, it would seem that the classic distinctions among psychosis, neurosis, and reactive disorder roughly correspond with these three types of mazeway inadequacy.

Pseudoneurotic and pseudopsychotic mazeway disorders can be seen in certain persons. Important elements or areas of these individuals' mazeways are suddenly revealed as inconsistent with the "real" world. Thus a bereaved person sees suddenly that an important mazeway element no longer has a corresponding "real" figure; the victim of a disaster perceives that a large section of the material and human objects of his environment have been destroyed or rendered inoperative; the disillusioned member of a society realizes that the sociocultural system no longer does, or perhaps never did, operate according to the principles which his mazeway assigned to it. Such individuals often respond initially to disappointment as if the "whole world," that is, the whole mazeway, had been destroyed, and may temporarily display the same blocked or unsystematic behavior characteristic of chronic neurotics and psychotics.

Normally, however, in persons suffering from such primarily reactive disorders, the mazeway is reconstituted, incorporating new cognitive residues based on the new information, and employing various devices to restore system and consistency. Unless this can be done, mental chaos remains, for the presence of contradictory learned generalizations makes orderly behavior impossible.

All human beings, however, and not merely unfortunate victims of catastrophe, from time to time experience the impact of new information that reveals discrepancies between mazeway and reality, thereby increasing mazeway inconsistency. Many of these day-to-day experiences are serious enough to arouse anxiety and to threaten temporarily the integrity of the mazeway. Mental health thus requires a constant expenditure of energy to resist the tendency toward increase of disorder, as measured by frequency of conflict or repression, in the mazeway system. One can speculate that there may also be a purely physical "leakage" that tends to increase disorder even in the absence of new sensory input. A considerable part of the average human's day's energy is probably spent in more or less deliberate mazeway maintenance: checking remembered sensory data to be sure that mazeway generalizations approximately agree with the evidence, checking the mazeway itself for internal consistency, working out formulas to resolve inconsistencies, and ensuring that communication is at an adequate level by checking to see that "factors" have not been left out of account. The brain, a problem-solving organ, works hard to ensure that the mazeway—its archive of problem solutions—is internally communicating, consistent, and realistic.

A special problem exists in the case of people who, without necessarily having been exposed to intolerable catastrophes of bereavement, disaster, or disillusionment, suffer from gradually increasing mazeway disorder. In these chronic mental invalids, the brain fails in its task of maintaining order in the mazeway. It may be argued that it is a physiological deficit of some kind that is the necessary and sufficient cause of this kind of chronic mental disorder, a deficit that interferes with the normal process of mazeway repair and resynthesis. Traumatic experience, in this view, would be traumatic only to the extent that the organism was unable to reduce the disorder increase resulting from the entrance of inconsistent learning into the system and, possibly, from internal leakage. Variation in the incidence of trauma would account only for minor variations in incidence of chronic mental disorder, although it would account for major variations in the incidence of reactive disorders. There is some evidence, in such sources as Kallmann's twin studies (Kallmann 1948) and in the studies by Selye, Hoagland, and others of adrenocortical function (Hoagland

1944 and 1950; Hoagland et al. 1950; Selye and Fortier 1950), to support the theory that a fundamental variable in *chronic* mental disorder is neither situational nor historical but physiological, although situational and social factors determine the "content" of the disorder by posing perceptual inconsistencies, the failure to resolve which precipitates the collapse of the mazeway.

Regarded from this point of view, "paranoid" system building of all kinds, including "normal" participation in conventional paranoid systems, religious and political, the idiosyncratic systems of institutionalized psychotics, and the revitalization systems of prophets (Wallace 1956b), is an effort to reestablish communication and consistency in a disordered mazeway. The "falsity" of any paranoid system is a matter of degree, all mazeways being "false" in the sense of not being completely true and complete representations of reality, and of convention, since it is only the unconventional mazeway that is recognized as false. All mazeways are compromises between the demands of reality representation, on the one hand, and of internal order and consistency on the other. The "paranoid" mazeway simply sacrifices so much reality representation in the interest of preserving internal communication and consistency that "normal" persons recognize the mazeway as "unrealistic." Hence the paranoid process and the process of mental disorder are to be regarded as opposed in an almost dialectical sense: the disease process is the process of order decrease, the paranoid process is the process of order increase.

MAZEWAY RESYNTHESIS IN RELIGIOUS PROPHETS

Let us return now to our original problem, the understanding of religious inspiration in prophets. When one examines the lives of prophets, one finds that many of them are reported to have been, in various ways and degrees, sick persons. They display, prior to their revitalization experience, such symptoms as depression, extreme sense of guilt, inactivity, alcoholic addiction, and various somatic illnesses. They may complain of the pressures of bereavement, of failure in career, of uncongenial social demands, although their personal difficulties seem no different from those of others who are not ill. They are people of whom it can be fairly said that they suffer severe stress and that they show evidence of mazeway disorder. Following the mazeway resynthesis, that is, the experience of religious inspiration, they display a remission of symptoms of distress. The process of mazeway resynthesis, then, seems to have the function of restoring an internal biopsychic equilibrium. It is, in a word, an autotherapeutic process that reduces stress.

The stress from which prophets suffer, it is important to emphasize, is a function not of the specific content, but of the degree of disorder of the mazeway. The mazeway order level—as measured, let us say, by the probability of finding nonambivalent objects in it—is a function of the order level of the environment. Any person living in a society that is, in reality, in a state of high disorder, will most probably, unless he undertakes a mazeway resynthesis, have a correspondingly high level of disorder in his own mazeway. This high level of disorder will elicit the symptoms of stress because stimuli will be constantly evoking uncertainty and conflict. Hence we may expect that disorganized societies will contain many persons suffering from rather severe stress, for whom unusually severe personal danger or past trauma may be difficult to demonstrate. Prophets generally emerge in societies that are extremely disorganized, and their prophecies deal with reform. The concern for social reform during mazeway resynthesis is the direct expression of a "striving" for mazeway order.

The relationship between stress and mazeway resynthesis, however, is not to be conceived as a simple motivational one in which stress is a cue indicating that mazeway resynthesis is necessary. The process is somewhat more complex, with stress playing a trigger role. Chronic stress mobilizes the general-adaptation syndrome, which stabilizes on the stage of resistance, to use Selye's terminology. This relative stabilization may persist for years, but the prophet is anxious, his bodily system begins to show signs of psychosomatic wear and tear, and his behavior first becomes rigid, then neurotic and/or regressive, setting up a slowly descending spiral. The critical point is reached when the psychosomatic disorganization becomes so severe that the physico-chemical milieu for resynthesis is automatically established and, at this point, the convulsive effort to redesign the mazeway takes place. When the prophet is close to this point, any temporary—and often irrelevant—increase in stress may precipitate the reaction. Such an increase could be caused by disease, bereavement, hunger and thirst, or the "end phenomenon," so called, after escape from a danger. The fact that the resynthesis occurs in a hallucinatory form very possibly may have something to do with associated changes in adrenalin metabolism. Adrenochrome, a deteriorated form of adrenaline thought to be produced by the body in the process of its detoxification, is a hallucinogenic agent. Certain normal persons respond to clinical administration of adrenaline with hallucinatory episodes (Hoffer, Osmond, and Smythies 1954). The hallucinatory nature of the experience may thus be an incidental attribute or psycho-physiological by-product of extreme stress, and its psychopathological significance may be greatly overemphasized (Boisen 1936).

The therapeutic resynthesis that occurs during the experience of religious inspiration would seem to be best described as a sorting process. Cognitive residues or assemblages are subjected to an extremely rapid scanning procedure, involving checking through a very large number of permutations and combinations, and identifying ambivalences. As we observed earlier, the mazeway assemblages of a prophet under stress are characterized by a high degree of ambivalence. That is to say, many objects and techniques are associated with two equally possible but opposed value connotations. Putting this in another way, at many points the mazeway splits, with a single assemblage being parts of two incompatible local systems. Thus liquor, for Handsome Lake, was part of systems of behavior leading both to gratification and to punishment. The first task of resynthesis seems to be the breaking up of many such local ambivalent systems by damping either "good" or "bad" value connotations. In Handsome Lake's case this was done by leaving an object such as liquor with only a "bad" connotation. The second task is the forging of new associative links between the now-monovalent local systems, so as to make two more or less self-contained "good" and "bad" systems. In this second task, certain assemblages collect into new groupings that amount to the postulation of the existence of supernatural beings or of different frequencies or degrees of importance of familiar objects and techniques. We can, I think, dispense with the notion of a central ego that is controlling these processes of organization. Hypothetically, this sorting and organizing could proceed automatically on the basis of association if one assumes a factor that destroys ambivalent linkages. This factor, if we may speculate further, may be a physiological one associated with the stage of exhaustion of the general adaptation syndrome.

SUMMARY

The mazeway is the brain's organized and codified archive of cognitive residues of perception bearing on the characteristics of the extrabodily environment, the body itself, techniques, and values. The mazeway thus contains the individual's perception of the sociocultural and natural system of which he is a part, and the mazeway determines his behavior in it.

When the mazeway is in a state of disorder, as defined by low levels of communication and consistency, the individual experiences stress. The process of mazeway resynthesis, with physiological mechanisms probably playing a facilitating role, reestablishes order by sorting assemblages into two or more systems on the criterion of goodness or badness. This reduces ambivalence and conflict, but necessarily involves a change in the individual's perception not only of himself but also of the environment, and it may involve his taking action to ensure correspondence between the new mazeway and reality.

Research is necessary to justify empirically the speculative conceptions presented here. We are in quest of an adequate theory of social perception that will take into account the way in which individuals perceive sociocultural systems. The writer believes that the mazeway concept will facilitate the formulation of hypotheses subject to testing in this area.

NOTES

1. This paper was presented at a meeting of the [Anthropology] Section [of the New York Academy of Sciences] on April 23, 1956.

10
Mazeway Disintegration

The Individual's Perception of Socio-Cultural Disorganization

One winter's day in 1649, a band of warriors from the Petun Indian village of St. Jean, south of the Georgian Bay, went out to intercept an invading war-party of Iroquois. They did not find the enemy. When they returned to the village, four days later, they saw only the ashes of their homes and the charred and mutilated bodies of many of their wives, children, and old men. Not one living soul had escaped death or capture; not one cabin had been spared from the flames. The Petun warriors sat down in the snow, mute and motionless, and no one spoke or moved for half a day; no one even stirred to pursue the Iroquois in order to save the captives or to gain revenge.

Temporary paralysis is one of the modalities of human reaction to disaster. The Petun warriors had in reality lost virtually all the objects (human and material) which were dear to them. But even in less tragic disasters, where damage and casualties are not so complete, and relief speedily arrives, a similar, temporary paralytic response frequently occurs. Beyond reaction to personal injury and loss, the sudden perception of physical destruction of the natural environment, fellow citizens, and material culture with which one is identified, seems to elicit fundamentally the same paralytic response as the Petun warriors showed in the sight of what might be called "total" disaster. It is the purpose of this paper to develop a theory of the individual's identification with his culture which will account for this response.

THE DISASTER SYNDROME

It is often reported after major physical disasters that many survivors in the impact area are initially found by rescue workers in a state variously described or denoted by such words as "shock," "dazed," "stupor," "apathy," "stunned," "numbed." In such persons, awareness of the extent and severity of damage to self, family, and community is limited. Efforts at first aid, rescue, and evacuation are often perfunctory and inadequate, and sometimes virtually absent, especially in regard to helping non-relatives and the community at large. Some people simply sit or stand motionless, or wander aimlessly, or "putter about" at inconsequential tasks. Expressions of strong emotion and feeling (pain, grief, fear, anger) are missing or sporadic and inadequate. This shock may persist for minutes or hours.

As organized rescue workers from the filter area and the community begin to arrive in quantity, the pattern changes. Uninjured survivors emerge somewhat from the cocoon of apathy and take some part in extrication, fire fighting, first aid, evacuation, and communication. Injured persons, however, tend to remain longer in the dazed state. Both groups are relatively docile and obedient, are extremely anxious to hear that others have survived too, are grateful for help and for gestures of concern, and are anxious that others be cared for first. This docile state may persist for hours or days.

After a day or two, both injured and uninjured survivors often show a mild (and perhaps rather superficial) euphoria, marked by thankfulness for survival and by intense public spirit and eagerness to work for the community's welfare; people give up old grudges, ignore barriers of social distance, and merge themselves in a kind of neighborhood revival or revitalization movement. Structures symbolic of community solidarity, such as churches, are cleaned up and put into temporary repair; neighbors help one another in rehabilitation. At the same time, however, considerable complaint is apt to be directed at mass care organizations and at relief and rehabilitation services furnished by persons outside the impact area: the mass care organizations are accused of being cold and indifferent to personal feelings; the necessity of applying for aid is sometimes resented; charges of looting, profiteering, and general inefficiency are voiced. Furthermore, many persons suffer from feelings of depression, from sleeplessness, nightmares, and general "edginess."

These three stages of behavioral reaction to disaster I have called the "disaster syndrome" because they are reported so widely and because they seem to have a coherence of process. The shock state can be called a regression to an extremely disorganized, pseudo-infantile level of adaptive behavior, and the other two stages can be described as a restitution of more adult modalities of action, with a notable emphasis on the individual's identification with the community and its way of life. We do not, however, have adequate statistics on how many persons in any particular disaster could be described as showing any one phase of this syndrome; and because the interviews on which I depend were taken before this syndrome had been delineated as an hypothesized type of prolonged reaction, no single case history in my files shows it clearly in all its stages, except perhaps for one case. Nevertheless, I am confident that inquiry of disaster survivors, pointed to the syndrome's evolution over a two-week period, would show it occurring in full form in many individual instances.[1]

CULTURAL LOSS AND MOURNING

In view of the difficulty of documenting the occurrence of the full syndrome, let us consider for the moment only the first two stages, which have been observed in sequence in the same individuals (shock and docility). It is interesting to ask what, specifically, it is that so "shocks" the individual that he is at first immobilized and then docilized. Physical injury is not necessary in its production: uninjured persons display it as well as the injured, and many severely injured accident victims often do not display the second (docile) stage at all. The loss of near relatives or close personal friends is not a necessary factor: it is shown in those with injured or dead relatives and in those whose friends and relatives escaped injury. Loss of personal property, is not a necessary condition: it is displayed on occasions, like the plane crash at Flagler, Colorado, where there was no damage or even threat to bystanders' homes, businesses, or other major property. But all persons displaying the disaster syndrome have seen a part of their community destroyed and a part of their culture rendered or revealed as inadequate.

Furthermore, it is curious that all three stages taken together have (to this observer's eyes at least) a similarity in pattern to the mourning process as it occurs in at least some persons in some cultures: an initial stage of stunned disbelief, inability to express emotion, random movement; a stage of passivity, dependence, acceptance of sympathy and help from family and friends; and finally a stage of joining with the community in burying the dead and of taking up a new life more or less free of disabling grief over the deceased.

CULTURAL CRISES AND REVITALIZATION MOVEMENTS

There is a type of social movement, precipitated not by physical disaster but by socio-economic pressures, some of whose aspects have a similarity to the disaster syndrome. In many societies, after a period of declining welfare (the decline being induced by domination by a foreign power, economic hardships, the increasing obsolescence of certain cultural devices, and perhaps by other factors difficult to specify or measure), a social crisis is reached in which many people feel acutely uncomfortable, and there may be overt symptoms of widespread personal and social disorganization (such as an increasing incidence of alcoholism, of venality in public officials, of delinquencies of various kinds). In such sick societies, it not infrequently happens that religious prophets arise. Such prophets generally have an ecstatic vision or revelation. In this revelation, a divine being appears, who promises aid and protection if certain injunctions are followed, and who presents an unfavorable analysis of the existing characterological and cultural pattern. It is thereupon recommended that the society be revitalized, by the new ways, or (usually) by a syncretism of both ancient and new-fangled elements. Following the vision or visions, the prophet is personally rejuvenated, and he begins to preach and proselytize. A movement develops which, as it institutionalizes, frequently effects massive reforms. An aura of euphoria, of brotherly love, of altruistic endeavor usually surrounds the movement during its early phases, although it may quickly sour into witch-hunting and militant defensiveness. It is notable, in the doctrines of these movements, that invariably there is one major problem, both intellectual and emotional, to be solved: the problem of identification. Shall the prophet and his followers identify with what they conceive to be a traditional way or some new or foreign way; shall they identify themselves with their own present native leaders or with new or foreign leaders? Until this problem of group identification has been solved by selection and compromise, orderly social life and individual comfort are alike impossible. Its actual solution is attended by a dramatic release of energy and by a sense of well-being.

The cultural crisis, then, appears to imply a collapse of cultural identification, with attendant depression and deterioration of behavior; the crisis is resolved by a reaffirmation of identification with some definable cultural system.[2]

A THEORY OF CULTURAL IDENTIFICATION

It is the thesis of this paper that in major physical disasters many persons will suffer "shock" and the subsequent characteristics of the disaster syndrome, partly or wholly as a result of the perception that *a part of their culture is inef-*

fective or has been rendered inoperative, and that the person reacts (unrealistically as it may be) to this perception as if a beloved object were dead. All survivors perceive cultural damage. Many survivors perceive also that they themselves, or their family, friends, and personal property have been injured, and these perceptions too call for the reactive behavior, so that the etiology in many individual cases will include not merely cultural loss, but also loss of beloved persons and valued property. But for a great many persons, I believe, the emotional impact of the perception of cultural damage is as "shocking" as, and for some is more shocking than, private loss; and conversely, many persons will suffer any degree of private loss, even death of self and family, before permitting loss of identification with their culture.

The word "identification" has suffered from almost as many definitions as the word "culture." I should like to postpone definition, therefore, until I have laid out a theoretical structure which does not depend entirely on the use of either term. Let us begin with a couple of analogies. They are liable to various qualifications, some of which I shall state, and which will be apparent both to psychologists and culturologists. One analogy is between non-material culture and "the way" a laboratory animal learns to run a maze in order to satisfy a want, like hunger. The other analogy is between material culture, natural environment, and persons and the maze itself. Human beings can be described as organisms whose peculiarity it is to construct and modify, slowly and laboriously, over centuries, very complicated sets of mazes for themselves and their posterity, with elaborate interconnecting doors and pathways; and also to construct complex rules for interaction and even mutual aid in operating the maze, as "the way" to satisfy their multifarious wants. Both kinds of maze-runners — men and laboratory animals — learn "the way" in response to cues presented by the *Gestalten* of successive positions in their respective types of maze. Both kinds of maze-runner are able to remember "the way" apart from the maze itself. And, I suspect, in both kinds of maze-runner, there is a tendency for both the maze itself, or at least parts of it, and the way it is run, to become objects of wanting. In man, certainly, various positions in the maze and various instrumental responses to these positions, which have no biological satisfiers in them become satisfying, and men will (provided certain minimal biologic wants do not become critical) work very hard merely to be able to sit (literally and metaphorically) in a biologically arid corner of the maze. Man, in other words, falls in love with his maze and his way of running it because they are associated with every satisfaction he derives from life, and, indeed, with the maintenance of life itself. The mazeway is "loved" whereas the "rewards" are merely enjoyed.

At this point I should like to make some of the qualifications I suggested before. Cultural mazes are much more complex than laboratory ones, and no doubt the extrapolation of discoveries about how rats learn and unlearn "the way" in their simple mazes must be gingerly applied to human affairs. Human beings are also bigger-brained, and, I trust, more complex intellectually and emotionally than rats. In man at least there is considerable variation among individuals in "the way" the maze is run, probably more so than in rats, and correspondingly, in how the maze is conceived to exist. Furthermore, different persons come into contact with different parts of "the" maze common to their group. Human beings, however, are loath to admit that they do not all run the same maze in the same way (i.e., they do not like to recognize that the same cue elicits a different response from different people). Some humans can see only two "ways" of responding to the cues: the right way and the wrong (or "deviant") way. (Military folk are more sophisticated: there is the right way, the wrong way, and the army way). Furthermore, people are always tinkering with the maze: opening a door here, digging a tunnel there, changing the rules for what to do when. . . . The maze analogy therefore does not imply any severe cultural determinism: the maze can be and is run in many different ways in the same community, and both maze and way are furthermore always being changed.

Man, in addition, has the capacity—which is implied in the foregoing remarks—to perceive not only the maze but also the way it is run, as if that way were an external object. The way itself can be remembered, analyzed, described verbally, and reified into something with a name. The maze itself as something physical—nature, material, and people—can be cathected in such a way that the mere perception of these objects is satisfying, and their mere absence, or presence in damaged form—can set in motion responses of anxiety. The way itself, however, can be cathected too, as if it were an object, and the conviction that *the way* has been forgotten or abandoned, or that it has somehow changed and betrayed one, can also arouse anxiety.

The nature of the emotional relationship of the individual both to the maze and to the way, and *their* interrelationship, is determined, I suspect, by a process of generalization (some forms of which are labeled "transference," "displacement," "sublimation," and "symbolization," I believe, in psychoanalytic writing) that begins in infancy when the maze is the limited circuit of the mother's body. I suggest that, whether consciously or no, the maze itself remains for the adult as a complex final extension of the original "maze" (the mother), and of course of intermediate extensions, too, and that the mazeway of the adult (his culture) retains similarly some at least of the emotional meanings of the infant's original mazeway. The individual's attitude toward his mazeway should theoretically pass through as complex an evolution as does his attitude toward a parent (or any other class of objects), so that in the adult he should have actually many attitudes, varying in level of awareness, ranging from "mature" love of country to querulous complaint, and susceptible to internal contradictions and ambivalences. Individuals should also differ as much among each other in their relationship to their mazeways as they do in their relationship to other objects. Insofar as the way does become reified by the individual, it becomes virtually indistinguishable from the maze itself, having become a sort of autochthonous system of cues. (The concepts of super-ego and ego-ideal come to mind here.) Under "normal" circumstances, however, this underlying relationship between the individual and his maze and his way does not so much obtrude itself as provide a relatively secure foundation for more intricate and more conscious behaviors.

To summarize, then, this formulation, which combines elements of culture, learning, and psychoanalytic theory: it is proposed that we regard physical objects external to the individual's perceptive apparatus, including natural objects, elements of material culture, and human bodies, as constituting a "maze," which presents the individual with cues. This maze is for the adult infinitely more complex than the mazes run by laboratory rats, and it has various characteristics, such as mobility, changeability, and inconsistencies; furthermore, it can be mapped as if it were a group of a great many component, but also elaborate, mazes. The infant's "maze" is much more limited, centering in the mother, whom the child learns *about* before he learns *from*. As the maze elaborates for the child, it retains for him nevertheless the affective significance of the mother, and of other early maze objects, of which it is in a sense merely an extension. The individual's behavior in running the maze in order to obtain satisfactions is the learning of a *way* (systems of action sequences), and to the extent that the way of using the same maze is similar among many persons, the anthropologist can denote the modalities of individual ways as elements of culture or national character. These ways, furthermore, can in man be abstracted, analyzed, verbally described, and reified, and be presented as cues by persons, by writing, and so forth. The perception of the maze itself, or parts of it, and of the way as a reified abstraction, constantly maintains in the individual, to a greater or lesser degree, a sort of conditioned satisfaction, which derives both from developmental associations and from current reinforcements.

Now the individual's way is a system of behavior which articulates very neatly, and preponderantly but not perfectly to his satisfaction, with the cues presented by the maze about him. His *way* and the maze itself, in other words, are complementary functions, even though his way may not be the same as that of his neighbor. When the individual has reified his way, furthermore, he considers that it is part of the maze itself (and hence shared by others), and responds to it as if it were an external cue, so that for him maze and way are identified. In this sense, therefore, I am using the phrase, "the individual's identification with his culture."

THE DISRUPTION OF CULTURAL IDENTIFICATION

The identification of the individual with his culture can be disrupted under various conditions. One condition of disruption is sudden physical destruction of the maze itself, or of a part of it. Another condition of disruption is the introduction of systematic changes in the maze by substitution rather than destruction, such that the individual is no longer able to employ his way in obtaining rewards. In the former case, the individual experiences a shock comparable to sudden and drastic bereavement, which temporarily interferes with his capacity to act with insight or to carry out such elements of his way as the remaining portions of the maze permit. His reactive depression is apparently disproportionate to the "real" situation: in other words, in a maze large enough for most visible (from a given point) portions to be destroyed or damaged without the whole maze actually being destroyed the destruction of part results in a reaction as if the whole maze were gone. The impact, furthermore, precipitates a regression to a very early, infantile, and primitive way, and the restitution of more mature learned ways should come about as he discovers, to his great joy, that the maze has not in fact been entirely destroyed after all.

In the case of the individual faced by a changing maze, there is first of all a considerable reluctance ("drag") to changing the old way, because of its symbolic satisfying value. As the old way, however, leads to less and less reward, and as frustrations and disappointments accumulate, there are set in motion various regressive tendencies, which conflict with the established way and are inappropriate to the existing maze. The individual can act to reduce his discomfort by several means: by learning a new way to derive satisfaction from the new maze; by encapsulating the regressive strivings in a fantasy system; and by reifying to himself his current way and maze, regarding a major portion of it as dead, and selecting (from either traditional or foreign regions, or both) part of the existing mazeway as vital, meanwhile mourning the abandoned (or abandoning) portion.

A major qualification, however, must be made here. If the individual has learned a way to use destroyed or rapidly changing mazes as a special type of maze itself, with its own system of cues and rewards, he is able to act in maze-destruction or mazeway-inconsistency situations with less shock, in the one case, and less tendency to regress, in the other, than the untrained individual.[3]

IMPLICATIONS FOR DISASTER CONTROL

Assuming for the moment that the foregoing considerations are valid, certain corollaries can be deduced for application to disaster control planning. An obvious one, and one intuitively recognized in practice, is the value of indoctrination and training in reducing emotional shock, and in increasing efficiency in the carrying out of verbally defined tasks. The person who is trained so as to view maze-destruction situations simply as mazes of a different kind, which present recognizable cues which he has a way of running, and which lead to rewards of one sort or another, particularly rewards of social approval and esteem, ought to experience far less shock than the person who is not so trained. Training of combat troops by exposing them to "infiltration courses," and the like, and the expectation of behavioral differences between "green" and "veteran" units, illustrate this principle. Similarly, Schneider's paper on "Typhoons on Yap" [1957] indicates the extent to which chronic disaster may be purged of its shock functions by phrasing it in terms of familiar cultural processes. Two further corollaries should follow: If the *specific* cues in a "real" disaster are to evoke the response called for, the training process must be carefully designed so that the individual can generalize without difficulty; and the nature of the reward should be such that it adequately replaces the loss anticipated from the sight of destruction. In regard to the latter point, it should theoretically be more effective to couch disaster training suggestions (such as Civil Defense popular instructions) in terms of "you *ought* to do thus and so for your community as well as yourself" than in terms of "take it or leave it: if you want to survive personally, send 25 cents for booklet X." In the former case, it is being suggested that the individual *can* lose his mazeway, but that if he does thus and so, no matter what happens, "somebody" will be appreciative. In the latter case, there is no mention of the danger of loss of the mazeway, and the issue is reduced to the level of accident safety warnings.

It would seem also reasonable to infer from the theoretical outline that therapy for "cases" of disaster syndrome should be based on "tender loving care," on reassurances that the mazeway is not in fact completely destroyed, on demonstration that it (or a visible substitute) does still work, and on permitting people as much as is possible to remain in the area to repair and to "make-do" with the remains. While evacuation may be dictated by other needs, it would seem that in itself evacuation is a kind of second disaster which intensifies the disruption of the individual's identifications. Furthermore, evacuation interferes with the survivor's learning to regard the destruction situation as a runnable maze. Evacuees should, other things being equal, display more severe and more prolonged symptoms of emotional trauma than non-evacuees.

Still further, the sooner the isolation period is ended, the shorter should be the duration of the disaster syndrome, since the appearance of rescue and relief workers is in itself a visible evidence of part of the mazeway still being in existence, and of the love and concern of surviving persons.

TESTING THE THEORY

The foregoing broad theoretical formulations were stimulated largely by examination of field interviews with disaster survivors and by reading historical data concerning revitalization movements. They have interest as explanations of phenomena hitherto not regarded as being necessarily related. I have also felt diffident in using, as an anthropologist, some features of Hullian learning theory. It would seem, however, that a number of specific testable hypotheses can be derived from these formulations, some requiring laboratory experiment and others appropriate field observations.

The general theory of the mazeway can, I think, be subjected to laboratory test, both with human subjects and at least some species of laboratory animals. One might, for instance, infer that human beings who have been trained to do some task which leads to significant emotional reward, will display a decline in efficiency of performance if certain physical circumstances which are not material to the task, but which have been regularly present during its learning, are removed. Numerous modifications of this design suggest themselves: the use of laboratory animals in such situations; comparing effects of evacuation and non-evacuation procedures; the differential effect of various ways, speeds, and degrees of "removing" parts of the maze; the effect of different learning experiences and associations; and so on. Possibly small group experiments might be designed to test similar hypotheses. For instance, one might hypothesize that a group performing a team task in a complex technological context should experience a period of morale dissolution and individual regression to pre-group norms following the experimenter's manipulation of the context so as to make the way inappropriate to the changed maze; there should be observable a stage of "cultural crisis," a moment of insight by someone into the nature of the defect in the mazeway, an emotional rejection of some elements of the old (or new) maze and a positive identification with others, leading to a minor euphoria. Groups could be varied in such matters as personality type and experience or lack of training in what to do in mazeway inconsistency situations; the maze context could be subjected to measurable different degrees of distortion; and so on. In regard to field observation, it would be desirable to obtain much more information about people who do and people who do not suffer from the disaster syndrome, looking particularly for the role of training in determining reaction, as well as to other conditions possibly associated with differences in reaction. It should be possible to verify or disprove, on a description level, my impression from casual reading that the syndrome can occur in any society.

Such research, in addition to being of value in the understanding of human behavior in extreme situations, should also contribute to the bridging of the gap between laboratory grounded learning theory and what anthropologists, sociologists, social psychologists, and psychiatrists know, in different terms, about such matters as the development of personality, socialization, the taking of roles, culture change, and the nature of morale. It is intriguing to me, at least, as one who has worked chiefly in field and library, to consider the possibility of integrating field and laboratory research in attack on theoretical problems in anthropology.

NOTES

1. See Wallace 1956c (chapter 8, this volume).
2. See Wallace 1956b (chapter 1, this volume).
3. For a later elaboration of the mazeway concept, see Wallace 1956d (chapter 9, this volume).

11

Dreams and the Wishes of the Soul

A Type of Psychoanalytic Theory among the Seventeenth Century Iroquois

Anthropologists have traditionally paid attention to the dreams and dream-related behavior of primitive peoples.[1] Three sorts of anthropological interest may be distinguished: the ethnographic, the historical, and the psychoanalytic. The ethnographer describes the beliefs and customs of his subjects, including the customary way in which they regard and use dream experiences. The ethnologist may look to dreams as the point of origin for innovations, or—and I think here particularly of Tylor—he may regard primitive theorizing about the meaning of dreams as the source of fundamental and widely distributed assumptions about the nature of the world; Tylor thought the experience of dreaming of distant or deceased persons might have suggested to early man the concept of the soul, and thus have contributed to the "theory" of animism. Finally, the cultural anthropologist of this generation has sometimes used reported dreams as data for psychoanalytic types of interpretation, with a view to determining what personality organizations might be regarded as typical of whole peoples or even of mankind, or as a portal to the understanding of the individual's relationship to his culture.

This paper is essentially ethnographic; it describes the theory and practice, relative to dreams, reported by Jesuit missionaries among the seventeenth-century Iroquois. However, the data raise questions of both theoretical and historical interest: for we find here a "primitive" people actively using a theory of the mind similar in many essentials to that expressed by Sigmund Freud and his intellectual heirs in Western European cultural tradition of two centuries later. It is at least an interesting case of independent invention (for I see no evidence of Iroquois dream theory having influenced Freud, directly or indirectly). It emphasizes again the probable importance of dreams as sources of innovation in human cultural history. And it poses an interesting question in the sociology of knowledge: what (if any) common sociocultural forces can be found to explain the existence of such similar psychological theories in two such different societies as Vienna and Iroquoia? While it is evident that Iroquoian and Freudian dream theory are not precisely the same (and the Iroquoian theory introduced an animistic thesis as well as the psychoanalytic one), the differences are not much more marked than the differences between, for instance, Jungian and Freudian varieties of psychoanalytic theory. It seems to the writer that this curious case of independent invention, in two such different cultures and in an area of culture peculiarly subject (so one might think) to functional explanations of various kinds, raises the dormant theoretical question of the nature of the psychic unity of mankind, and suggests the importance of the now unfashionable interest in the philosophical activities of "primitive" peoples for the evaluation of psycholinguistic studies and theories of "primitive" thought. [2]

The blackrobed Jesuit fathers began the preaching of the gospel to the Seneca nation in the year 1668. They quickly found that the Seneca were rigidly attached to Iroquoian religious traditions and were particularly obstinate in looking to their dreams for guidance in all the important affairs of life. Father Fremin wrote:

The Iroquois have, properly speaking, only a single Divinity—the dream. To it they render their submission, and follow all its orders with the utmost exactness. The Tsonnontouens [Seneca] are more attached to this superstition than any of the others; their Religion in this respect becomes even a matter of scruple; whatever it be that they think they have done in their dreams, they believe themselves absolutely obliged to execute at the earliest moment. The other nations content themselves with observing those of their dreams which are the most important; but this people, which has the reputation of living more religiously than its neighbors, would think itself guilty of a great crime if it failed in its observance of a single dream. The people think only of that, they talk about nothing else, and all their cabins are filled with their dreams. They spare no pains, no industry, to show their attachment thereto, and their folly in this particular goes to such an excess as would be hard to imagine. He who has dreamed during the night that he was bathing, runs immediately, as soon as he rises, all naked, to several cabins, in each of which he has a kettleful of water thrown over his body, however cold the weather may be. Another who has dreamed that he was taken prisoner and burned alive, has found himself bound and burned like a captive on the next day, being persuaded that by thus satisfying his dream, this fidelity will avert from him the pain and infamy of captivity and death, which, according to what he has learned from his Divinity, he is otherwise bound to suffer among his enemies. Some have been known to go as far as Quebec, travelling a hundred and fifty leagues, for the sake of getting a dog, that they had dreamed of buying there. . . .

Father Fremin and his colleagues were appalled: some Seneca might, any night, dream of their deaths! "What peril we are in every day," he wrote, "among people who will murder us in cold blood if they have dreamed of doing so; and how slight needs to be an offense that a Barbarian has received from someone, to enable his heated imagination to represent to him in a dream that he takes revenge on the offender" (letter of Father Fremin, in Kenton 1927, 2:191–92). It is small wonder that the Jesuits early attempted to disabuse the Seneca of their confidence in dreams, propounding various subtle questions such as, "Does the soul leave the body during sleep?" and "Can infants in the womb dream?", either affirmative or negative answers to which would involve the recognition (according to the Jesuits) of logical contradictions in native theory (Relation of Father Carheil, 1669–70, in Kenton 1927, 2:186–89).

But Jesuit logic did not discourage Seneca faith. The Quaker missionaries who reached the Seneca one hundred and thirty years later found in them much the same "superstitious" respect for dreams which their unsuccessful predecessors had discovered. "They are superstitious in the extreme, with respect to dreams, and witchcraft," wrote Halliday Jackson (1830) "and councils are often called, on the most trifling occurrences of this nature. To elucidate in the winter of 1799, while one of the Friends was engaged in instructing the children in school learning, a message came from a confederate tribe, eighty miles distant, stating that one of their little girls had dreamed that 'the devil was in all white people alike, and that they ought not to receive instruction from the Quakers, neither was it right for their children to learn to read and write.' In consequence of this circumstance, a council was called, the matter was deliberated on, and divers of them became so much alarmed, as to prevent their children from attending the school for some time."

This faith in dreams is still alive, although somewhat diminished in strength, in the twentieth century. For many Seneca, dreams even today control the choice and occasion of curing ceremonies, membership in the "secret" medicine societies, the selection of friends, and degree of confidence in life.

At the New Year's ceremony, people still go about asking that their dreams be guessed, and a particularly vivid dream still is brought to a clairvoyant (usually a woman) for interpretation (Fenton 1953; and personal communications from M. H. Deardorff). Over the course of nearly three hundred years and probably longer, the Seneca—like the other Iroquois—have let dreams direct their lives.

The Iroquois theory of dreams was basically psychoanalytic. Father Ragueneau in 1649 described the theory in language which might have been used by Freud himself:

> In addition to the desires which we generally have that are free, or at least voluntary in us, [and] which arise from a previous knowledge of some goodness that we imagine to exist in the thing desired, the Hurons [and, he might have added, the Seneca] believe that our souls have other desires, which are, as it were, inborn and concealed. These, they say, come from the depths of the soul, not through any knowledge, but by means of a certain blind transporting of the soul to certain objects; these transports might in the language of philosophy be called *Desideria innata,* to distinguish them from the former, which are called *Desideria Elicita.*
>
> Now they believe that our soul makes these natural desires known by means of dreams, which are its language. Accordingly, when these desires are accomplished, it is satisfied; but, on the contrary, if it be not granted what it desires, it becomes angry, and not only does not give its body the good and the happiness that it wished to procure for it, but often it also revolts against the body, causing various diseases, and even death. . . .
>
> In consequence of these erroneous [thought Father Ragueneau] ideas, most of the Hurons are very careful to note their dreams, and to provide the soul with what it has pictured to them during their sleep. If, for instance, they have seen a javelin in a dream, they try to get it; if they have dreamed that they gave a feast, they will give one on awakening, if they have the wherewithal; and so on with other things, And they call this *Ondinnonk*—a secret desire of the soul manifested by a dream (Kenton 1927, 1:503–04).

But the Hurons recognized that the manifest content or emptiness of a dream might conceal rather than reveal the soul's true wish. And so:

> . . . just as, although we did not always declare our thoughts and inclinations by means of speech, those who by means of supernatural vision could

see into the depths of our hearts would not fail to have a knowledge of them—in the same manner, the Hurons believe that there are certain persons, more enlightened than the common, whose sight penetrates, as it were, into the depths of the soul. These see the natural and hidden desires that it has, though the soul has declared nothing by dreams, or though he who may have had the dreams had completely forgotten them. It is thus that their medicine-men . . . acquire credit, and make the most of their art by saying that a child in the cradle, who has neither discernment nor knowledge, will have an *Ondinnonk*—that is to say, a natural and hidden desire for such or such a thing; and that a sick person will have similar desires for various things of which he has never had any knowledge, or anything approaching it. For, as we shall explain further on, the Hurons believe that one of the most efficacious remedies for rapidly restoring health is to grant the soul of the sick person these natural desires (Relation of Father Ragueneau, 1647–48, in Kenton 1927, 1:503–04).

According to Iroquois theory, disease or bodily infirmity could arise from three sources: from natural injuries, such as the wounds of war or physical accident; from witchcraft, by which certain foreign articles such as balls of hair, splinters of bone, clots of blood, or bear's teeth were projected magically into a victim's body; and from

the mind of the patient himself, which desires something, and will vex the body of the sick man until it possesses the thing required. For they think that there are in every man certain inborn desires, often unknown to themselves, upon which the happiness of individuals depends. For the purpose of ascertaining desires and innate appetites of this character, they summon soothsayers, who, as they think, have a divinely-imparted power to look into the inmost recesses of the mind. These men declare that whatever first occurs to them, or something from which they suspect some gain can be derived, is desired by the sick person. Thereupon the parents, friends, and relatives of the patient do not hesitate to procure and lavish upon him whatever it may be, however expensive, a return of which is never thereafter to be sought . . . (Relation of Father Jouvency, 1610–13, in Kenton 1927, 1:7).

The Huron, Seneca, and other Iroquoian peoples ascribed to the soul several faculties which are not unlike the faculties which European psychologists of the day (i.e., the theologians) recognized. The Huron considered that the human body was inhabited by a single soul with several functions, and depending on the function which was being alluded to at the moment, a different name was used. There was a name for the soul in its capacity to animate the body and give it life; in its capacity to have knowledge; in its capacity to exercise judgment; in its capacity to wish or desire; and in its capacity to leave the body, as it might during dreams or after death. The soul occupied all parts of the body, and so had head, arms, legs, trunk, and all the rest of the anatomy (in ethereal counterpart) of the corporeal body (Relation of Father LeJeune, 1636, in Kenton 1927, 1:255–56).

Intuitively, the Iroquois had achieved a great degree of psychological sophistication. They recognized conscious and unconscious parts of the mind. They knew the great force of unconscious desires, and were aware that the frustration of these desires could cause mental and physical ("psychosomatic") illness. They understood that these desires were expressed in symbolic form by dreams, but that the individual could not always properly interpret these dreams himself. They had noted the distinction between the manifest and latent content of dreams, and employed what sounds like the technique of free association to uncover the latent meaning. And they considered that the best method for the relief of psychic and psychosomatic distress was to give the frustrated desire satisfaction, either directly or symbolically.

The dreams reported by the Jesuit fathers, and in the ethnological literature up to the present time, provide a measure of the range and types of manifest content, and to a degree of the latent content, of Iroquois dreams. Dreams involving overt sexuality were not rare, and since they were freely reported and often acted out in therapeutic orgies, they gave the fathers great concern. Normally the Iroquoian peoples were modest in dress, often rather shy in heterosexual contacts, and although premarital affairs were freely permitted to the young people and divorce and remarriage were easy for adults, chastity and marital fidelity were publicly recognized ideals. The fulfillment of dream wishes, however, took priority over other proprieties.

In 1656, at Onondaga, three warriors came to the village during the Midwinter Ceremony. They had been absent for a year in an unsuccessful campaign against the Cat, or Erie, Nation. One of the warriors "was as wasted, pale, and depressed, as if he had spoken with the Devil. He spat blood, and was so disfigured that one scarcely dared to look him in the face." This man, when he arrived, announced that he had a matter of great importance to communicate to the elders. When they had assembled, he told them that during the campaign he had seen Tarachiawagon, He-who-holds-up-the-sky, the culture hero, in the guise of a little dwarf. Tarachiawagon had addressed the warrior thus:

> I am he who holds up the Sky, and the guardian of the earth; I preserve men, and give victories to warriors. I have made you masters of the earth and victors over so many Nations: I made you conquer the Hurons, the Tobacco Nation, the Ahondihronnons, Atiraguenrek, Atiaonrek, Takoulguehronnons and Gentaguetehronnons; in short, I have made you what you are: and if you wish me to continue my protection over you, hear my words, and execute my orders.
>
> First, you will find three Frenchmen in your village when you arrive there. Secondly, you will enter during the celebration of the Honnaouroria. Thirdly, after your arrival, let there be sacrificed to me ten dogs, ten porcelain beads from each cabin, a collar [belt of wampum] ten rows wide, four measures of sunflower seed, and as many of beans. And, as for thee, let two married women be given thee, to be at thy disposal for five days. If that be not executed item by item I will make thy Nation a prey to all sorts of disaster,—and, after it is all done, I will declare to thee my orders for the future (Father deQuens, Relation of 1655–56, in Kenton 1927,2:80–81).

The dreamer's demands were fulfilled.

The Jesuits noted also, among the Huron, a formal ritual of gratification of sexual wishes expressed in dreams. In 1639, Father LeJeune met an old man ("in the common opinion of the Savages, . . . one of the most respectable and virtuous men of the whole country") who was dying of an ulcer which had spread from his wrist to his shoulder and finally had begun to eat into his torso. This man's last desires were "a number of dogs of a certain shape and color, with which to make a three day's feast; a quantity of flour for the same purpose; some dances, and like performances; but principally . . . the ceremony of the 'andacwander,' a mating of men with girls, which is made at the end of the feast. He specified that there should be 12 girls, and a thirteenth for himself" (Relation of Father LeJeune, 1639, in Kenton 1927, 1:388).

During the dream guessing rites at Midwinter and, on occasion of illness, at other times of the year, persons propounded riddles in a sacred game. Each person or a group announced his "own and special desire or 'Ondinonc'—according as he is able to get information and enlightenment by dreams—not openly, however, but through Riddles. For example, someone will say, 'What I desire and what I am seeking is that which bears a lake within itself'; and by this is intended a pumpkin or calabash. Another will say, 'What I ask for is seen in my eyes—it will be marked with various colors'; and because the same Huron word that signifies 'eye' also signifies 'glass bead', this is a clue to divine what he desires—namely, some kinds of beads of this material, and of different colors. Another will intimate that he desires an Andacwandat feast that is to say, many fornications and adulteries. His Riddle being guessed, there is no lack of persons to satisfy his desire" (Father LeJeune, Relation of 1639, in Kenton 1927, 1:398).

Nightmares of torture and personal loss were apparently not uncommon among warriors. In 1642 a Huron man dreamed that non-Huron Iroquois had taken him and burned him as a captive. As soon as he awoke, a council was held. "The ill fortune of such a Dream," said the chiefs, "must be averted." At once twelve or thirteen fires were lighted in the cabin where captives were burned, and torturers seized fire brands. The dreamer was burned; "he shrieked like a madman. When he avoided one fire, he at once fell into another." Naked, he stumbled around the fires three times, singed by one torch after another, while his friends repeated compassionately, "courage, my Brother, it is thus that we have pity on thee." Finally he darted out of the ring, seized a dog held for him there, and paraded through the cabins with this dog on his shoulders, publicly offering it as a consecrated victim to the demon of war, "begging him to accept this semblance instead of the reality of his Dream." The dog was finally killed with a club, roasted in the flames, and eaten at a public feast, "in the same manner as they usually eat their captives" (Father Lalemant, Relation of 1642, in Kenton 1927, 1:455–56). In the period 1645–49, Father Francesco Bressani saw a Huron cut off a finger with a sea-shell because he had dreamed that his enemies had captured him and were performing this amputation (Bressani's Relation of 1653, in Kenton 1927, 2:42). In 1661–62, Father Lalemant describes three similar cases among the Five Nations. One man, in order to satisfy the dictates of his dream, had himself stripped naked by his friends, bound, dragged through the streets with the customary hooting, set upon the scaffold, and the fires lit. "But he was content with all these preliminaries, and, after passing some hours in singing his death song, thanked the company, believing that after this imaginary captivity he would never be actually a prisoner." Another man having dreamt that his cabin was on fire, "could find no rest until he could see it actually burning." The chief's council in a body, "after mature deliberation on the matter," ceremoniously burned it down for him. A third man went to such extremes of realism, after a captivity nightmare, that he determined "that the fire should be actually applied to his legs, in the same way as to captives when their final torture is begun." The roasting was so cruel and prolonged that it took six months for him to recover from his burns (Father Lalemant, Relation of 1661–62, in Kenton 1927, 2:74 fn.).

Some dreams were violently aggressive. One Huron dreamed that he killed a French priest. "I killed a Frenchman; that is my dream. Which must be fulfilled at any cost," he yelled. He was only appeased by being given a French coat supposedly taken from the body of a dead Frenchman. A Cayuga man dreamed that he gave a feast of human flesh. He invited all the chief men of the Cayuga nation to his cabin to hear a matter of importance. "When they had assembled, he told them that he was ruined, as he had had a dream impossible of fulfillment; that his ruin would entail that of the whole Nation; and that a universal overthrow and destruction of the earth was to be expected. He enlarged at great length on the subject, and then asked them to guess his dream. All struck wide of the mark, until one man, suspecting the truth, said to him: 'Thou wishest to give a feast of human flesh. Here, take my brother; I place him in thy hands to be cut up on the spot, and put into the kettle.' All present were seized with fright, except the dreamer, who said that his dream required a woman." A young girl was adorned with ornaments and, unaware of her fate, led to the dreamer-executioner. "He took her; they watched his actions, and pitied that innocent girl; but, when they thought him about to deal the death-blow, he cried out: 'I am satisfied; my dream requires nothing further'" (Father deQuens, Relation of 1655–56, in Kenton 1927, 2:69–75). During the "Feast of Fools," the annual *Ononharoia* or "turning the brain upside down," when men and women ran madly from cabin to cabin, acting out their dreams in charades and demanding the dream be guessed and satisfied, many women and men alike dreamt of fighting natural enemies. Dreams in which hostility was directed at members of other nations were properly satisfied by acting them out both in pantomime and in real life; but bad dreams about members of the same community were acted out only in some symbolic form, which had a prophylactic effect. Thus, someone on the Cornplanter Seneca Reservation (during the nineteenth century) dreamed that a certain young woman was alone in a canoe, in the middle of a stream, without a paddle. The dreamer invited the young lady to a dream-guessing ceremony at his home. Various people gathered and each one tried to guess what the dream was. Finally the dream was guessed. A miniature canoe with a paddle was thereupon presented to the girl. This ceremony was expected to forestall the dream disaster from happening in real life (Skinner Ms: 13–14).

Dreams were very common in which the dreamer met a supernatural being who promised to be a friend and patron and to give his protégé special powers and responsibilities. They were often experienced by boys at puberty who deliberately sought such guardian spirits. One case was described in some detail by the Jesuits. At the age of fifteen or sixteen, the youth retired alone into the woods, where he spent sixteen days without food, drinking only water. Suddenly he heard a voice, which came from the sky, saying, "Take care of this man, and let him end his fast." At the same time, he saw an old man "of rare beauty" descend from the sky. This man approached, gazed kindly at him, and said, "Have courage, I will take care of thy life. It is a fortunate thing for thee, to have taken me for thy master. None of these Demons who haunt these countries, shall have any power to harm thee. One day thou wilt see thy hair as white as mine. Thou wilt have four children; the first two and the last will be males, and the third will be a girl; after that, thy wife will hold the relation of a sister to thee." As he concluded speaking, the old man held out to him a piece of raw human flesh. The youth turned aside his head in horror. "Eat this," then said the old man, presenting him with a piece of bear's fat. When the lad had eaten it, the old man disappeared. On later occasions, however, he frequently reappeared with assurances of help. Most of the old man's predictions came true: the youth, become a man, had four children, the third of whom was a girl; after the fourth, "a certain infirmity compelled him to . . . continence"; and, as the eating of the bear's meat augured, the man became a noted hunter, gifted with a second sight for finding game. As an old man, looking back, he judged that "he would have had equal success in war had he eaten the piece of human flesh that he refused." In his later years this man became a Christian and was baptized (Father Lalemant, Relation of 1642, in Kenton 1927, 1:453–54).

Dreams of supernatural protectors (or persecutors) also came often to sick persons, and the appropriate therapeutic ritual was deduced from the identity of the spirit. Thus, dreams of false-faces called for the curing rituals of the Society of Faces; dreams of birds (in recent years, particularly of bloody or headless chickens) indicated that the Dew Eagle Ceremony was required. Sick persons often dreamed of someone (or a relative of the sick person dreamed), and the dream was interpreted to mean that the sick person "wants a friend." During the Eagle Society Ceremony, the sick person is given a "ceremonial friend"; thereafter the two treat one another as kinfolk, and the relationship of mutual helpfulness is life-long. If a boy's friend, for instance, is an older man, he

. . . must help the child to grow up to be a man. He must advise the boy, acting as his counsellor. . . . When one is ill, they choose a friend for him from the other side (moiety). It is believed that the ceremony of making friends merges the relatives of the two principals into one kindred unit: the relatives of the man are linked with the relatives of the child. The older man must act as an example to his junior friend. The older man's conduct shall be observed by the younger boy who considers the older friend a model of behavior. The creator has ordained that these two be friends and it is hoped the younger one will grow up to be the fine man his older partner is supposed to be. Whatever he observes the older man doing, he shall do it. The old man bears the onus of the child's future. As a reward he will see the Creator when he dies. When the two meet on the road, the older person speaks first. "Thanks you are well my friend?" The younger one answers, "Truly thank you I am well my friend." Every time he sees me, he calls me "friend" (Fenton 1953:126–14 quoting Seneca informant, He-strikes-the-rushes).

The force of the unconscious desires of the individual, which are so compelling that "it would be cruelty, nay, murder, not to give a man the subject of his dream; for such a refusal might cause his death," sometimes was reinforced by the fact that in native theory they were the vehicle for expressing the desires and commands of the supernatural beings whom his wandering dream-soul had met. Some of these supernatural dreams have already been mentioned. Those involving powerful supernaturals like Tarachiawagon were apt to achieve a great notoriety, and (if the chiefs considered the dream ominous) the whole nation might exert itself to fulfill the dreamer's demands; neglect invited national disaster. In the winter of 1640, during an epidemic of smallpox among the Huron, a young fisherman had a vision: a demon appeared to him under the form of a tall and handsome young man. "Fear not," said the being, "I am the master of the earth, whom you Hurons honor under the name of Iouskeha. I am the one whom the French wrongly call Jesus, but they do not know me. I have pity on your country, which I have taken under my protection; I come to teach you both the reasons and the remedies for your misfortune. It is the strangers who alone are the cause of it; they now travel two by two through the country, with the design of spreading the disease everywhere. They will not stop with that; after this smallpox which now depopulates your cabins, there will follow certain colics which in less than three days will carry off all those whom this disease may not have removed. You can prevent this misfortune; drive out from your village the two black gowns who are there." The demon continued with prescriptions for distributing medicinal waters to the sick; but after a few days, apparently, the popular disturbance subsided and the priests were not expelled (Father Lalemant, Relation of 1640, in Kenton 1927, 1:254–55 fn.). In the winter of 1669–70, a woman at Oneida was visited in a dream by Tarachiawagon, who told her that the Andaste (southern enemies of the Five Nations) would attack and besiege the Oneida village in the spring, but that the Oneida would be victorious and that they would capture one of the most famous Andaste war captains. In her dream she heard the voice of this man coming from the bottom of a kettle, uttering wailing cries like the cries of those who are being burned. For a time, this woman became a prophet; every day people foregathered at her house to hear her pronouncements; and all she said was believed absolutely (Father Bruyas, Relation of 1669–70, in Kenton 1927, 2:80 fn.). Of course, prophetic dreams of this kind derived much of their impact from the conviction of the community that while some dreams expressed only the wishes of the dreamer's soul, others expressed the wishes of his personal guardian spirit or of various supernatural beings—particularly of Tarachiawagon, the Holder of the Heavens, the Master of Life, he who decided the fate of battles, the clemency of the seasons, the fruitfulness of the crops, and the success of the chase.

The effectiveness of the Iroquois dream therapy was sometimes admitted even by the Jesuits, who had neither psychological insight nor religious sympathy for the primitive dream theory. Father LeJeune described the case of a woman who had gone to live with her husband in a strange village. One moonlit night, during a feast, she walked out from her cabin with one of her baby daughters in her arms. Suddenly, she saw the moon dip down to earth and transform itself into a tall, beautiful woman, holding in her arms a little girl like her own. This moon-lady declared herself to be the "immortal seignior" of the Hurons and the several nations allied to them, and announced that it was her wish that from each of the half-dozen or so tribes she named, a present of that tribe's special product should be given to the dreamer—from the Tobacco Nation, some tobacco; from the Neutrals, some robes of black squirrel fur; and so on. She declared that she liked the feast then being given, and wanted others like it to be held in all the other villages and tribes. "Besides," she said, "I love thee, and on that account I wish that thou shouldst henceforth be like me; and as I am wholly of fire, I desire that thou be also at least of the color of fire," and so she ordained for her a red cap, red plume, red belt, red leggings, red shoes, red all the rest.

The moon-lady then vanished and the mother returned to her cabin, where she collapsed "with a giddiness in the head and a contraction of the muscles." Thereafter she dreamt constantly of "goings and comings and outcries through her cabin."

It was decided by the chiefs that this was an important matter and that every effort should be made to give satisfaction to the sick woman: not only her wishes but those of the moon-lady were involved. She was dressed in red; the disease was diagnosed (from the symptom of giddiness) as demanding the Dream Feast or Ononwharoria ("turning the brain upside down") and messengers collected for her the articles she required. The Jesuits sounded a sour note, refusing to contribute the blue blanket she wanted from a "Frenchman," but the lady went through the five-day ritual, supported on the arms of sympathetic friends. She hobbled in her bare feet through more than two hundred fires; she received hundreds of gifts; she propounded her last desire in dozens of cabins, relating her troubles "in a plaintive and languishing voice" and giving hints as to the content of the desire, until at last it was guessed. Then there was a general rejoicing, a public council, a giving of thanks and congratulations, and a public crowning and completing of her last desire (which Father LeJeune, exasperatingly, does not describe or even hint at).

An honest man, the father was compelled to admit that all this worked:

> It is to be presumed that the true end of this act, and its catastrophe, will be nothing else but a Tragedy. The devil not being accustomed to behave otherwise. Nevertheless, this poor unhappy creature found herself much better after the feast than before, although she was not entirely free from, or cured of her trouble. This is ordinarily attributed by our Savages to the lack or failure of some detail, or to some imperfection in the ceremony . . . (Father LeJeune, Relation of 1639, in Kenton 1927, 1:393–401).

Not all therapeutic dream-fulfillments ended in even a partial cure, of course, but this was not felt as any reflection on the principles of dream therapy. The whole village vied to give the sick person his every wish, for any frustration was a threat to life. A dying man might be surrounded by literally thousands of scissors, awls, knives, bells, needles, kettles, blankets, coats, caps, wampum belts, beads, and whatever else was suggested by the sick man's fancy or the hopeful guesses of his friends. If he died at last, "He dies," the people would say, "because his soul wished to eat the flesh of a dog, or of a man; because a certain hatchet that he wished for could not be procured; or because a fine pair of leggings that had been taken from him could not be found." If he survived, the gift of the last thing that he wished for during his illness was cherished for the rest of his life.

Looking over the material on Iroquois dreams, it is apparent that there were two major types of dreams or visions recognized by the society and separately institutionalized (although in many dreams the two types were blended). These two types may be called *symptomatic dreams* and *visitation dreams.*

A symptomatic dream expressed a wish of the dreamer's soul. This wish was interpreted either by the dreamer himself or by a clairvoyant, who for a fee diagnosed the wish by free association in reverie, by drinking a bowlful of herb teas while chanting to his guardian spirit, by consulting his guardian spirit in a dream or trance (sometimes going to sleep with a special herb under his head), by water scrying, and in later days by reading tea leaves and cards. Anyone could become a clairvoyant and there were many in each community, some occupying roles of repute—like famous doctors—and others of more humble pretensions helping their immediate families (See Fenton 1953: passim; Jesuit Relations, passim, in Kenton 1927). These diagnoses served as signals for the execution of various rather conventional patterns of acting out the wish, either literally or symbolically. Some of these acting out patterns were prophylaxes against the fate implicit in the wish—for example, the symbolic or partial tortures and the abortive cannibal feasts.

This sort of acting out seems to have been based on the idea that a wish, although irrational and destructive toward self or friends, was fateful, and that the only way of forestalling realization of an evil-fated wish was to fulfill it symbolically. Others were curative of existing disorders, and prophylactic only in the sense of preventing ultimate death if the wish were too long frustrated. The acting out patterns can also be classified according to whether the action required is mundane or sacred and ceremonial. Thus dreams of buying a dog, and then travelling a long distance to obtain the dog, involve no particular sacred ceremony revolving around the wish itself, nor would a dream of going on a war party require more than participation in the normal course of military enterprise. But most of the symptomatic dreams of mentally or physically sick people demanded a ceremonial action, often not only at the time of the dream, but periodically thereafter during the dreamer's whole life span.

The annual festival at Midwinter not merely permitted but required the guessing and fulfillment of the dreams of the whole community. There were probably several dozen special feasts, dances, or rites which might be called for at any time during the year by a sick dreamer: the *andacwander* rite, requiring sexual intercourse between partners who were not husband and wife; the *ohgiwe* ceremony, to relieve someone from persistent and troubling dreams about a dead relative or friend; the dream guessing rite, in which the dreamer accumulated many gifts from unsuccessful guessers; the Striking Stick Dance, the Ghost Dance, and many other feasts, dances, and even games. The repertoire could at any time be extended by a new rite, if the dreamer saw a new rite or a nonsacred rite in a dream, or if his clairvoyant divined that such a rite was called for; normally social dances became curative when performed for someone at the instigation of his dream. Some rites were the property of "secret" medicine societies, membership in which was obtained by having received the ministrations of the society upon dream diagnosis of its need. Visions of false faces called for the rituals of the False Face Society; visions of dwarf spirits indicated a need for the "dark dance" of the Little People's Society; dreams of bloody birds were properly diagnosed as wishes for membership in the Eagle Society; dreams of illness or physical violence and injury were evidence of need for the Medicine Men's Society Rite or for the Little Water Society. The relationship of dreams to ritual was such that the repertoire of any one community might differ from that of the next because of the accidents of dreams and visions, and any element might at any time be abstracted from the annual calendar of community rituals and performed for the benefit of an individual (See Fenton 1936; Speck 1949; Skinner Ms; Jesuit Relations in Kenton 1927, for details on the relation of ritual and dream).

The symptomatic dreams described above displayed, in their manifest content, relatively humble and mundane matters: wanted objects such as dogs, hatchets, knives, clothing; familiar dances and rituals, and their ceremonial equipment; familiar animals, birds, and plants. However, the second category of dreams showed powerful supernatural beings who usually spoke personally to the dreamer, giving him a message of importance for himself and often also for the whole community. Sometimes these were personality transformation dreams, in which the longings, doubts, and conflicts of the dreamer were suddenly and radically resolved; the dreamer emerged from his vision with a new sense of dignity, a new capacity for playing a hitherto difficult role, and a new feeling of health and well being. Such experiences were particularly common among boys at puberty. Retiring alone to the woods, fasting and meditating in solitude, the youth after a week or two of self-denial and thought experienced a vision in which a supernatural being came to him, promised aid and protection, and gave him a talisman. In a sense, the guardian spirit took the place of the parents upon whom the boy had hitherto depended, and from whom he had now to emancipate himself emotionally if he were to become a whole man. Guardian spirits varied in character and power: some gave clairvoyant powers; some gave unusual hunting luck and skill; some gave luck, courage, strength and skill in war. Clairvoyants possessed especially potent guardian spirits which enabled the shaman, simply by breathing on a sick man's body, to render it transparent. Prominent shamans claimed the power to foretell coming events, such as approaching epidemics and other great public calamities. A few such men became known as prophets, and were "apt to acquire great influence and their advice [was] usually followed without much question." This gift of prophecy was the endowment of a particularly good and powerful guardian spirit.[3]

In Iroquois theory, a dream could thus reveal the wishes not only of the dreamer but also of the supernatural who appeared in his dream. Frustration of the wishes of a supernatural was dangerous, for he might not merely abandon or cause the death of the dreamer, but bring about disaster to the whole society or even cause the end of the world. Hence, dreams in which such powerful personages as Tarachiawagon (culture hero and a favorite dream figure) appeared and announced that they wanted something done (frequently for the dreamer) were matters of national moment. Clairvoyants were called upon; the chiefs met, and discussed ways of satisfying the sometimes expensive or awkward demands of the dreamers (representing the powers above), or of averting the predicted catastrophe. Not infrequently this type of dream also bore elements of personality transformation for the dreamer, who in his identification with the gods assumed a new role as prophet, messiah, and public censor and adviser. Such prophets might make detailed recommendations about the storage of crops, the waging of war, diplomatic policy toward other tribes and toward the French or the English, measures to avert epidemics or famine. Rarely, however, did such prophets maintain a lasting influence.

The theory of dreams among the Iroquois is in evident accord with the theme of freedom in the culture as a whole. The intolerance of externally imposed restraints, the principle of individual independence and autonomy, the maintenance of an air of indifference to pain, hardship, and loneliness—all these are the negative expression, as it were, of the positive assertion that wishes must be satisfied, that frustration of desire is the root of all evil. But men are never equally aware and equally tolerant of all their desires; and dreams themselves, carefully examined, are perhaps the quickest portal to that shadowy region where the masked and banished wishes exist in limbo. What, if anything, can we learn about the unconscious of Iroquois Indians from the scattered dreams recorded by the Jesuits and other casual observers?

The manifest content of Iroquois dreams is probably as various as the wishes of mankind: there are dreams of love and hate, pleasure and pain, of lost loved ones and longed for guardians; inconsequential and absurd things happen, and trivial objects are transfixed by the arrow of desire; abhorrent actions and repulsive thoughts plague the restless sleeper. Dreams as reported in the literature seem to have held a prevailingly anxious tone, ranging from nightmare fantasies of torture to the nagging need to define the unconscious wish and satisfy it before some disaster occurs. The most dramatic and most frequently mentioned dreams seem to come from three groups of people: pubescent youths (who must renounce childhood's indulgences); warriors (who fear capture and torture); and the sick (who fear to die). These are perhaps the stress points which generate desire. Adolescent conflict, dreams of battle, and the silent panic of the sick: these are things of which men of many cultures, including our own, have experience.

The manifest content, and the conscious rationale the Seneca themselves give to dreams, are largely in active voice; such passivity as shows itself is laden with pain, unless it occurs in transformation dreams, where a man may be passive in relation to a god. But the latent content, representative of the underlying wish, may be seen in the acting out which is so often passive or self-destructive. Dreams are not to brood over, to analyze, and to prompt lonely and independent action; they are to be told, or at least hinted at, and it is for other people to be active. The community rallies round the dreamer with gifts and ritual. The dreamer is fed; he is danced over; he is rubbed with ashes; he is sung to; he is given valuable presents; he is accepted as a member of a medicine society. A man whose dream manifests a wish to attack and kill is satisfied by being given a coat; a man who dreams of sleeping with a woman does not attempt to woo his mistress, he is given an available female by the chief's council. Only in the personality transformation dreams of pubescent boys and adult prophets is passivity accepted in the dream; and these are the dreams of men in extremis.

This observation suggests that the typical Iroquois male, who in his daily life was a brave, generous, active, and independent spirit, nevertheless cherished some strong, if unconscious, wishes to be passive, to beg, to be cared for. This unallowable passive tendency, so threatening to a man's sense of self-esteem, could not appear easily even in a dream; when it did, it was either experienced as an intolerably painful episode of torture, or was put in terms of a meeting with a supernatural protector. However, the Iroquois themselves unwittingly make the translation: an active manifest dream is fulfilled by a passive receiving action. The arrangement of the dream guessing rite raises this dependency to an exquisite degree: the dreamer cannot even ask for his wish; like a baby, he must content himself with cryptic signs and symbols until someone guesses what he wants and gives it to him.

The culture of dreams may be regarded as a useful escape valve in Iroquois life. In their daily affairs, Iroquois men were brave, active, self-reliant, and autonomous; they cringed to no one and begged for nothing. But no man can balance forever on such a pinnacle of masculinity, where asking and being given are unknown. Iroquois men dreamt; and, without shame, they received the fruits of their dreams and their souls were satisfied.

NOTES

1. The data presented in this paper were in part assembled in the course of a study of the Handsome Lake religion conducted while the writer was a Faculty Research Fellow of the Social Science Research Council, and were analyzed in the course of a comparative study of religious movements supported by Grants M-883 and M-1106 from the National Institute of Mental Health and Grant 1769 (Penrose Fund) from The American Philosophical Society. Research assistance was provided by Josephine Dixon; W. N. Fenton gave valued criticism. It should be noted that I use the word, "psychoanalytic" in this paper to denote a group of theories rather than a specific one. Rigorous usage would exclude many variants and dilutions which, for want of a better term, I gather under the rubric "psychoanalytic." Psychoanalytic in this usage thus includes any theory of dreams which regards the dream as the symbolic expression of unconscious wishes. As the following pages will indicate, the Iroquois theory differed from Freudian theory in regard to substantive interpretation: the Iroquois did not use the incest (Oedipus) formulation, did not give a central role to the concept of intrapsychic conflict, and did not reduce content regularly to sexual symbols. The Freudian theory of course did not use the concept of a detachable soul nor did it admit the presence of supernatural beings.

2. There is another area of Iroquois psychological theory which neatly parallels current psychiatric formulations: the process of mourning.

3. See Jesuit Relations, in Kenton 1927: passim; and Ely S. Parker Ms [n.d.] on medicine men and Indian dances, in Parker Collection 1802–1846, in the Henry E. Huntington Library.

12

The Psychic Unity of Human Groups

Mazeway is to the individual what culture is to the group. Just as every group's history is unique, so every human individual's course of experience is unique. As a product of this experience, every human brain contains, at a given point of time, a unique mental image of a complex system of dynamically interrelated objects. This mental image—the mazeway—includes the body in which the brain is housed, various other surrounding things, and sometimes even the brain itself. It consists of an extremely large number of assemblages or cognitive residues of perception and is used by its holder as a true and more or less complete representation of the operating characteristics of a "real" world.

The mazeway may be compared to a map of a gigantic maze with an elaborate key or legend and many insets. On this map are represented three types of assemblage: (1) goals and pitfalls (values, or desirable and undesirable end-states); (2) the "self" and other objects (people and things); and (3) ways (plans, processes, or techniques) that may be circumvented or used, according to their characteristics, to facilitate the self's attainment or avoidance of values. For heuristic purposes, let us crudely categorize the content of the mazeway, recognizing that these categories (like the categories represented by different colors, shadings, shapes, or thicknesses of line on a map) do not represent the only possible analytical divisions and relationships. The normal human mazeway, then, may contain representation of at least the following phenomena:

I. Values (images of situations associated with pleasant or unpleasant feeling-tone)
   A. Positive organic values
      1. Eating and drinking
      2. Sleeping, rest, relaxation, absence of discomfort or bodily tension
      3. Sexual satisfaction

      4. Optimal temperature maintenance

      5. Elimination of wastes

      6. Breathing

   B. Positive symbolic values

      1. Testimonials of love, admiration, and respect from human objects

      2. Enactment of behavior sequences satisfying "in themselves" (for example, a game or sport, conversation, meditation), or satisfying because they are instrumental to other values

      3. Presence of objects associated with organic and symbolic consummations (including human and nonhuman objects)

   C. Altruistic values (images of situations in which the primary and secondary values of others are satisfied)

   D. Negative values (associated with pain, discomfort, anxiety): the reverse of consummations outlined above

II. Objects (images, with associations, of animate and inanimate objects)

   A. Self

      1. Body image

         a. surface of body

         b. bodily adornment (clothing, cosmetics, perfume, and so forth)

         c. organs and organ systems

         d. prostheses (for example, false teeth, wooden leg)

         e. defects or injuries (for example, "weak back," "shortness of breath")

      2. Self image

         a. physiological processes (for example, digestion, sexual desire)

         b. psychological process (nature of thoughts, dreams, emotions, and so forth)

         c. personality (characteristic impulse and action patterns recognized in self)

         d. evaluation (for example, good-bad, strong-weak) of parts or whole

         e. conception of the soul

   B. Human environment

      1. Particular persons

         a. values of others

      b. characteristics of behavior of others (in relation to self and to others)
    2. Classes of persons
      a. particular classes defined (for example, on basis of residence, kinship, race, political affiliation, wealth, and so forth)
      b. values and characteristics of classes (in relation to self and others)
    3. Sociocultural system as a whole
  C. Nonhuman environment
    1. Animals
    2. Plants
    3. Tools and equipment ("material culture")
    4. Natural phenomena (for example, fire, weather, topography, and terrain)
    5. Natural system as a whole
  D. Supernatural environment
    1. Particular supernaturals (for example, ancestors' spirits, deities, ghosts, demons, and so forth)
    2. Classes of supernaturals
    3. Supernatural processes (for example, mana and taboo, witchcraft, and magic)
  E. Statements of how entire sociocultural, self, natural, and supernatural system works
III. Techniques (images of ways of manipulating objects in order to experience desired end states or values)
  A. Techniques themselves (an extremely large number of interlocking and alternative statements of "what to do when . . .")
  B. Priority systems among values (statements of which to enjoy first, or which to do to the exclusion of something else)
  C. Priority systems among techniques (statements of which technique to use in order not to obstruct use of another, or the attainment of some other value)

These elements can be combined in an almost infinite variety of "imagined" action sequences.

The concept of mazeway thus embraces, in an organized fashion, several phenomena already generally recognized as common to human awareness:

the "body image" (Schilder 1935); "role," "self," "the other," "the generalized other" (G. Mead 1934); "behavioral environment" (Hallowell 1955b); the
"world view" (Redfield 1953). It is reminiscent of E. D. Tolman's "cognitive
maps" (1948) and of the topological concept of "life-space," and closely resembles certain concepts in cognitive theory: the "image" (Boulding 1956)
and "plan" (Miller et al. 1960). And the mazeway concept borrows from traditional psychological notions of perception, association, "integration," and
patterning of experience. Evidently, the mazeway includes in one field images of phenomena that, to many an outside "absolute" observer, would fall
into conceptually distinct and sometimes incommensurable categories: personality, culture, society, natural environment, values, and so on. From the
standpoint of the individual mazeway-holder, however, all these phenomena
normally constitute one integrated dynamic system of perceptual assemblages.
Within this system, self and nonself interact according to predictable (if more
or less idiosyncratic) "laws," the description of which in generalized form is
the business particularly of personality psychology and of dynamic psychiatry.

REDUCTIONISM AND THE RELATION OF
PERSONALITY AND CULTURAL SYSTEMS

Anthropologists sometimes like to think of culture as a closed system and
regard most efforts to consider the relation between cultural and noncultural
(for example, psychological and physiological) data as "reductionism." Leslie
White has been the most systematic and eloquent exponent of this tendency,
and consequently a discussion of White's position on this matter offers a direct way of coming to grips with the issue. We cannot help but agree with
White's essential position — that culture is "real," that cultural evolution is a
major subject matter of anthropology, and that the anthropologist should be
interested in culture. But some of White's arguments in justification of this
position seem to be not only unnecessary, but fallacious. There are, first of all,
certain questionable ontological claims: on occasion he insists upon settling
the question of what culture is by philosophical arguments ("A thing is what
it is . . .") and dogmatic assertions that he *knows* what culture is and is not.
Second, he explicitly regards the human organism and indeed all the physical
universe as constant parameters without which culture could not exist, but
which, once given, have no bearing on the variables involved in cultural process. "A consideration of the human organism, individually or collectively, is

irrelevant to an explanation of the processes of culture change" (White 1959). This position could only be successfully maintained if it were the case that "the human organism, individually or collectively," which White has already admitted is a parameter (albeit, in his view, a single-valued one) of cultural process, were indeed a changeless, uniform, absolute, univalued parameter. But the human organism, individually and collectively, is not uniform. It has been grossly variable, in physical evolution, synchronically in any population in response to genetic, ecological, and cultural circumstances, and in the individual in response to growth, accident, and disease. Indeed, the anthropologist must take the position that the processes of culture change (including the process by which human culture emerged) cannot be explained adequately without a consideration of the human organism, individually and collectively, and of that organism's physical environment, as well as of culture, per se. Any other position will inevitably yield a science of culture that is no science at all, but rather a sterile catalogue of cultural forms.

What sort of consideration of "the human organism" does culture and personality undertake in the interest of extending our knowledge of cultural process? First of all, the physiology of the organism is considered, insofar as it is relevant. The areas of relevance, however, are broad: endocrinology; neurophysiology, particularly of the limbic system; diet and nutrition; sickness and health; physical evolution; the general adaptation syndrome (of Selye [1956]); maturation, sexual differentiation, and aging; psychopharmacology (particularly in relation to narcotics and hallucinogenic agents like peyote). All of these, and more, are intimately related to both psychological and cultural processes. In regard to specifically psychological subjects a number of traditional areas are relevant: learning, perception, cognitive process, group dynamics, the structure of affect distribution (a conventional sense of "personality"), and existential phenomenology (the attempt to describe what another person perceives in categories isomorphic with those in which he perceives it). And, most importantly, the human organism is creative: it selects, rejects, seeks information, thinks, makes decisions, and ultimately modifies the systems of which it is a part. In addition to "interacting" externally with other components of social and other systems, the human organism does systematic internal work, the magnitude of which, even in a grossly physical sense, is measured by metabolic assays.

In culture and personality analysis, as was implied in the discussion of operational definitions, a society is usually considered to be a system on a higher level of organization than are the individual organisms, or even the social groups, that are the components of that society. There are available to the student of culture and personality two major, and to a degree antithetical, conceptions of the nature of the relation between cultural and personality systems; and at this point, perhaps, the dialectic should be presented, for it will sooner or later be translated into the student's research operations. These conceptions may be construed, respectively, as emphasizing the *replication of uniformity* and the *organization of diversity*. We shall discuss them at greater length later; for the moment, it will suffice to contrast the world view behind each.

THE REPLICATION OF UNIFORMITY

In many investigations, the anthropologist tacitly, and sometimes even explicitly, is primarily interested in the extent to which members of a social group, by virtue of their common group identification, behave in the same way under the same circumstances. For the sake of convenience in discourse, they may even be considered to have learned the "same things" in the "same cultural environment." Under such circumstances, the society may be regarded as culturally homogeneous and the individuals will be expected to share a uniform nuclear character. If a near perfect correspondence between culture and individual nuclear character is assumed, the structural relation between the two becomes nonproblematical, and the interest of processual research lies rather in the mechanisms of socialization by which each generation becomes, culturally and characterologically, a replica of its predecessors. This viewpoint is particularly congenial to the world view associated with dynamic psychology, ultimately based on Freud's psychoanalytic theories but modified by conceiving the personality to reflect faithfully the culture in which it was formed and not merely universal constants, such as the Oedipus conflict and the stages of psychosexual maturation. The sense of tragedy implicit in this world view is, as everyone knows, very different from that which preceded it. From the days of the Greeks to the Industrial Revolution, Western man had, most commonly, conceived of the essence of tragedy as lying in the inevitability of sin, that is, of sacred crime, the intentional or unintentional violation of "the Law." Different as the Greek plays are from the Christian gospels, they agree on one theme: sin is unavoidable. Beginning with Freud, and increasingly with his successors, the inevitable tragedy of man's situation was seen not as sin, but as the conflict of wishes, in themselves neither evil nor good, and often growing from contradictions inherent in the person's culture. Thus, to the student who emphasizes the replication of uniformity, the point of tragic concern is the fate of those whose cultures, internally rent with contradictions, unavoidably instill painful conflict.

THE ORGANIZATION OF DIVERSITY

In other investigations, it is sometimes more interesting to consider the actual diversity of habits, of motives, of personalities, of customs that do, in fact, co-exist within the boundaries of any culturally organized society. When the fact of diversity is emphasized, the obvious question must immediately be asked: how do such various individuals organize themselves culturally into orderly, expanding, changing societies? When the process of socialization is examined closely, it becomes apparent that, within the limits of practical human control and observation, it is not a perfectly reliable mechanism for replication. And culture, far from being, with the one exception of recent Western civilization, a slowly changing, sluggish, conservative beast, appears to be a turbulent species, constantly oscillating between the ecstasies of revitalization and the agonies of decline. Culture shifts in policy from generation to generation with kaleidoscopic variety and is characterized internally not by uniformity, but by diversity of both individuals and groups, many of whom are in continuous and overt conflict in one subsystem and in active cooperation in another. Culture, as seen from this viewpoint, becomes not so much a superorganic entity, but policy, tacitly and gradually concocted by groups of people for the furtherance of their interests, and contract, established by practice, between and among individuals to organize their strivings into mutually facilitating equivalence structures. Nor can the phenomenological world of an individual, or of a people, be assumed to be understood by the anthropologist once he can predict the movements of their bodies; rather, he must recognize the possibility of a radical diversity of mazeways that have their orderly relationship guaranteed not by the sharing of uniformity, but by their capacities for mutual prediction.

From this organization of diversity viewpoint grows a different sense of tragedy. The unwanted inevitability is not sin, nor conflict, but loneliness: the only partly bridgeable chasms of mutual ignorance between whole peoples and the failures of understanding between individuals. A modicum of this loneliness would appear to be as irreducible in interpersonal relations (including the relation of the anthropologist to his subjects) as is the complementarity of perceptions in physical observation.

THE PSYCHIC UNITY OF HUMAN GROUPS

One of the most hoary assumptions of the uniformitarian viewpoint is the belief that a society will fall apart and its members scatter if they are not threaded like beads on a string of common motives. Numerous sources may be quoted that attest to the "common thread" belief. Thus Aberle, Cohen, Davis, Levy, and Sutton (1950) in an essay on the functional prerequisites of a human society, include as prerequisites a "shared, articulated set of goals." Erich Fromm asserts that a nuclear character structure must be shared by "most members of the same culture" in order for the culture to continue; socialization must make people "want to act as they have to act" (In Sargant and Smith 1949:5). Émile Durkheim's thesis that society depends for integration upon the "common sentiments" of its members is a similar view (1915). John Honigmann expresses the position in the plaintive assertion, "In any community, there must be some congruence between what different people do, believe, and feel, otherwise social order would be impossible" (Honigmann 1954:220). Margaret Mead has carried the argument to the point where cultural heterogeneity is conceived as almost ipso facto pathogenic: "in a heterogeneous culture, individual life experiences differ so markedly from one another that almost every individual may find the existing cultural forms of expression inadequate to express his peculiar bent, and so be driven into more and more special forms of psychosomatic expression" (M. Mead 1947:72). Social philosophers, less humane than the scientists quoted above, but equally disturbed by the problems of their societies, at times have found the "common motive" theme a congenial one and have used the threat of social disintegration and individual degeneration to justify draconian measures for the standardization of sentiments.

It is, however, impossible to demonstrate empirically that any social system is operated by individuals all driven by the same motives; indeed, the data of personality and culture studies, as well as clinical observation, show conclusively that a sharing of motives is not necessary to a sharing of institutions. But is cognitive sharing a functional prerequisite of society? Here we enter the domain of the ethnographer who may not wish to tread the spongy ground of motive analysis, but who finds it both necessary and painless to make inferences from overt behavior about cognitive matters, such as the criteria for discrimination of kinsmen by terminological category, the substantive beliefs about the order of the cosmos, and the rules of procedure by which a shaman arrives at his differential diagnosis over a sick child. The minimum task of the ethnographer, of course, is simply to describe overt human behavior. "Description," in this minimum sense, is the formulation of a set of statements that will predict, for the ethnographer, what a class of subjects will do and say under various circumstances. Accordingly, any complete ethnographic statement will include a specification of both a configuration of circumstances and of a behavior sequence that a class of subjects produces (presumptively as a result of learning) whenever that configuration presents itself. Usually, the "circumstances" that elicit a certain behavior sequence on the part of one class of subjects will include the acts and utterances of another class. Therefore, most ethnographic descriptions primarily concern repetitive patterns of reciprocal interaction in which the behaviors of each class are the circumstance for the behaviors of the other class.

It has been sometimes assumed that such systems of reciprocal interaction, in which different classes of subjects play specialized roles, as well as general norms describing constant act and circumstance relations for a single class of subjects, require not merely a set of cognitive maps, but a uniformity of cognitive maps among the participants for their continued successful operation. For example, in their previously quoted essay on the functional prerequisites of a human society, Aberle, Cohen, Davis, Levy, and Sutton postulate the necessity of "shared cognitive orientations," as well as a "shared, articulated set of goals" (1950). Yet what few formal attempts have been made, by techniques such as componential analysis, to define the cognitive maps necessary to culturally correct behaviors have demonstrated unambiguously that it is often possible for the ethnographer to construct several different maps, each of which will predict adequately the overt behavior of subjects. Let us therefore now ask the question directly: is it necessary that all participants in a stable sociocultural system have the same "map" of the system in order that they may select the correct overt behaviors under the various relevant circumstances?

1. Minimal Sociocultural Systems

A system may be defined as a set of variable entities (persons, objects, customs, atoms, or whatever) so related that, first, some variation in any one is followed by a predictable (that is, nonrandom) variation in at least one other;

second, that there is at least one sequence of variations which involves all of the entities.

Let us define the properties of the least complex system that an ethnographer might describe. Such a system must satisfy the following minimum requirements: first, that two parties, A and B, the initiator and respondent, respectively, interact; second, that each completion of one sequence of interactions be followed, sooner or later, by a repetition of the same sequence. Representing the acts of A by the symbols a_i, those of B by the symbols b_j, and temporal relationship by the symbol $\rightarrow$, to be read "is followed by," we assert that the simplest such system has the following structure:

$$a_1 \longleftrightarrow b_1$$

Since it is legitimate to regard the sense of the symbol $\rightarrow$, "is followed by," as a reasonable interpretation of the logical relationship of material implication (whenever x, then y), we may refer to the structure $a_1 \leftrightarrow b_1$ as a *primary equivalence structure* (ES_1). In such a structure, whenever A does a_1, then (sooner or later) B does b_1; and whenever B does b_1, then (sooner or later) A does a_1.

Interaction structures of ES_1 type seem too simple to serve as useful models of the components of sociocultural systems. The *secondary equivalence structure* (ES_2), however, looks more interesting:

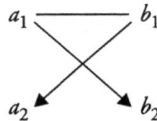

Here we may interpret acts a_1 and b_1 as instrumental acts and acts a_2 and b_2 as consummatory acts. The distinguishing feature of ES_2 is that the consummatory act of each party is released by (but is not necessarily exclusively conditional upon) the instrumental act of the other. The equivalence between a_1 and b_1 describes the repetitive nature of the interaction. A little ritual commonly found among the present inhabitants of the eastern coast of the United States (its wider distribution, in time and space, is unknown to me) provides a whimsical but culturally valid example of a secondary equivalence structure. When a child loses one of his baby teeth, he places the tooth under his pillow at night when he goes to bed; the parent, after the child has fallen asleep, comes and replaces the tooth with a coin ($a_1 \rightarrow b_1$). The child, on awakening, takes the coin and buys candy with it ($b_1 \rightarrow a_2$). (Possibly, he thereby loosens another tooth, if it is caramel candy!) The parent, meanwhile, after replacing the tooth with a coin, delightedly reports the transaction to his spouse $(a_1 \rightarrow b_1 \rightarrow b_2)$. And with the next tooth he sheds, the child, who has observed that tooth-placing is followed by candy and who likes candy, repeats a_1 and thus continues the process $(b_1 \rightarrow a_1)$. This simple custom is (for reasons that I shall mention later) not unlike the silent trade, so widely reported among primitive peoples. It may be diagrammed as follows:

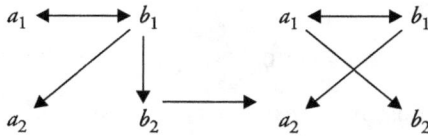

More complex structures, involving two parties, can obviously be constructed out of the same relationships. Thus a tertiary equivalence structure (ES_3) has the form:

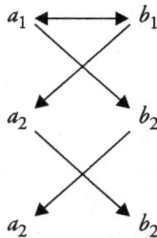

Structures of quaternary and still higher degree evidently can be made by a simple process of extension. Structures involving more than two persons also can be designed, although they are more difficult to represent on a plane surface. In general, we can consider that the two-party secondary equivalence structure, which we have suggested as the smallest practical model of a stable sociocultural system, is only one of a class of equivalence structures ^mES_n, where $m > 1$ denotes the number of parties to the system, and $n = 1$ denotes the number of levels of equivalences $a_i \leftrightarrow b_j$ incorporated. It would be interesting to investigate in detail the logical properties of these systems and to speculate that, in principle, *any* sociosystem involving m parties in repetitive interaction, can be described by some equivalence structure of the class ^mES_n. However, these exercises would carry us beyond the purposes of this discussion.

We now conclude that the simplest possible social interaction system that an ethnographer might describe has the form of a two person secondary equivalence structure. This structure is, however, a model of what the ethnographer perceives; it is the ethnographer's cognitive map. We wish now to discover with what combination of maps, α_i and β_j held by the two parties A and B, the ethnographer's model is compatible.

2. Minimal Cognitive Maps of Participants in Sociocultural Systems

At this point, we must make explicit two conventions that have been employed in the foregoing analysis. These are: first, that the ethnographer's map is valid ("true"); second, that the systems are "perfect," in the sense that there are no exceptions to the regularity of the relationships indicated by the symbols $\rightarrow$. We know, of course, that in "real life" ethnographers make errors and that human behavior is not perfectly predictable. Although it would not invalidate the reasoning to introduce these qualifications (since a probabilistic logic would do just as well as the strict two-valued logic we are using), it would make the demonstrations more tedious. These conventions are now also applied to the cognitive maps maintained by the participants: we assume that the relationships are two valued ("yes" or "no" rather than a probabilistic "maybe").

We have suggested already that a_1 and b_1 be regarded as "instrumental" acts and a_2 and b_2 as "consummatory." It is important to recognize that this classification is only a relative one; that is, a_1 is instrumental with respect to a_2, and b_1 with respect to b_2. In teleological terms, A does a_1 "in order to be able" to do a_2, and B does b_1 "in order to be able" to do b_2. But we do not actually need to invoke any panel of needs, drives, tensions, instincts, or whatever, the satisfaction of which makes an act ultimately consummatory, since we assume that the maps validly describe real events. It is therefore true by definition that neither A nor B will continue to participate in the system unless, first, each perceives that, *within the limits of the system,* his ability to perform his own consummatory act depends upon his partner performing his instrumental act; second, that when he performs his own instrumental act, its function is to elicit his partner's instrumental act; third, that he repeatedly performs his own instrumental act.

The simplest (but not the only) possible cognitive maps for A and B, respectively, which satisfy the foregoing requirements, are the following:

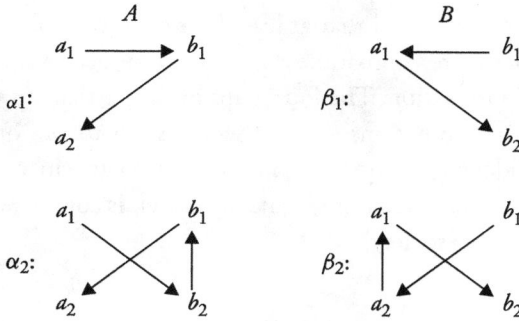

These maps are to be interpreted as follows:

α_1: *A* knows that whenever he does a_1, *B* will respond with b_1, and *A* will then perform a_2.

α_2: *A* knows that whenever he does a_1, *B* will respond with b_2 and then b_1, and *A* will then perform a_2.

β_1: *B* knows that whenever he does b_1, *A* will respond with a_1, and *B* will perform b_2.

β_2: *B* knows that whenever he does b_1, *A* will respond with a_2 and then a_1, and *B* will then perform b_2.

Each possible combination of these cognitive maps will yield a structure that is identical with, or logically implies, $^2ES_2$. Thus:

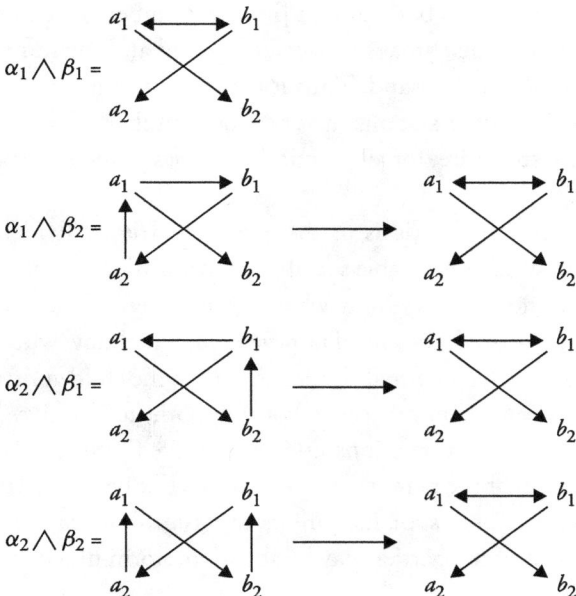

We have now demonstrated that at least four cognitive maps, in addition to the ethnographer's, are compatible with the continued existence of a simple system of social interaction. The four maps of the participant parties can exist in four possible combinations, each of which sums to $^2ES_2$ or to a form that implies $^2ES_2$. Evidently, it is not *necessary* that both participants share the same map; and we have answered our original question: is cognitive sharing a functional prerequisite of society?

HOW MANY COMBINATIONS OF COGNITIVE MAPS WILL YIELD THE SECONDARY EQUIVALENCE STRUCTURE?

Even a casual comparison of the ethnographer's model with the four partici-pants' models will suggest that a number of unique cognitive maps are possible which are different from, but contain, either or both of the A structures and/or either or both of the B structures. The basic model of $^2ES_2$, itself, for instance, contains both α_1 and β_1; $^2ES_2$ added to itself will yield $^2ES_2$; $^2ES_2$ added to α_1 will yield $^2ES_2$; $^2ES_2$ added to β_1 will yield $^2ES_2$ and so on. Let us therefore inquire, out of curiosity, just how many unique combinations of α-maps and β-maps there are where the sum equals, contains, or implies $^2ES_2$ the proviso that each component α-map include either or both α_1 and α_2, and each component β-map include either or both β_1 and β_2. The number is well over a million. The number of unique α-maps is over a thousand and the number of unique β-maps is also over a thousand. Thus it is apparent that even when one con-siders extremely simple systems, a very large number of different cognitive maps of such systems are, for all practical purposes, interchangeable as system components.

What are the implications of these considerations? Evidently cognitive sharing is not *necessary* for stable social interaction. The two parties to systems of form $^2ES_2$ do not need to know what the "motives" of their partners in the interchange are. Indeed, they need not even correctly know who their partners are. In the tooth exchange ritual alluded to earlier, the child at first believes that a good fairy, whom he never sees, takes the tooth, for motives unexplained, and leaves the coin. This relationship is not unlike the silent trade. Later, the child may know that the parents are responsible, but he does not "let on" from a benevolent wish not to spoil his parents' fantasies about *his* fantasies. One or the other or both of the parties may be able to perform his consummatory act *only* after the partner performs his instrumental act; or other circumstances may also permit it.

But, the advocate of togetherness may argue, whether or not it is necessary that *all* members of society share all cognitive maps, they must share at least *one*. Such an argument, however, is not convincing. I know of no criteria that would specify the one map all members of a given society should share. One cannot argue empirically that all members of all societies are *known* to share at least one map, for the data to support such an argument do not exist. And merely demonstrating that some defined group of human individuals, or even all the members of some one society, share a particular map, is irrelevant to the discussion. (Such a society would have to be peculiarly simple and at the same time clairvoyant.) Two or more parties may indeed share a common cognitive map, but such a circumstance is, in a sense, wasteful, since at least two, and therefore all, of these maps must be larger than the minimally necessary ones. And only when each actor is cognizant of the other's "motive" (consummatory act), can the actors' cognitive maps be identical and still contribute to system maintenance.

It may appear to be a bleak prospect to consider that human beings characteristically engage in a kind of silent trade with all their fellow men, rarely or never actually achieving cognitive communality. Indeed, one may suspect that the social sciences have nourished the idea of cognitive sharing for so long, just because the world may seem rather a lonely place if the wistful dream of mutual identification is abandoned. Still another anxiety may now arise: for an implication of our researches is that individuals can produce a sociocultural system that is beyond their own comprehension. If, for instance, α_k is as complex a map as A can maintain, and β_1 is as complex as B can maintain, their sum (*unless* they are identical) will be a structure *containing* $^2ES_2$, but in its totality *more* complex than one or both of them can grasp. If one of these parties is an anthropologist, who is attempting to construct a general ES that he will call "culture," then, alas, he may be a participant-observer in a sociocultural system that is more complex than he can describe ethnographically! Even if he cannot describe the system fully, he must be able to construct a cognitive map that is more complex than that of any of his subject's.

But perhaps the most significant point to be made is a relatively practical one, growing out of concerns with the application of anthropological knowledge to psychiatric research. A principle problem for the research anthropologist, in a mental hospital setting, is to explain how a person comes to be extruded from his sociocultural system. Is it because he is a "deviant," one whose cognitive maps are not shared by other members of the community? Or is it because he has been unable to maintain stable cognitive maps sufficiently complex for them to sum to an equivalence structure with those of his fellows? From the viewpoint of the organization of diversity, it would appear that the most generally adequate explanation is the latter: particularly in a large and complex society, equivalence structures normally will be the articulation of uniquely private cognitive worlds. The measure of individual value will not be conformity, but complementarity.

IS COGNITIVE NONSHARING A FUNCTIONAL PREREQUISITE OF SOCIETY?

Finally, we ask whether the fact that cognitive sharing is not a *necessary* condition of society does not mask an even more general point. Not only *can* societies contain subsystems, the cognitive maps of which are not uniform among participants, but they *do,* in fact, invariably contain such systems. Ritual, for instance, is often differently conceptualized by viewers and performers; public entertainment similarly is variously perceived by professional and audience; the doctor (or shaman) and patient relationship demands a mutual misunderstanding. Even in class and political relationships, complementary roles (as, for instance, between the holders Of "Great" and "Little" Traditions) are notoriously difficult to exchange. Administrative personnel and leaders generally, must understand the system on a "higher" level of synthesis than their subordinates, a level that demands a different, because more abstract, cognitive map. Indeed, we now suggest that human societies may characteristically *require* the nonsharing of certain cognitive maps among participants in a variety of institutional arrangements. Many a social subsystem simply will not "work" if all participants share common knowledge of the system. It would seem therefore that cognitive *non*uniformity may be a functional desideratum of society (although, by the criteria we have used above, it is certainly not a formal prerequisite any more than is uniformity). For cognitive nonuniformity subserves two important functions: (1) it permits a more complex system to arise than most, or any, of its participants can comprehend; (2) it liberates the participants in a system from the heavy burden of learning and knowing each other's motivations and cognitions.

If sociocultural organization is not necessarily dependent upon a community of motives or cognitions, then by what psychological mechanism is it achieved and maintained? This mechanism is evidently the perception of partial equivalence structures. By this is implied the recognition—as the result of learning—that the behavior of other people under various circumstances is predictable, irrespective of knowledge of their motivation, and thus is capable of being predictably related to one's own actions. Evidently, groups as well as individuals can integrate their behaviors into reliable systems by means of equivalence structures without extensive motivational or cognitive sharing. The equivalence structure model should be congenial to that tradition in social anthropology which interests itself in the relations between organized groups. Thus reciprocal interactions between the representatives of geographically separate groups as alien as American Indian tribes and colonial or state governments have proceeded for centuries, with only minimal sharing of motives or understanding, on a basis of carefully patterned equivalences. Similar observation might be made of the relations between castes, social classes, professional groups, kin groups, factions, parties, and so forth. In no case is it necessary that a basic personality or a basic cognitive framework be shared, but it is necessary that behaviors be mutually predictable and equivalent.

We may say that as any set of persons establish a system of equivalent behavioral expectancies, an organized relationship comes into existence. Such a system of equivalent mutual expectancies may be termed an *implicit contract,* in the general sense of the word "contract." In this sense, and not in the sense of any formal document, society is, as Rousseau intuited, built upon a set of continually changing social contracts that are possible only because human beings have cognitive equipment adequate to their maintenance and renewal. Culture can be conceived as a set of standardized models of such contractual relationships, in which the equivalent roles are specified and available for implementation to any two parties whose motives make their adoption promising. The relationship is based not on a sharing, but on a complementarity of cognitions and motives. Marital relationship, entry into an age grade, the giving of a feast—in all such contracts the motives may be diverse, but the cognitive expectations are standardized. Thus the relationship between the driver of a bus and the riders is a contractual one, involving specific and detailed mutual expectancies. The motives of drivers and riders may be as diverse as one wishes; the contract establishes the system. From this standpoint, then, it is culture that is shared (in the special sense of institutional contract) rather than personality, and culture may be conceived as an invention that makes possible the maximal organization of motivational and cognitive diversity. This it is able to accomplish because of the human (not uniquely human, but preeminently so) cognitive capacity for the perception of systems of behavioral equivalence.

NOTES

This is an excerpt from a longer chapter and contains minor alterations to the text and notes.

13
Mental Illness, Biology, and Culture

Do different cultures encourage different styles of mental illness? Are there societies in which mental illness is absent, or at least rare in comparison with our own? Have either style or frequency of mental illness, or both, changed during the history of Western civilization? These and similar questions, prompted by practical concern with the mental health of our contemporary world populations, have evoked answers from anthropologists. *Yes,* different cultures do encourage different styles of mental illness, *but* the major categories of mental illness (the organic psychoses, the functional psychoses, the neuroses, the situational reactions, etc.) seem to be universal human afflictions. *No,* there are no societies of whom it can be said with confidence that mental illness is absent or, with certainty, that it is even rare, *but* there are certainly differences in the frequencies of illness and in the readiness of different social systems to recognize what Western psychiatry would call illness as significant disorder. *Yes,* styles and frequencies of various mental illnesses have changed in recent western history (hysteria, for instance, is now a relatively rare diagnosis, and devils and demons have been replaced by radio and radar in paranoid delusions), *but* we do not know all of the reasons for such changes over time nor for the differences between social classes and between regions.

Thus, the relation between culture and mental health remains an intriguing problem for anthropologists, a promising field for research, and perhaps some day a richly rewarding field for application. At the present time, like other scientists interested in mental illness, anthropologists are still searching for more adequate concepts, more powerful theories, and more effective techniques of observation. One of the avenues of research which has been under rapid construction outside of anthropology is biological in concept and method; and since this approach is relatively unexploited by anthropologists, yet is potentially of great significance for anthropological theory, a considerable part of this chapter will be devoted to considering the ways in which the current cultural anthropological work in this area can assimilate and exploit what may be regarded, in the context of anthropology, as a physical anthropological position.

CERTAIN LIMITATIONS OF CONVENTIONAL ANTHROPOLOGICAL THEORIES OF MENTAL ILLNESS

The culture and personality tradition in anthropology has borrowed its models of personality development, its characterology, and its conceptions of mental illness almost exclusively from a combination of learning, *Gestalt*, and psychoanalytic theories. This is in part a historical accident: these functional approaches were developing most vigorously in American psychology and psychiatry just at the time, in the late 1920's and early 1930's, when cultural anthropologists were first turning their attention seriously to the individual. Anthropologists found these psychologies readily applicable to an understanding of the individual in culture; and the psychologists and psychoanalysts found in cross-cultural materials useful corroborative evidence for their theories. But the more recently developed biological approach, while it has not yet (anymore than the functional approach) provided a spectrum of "cures" of such refractory disease clusters as schizophrenia and cerebral arteriosclerosis, has already yielded a considerable body of knowledge of processes (in this case, of organic mechanisms) which are implicated in one or another type of psychopathology. This knowledge should be incorporated without delay, in general outline, into the conceptual armamentarium of every anthropologist concerned not only with mental disease but also with normal personality development and function.

At the present time, anthropological treatments of mental disease topics, particularly by culture and personality scholars, generally depend on a simple paradigm: The symptomatology of the illness under scrutiny is assumed to be motivated behavior expressive of psychological conflicts and to some degree effective in reducing tension and anxiety; the symptoms are "interpreted" in terms of some deductive schema intended to lay bare the (usually assumed to be unconscious) conflict; cultural *Anlagen* in the symptomatic behavior are pointed out; and finally, the source of the conflict is sought in traumatic emotional and/or cognitive dilemmas imposed by the victim's culture. This procedure almost completely neglects the victim's body; or, rather, it attributes to the victim's psyche a virtually magical ability to control the state of its body, by uncritically assuming that almost any somatic expression can be satisfactorily explained merely by asserting a plausible concomitant intrapsychic conflict. Even the "psychosomatic" position, it must be emphasized, is not "organic" in the sense indicated above, for it seeks the explanation of both somatic and behavioral disorder in antecedent psychological and cultural rather than in antecedent physiological conditions: thus the ulcer is explained by reference to the autonomic discharge attendant upon intrapyschic conflict, and the existence of intrapsychic conflict is explained by reference to culturally enjoined learning experiences rather than by any neurophysiological process.

Thus, even with regard to syndromes familiar to Western clinicians and conventionally (if not invariably) conceived as functional in etiology, the assumption that biological determinants are negligible is becoming an increasingly hazardous one to make. But the anthropologist is peculiarly vulnerable to criticism when he utilizes the functional paradigm without qualification to explain exotic forms of mental illness, such as the *pibloktoq* of the Polar Eskimo and the *windigo* psychosis of the northern Algonkian hunters. Here, in addition to the difficulties engendered by the fundamental ambiguity of current psychiatric theory over the respective causal roles of psychological and organic factors in clinically familiar syndromes, there are (or ought to be) serious uncertainties introduced by recognition of the extreme climatic, epidemiological (in respect to infectious diseases), and nutritional conditions to which technologically primitive populations are at times exposed (see, for example, Tooth's discussion [1950] of the difficulty even psychiatrists experience, when using purely behavioral criteria, in making the differential diagnosis between schizophrenia and certain types of trypanosomiasis in West Africa).

This paper is not intended, however, as an admonition to anthropologists to abandon an obsolete dogma for the sake of embracing a new scientific faith. Rather, the necessity for incorporating a new viewpoint into an existing tradition is pointed out. That this incorporation will entail modification of some beliefs and procedures may be expected; but the new theoretical position should be a strong synthesis rather than a weak substitute.

THE ORGANIC APPROACH IN PSYCHIATRY

The year 1927 may be taken as the beginning of codification of the culture and personality position in anthropology, for in that year Sapir's pioneering paper "The Unconscious Patterning of Behavior in Society" was published in a symposium on *The Unconscious* (Mandelbaum 1949). Sapir's paper, probably the first major piece of theoretical writing in the culture and personality tradition, set, or at least prefigured, the frame of reference of later anthropological work in this area. This frame of reference was predominantly psychological rather than biological: it implied that the fundamental, and often unconscious, organizations of individual behavior which are conventionally labeled "personality" are molded, not by physical constitution, but by a combination of cultural milieu and individual experience. The correspondingly functional character of the conventional culture and personality view of mental disorder, as it developed in the next few years in the work of Sapir, Benedict, Mead and others, can be readily explained by the absence of any substantial competing body of thought; for the biological approach in psychiatry did not even begin to make headway until after 1927.

The most impressive body of psychiatric theory in 1927 was psychoanalytic. This theory, although it gave lip service to biological thinking, and although its builders were well grounded in neurology, was in operation uncompromisingly psychological. Accordingly, the published case histories provided very little information concerning the physiological status of the patients. The analyst sometimes used physical metaphors (like "the economy of psychic energy"), invoked constitutional predispositions, and made assumptions about organically grounded instincts, erogenous body zones, and stages of sexual maturation. Freud, himself a neurologist of distinction, even asserted that behind the analyst stood the man with the syringe. But the psychoanalytic physiology, as it grew beyond Freud's control, was increasingly a pseudophysiology. Biological man was for all practical purposes constant in the psychoanalytic equation, and "psychological" events (leanings, communications, fantasies, motives, defense mechanisms, etc.) were the variables.

Most of the currently prominent "organic" methods of treatment were developed after psychoanalysis reached its theoretical maturity. In 1927 psychiatry had little else to offer in treatment beyond psychological (including psychoanalytic) methods for the well-to-do and custodial care (eked out by sedatives, hydrotherapy, and work therapy) for the poor. The insulin coma treatment for schizophrenia was introduced about 1930 and metrazol convulsive therapy in 1936; electroshock was not developed until 1938 (and all of these treatments were first publicly described in Europe). Psychosurgery was seriously developed in Portugal about 1935 and in this country in 1936. Psychopharmacology, hitherto a somewhat exotic specialty, began to flourish only during World War II. The use of drugs for abreaction of emotional conflict in combat neuroses became prominent during the early years of the war; and the intensive study of the psychotomimetic drugs (principally hallucinogens) and their experimental use for therapeutic purposes has developed chiefly since World War II. The new tranquilizing (or "ataractic") drugs were first offered to the medical profession in 1952, and the energizers (or "psychostimulants") have come even later.

Basic science contributions, apart from psychoanalytic theory, were equally uninspiring in 1927. Inspired by the discovery of the role of syphilis in paretic psychoses, early speculations about the role of focal infection in the etiology of the other psychoses were failing to find clinical confirmation. Berger's first report on the use of the electroencephalograph (EEG) for recording "brain waves" (electrical potentials originating in the cerebral cortex and in other parts of the brain as well) was not published in Germany until 1929; not until 1935 did American scientists publish confirmatory findings. Clinical chemistry had only in the preceding fifteen years developed the basic techniques for analysis of small samples of blood; prior to World War I, investigations of human metabolic processes had had to depend largely on studies of diet and urine, because the quantities of blood required for chemical analysis were so large as to prohibit their use as routine clinical procedures. The application of these new techniques of blood analysis to problems of psychiatric research, and the biochemical findings based on their use, came almost entirely after 1927. Thus, for instance, endocrinology was still in its infancy in 1927. The importance of hormones of the adrenal cortex, which play a role in regulating the carbohydrate metabolism and the balance of mineral electrolytes in the body fluids, and which in excess can precipitate psychotic states, was not realized until the late 1920s. Research in that area was so slow in diffusing into other branches of knowledge that as late as 1944, in a widely read two volume symposium entitled *Personality and the Behavior Disorders* (Hunt 1944), the adrenal cortex is given one paragraph (and no mention in the index). Thus Selye's first publication on the celebrated stress or general adaptation syndrome concept was first published in *Nature* in 1936 (*vide* Selye 1956); and the "cortisone psychoses" did not even exist until cortisone was isolated, synthesized, and finally used in the treatment of arthritis about 1945. Franz Kallmann's early report on his genetic studies of schizophrenia utilizing pairs of identical twins was published in 1938 (Kallmann 1938). The more modern theories of nerve impulse transmission emerged during and after World War II, some of them stimulated by investigations into the action of the so-called "nerve gases" by the Army Chemical Center.

But there is no reason to continue the demonstration farther. The major point is clear: a large part of the modern knowledge of the physiological parameters of the behavior of the central nervous system in man has been accumulated since the original conceptual structure of the culture and personality viewpoint was built by Sapir, Mead, and other pioneer scholars. Whole literatures, rivaling in size the entire body of culture and personality writings, now exist on such topics as the relation between the adrenal hormones and mental function, the localization of labor in the brain as revealed by electroencephalographic and derivative techniques, and the effects of drugs on mood and cognitive process. And the major portion of all of these fields of knowledge had been contributed well after culture and personality committed itself to a functional approach.

As yet, the various special lines of the new organic approach have not achieved synthesis either among themselves or with the (actually older) psychosocial tradition in psychiatry and the social sciences. Nevertheless, a general philosophy would seem to animate the approach and to determine the nature of any future synthesis with the functional position. The philosophy would seem to reside in four principles:

1. Statements about "behavior," "mind," "personality," "psyche," "mental illness," and other "psychological" entities are statements about physical systems which include brain (for the brain *is* the mind).
2. Any physical dysfunction of brain implies some mental dysfunction.
3. Some physical dysfunctions will produce disorganizations of neural systems most of whose components will remain individually undamaged.
4. Most cases of chronic, and many of acute, behavior disorders (including the functional psychoses) are the symptomatic consequences of chronic, or acute, physical dysfunctions of brain.

The reader will note that the organic approach, as thus stated, does not claim that every socially undesirable mental state, attitude, or motive necessarily implies a physical dysfunction; thus, evidences of hostility and anxiety, "neurotic" defenses, suicide, antisocial acting out, and so forth may in principle be produced by brains which function perfectly well but have been subjected to environmental pressures (including faulty communication) to which these "symptoms" are "normal" responses. But the organic approach would differ from the functional approach in claiming that an adequately functioning brain will be able to adapt to, or reduce, environmental pressures, and that *chronic* mental dysfunctions are therefore preponderantly the consequence of a chronic physical dysfunction which existed prior to, or independently of, the organism's embarrassment by environmental pressures. A radical functional theory, by contrast, would ascribe a far smaller role to organic factors as causal agents in all except the gross and obvious types of organic brain damage; but most functionalists would probably concede that chronic psychogenic stress can on occasion elicit physiological alterations, sometimes irreversible, which aggravate functional mental disorders (just as chronic psychogenic stress can lead to non-mental organic disorders such as duodenal ulcer).

More specifically the organic approach can be divided into such main topical areas as:

1. The study of the anatomy and physiology of the central nervous system (including the autonomic system) considered as an entity.
2. The study of the localization and organization of labor in brain (including the logical structure of nerve nets).
3. The study of nerve and nerve impulse.
4. The study of the relation of metabolic (including digestive, excretory, circulatory, endocrine, and intracellular biochemical) processes to cerebral function.
5. The study of the genetics of mental disorders.
6. The study of the effect of hypoxia, hypoglycemia, and electrolyte imbalance on cerebral function and the various processes responsible for hypoxia, hypoglycemia, and electrolyte imbalance.
7. Psychopharmacology (including the study of tranquilizers, energizers, and psychotomimetic agents).
8. The study of the effect of nutritional variables on cerebral function.
9. The study of the shock therapies (principally insulin coma and electroshock).
10. The search for blood fractions containing suspected psychopathogenic (toxic) substances spontaneously produced by the body.

The disciplines involved in these and other studies of psychopathology range from mathematical physics and computer design, through such laboratory sciences as physical chemistry, biochemistry, clinical chemistry, physiology, experimental psychology, and neuropsychiatry, to those areas of anthropology and sociology which can contribute data, method, or theory to organically oriented investigations.

A major problem in the organic approach has, of course, been its relative insularity from psychosocial knowledge (this has not been a problem of the functional approach alone). Accordingly a major need of both approaches is a better understanding of how knowledge and speculation concerning the physical aspects of human systems can best be related to knowledge and speculation concerning the psychological and social aspects of these systems. This is imperative because, although cases of mental illness are usually first identified in the community by laymen using social criteria rather than criteria of physical science, and although some part of the total disease process is invariably a function of social system interacting with individual personality, if the development of many of these cases is dependent on organic processes, then very careful analysis must be made of the interaction of social and organic events. And anthropology, by both theory and field investigation, can contribute significantly to the advancement of this kind of analysis.

AN ILLUSTRATIVE PROBLEM: PIBLOKTOQ

In its simplest form, the problem faced by anthropological theory in the area of mental illness can be illustrated by the syndrome *pibloktoq*[1] among the Polar Eskimo of the Thule District of northern Greenland. The classic course of the syndrome, as judged from cases described by various travelers in the north (MacMillan 1934; Peary 1907; Rasmussen and Rasmussen 1915; Whitney 1911) and from photographs of one attack (American Museum of Natural History 1914), is as follows:

1. *Prodrome.* In some cases a period of hours or days is reported during which the victim seems to be mildly irritable or withdrawn.
2. *Excitement.* Suddenly, with little or no warning, victims, mostly women, become wildly excited. They may tear off clothing, break furniture, shout obscenely, throw objects, eat feces, or perform other irrational acts. Usually they finally leave shelter and run frantically onto tundra or ice pack, plunge into snowdrifts, climb onto icebergs, and may actually place themselves in considerable danger, from which pursuing persons usually rescue them, however. Excitement may persist for a few minutes up to about half an hour.
3. *Convulsions and Stupor.* The excitement is succeeded by convulsive seizures in at least some cases, by collapse, and finally by stuporous sleep or coma lasting for up to twelve hours.

4. *Recovery.* Following an attack, the victim behaves perfectly normally; there is amnesia for the experience. Some victims have repeated attacks; others are not known to have had more than one.

The epidemiological parameters seem to be:

1. *Geographical. Pibloktoq* (or, in Danish usage, *Perdlerorpoq*) is known to occur among the Polar Eskimo of the Thule District. Whether the same syndrome (whatever it is called) occurs elsewhere is uncertain. Hoygaard, in a dietary and medical study of the Angmagssalik Eskimo in 1936–37, reported that "*Hysterical fits* accompanied by strong mental and physical excitation were frequent, especially in women" (Hoygaard 1941:72). It does not seem to have been noted, however, among Canadian or Alaskan Eskimo, nor is it certain that it occurs in Asia or northern Europe. Thus we can only say that it *certainly* occurs in northwest Greenland; that it *probably* occurs elsewhere in Greenland; and that it *may* occur anywhere in the world. Whether or not the syndrome is to be considered a uniquely arctic or even Polar Eskimo affliction depends on whether it is a unique disease.

2. *Seasonal.* Reports describe cases occurring at all seasons of the year but cases are said to be fewer in the summer.

3. *Historical.* As might be expected, since the Thule Eskimo were not visited by white men until 1818, the case notes and descriptions are recent, the best of them dating from the time of Peary's visits to the Polar Eskimo in the first decade of the twentieth century. Detailed accounts have been provided by Peary (1907), MacMillan (1934), Knud and Niels Rasmussen (1915), and Gussow (1960), and others familiar with the Polar Eskimo. It is probable, however, that the disorder is fairly ancient in the area. As early as the mid-eighteenth century, northwest Greenlanders (possibly including the Polar Eskimo) were reported to be peculiarly subject to the "falling sickness." And in the 1850's the crew of Elisha Kane's icebound ship, twice wintering north of Thule, were afflicted by a strange "epileptotetanoidal disease" which, in combination with scurvy, killed at least two men, incapacitated others, and rendered their dogs worthless (Kane, 1856). "Epileptotetanoidal" is a reasonably accurate descriptive phrase for *pibloltoq*.

4. *Frequency. Pibloltoq* can apparently reach epidemic proportions: eight of seventeen Eskimo women associated with Peary's 1908 expedition

were afflicted during one winter season; other observers have claimed that at certain times cases could be seen almost every day in a single village.

5. *Racial Nonspecificity.* As was noted above, several probable cases of *pibloktoq* among scorbutic whites were observed by Kane and Hayes in the 1850's in the same region.

6. *Possible Species Nonspecificity.* "Fits" among sled dogs, with social withdrawal, snarling, fighting, and convulsive seizures, but usually ending in death, are said to be regarded by Eskimo as the same syndrome and are given the same name, *pibloktoq,* as the human attacks.

THE HYSTERIA HYPOTHESIS

The major psychological explanation of the *pibloktoq* syndrome has been psychoanalytic. In 1913 A. A. Brill, Freud's self-appointed American apostle, wrote a paper on the subject based on a reading of one of Peary's books and on personal discussion with Donald MacMillan, the naval officer who accompanied Peary (Brill 1913). Brill considered the syndrome to be classic hysteria major. Following a somewhat simplified Freudian model, he interpreted the seizures as expressions of frustration at lack of love and cited as the type case a female who displayed particularly flamboyant attacks. This attractive young woman had not succeeded in getting a husband because she was a poor seamstress; she was consequently frustrated in her emotional need for love in all but the most crudely physical sense. More recently, Gussow (1960) has extended Brill's formulation, interpreting the hysterical flight as a seductive maneuver, an "invitation to be pursued," in persons whose chronic insecurities have been mobilized by some precipitating loss or fear of loss, and who seek loving reassurance in a "primitive and infantile, but characteristically Eskimo, manner." Indeed, he feels that such reactions are a manifestation of the basic Eskimo personality. The greater frequency of *pibloktoq* in women he explains culturally as the result of "the socially subservient position of women . . . and their added helplessness in the face of culturally traumatic experiences." The nudity is in part explained by the common tendency of Eskimo to undress indoors and to chill the naked body out of doors after the sweat bath. The glossolalia, mimetic behavior, shouting, weeping, and singing sometimes observed he also explains culturally by pointing out that these behaviors are found in shamanistic performances and religious ceremonies, not only among the Eskimo, but also in Korea. The flight is considered to be a hysterically motivated invitation to be taken care of, rather than a component of an involuntary psychomotor seizure pattern, because no cases of flight have been reported in which the victim was not seen, followed, and rescued. The asserted tendency for *piblokloq* to occur in winter is illuminated by the observation "that winter, more than other seasons, intensifies Eskimo insecurity—and hence their proneness to derangement—through increased threat of starvation, high rate of accidents, fear of the future, and so forth."

These psychoanalytic and psychocultural explanations, however, are for several reasons not entirely satisfying. Nudity, for instance, is indeed culturally prefigured, since it is the only means of reducing body temperature in persons who have no clothes to wear other than heavy furs in poorly ventilated dwellings where the temperature may rise to over 100° F. But this suggests that the denudation may be merely a response to a sudden somatic sensation of extreme heat. The fact that most reported victims of hysterical flight were rescued from danger without injury may obviously be an artifact of observation: any victims who froze, drowned, lost themselves, were carried away on drifting ice, fell and died alone in the snow, and so on, would by definition be those who were not observed. Furthermore, in at least one case, a rescued woman *was* injured; she suffered a frozen hand and breast, a serious condition in the absence of European medical technology. Two of Kane's men died and the dogs often die. Glossolalia, singing, and so forth are hardly evidence for an influence of *Eskimo* culture on the form of this hysteria, since these behaviors are virtually pandemic. The evidences of extreme physiological stress (bloodshot eyes, flushing of face, foaming at mouth, convulsive movements) and the demented behavior (attempting to walk on the ceiling, eating of feces, and ineffectual destructiveness) are not prefigured in the culture. And finally, the Eskimo are not reported to explain these fits (in contrast to psychotic disorders) by supernatural theories of disease (such as possession, witchcraft, punishment for taboo violation, or soul loss) but seem to regard them as natural ailments, experienced by dogs and men alike, comparable perhaps to the common cold, the broken limb, and other ills that the flesh is heir to. This phlegmatic response would not provide very much in the way of reward for a hysterical fit

THE CALCIUM DEFICIENCY HYPOTHESIS

An alternative, and in part biological, hypothesis can be suggested which explains *pibloktoq* with at least equal plausibility. Low concentrations of ionized calcium in the blood (hypocalcemia) produce a neuromuscular syndrome known as tetany which is often complicated by emotional and cognitive disorganization. The neurological symptoms of tetany include characteristic muscular spasms of hands, feet, throat, face, and other musculature, and in severe attacks, major convulsive seizures. The tetanic syndrome may be precipitated by trivial stimuli and is usually brief and sporadic rather than continuous (continuous tetany may of course be fatal). Although the information available in the photographs and literature is not sufficient in itself to establish the diagnosis, the symptoms of *pibloktoq* are compatible with the clinical picture of hypocalcemic tetany, and several authorities have suggested the calcium deficiency hypothesis (Hoygaard 1941:72; Baashuus-Jensen 1935:344, 388; and Alexander Leighton in a personal communication). Observation and testing in the field would be required to confirm the hypocalcemic hypothesis and to rule out alternative diagnoses (hypoglycemic shock, hysteria, food poisoning, virus, encephalitis, etc.).[2] It is also possible that a tendency toward epilepsy may have been genetically determined by inbreeding in this small isolated group; this is suggested by reports that epilepsy is more common in northern Greenland than elsewhere on the island. The hypocalcemia and epilepsy theories are not mutually exclusive, however, since hypocalcemia probably would tend to precipitate a latent seizure in persons prone to epilepsy. Observation and testing for differential diagnosis would require both the eliciting of neurological signs in victims during attack, or in persons with a history of attacks, and blood tests on victims and on samples of *pibloktoq*-prone and *pibloktoq*-free persons for serum calcium, serum potassium, and possibly other constituents.

The plausibility of the calcium deficiency hypothesis is supported not merely by the opinions of certain authorities and by the compatibility of the *pibloktoq* syndrome with the syndrome of hypocalcemic tetany, however. It is also suggested by indirect evidence, both medical and ecological.

Medically, the Eskimo of Greenland (including the Thule District) are characterized by a proneness to hemorrhage and slow coagulation (Hoygaard 1941:83–85, and Cook 1894:172). Such a tendency toward bleeding might conceivably be associated with low serum calcium levels (although vitamin K deficiency is more likely to lead to this condition). At Angmagssalik, convulsions in infants, suggestive of hypocalcemic tetany, were reported by Hoygaard to be frequent (Hoygaard 1941:78, 135), and Bertelsen noted in a medical report on the Greenland Eskimo that there was a high frequency of cramps, especially of the legs, even in adults (Bertelsen 1940:216). These observations are reminiscent of the account by Kane of the "strange epilepto-tetanoidal disease" which incapacitated his crew north of Smith Sound in the 1850's. He diagnosed two fatal cases of "tetanus" displaying laryngospasm (these could have been actually hypocalcemic tetany going into *status eclampticus*), two fatal cases of the "epilepto-tetanoidal disease," and numerous cases of cramps and muscular pains, sometimes accompanied by "mental symptoms" of disorientation and confusion, both in dogs and man (Kane 1856).

Ecologically, it may without hesitation be stated that the high arctic environment does not provide rich sources of nutritionally available calcium during all seasons of the year to technologically primitive populations. Hoygaard found that nearly half of the annual calcium intake at Angmagssalik was provided by dried capelin (the bones of dried capelin being edible). When dried capelin was available, the calcium intake was low but above the level asserted by medical authorities to be the minimum for maintenance of health. But without dried capelin (a circumstance which periodically occurred as a result of unavailability of the fish or unsuitability of the weather for drying them), calcium intake dropped well below the minimum (Hoygaard 1941). Rodahl also found the dietary of certain Alaskan Eskimo groups to be relatively low in calcium (Rodahl 1957). At Thule, although no careful dietary studies have been found, it is reported that little fishing is done because fish are sparse and consequently capelin is not caught in substantial quantity. Probably substituting for dried capelin, however, are birds—the "little auks"—which, after storage in seal oil, can be eaten whole, including, apparently, some of the bones (MacMillan 1918). A further ecological complication may be a product of the high latitude itself. Man requires a certain quantity of vitamin D_3 in order to absorb and utilize dietary calcium efficiently (and possibly also to metabolize carbohydrate efficiently). This vitamin is formed in the human and animal skin when ultraviolet light activates certain cholesterol-containing oils. In the high arctic, however, a combination of low sun angle during summer, a long period of winter darkness, and the need for heavy clothing during most of the year, must prevent the human body from synthesizing much of its own vitamin D_3. Whether sufficient vitamin D_3 can be secured from sea fauna at this latitude is uncertain. Seal oil contains significant quantities of vitamin D_3 but, at Thule, the fish oils rich in vitamin D_3, such as cod liver oil, are probably not a major source of supply because of the aforementioned lightness of fishing in that region. To summarize the ecological problem briefly, even if sufficient vitamin D_3 is available to allow maximum efficiency in calcium absorption and utilization, it is still highly probable that some people, at some seasons of the year, will be unable to secure sufficient dietary calcium to meet published medical standards. If such a low calcium intake were coupled with a high protein and high potassium intake, the neurological consequences would be intensified, and the heavy meat consumption of Polar Eskimo entails a large intake of protein and potassium.

One fact, however, militates against a simple dietary calcium deficiency hypothesis: the reported extreme rarity of rickets in Eskimo infants and of osteomalacia in Eskimo adults (for example, in pregnant and lactating women) (Bertelsen 1940). These are diseases in which, as a consequence of inadequate calcium intake or utilization, or both, the bones yield their calcium to the blood and, eventually, to the urine, with the sufferer thus gradually losing calcium from the body at the expense of bony tissue. In temperate latitudes, rickets and osteomalacia are normally forestalled by milk, sunlight, and supplementary vitamin D_3 preparations in cod liver oil and vitamin pills. If one hypothesizes that the Eskimo diet is low in calcium, and perhaps in sun-formed vitamin D_3, how is it that rickets is not evident? The answer to this question requires another hypothesis concerning hormonal function. It would seem that if calcium and/or vitamin D_3 intake is chronically low in the high arctic environment, then the Eskimo physiology must for generations have been forced to "choose" between tetany and rickets—and, unlike more southerly populations, it has "chosen" tetany as the lesser of two evils. (More precisely, of course, it is the environment which has selected the better-fitted physiological alternative.) Rickets and osteomalacia would in a primitive Eskimo economy be fatal because they are physically crippling. Sporadic attacks of tetany, even if occasionally damaging or even fatal, would be by comparison merely an annoyance. Hence the hypocalcemia hypothesis requires the corollary that the Polar and perhaps other Eskimo tend to be mildly hypoparathyroid (or, more exactly, again, that in this cultural-ecological matrix, optimum parathyroid function requires a lower activity than does optimum function under the conditions of European and American medical practice). Such a mild "hypoparathyroidism" would be conceived as a product of natural selection for primitive life in an arctic environment, yielding a type of hormonal balance which retains calcium in the bones even if calcium levels in serum fall occasionally. There is, as a matter of fact, some evidence to support this hypothesis. The doomed medieval Norsemen, not preadapted to a high arctic environment, who settled along the west coast of Greenland, and who finally died out and were replaced by ricketless Eskimo, *did* suffer from rickets and osteomalacia (Maxwell 1930:20).

But if we propose a hypocalcemia hypothesis, do we ignore Eskimo culture? Certainly not. Consideration of cultural factors is, in fact, already implicit in the hypothesis as enunciated. This hypothesis rests on the assumption that the subsistence technology is "primitive," that is, in this application of the concept, that manufactured vitamins and imported or specially processed calcium-containing foods are not available and that, to hunters, a strong and undistorted skeletal structure is of greater survival value than freedom from occasional attacks of tetany. These cultural characteristics render the population vulnerable to a local dietary calcium and/or vitamin D_3 shortage and select the nervous and muscular system rather than the skeleton as the target tissue of any calcium and/or vitamin D_3 nutritional deficiency.

But Eskimo culture also functions to minimize, within the limits stated above, the frequency and severity of attacks, *via* the customs of securing, processing, and storing of large quantities of calcium-containing birds (the "little auks"); of obtaining, preserving, and making extensive use of vitamin-D_3-containing seal oils; of stripping and exposing the body to direct sunlight whenever the weather permits; of weaning children late (thus ensuring them maximal calcium intake in mother's milk during the rickets-vulnerable period of infancy); of securing to pregnant women (who are particularly vulnerable to osteomalacia) and children preferred access to fresh and stored foods high in calcium (specifically, the little auks and whatever dried fish are available) by making women and children chiefly responsible for netting the birds and collecting the eggs, and (to judge from taboos reported from Eskimo groups other than Thule) by maintaining food taboos which have the effect at certain times of substantially restricting the pregnant or lactating mother to the use of dried fish, birds, or other stored foods high in calcium.

It is possible that, apart from its role in etiology, Eskimo custom also affects the details of overt symptomatology. Conceivably the frequently reported impetuous flight from the group during the initial phases of an attack may reflect a personality trait common among Eskimo: withdrawal from, rather than aggression in, a situation when the individual's confidence in his ability to master it has been shaken. Such a tendency may be reflected in the tendency for Eskimo men to abandon kayak hunting if their confidence has once been disturbed ("kayak-phobia"); by the practice of *kiviktoq,* or "going into the mountains" to live a hermit's life, in men and women alike who feel rejected by their communities; by the reported willingness of the aged and infirm to be abandoned to die; and by the anxiousness of Eskimo parents not to disturb the confidence of their children, even when playing dangerously, by frustrating negative commands. Such a psychological interpretation—which is, in a sense, directly contradictory to the hysteria hypothesis—rests on the assumption that any incipient neurological dysfunction is susceptible to different interpretations by the victim and his associates and can therefore precipitate different overt responses, depending on particular customs of the individual and group.

And finally, with regard to its handling of cases of *pibloktoq,* Eskimo custom obviously plays a very important role. An attack of *pibloktoq* is not automatically taken as a sign of the individual's general incompetency. Victims are, if necessary, prevented from injuring themselves or others; otherwise they are left alone while the attack spends itself. The attack may be the subject of good-humored joking later but is not used to justify restriction of the victim's social participation. There is, in other words, little or no stigma; the attack is treated as an isolated event rather than as a symptom of deeper illness. Such a phlegmatic approach would seem well calculated once again to minimize any damage to the individual's personal confidence and thus would work to forestall the development of chronic psychological invalidism. The impact on chronicity of differential handling of such episodic disorders is well illustrated in the history of American combat psychiatry, which between World War II and the Korean War achieved a 50 percent reduction in the rate of chronic psychoneurosis developing out of combat breakdown simply by refusing to treat the breakdown as a symptom of illness (Glass 1953).

IMPLICATIONS OF THE ALTERNATIVE THEORIES

Two alternative armchair theories of *pibloktoq* have been presented. Although the "organic" (hypocalcemia) theory seems preferable, the organic theory is just as much concerned with analysis of cultural factors as is the "psychological" (hysteria) theory. In order to choose between the two, field investigation will be necessary. Such field investigation will have considerable significance for anthropological theories of mental illness (and professional psychiatric theory, for that matter). For not only will it contribute to the solution of a particular—and to some eyes, perhaps, an unnecessarily exotic—diagnostic problem, it will also bear on two major theoretical issues.

One of these major issues is the understanding of hysteria itself. As is well known, psychoanalysis was originally conceived as a means for treating hysteria, and upon the analysis of cases diagnosed as hysteria much of its theoretical structure has been erected. Since Freud's time, hysteria has become a rare disorder in most of Europe and America. This may be the consequence of culturally determined changes in modal personality structure in Western countries and in preferences for various styles of psychosomatic expression. It may also be the result of changes in diagnostic practice (it has been suggested, for instance, that "hysteria has vanished right into the diagnosis of epilepsy" (Peterson 1950)). And it may be the result of culturally determined changes in such matters as style of dress and housing, hours of work, methods of lighting, and diet, which could affect, in particular, calcium intake and utilization in persons vulnerable to tetany and rickets. Certainly rickets has become more rare in precisely those groups once most prone to grand hysteria: the Western European urban populations. But now we are suggesting that at least one type of hysteria (the "grand hysterical attack") may not be purely psychogenic!

Such an implication demands support by way of empirical investigation—an investigation which, in fact, takes up again an abortive line of inquiry into the relationship between tetany and hysteria that began in Europe before the psychoanalytic theories of hysteria swept competing approaches from the field (Barrett 1919–1920:385–386). It is of more than antiquarian interest to recall that between 1880 and 1895 there was a veritable endemic of tetany among the working class of Vienna, Paris, and other European cities (Shelling 1935:115–116). This plague of tetany was, at the time, not understood etiologically, for the role of calcium in tetany had not been established. During the same period, the work of French and Viennese neuropsychiatrists on hysteria was being pursued most intensively, and it culminated, as everyone knows, in Freud and Breuer's *Studies in Hysteria,* which was published in 1895 after a preliminary publication in 1893. This study revealed the psychological connection between the hysterical symptom and traumatic emotional conflict and suggested a technique of "talking" therapy which soon developed into the method of psychoanalysis. We might now ask, however, whether the physiological milieu of hypocalcemia may not have been a conditioning factor in hysteria. The most serious endemics of rickets and of hypocalcemic tetany—determined by constraints of custom and/or economy on food, dress, interior lighting, working hours, and access to open spaces not only among working people but among all classes in late nineteenth-century Europe—came at precisely the same time that hysteria reached its peak as a psychiatric problem. The discovery of the value of sunlight, milk, and vitamin-D_3-containing foods, and the general amelioration of social conditions, during the early twentieth century, was accompanied by a drastic reduction in the frequencies of rickets, of tetany, and of hysteria. Thus we may suggest, as a hypothesis for medicohistorical investigation, that the hysterical attack and perhaps even hysterical conversion will occur most readily in persons with low levels of serum ionized calcium and that chronically low levels may maintain a neurophysiological milieu in which either tetany, hysterical attacks, hyper-suggestibility, or hysterical learning of conversion symptoms is sooner or later inevitable, the choice of disorder depending on various conditioning factors of situation, personal history, and biochemical individuality.

Suggesting that the late-nineteenth-century European hysterias may have been in considerable proportion undiagnosed cases of serum calcium deficiency raises a major issue in psychiatric theory, for psychoanalysis was founded on the analysis of hysterics. In view of this fact, it may be well to evaluate further the culture-historical dimensions of the issue. The late-nineteenth-century students of hysteria—including Freud—were aware that hysterics might display unusual physiological profiles as well as disordered behavior, and some felt that hereditary predisposition played a role in the pathogenesis of the disease. But these psychiatrists of the 1890's were in somewhat the same position vis à vis physiological explanations of hysteria as the anthropologists of the 1920's were vis à vis explanations of psychopathology in general: physiological investigations had not advanced far enough to provide a base for framing testable physiological hypotheses.

Thus the first demonstration that tetany was associated with reduced concentration of calcium in the blood was not made until 1908; hitherto the diagnosis depended on the finding of positive neurological signs. Not until 1921 did the development of micrometric methods of determining quantities of serum calcium make possible widespread testing for serum calcium level (Shelling 1935: 114–116). Differential diagnosis in certain cases between hysteria and tetany was extremely difficult, and in fact probably was arbitrary, before the development of the serum calcium and tetany hypothesis and the provision of appropriate methods of clinical chemistry. Consequently, some cases which today would probably be regarded as unequivocally tetany (e.g., the tetanic syndrome following thyroidectomy) were in 1904 diagnosed as mixtures of tetany and hysteria (*cf.* Curschmann 1904). Thus it is *impossible* that Freud could have considered the possibility that hysteria might be a symptomatic consequence of low serum calcium. The cultural milieu in which he worked had not provided him with the concepts or tools by which the question could have been asked or answered. Inasmuch as we cannot return to the nineteenth century to do serum calcium determinations on Freud's original patients, we cannot say what the results would have been, nor can we estimate the impact on the development of psychoanalysis if the findings had been positive. But at least we have still another historical answer to the question "Why has hysteria virtually disappeared in Europe and the United States?" Our (metaphorical) answer is, "It dissolved in bottles of milk and cod-liver oil—that is to say, the cultural changes associated with an appreciation of the importance of sunlight, vitamin D_3, milk, and various other factors for maintaining proper calcium balance, together with a general improvement of nutritional standards, has virtually eliminated (except in certain rare medical conditions) a total syndrome, one symptom cluster of which was once (and still is) called tetany, and another symptom cluster of which was once (but no longer is) called "grand hysterical attack."

The need for empirical evidence bearing on the hypotheses outlined above leads immediately to a consideration of the second major issue: the larger theoretical structure which should guide such an investigation. It is evident that even if it is possible to identify a specific physiological variable as the *precipitant* of the overt symptomatology, an adequate explanation of the frequency of the syndrome in the population, its geographical range, its racial and species distribution, its seasonal variation, its history, and the severity and details of form of the symptoms themselves, must depend on evaluating other variables, physiological, psychological, and cultural. It is the interaction of these other variables with the immediately precipitating physiological variable which provides the necessary and sufficient conditions for a type of mental illness to occur in a particular group with a particular frequency. We have already suggested some of these conditions in the *pibloktoq* analysis. Let us now turn our attention to the development of a frame of reference which can guide the refinement of theory and the acquisition of relevant empirical data. We shall begin, in the next section, with a further discussion of a point introduced in the *pibloktoq* analysis: the importance of the "theory of illness" in the formation of a symptomatic structure. And finally we shall attempt to generalize the line of thought represented in the *pibloktoq* analysis, and in the following discussion, into a rough model of a biocultural approach to mental illness.

THE IMPORTANCE OF CULTURALLY INSTITUTIONALIZED THEORIES OF ILLNESS AS DETERMINANTS OF RESPONSE TO ORGANICALLY BASED PSYCHOPATHOLOGY

Mental illness is an episode in a life program, usually following a more or less extended period of normalcy (as defined by both the person and his community), and terminated either by death or by a return (temporary perhaps) to normalcy. In the biocultural model, a conjunction of pathogenic, organic, and psychological events is considered to abort a life program normal to the society by crippling the victim's apparatus for cognitive organization. With the onset of the physiologically determined desemantication (reduced cognitive organization capacity) the victim is unable to organize his perceptions, his motives, and his actions meaningfully so as to satisfy his own wishes without frustrating those of others or vice versa. His more or less desperate efforts to protect himself from the consequences which he expects to follow the drastic reduction of cognitive capacity are apt to be the most conspicuous symptoms of the disorder: withdrawal, aggression, paranoid delusion, and the bizarre use of the familiar mechanisms of defense like repression, sublimation, denial, etc. And simultaneously, the victim's community is responding to this overt symptomatology with its own procedures of withdrawal, aggression, therapy, and so forth.

What will determine the victim's and the community's expectations of consequences and their choices of defensive strategy? Evidently the frequency, duration, and predictability of periods of desemantication, and their commonness in the population, will be data of extreme importance in the evaluation of self by the victim and of victim by community. If the period of desemantication is relatively brief (not more than a few days), is relatively infrequent (not more than once a month), is predictable (either by a calendrical device or by association with other scheduled events), and is commonly observed to occur in others without dire consequences, then even severe degrees of desemantication with considerable associated inconvenience and discomfort may be tolerated by the personality. Similarly, brief, infrequent, predictable, and common overt disorders may be tolerated by the community. Such situations (to give some familiar examples) are premenstrual tension, drug and alcoholic intoxication, ritually induced dissociation, exhaustion, and the Polar Eskimo *pibloktoq*. The more delayed in the life program, the more frequent, the more prolonged, the less predictable, and the less common the event, the more threatening it will be to the personality and to the community, and the more desperate and (for the victim) the more ill conceived their complementary defensive strategies will become. Where the desemantication is severe and irreversible, as in chronic brain syndromes, the victim may be so preoccupied with maintaining the former sense of competence that even trivial *contretemps* precipitate "catastrophic" reactions (Goldstein 1940). Schizophrenia and perhaps the affective psychoses (such as involutional melancholia) would appear to have an intermediate status between chronic syndromes and brief episodic attacks. The desemantication is not fully continuous and the victim is consequently able to retain for a considerable period an intermittent normalcy of function, but the episodes are sufficiently frequent, prolonged, and severe to result in an accumulation of permanent defensive strategies which eventually in themselves make adequate social participation almost impossible during the clear periods, and, sometimes, even after the desemantication phase itself has ended.

But it is not merely the timing and conventionality of the disorder which will affect the defensive response of the victim and his community. The personality of the victim and the culture of the group provide models of the experiences and symptoms of the event which assign to them definite meanings and provide recipes for handling the situation. These models are, in the individual's case, a function of the history of his learnings, and in the community's case, a function of other aspects of the culture, its social structure, and its history. They are widely variable in form and are not entirely predictable from a knowledge of the timing and conventionality of the disorder. While the anthropologist may or may not undertake the solution of problems of differential diagnosis and etiology (which, as we observed earlier, unavoidably involve questions of biological as well as psychological dynamics), he can certainly investigate the patient's and the community's theories of illness and its treatment. Thus his most immediately relevant contribution can be an analysis of how, in the society in question, symptomatology and its programming are normally conceptualized. As we have indicated above, whatever its etiology, the course of an illness occurs in a social matrix and is observed both by the victim and his associates. Their conception of what is happening will play an important part in determining what will be their response to the symptoms (see Wallace 1959a). Thus, even if etiology and the primary symptoms of an illness were, except in an epidemiological inquiry, to be considered as physiological accidents and thus as largely independent of culture, the efforts of the victim and of his fellows to cope with the illness must be recognized as being highly dependent on culture, for these responses to illness are very considerably determined by what may be called the native—and in particular, the patient's—theory of illness. In short, since the cause of illness even if physiologically initiated is progressively modified by feedback via the victim's and the community's conception of the illness, the victim's personality and the community's culture play a determining role.

Some of the recent literature in social psychiatry has directed attention to theory of illness as a significant variable. Of particular interest are the studies of psychiatric illness in New Haven summarized in Hollingshead and Redlich's book *Social Class and Mental Illness* (1958). These studies demonstrate again not only class differentials in prevalence of certain kinds of treated mental illness (for example, that schizophrenia is about nine times as prevalent in the lowest socioeconomic group as in the highest, even after standardizing for population size), but also class differentials in methods of treatment (that is, that lowest class schizophrenics receive either organic treatment or no treatment at all, while highest class schizophrenics receive psychotherapy and/or organic treatment). These differences are doubtless partly a function of differential access to economic resources; but, as Hollingshead and Redlich carefully show, they are also partly a function of differences in the conceptions of illness and of treatment between lower class and higher class patients. Specifically, the dissonance between the lower class patients' and their middle class physicians' theories of what illness is, how it originates, and how it is cured, interferes with free communication. These differences make mutual acceptance, liking, trust, and intelligent cooperation difficult, and often result in either mutual withdrawal or the patient's refusal to enter into a psychotherapeutic relationship at all.

Other sources have approached the problem of theory of illness from various standpoints. Cannon and others, for instance, have analyzed the phenomenon of "voodoo death" as a type of overresponse to a "realistically" trivial trauma by a victim who is convinced that he will die because he has been bewitched by an enemy or doomed for the infraction of some taboo (Cannon 1942). Comparable, if less dramatic, studies have revealed that bodily injuries and mental infirmities of one sort or another lead to different responses depending on the culturally defined meaning of the situation. For instance, in their collection of papers reporting on investigations by the National Institute of Mental Health of the impact of mental illness on the family, Clausen and Yarrow (1955) describe in some detail the differences in the "meaning" of mental illness to various persons, including the patient, and the effect of these semantic positions in shaping the path to, through, and from the mental hospital. In their study of thirty-three families in which the husband was the patient, they found that nearly half of the husbands were never seen by a psychiatrist before hospitalization was arranged. The difficulty, and usually the reluctance, with which the patient's family came to define his problem as one requiring psychiatric care, and the slowness and uncertainty with which they proceeded to secure that care, meant that "discontinuities of action were frequent, and paths to the hospital were beset with obstacles and traumata for husband and wife" (Clausen and Yarrow 1955:32). And in our own research at the Eastern Pennsylvania Psychiatric Institute, we have been concerned with the problem of how the patient's theory of the mechanism of hallucination affects his and his fellows' response to that experience. We have worked with cross-cultural materials in the literature and have pointed out, for instance, the contrast between the responses to mescaline intoxication of normal white volunteers and of American Indian religious peyotists (Wallace 1959b).

A MODEL FOR THE ANALYSIS OF THEORIES OF MENTAL ILLNESS

We conceive that among the set (mazeway) of cognitive "maps" which each individual maintains, describing and interpreting the world as he perceives it, is his theory of mental illness. This map gives meaning to experience, by defining the possible states which a person can occupy in a mental health context, and by relating the possible states which the person can occupy to one another via various transfer mechanisms, so as to provide the rationale for decision. Such a map can therefore be conceived of as having three aspects: (1) the *states* specified; (2) the *transfer mechanisms* which are conceived to effect change from one state to another; and (3) the *program* of illness and recovery which is described by the whole system. We confine our attention here to the patient's program for the patient himself; his programs for other persons, and the program of others for him, may (or may not) be different. Thus in the following analyses the entity to which each state description refers is constant, being ego, even though ego is variable in the sense of having different properties at different stages of the program, and in the sense of being "now" at one or another of these stages in ego's own (not necessarily correct) opinion (interesting possibilities of programs involving multiple referent entities, because of the logical complexities of such schemas, are not considered here).

Evidently, one can "plug in" on an individual's program at a number of different levels of abstraction. In order to minimize partly the unreliability of reporting which ensues if level of abstraction is left unspecified, we have found it useful to base analysis on five "states," which will constitute stages of every program: "normalcy," "upset," "psychosis," "in treatment," and "innovative personality." These are always to be understood as the subject's concepts of his own possible states and not as the observer's concepts of the subject's condition. The terms are unimportant; they simply label positions in the model. *Normalcy* refers to a state in which the person is performing to his own and other's satisfaction the roles appropriate to his situation in society. *Upset* refers to a state where role performance has been reduced to a level of minimal adequacy, with noticeable personal and/or group discomfort. *Psychosis* is a state where role performance has become so inadequate that in order to reduce personal and group discomfort, some degree of social isolation (either self- or group imposed) must be instituted. *In treatment* is a state where the person is receiving ministrations from specialists, designed to remove the conditions responsible for personal and group discomfort, and to return the patient to full social participation. *Innovative personality* is a state in which the person is again able to perform roles to his own and group satisfaction, but roles different to a greater or lesser degree from those performed in state N (as the difference approaches insignificance, P approaches N). These five states may be conceived as arranged in a graph whose starting point is N, with "goodness" of state decreasing in order of position to the right of N:

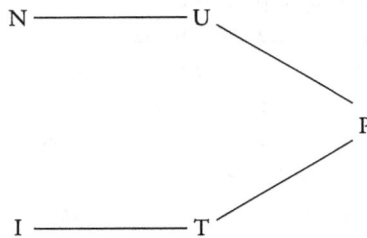

We assume that any individual classification of states will include these five except where concept I is equivalent to N, in which case the graph reduces to:

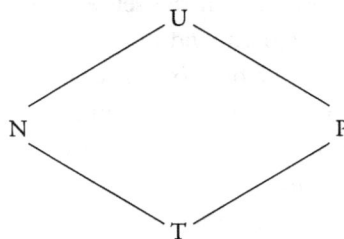

We also assume that between any two states one of four transfer relations may be conceived: no transfer possible (symbolized by open space); one directional transfer($\rightarrow$); one directional transfer($\leftarrow$); and reversible transfer($\leftrightarrow$). Definition of the states and of the transfer mechanisms can usually be best represented not on the graph but in appended tables in order to avoid cluttering the graph with written notations. The reader will note that any two states may stand, in relation to one another, as positive and negative goals depending on their relative position on the value dimension. For instance, U may be a negative goal for a person who is in state N, but a positive goal for a person in state P. And finally, depending on the circumstances, additional states may be added to the model if they are part of the subject individual's or culture's phenomenological world.

A given patient's theory of illness can be inferred from several types of behavior:

1. Plain statements ("It's worrying that makes people lose their minds").
2. Comparative statements ("Joan was real sick when they brought her in, but now that she's been here awhile, she's quieted down a lot").
3. Differential motor behavior (avoiding certain patients while socializing with others).
4. Case history material (information that experiencing hallucinations first convinced the patient that he was seriously ill and required psychiatric help).

These and other data, obtained from tape recorded interviews with the patient and his family and associates, records kept by social workers and therapists, direct observation on the ward, and so on, permit the classification of concepts and beliefs, and the working out of their interrelationships in the subject's mazeway. The investigator must keep constantly in mind that these belief structures can change and (this is often difficult) that it is the subject's (or the community's) belief system, and not the patient's "true" condition as perceived by the clinician, that is being studied (and if the clinician's belief system is being studied, the validity of the clinician's beliefs is technically irrelevant). The tediousness of the task should not be underestimated. A satisfactory case history, for instance, covering day-by-day events for months prior to hospitalization, and during the hospital stay itself, requires extensive checking and cross-checking with dozens of sources of information. The process is comparable to the compilation of data for a biography. Discrete items of information, culled from various sources, are ordered first chronologically and then by topic until an internally coherent process appears in which the subject's decisions and attitudes are demonstrably related to his current situation and past experience. Thus one source may reveal that on a certain date the patient, a ritually faithful Catholic, failed to go to Mass; another source may show that the day before, he had an interview with his priest, who counseled him to exercise will power and to cease wallowing in self-pity; a third source reveals that next week the patient went to his family doctor and received a prescription for tranquilizers; and a fourth source finally shows that some time during the week preceding the visit to the priest, the patient experienced a frightening impulse to kill his wife and child. These details fit into the pattern of a process. With increasing fear of losing self-control, the patient, who still regards his "upset" state as one of moral uncertainty, turns to the priest for help; but the priest's advice does not help to resolve the uncertainty, and he redefines his state as an "illness" requiring medical attention.

ILLUSTRATION: A ZULU THEORY OF MENTAL ILLNESS

Among the Zulu known to Canon Callaway in South Africa, about the middle of the last century, a complex and rather sophisticated theory was held which, in its formal structure, is not dissimilar to some varieties of current psychiatric theory. The structure of this theory is given in the following formula:

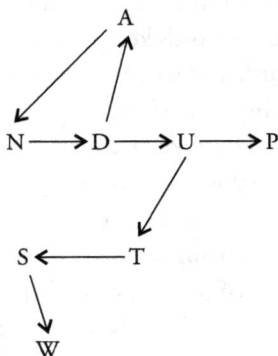

The definition of the states, as given in Callaway's translation of the Zulu text (Callaway 1931) is as follows:

N: "Robust"; good appetite; not choosy about food.
D: "Delicate, not having any real disease, but delicate."
A: "Ill"; choosy about food; loss of appetite; suffers vague pains; anxious dreams; possessed by spirits of ancestors.
U: "Ill"; choosy about food; loss of appetite; suffers vague pains; anxious dreams; possessed by a class of spirits known as *Amatongo*.

P: "A fool," "unable to understand anything," "mad," not a "man."

T: Continued ill health, sleeplessness, loss of weight, skin diseases, but hopeful of becoming a shaman.

S: Good physical health; the state of being a shaman or *inyanga,* i.e., one with a "soft head" who, with the help of his familiar spirits among the *Amatongo,* performs the respectable special role of "diviner" (finder of lost objects and physician to possessed persons).

W: "Always out of health," unable to divine, but of unusual wisdom, and able to work.

The transfer operations, to the extent that they are described in Callaway's text, are:

N→D: Initial possession by either *Amatongo* or ancestral spirits.

D→A: Completion of possession by ancestral spirits.

A→N: Relinquishment of possession by ancestral spirits after being exorcised by sacrifice of cattle under direction of shamans.

D→U: *Amatongo* increase control over victim but divide into two groups, one group (under influence of medicines and cattle sacrifice exorcism) objecting to complete possession and the other insisting on complete possession.

U→P: Continued "blocking the way" of the *Amatongo* by exorcism and by medicines taken by mouth.

U→T: Patient's family, patient, and community, recognize that *Amatongo* are struggling to possess patient, and terminate medicines and exorcism.

T→S: Patient seeks communication with *Amatongo* in his dreams and singing; community participates in his singing and ask him questions for *Amatongo* to answer.

S→W: A "great doctor" can "lay the spirit" of *Amatongo* to the extent of preventing the patient from remaining a diviner but only at the cost of leaving him chronically in state W.

Notable features of the model are, first, the importance of the differential diagnosis (by a shaman) between possession by the relatively benevolent ancestors and by the dangerous *Amatongo;* and second, the irreversible nature of *Amatongo* possession, which eventuates in a state of dementia unless the victim accepts his fate and undergoes the complete course of training as an *inyanga.*

APPLICATION TO CLINICAL CASE MATERIAL

In the application of the foregoing concepts to clinical case material, it must be borne in mind that the structure and development of a patient's theory of illness may be related to, but is nevertheless distinct from, the structure and development of his conflict structure ("neurosis") and of his therapeutic regime. In one of the two cases which we have analyzed in some detail by the help of the model, we found the model to be helpful in understanding a temporary impasse, with an associated flurry of disturbed behavior, reached at a certain stage in therapy. The crucial problem in treatment, from the therapist's viewpoint, was the patient's unwillingness to accept the presence in himself of hostile feelings toward various close relatives. The therapist defined the goal of treatment (I) as a less repressive personality and he encouraged the patient to assert himself and his needs more freely and to recognize that these needs, and the hostilities generated by their frustration, were not evil but merely human. The patient was stubbornly resistant, not merely because of the psychodynamics of the situation, but also because the therapist was suggesting that he "act out" in somewhat the same way as his own psychotic father had acted out before his hospitalization some years before. The therapist thus was suggesting to the patient a state I which, in the patient's theory of illness, was hard to distinguish from P. The patient's conscious attention was, at this time, centered on a struggle to avoid entering state P; hence the therapist's suggestions were terrifying, not only because they may have aroused unconscious resistance (in the conventional psychodynamic sense), but because they pushed him toward a self-identification with a psychotic father.

The resolution of the impasse was provided by his development of a compromise, which the therapist was willing to accept, between his original theory and the therapist's theory. This compromise took the following form:

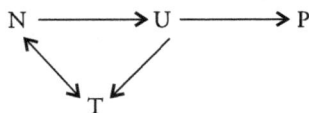

$$N \longrightarrow U \longrightarrow P$$
$$\nwarrow \qquad \nearrow$$
$$\searrow \quad \swarrow$$
$$T$$

He steadfastly retained the belief that the object of his efforts was a return to his normal, presymptomatic, good-husband-and-father self (N). But he accepted T as a necessary way station on the path to N and as a means of avoiding the alternative state P. His acceptance of the existence and value of T was followed almost immediately by release to the outpatient department.

APPLICATION TO THE CLASSIFICATION OF CULTURES

Because of the ubiquity of the major types of mental disease, and because of the uncertainty of etiological understanding, it is hazardous to classify cultures as more or less pathogenic in respect to any particular mental illness or to mental illness in general. In all likelihood, as knowledge of the causes of mental illness is extended, it will become easier to discern the relation between culture and etiology. Thus in the future it may be possible to regard the frequency, distribution, and forms of mental illness in a society as an index of its culture. But at the present time, despite the currency of certain hypotheses based on psychodynamic assumptions about the relation between culture and mental illness, it is not feasible to establish a classification based on demonstrated etiological processes.

It is however reasonable to suggest that cultures may, even on the basis of present knowledge, be classified with respect to such culturally institutionalized responses to various types of mental illness as the society's taxonomy and definitions of mental illness, its theory or theories of illness, and its techniques of therapy and their rationale. Such a classification must, in effect, form a matrix of intersection of a constant typology of mental illness (that is, a typology defined by the investigator and used as a constant referent for controlling cross-cultural comparisons) and of alternatively possible responses available cross-culturally. The types so defined may then be investigated in order to discern whether or not a correlation exists between response type and other aspects of culture. If such correlations can be shown to exist, then at least *response to mental illness* may be considered an index of culture.

Evidently a number of possible schemes, of varying degrees of complexity and abstraction, can be created, based on different constant typologies and different panels of alternative responses. One typological system based on theoretical considerations introduced in the preceding sections will be outlined here. For the constant typology, the two dichotomous dimensions of severity and chronicity rather than Western diagnostic categories will be used (mild versus severe, and intermittent versus continuous). For the response typology, two dichotomous dimensions will be used: episodic versus symptomatic interpretations of illness, and treatment versus extrusion as a method of handling illness. These concepts may be defined further as follows: Mildness and severity refer to the degree of abnormality of the overt behavior itself and not to its duration or frequency of occurrence; intermittency and continuousness refer to halves of a continuum, intermittency being the half in which the disorder can best be characterized as discrete attacks separated by intervals of normalcy, and continuousness as the half in which the disorder can be characterized as a period of uninterrupted dysfunction. Episodic interpretations of illness confine attention only to the overt disorder itself and regard it as an isolated episode in an essentially normal life program, whereas symptomatic interpretations construe the overt disorder as a sign of a more serious underlying inadequacy which threatens to recur, possibly in a more undesirable form, on later occasions. Treatment as a method of handling illness implies a policy of attempting to cure, to improve, or to tolerate (even by ignoring the behavior) and make the best use of the victim, in contrast to the method of extrusion, which by such devices as confinement, banishment, or even execution attempts to rid society entirely of an incompatible participant. The suggested dichotomies are, of course, divisions of continua, and the distinctions are easier to make in extreme than in intermediate cases. Thus a series of epileptic attacks is easy to classify in the constant typology as intermittent and severe, and a case of obsessive fear of heights as mild and continuous; but a given schizophrenic psychosis may be neither clearly continuous nor notably severe, yet seem by contrast with epilepsy and the fear of heights to require the continuous and severe classification.

The whole schema may be represented in the following diagram:

	Intermittent	Continuous
Mild	Episodic *or* Symptomatic Treatment *or* Extrusion	Episodic *or* Symptomatic Treatment *or* Extrusion
Severe	Episodic *or* Symptomatic Treatment *or* Extrusion	Episodic *or* Symptomatic Treatment *or* Extrusion

Thus any group, with respect to any given syndrome, may be classified as episodic-treatment, episodic-extrusion, symptomatic-treatment, or symptomatic-extrusion, within that cell which characterizes the syndrome on the constant typology. If we consider *pibloktoq,* for instance, we would classify this as intermittent-severe in the constant typology, and the Polar Eskimo handling of it as episodic-treatment in the response typology. The same syndrome in the context of, let us say, an operational wing of the U.S. Strategic Air Command would also be classified as intermittent-severe, but the handling of the condition would be classified as symptomatic-extrusion. And, again, this same intermittent-severe syndrome in the context of a liberal arts college campus would be handled either as episodic-treatment or symptomatic-treatment.

The number of possible cultural patterns established by this paradigm is quite large. Although, with regard to any single syndrome only four types of response are considered, there are four types of syndrome, with regard to each of which these four possibilities exist. Therefore the number of possible cultural patterns is 4^4 or 256. Furthermore, of course, any *description* of the way in which a society handles mental disorders will make many distinctions, even of a classificatory kind, that cannot be included in a pattern classification scheme. Thus, for instance, with respect to the "treatment" class, it will be noted in any description whether the condition in question is ignored, is recognized but tolerated, or is directly approached by a means of therapy. If therapy is employed, it can be medical (physiological) or psychological; and if psychological, it can be secular or religious, cathartic or repressive, and so on. Rather than attempt to embrace all of the 256 patterns, let alone the further elaborations and refinements desirable for any sort of descriptive account, therefore, it would appear to be useful to note that among the large number of possible patterns, several stand out as stock patterns which may be used for the purpose of seeking to establish whether or not, in principle, correlations may exist between a group's manner of handling behavior disorder and other aspects of its culture.

Four such ideal pattern types are offered below:

	Inc.	Cont.	Inc.	Cont.	Inc.	Cont.	Inc.	Cont.
Mild	Sy Ex	Sy Ex	Ep Tr	Sy Tr	Sy Tr	Sy Tr	Sy Tr	Sy Tr
Severe	Sy Ex	Sy Ex	Ep Tr	Sy Ex	Sy Ex	Sy Ex	Sy Tr	Sy Tr
	I		II		III		IV	

It is suggested—with the hope not so much that the suggestions will convince as provoke thought and consideration in empirical studies—that these four patterns of institutionalized response to mental illness are associated with definite types of social structures. Pattern I, for instance, would seem to be characteristic of aggressive and power seeking, self-selected, elite groups generally, whether they be kinship, military, political, economic, or religious. These elite groups extrude (screen out) all persons with visible behavioral anomalies (symptomatic of possible other disabilities as yet unrevealed) in order to maintain a maximally reliable and effective organization. Pattern II would seem to be characteristic of technologically primitive small communities that recognize disorder as a symptom of a hidden threatening weakness only when it is continuous, and that will resort to extrusion only when it is both continuous and severe. Pattern III would seem to be characteristic of pre-nineteenth-century Western civilization generally: all disorders are symptomatic, and all serious disorders require extrusion. Pattern IV, on the other hand, would seem to characterize the psychodynamic tradition in twentieth-century Western psychiatry, and an increasing number of other educated subgroups in Western populations, who regard all disorders as symptomatic, but also consider that all disorders should be treated rather than disposed of by extrusion.

Space does not permit further elaboration of these concepts; but enough has been said, perhaps, to indicate not only the problems in attempting to create a taxonomy of responses to mental illness with cultural index value, but also the possible value of such a taxonomy in establishing relations between responses to mental illness and other aspects of culture. To the extent that these patterns of response have a bearing on the course of various syndromes, whatever their etiology may be, a taxonomy of this kind may additionally have some utility as an evaluative index of social efficiency in handling the problems of mental illness. We may speculate, for instance, that a group whose response to a behavioral disorder is to regard it as symptomatic of an underlying and threatening chronic incompetency, rather than an episode in a normal life program, will induce in the victim a sense of his own inadequacy that is in itself directly pathogenic. We may further speculate that his anxious efforts to defend himself will markedly affect the form and course of the disorder itself. If these defensive efforts are not directed toward the securing of a validly effective therapy, then the pathogenic pressure of the culturally institutionalized definitions of and responses to mental illness will be uncompensated. In such an unhappy case, even if the etiology of the disorder were actually completely organic, the culture would be playing a contributory role in the mental disease process.

TOWARD A BIOCULTURAL THEORY OF MENTAL ILLNESS: THE INTEGRATION OF THE ORGANIC AND FUNCTIONAL APPROACHES

How can the cultural anthropologist relate his conceptions of the structuring of social behavior to biological theories of mental illness? The model of mental

illness advocated in this paper as an answer to this question is essentially homeostatic. A behavior system is considered to be disturbed when an independent
variable, organic in nature, passes certain boundary values; and the responses
of the various components of this system can be construed as motivated efforts
to restore equilibrium. These responses are prescribed by the system itself in
its theory of illness. But mere lip service to the ideal of an "interdisciplinary"
approach, and pleas for the recognition of the importance of biological or cultural factors, will not solve the scientific problem. Only an approach which
considers the *specific nature* of the interaction between biological and cultural
(psychosocial) variables can have high predictive value.

The specific nature of this biocultural interaction can best be investigated
by conceiving of the total course of the psychotic episode as a single event
and then analyzing it into stages. Each stage is defined by a change in one of
the major relevant dimensions of the event. A number of plausible programs
can be constructed by a priori reasoning from different assumptions about the
identity of the initial stage. One such program derives from the assumption
(not yet justified by empirical findings) that the initial event in the psychotic
episode is the occurrence of an organic dysfunction in a hitherto intact (even
if peculiarly vulnerable) individual.

If one makes this assumption, every episode of serious mental illness can
be divided into four stages (exclusive of therapeutic and rehabilitation stages).

In the first stage, the organism is functioning normally. In the second
stage, an intermittent or continuous, of greater or lesser severity, organic interference with normal brain function occurs. Presumably the oft-remarked tran-
scultural invariance of the major clinical entities and the absence of unique
ethnic psychoses result because the number of types of organic interference
is limited. Many sources of such interferences are known, however: cerebral
hypoglycemia or hypoxia, electrolyte disturbances, gross tissue change, hormonal autointoxication, toxic metabolites, drugs, viral invasion, anomalies
of enzyme action, and so on. These immediate sources in turn can theoretically depend upon many "final" prolonged states of psychodynamically
and socially determined stress (such as those revealed by psychoanalytic investigations) which may produce temporary, and conceivably sometimes even
irreversible, changes in body chemistry. Genetic factors may also be responsible for differential vulnerabilities within a population to the various noxious
factors. Thus even from an organismic position one can comfortably look
to social and psychological processes as "final" causes, particularly if the differential incidence of disorders rather than the understanding of individual

cases is of primary concern. Coincident with the neural dysfunction occurs psychological dysfunction. The quality of this dysfunction is best conceived as a relative difficulty in organizing cognitive content: difficulty in finding the "meaning" of perceptual data, difficulty in maintaining the structure of motives, difficulty in relating affect to "rational" considerations. These difficulties may be metaphorically described as desemantication: the shrinking of the semantic matrix. This kind of dysfunction can vary in severity from an almost imperceptible decrement to a decrement so catastrophic as to approximate decerebration, with attendant loss of perceptual contact with the environment, motor discharge, and release of autonomic functions. At an intermediate level between mild confusion and unconsciousness would seem to fall the experience of meaninglessness, described by some schizophrenics as a sense of unreality, depersonalization, and loss of identity. Desemantication may be briefly episodic, as in hysteriform attacks, or chronic, as (apparently) in schizophrenia. Also coincident with neural and psychological dysfunction is primary behavioral failure attendant upon the desemantication. This is failure as judged by either the victim and members of his group, or both, and may occur in a variety of sectors of life, both interpersonal and technological. While incompetence in interpersonal relations may be the most conspicuous consequence of desemantication in the eyes of the group, technical failures in performing essential routine tasks, such as walking, paddling a kayak, ironing clothes, and preparing food, may come first to the victim's own awareness. Such failures may vary in duration and in the social or individual importance of the area of behavior involved.

If negative self-evaluation by the victim follows the events of the second stage, then the third stage will occur, characterized by anxiety, depression, and other negative affects directed toward the self. All persons constantly monitor and evaluate their competence in attaining their goals, both by self-perception and by perception of others' response to their behavior. A person experiencing desemantication finds the performance of his tasks more difficult and in some instances impossible. If the desemantication is continuous and is relatively severe, he will be unable to deny the reality of his loss of competency. His evaluation of these failures, which is a complex function of his current experience, the responses of others, and past learning, will be less effective than normal precisely because of the desemantication itself. But it will be based, in every instance, in part on concepts available to him from his past learning of the culturally standardized interpretations of the specific experiences and incompetencies which he now recognizes in himself. Thus he may interpret the perplexing voices which he hears as religious revelations, as the delirium accompanying fever, as the result of overwork, as the consequence of emotional conflict, and so forth, depending on the content of the experience, the reactions of others, and the explanations offered by his own cultural background. To the extent that the self-evaluation is negative, he loses confidence in his ability to control his own behavior, to master his environment, and to relate his behavior systematically with others.

The fourth stage is cognitive damage incurred in the course of the victim's defensive response to the negative self-evaluation. The response to his own anxiety and depression is, because of the existence of physiological dysfunction, itself apt to be disorganized. But it is designed to improve the negative self-image and to protect the person from catastrophe, and may in some degree relieve the patient's anxiety and depression, albeit at the cost of cognitive damage in the form of paranoid delusions, self-limiting withdrawal from society, and so on. Part of the response may be "neurotic," in the sense of utilizing such mechanisms of defense as denial, repression, projection, paranoid oversimplification, and so on. Part of it may be impulsive fighting with, or withdrawing from, a now dangerous and exhausting world. Part of it may take the form of seeking help. The style in which the person goes about attempting to defend himself, maintain self-respect, and secure help will of course reflect his cultural learning.

Through the second, third, and fourth stages, the victim's community is also evaluating and responding to him as a "changed person." Even in a homogeneous community, the social evaluation and response may be considerably different from the victim's, both because the victim's desemantication constrains his behavior, and because his motives may be divergent from those of the group. Whether or not his motives diverge from the group will depend considerably on the nature of these beliefs. Thus, for instance, if mental illness as evidenced by hallucination is culturally defined as a degrading condition to which society responds by social extrusion, the victim will be strongly motivated to conceal his condition, to deny it, to withdraw from prying eyes, and to accuse others of conspiracy against him if the charge is made. If, on the other hand, hallucination is a sign of contact—uncomfortable perhaps—with the supernatural world, and is responded to with rituals of intensified social acceptance, the hallucinator's motives will in all likelihood not be directed toward denial, concealment, and defense, but toward maximum publicity.

This model of the process of becoming mentally ill, as an immediate consequence of neurophysiological dysfunction, in a social environment, may be succinctly represented in a paradigm. Such a paradigm, of course, represents only a canonical form or modal type. The symbols are read as follows: "O" represents level of neurophysiological function of brain; "S" represents level of semantic psychological function; "B" represents level of overt behavioral success in achieving goals in social context; "A" represents level of anxiety, depression, and other negative affect directed toward self; and "D" represents the degree of cognitive damage incurred in the course of the defensive responses of the individual to his own negative self-evaluation. The operator $\downarrow$ represents pathological change, and λ represents "and."

Stage 0: Eufunction (O, S, B,) λ (A) λ (D)

    If physiological injury occurs, then

Stage 1: Primary Dysfunction ($\downarrow$O, $\downarrow$S, $\downarrow$B) λ (A) λ (D)

    If negative self-evaluation occurs, then

Stage 2: Anxiety and Depression ($\downarrow$O, $\downarrow$S, $\downarrow$B) λ ($\downarrow$A) λ (D)

    If anxiety and depression are severe and prolonged, then

Stage 3: Cognitive Damage ($\downarrow$O, $\downarrow$S, $\downarrow$B) λ (A) λ ($\downarrow$D)

CONCLUSION

The importance of the organic factors in psychopathology has been largely ignored by anthropological theory, which has emphasized psychological factors almost exclusively. If the viewpoint is taken that organic events play a significant role in the etiology of many mental disorders, it is possible to see the role of cultural differences as particularly relevant to etiology via their influence in determining the frequency with which the pathogenic organic events occur. From this point of view also, the culturally institutionalized theories of illness and of therapy appear to be extremely important in deciding the nature of the victim's and his group's responses to the disorder. A model of mental illness as a type of event is offered which integrates the organic and psychosocial approaches.

It may be hoped that anthropologists who have occasion to make observations in the field on persons with mental illness will in the future be able to obtain and record more extensive information on the physical status and history of the victims. Data on nutrition, infectious diseases, head injuries, and autonomic symptomatology, both with regard to the individual cases and also with respect to the community as a whole, would be helpful in describing individual cases, in understanding group differences, and in putting the brakes on overly facile attributions of psychopathology to "social structure," "culture," and "basic personality."

NOTES

1. The description of the *pibloktoq* syndrome is based on a compilation of published and manuscript descriptions, both specific and generalized, by a variety of observers, from the missionary Hans Egede in 1765 to about 1940. Seventeen photographs of a woman during a *pibloktoq* attack at Etah were taken by Donald MacMillan in June 1914; we were able to use copies of these from the original negatives on file in the Photographic Division of the American Museum of Natural History. I am indebted to Mr. [now Dr.] Robert Ackerman, my collaborator in the *pibloktoq* study, who has collected many of the data and contributed heavily to their interpretation; to Dr. Zachary Gussow, who kindly permitted use of his unpublished manuscript on *pibloktoq;* and to Dr. Gilbert Ling, who reviewed the calcium hypothesis and contributed to its refinement.

2. Since conducted by Edward Foulks (1972) [Ed.].

14

The Trip

This man is on a journey from the City of Destruction to Mount Zion.
— John Bunyan, Pilgrim's Progress

Why is the psychedelic drug experience called a "trip"? And will understanding why this term is used help to understand the experience itself? The aim of this paper is to suggest answers to these two rather limited questions.

Descriptions of psychedelic drug experiences by users of LSD, marihuana, mescaline, opium derivates, and whatnot, are highly varied—and, indeed, there may be a good deal of difference in various stages of any one trip. Mood can range from black depression to ecstasy; the perceptual and thought content go from mild distortions of normal mental function to florid hallucination. But the *interpretation* of these highly varied primary experiences is much more standardized and conventional, at least among those seriously experimenting with drugs in the tradition of Aldous Huxley, Timothy Leary, and the hippies. This interpretation is, in effect, a cultural form. It defines the psychedelic drug experience as a process of self-discovery, of self-confrontation, of deep self-encounter, hopefully leading to self-acceptance, a heightened capacity to love, and spiritual harmony. Sometimes the awareness is painful, of course, but an experienced companion can help the novice through these difficult confrontations toward a more healthy synthesis.

Now this cultural form is not new, even though the high popularity of psychedelic drug use is apparently new. This cultural form is very old in western civilization. Furthermore, every culture possesses a formal schema for interpreting hallucinatory and mystical experience and, as we shall see, the psychedelic form has a certain similarity to some cultural forms, and certain differences from others, in exotic cultures too. Furthermore, this form is poles apart from the form that sees drug use as a device for preventing pain, such as the mental pain of anxiety or the physical pain of injury or of narcotic withdrawal. Let us go on to consider some of the other variants on this form in western cultures.

WESTERN SCHEMAS OF SPIRITUAL GROWTH

The Christian tradition has long contained a schema of spiritual growth, likened to a journey, both in popular and professional language. One of the most celebrated popular presentations of the schema was written by John Bunyan, who in the seventeenth century wrote *Pilgrim's Progress.* The salvation of the soul from religious melancholy and the threat of damnation, as it is tried by various burdens and temptations in the course of life, and as it improves in self-knowledge, is described metaphorically as a trip undertaken by the hero Christian. Although he lives comfortably in the world, he suffers from an agitated depression and from intense mental anguish. His children and friends, thinking him insane, try to restrain him, but he leaves home. On his journey from the City of Destruction to Mount Zion, he encounters people named for various virtues and vices (Pliable, Obstinate, Muckraker, etc.), traverses regions named for spiritual states (e.g., The Slough of Despond), discovers both weaknesses and strengths in himself, and gradually leaves weakness behind and travels on in mounting strength. The book was for some Protestants so meaningful that it and the Holy Bible were often the only books a household contained. It is said to have been, next to the Bible, the most widely read book in the English language. It was simplified for children; my grandfather, a minister, gave me a children's edition, embellished with colored plates, when I was very young.

For the professional religious person engaged in spiritual exercise, Christian tradition provided standard models of mystical experience. Here again the process of spiritual growth was described as a journey, in this instance, along the so-called "Mystic Way." The "Mystic Way" consisted of several stages of spiritual growth, metaphorically described as a spiral road with periodic oscillations between states of pleasure and states of pain. In one formulation, the "Way" consists of five stages: (1) the *Awakening* of the self to consciousness of divine reality (pleasurable); (2) *Purgation* of the self of internal impediments to spiritual growth (painful); (3) *Illumination* of the self by contemplation of the absolute (pleasurable); (4) the *Dark Night of the Soul* in which the ego disintegrates (painful); and finally (5) *Union* in which the self is re-experienced as an expression of the absolute (pleasurable to the degree of ecstasy). The final state is thus not, as in Oriental mysticism, formulated as the annihilation of the self and its dissolving into the real but absolute world, but as the perfection of the self in a kind of spiritual marriage with divinity.

These schemas, of course, are not embodied only in religious literature; they are repeated and adapted to all sorts of contexts in literature and folklore. Thus, for instance, a recurrent theme in secular literature is the actual trip undertaken for some worldly reason, or for the purpose of escape from self, which has as its unintended result a series of self-confrontation experiences which lead toward maturity, health, and happiness. Television serials are particularly apt to use the schema, for their episodic format fits comfortably with the successive adventures of a voyaging soul connected not so much by external plot as by the internal problems of spiritual growth of the protagonist. Consider, for instance, *The Fugitive, Run for Your Life, Route 66, The Rebel,* all of which have—or had—as their theme the wanderer who discovers himself a little more fully in each new environment. And it may be this theme which is behind the old prescription of a long trip as therapy for "nervous conditions" and of a "Wanderjahr" for youth.

PROGRAMS OF SPIRITUAL GROWTH IN OTHER CULTURES

We have already remarked that the mystical tradition in Oriental religions—including Islam, Buddhism, and Hinduism—has certain formal resemblances to the western tradition. A central theme in all is the notion of renunciation of worldly cathexes and a finding of the self in the process of losing the self. The concept of pilgrimage as a means of spiritual improvement, and of travel away from the "City of Destruction" in order to find salvation, is also common.

But the worldwide currency of this symbolism, and its great antiquity, are revealed even more plainly in four other kinds of widely distributed motifs: the motif of shamanism, the motif of prophecy, the motif of the culture hero and of the trickster, and the motif of the initiation ceremony.

The role of shaman—the individual who practices religio-magical therapy and divination for a fee—is a culturally universal occupation which goes back into the Old Stone Age. The shaman's power, in general, comes from his ability to communicate with familiar spirits, and he often attains this power as a resolution of a spiritual crisis not unlike that described by John Bunyan. In the Siberian shamanistic tradition, the shaman is thereafter able to go into a trance during which his soul travels to visit distant places or even to the abode of the gods. His route is sometimes the world tree, or a similar structure—the so-called *axis mundi* which connects the material and spiritual worlds. Thus the shaman's trip spans the two orders of reality and is the means by which otherwise inaccessible but vital information from sacred realms is brought back to profane reality.

The religious prophet who launches and leads revitalization movements frequently experiences his revelations about the nature of good and evil and man's obligations with regard to them as a vision. These prophetic visions usually involve both a visual and auditory aspect. A not uncommon "program" for these visions is a trip to heaven, where the prophet is lectured by divinity and sent back with the gospel for mankind. Thus Handsome Lake, the Seneca Indian prophet (1749–1815), was escorted on a tour of heaven and hell by three angels, who educated him in god's purposes toward man. Sometimes the mechanism of salvation for the society as a whole is conceived as a trip or voyage, as in the Melanesian cargo cults and the South American *terre-sans-mal* movements. In the former, the ghosts of the ancestors are believed to be on their way in a ship or airplane, bearing a cargo of European goods; in the latter, the followers of the prophet believe that they can find a kind of Shangri-La—a land without evil—by actual migration into the jungle.

The culture hero—the bringer of the arts of civilization, and the wisdom of the gods, to mankind—is another widely known archetype. The culture hero in our religious tradition is exemplified by Moses, who, as we all know, spent a good deal of time traveling and who in one climactic trip went up onto the mountain and returned with the Ten Commandments directly engraved by God on the sacred tablets. In western cultures the hero is apt to be identified as an historic personage (as indeed he may be) and the archetypal myth is woven, as it were, around the skeleton of his biography. In preliterate cultures, the culture hero is often depicted as the trickster, a being in animal form who endures a series of adventures in the course of his travels, brings wisdom and skills back to the people. But the most important message conveyed by the culture hero, and the trickster, is the message of how to achieve spiritual growth. The trickster, in his ridiculous adventures, again and again is confronted by the embarrassing consequences of his immaturity (i.e., his vanity, his gluttony, his incestuousness, his pride, and so forth) and is required to abandon his frailties. Hammered thus by fate into some semblance of a human being, he at last returns from his journeys chastened but a whole person at last. The trickster cycle among the Winnebago Indians, for instance, has been well analyzed in the Jungian tradition, which is in some ways better attuned to these themes than the Freudian.

The fourth universal theme is the rite of passage, particularly the initiation rite, of which the classic examples are the puberty ceremonies of Australian and African tribal cultures. Here too, in order to achieve spiritual growth, the youthful initiate is physically separated from less familiar surroundings by some travel, is forced to renounce various pleasures and to suffer mortifications of the flesh, and is eventually re-introduced to the world as a more or less mature adult. In this case, the symbolism of death and rebirth is often explicitly used.

WHY IS IT CALLED A TRIP?

Examples of the motifs I have been sketching forth could be multiplied indefinitely but there is no point in obscuring the point with unnecessary detail. It is very plain that, in many cultures on all the continents, and from a time far back in the Stone Age, human beings have likened the process of spiritual growth to the experience of making a trip. The metaphor is so regularly used that one suspects that more than simple diffusion of a metaphor from a remote point of origin is responsible. There may be something about this process in human nature which can best be communicated to those who have not undergone it by likening it to a trip. Let us consider, then, what there is about trips real and spiritual which makes the one the proper metaphor for the other.

At first, the relationship appears to be simply explained. Both kinds of trip have in common the fact that they bring the traveler new information. One imagines the ego as a kind of shell, surrounded by an outer space and surrounding an inner space; as it makes forays in either direction, it gains knowledge.

But as one looks more closely, this simple model begins to dissolve. The circumstances of the two kinds of trips seem to be so grossly different that the metaphor hardly seems apt. In the one, the new information concerns the outside world; in the other, the world within. In the one case, there is the expenditure of physical energy, transporting the body from one place to another; the mode is active and outgoing. In the other, there is conservation of physical energy, the body remaining where it is; the mode is passive and introversive.

In the one, the senses are constantly stimulated with vivid and changing new sights and sounds; in the other, there is sensory isolation, achieved by darkness, monotonous alterations of sounds and lights, and the action of drug or trance or sleep itself. In the one, the ego is maintained; in the other, the ego is dissolved. To view the ego as a shell between two similar types of space, poking pseudopods in either direction to gain information hardly seems to lead to much in the way of insight into the reasons for choosing the metaphor. There are, after all, other ways of gaining external, worldly information than going on a trip: one can send a spy, receive a messenger, read a book, or simply sit and watch and listen.

So let us go further by recognizing a series of paradoxes. Some of the features which we have just listed as obviously distinguishing outer and inner trips do not, on closer inspection, seem to distinguish them at all. Thus the traveler in a strange place, as anthropologists well know, can suffer a real identity loss (the so-called "culture shock" syndrome) as he fails to receive those confirmations of the self which in his old surroundings he was able to take for granted. Like the paranoid, he may be unable to know whether the trouble is within himself or in the unpleasant world outside. And the "real" traveler too may be isolated from meaningful stimulation, unable to speak the language or understand the music, sleeping by himself, as semantically deprived as the prisoner in a cell. And the "real" traveler is, in fact, often in a very passive situation, forced to depend upon guides and purveyors of transportation, at the mercy of a community upon which he can make little claim and in which his status in uncertain. And finally, the "real" traveler is indeed often forced into real confrontation with self. Lonely, bored, and dependent, he must call upon inner resources, and overcome inner weaknesses and fears, with which he may have had little call to acquaint himself back home. Thus, like the traveler on a psychedelic trip, the real wayfarer may come back "a changed man."

But in another sense there is a paradox, too, for the spiritual traveler may report an exquisitely heightened sensitivity to sensory stimulation of all kinds. Far from feeling socially isolated, he may experience an intense communion with others, a heightened awareness of this feeling and being, and of his real closeness to them. Barriers to communication may fall and mutual confidence replace dependency, fear and mistrust; sexual "hang-ups" may be left behind and a capacity for satisfying sexual love achieved. The significance of the spiritual trip may on occasion be less an increase in insight and acceptance of self as a heightened awareness of the real world around the self. And, on "bad trips," he may be unable, as the paranoid is not, to be sure whether the City of Destruction is within himself or in the world outside. The merging of the inner and the outer world in fact would seem to be a tendency shared by primitive and civilized alike, for in many primitive cultures, at least, the dream is conceived to be no more than a real trip by the soul out into a real world.

Thus the paradox is resolved by the use of a single metaphor: that every real trip is also a trip of spiritual growth, and every spiritual trip brings a heightened awareness of the real world.

CONCLUSION

Every society needs to provide means for spiritual growth. In twentieth-century America, perhaps, these measures have been increasingly denied the young. The prolongation of education, the postponement of commitment to the real world, the bureaucratization of community life, the exclusion, intended or not, of whole classes of people from the possibility of responsible adult participation in the life of the society, make maturation and spiritual growth very difficult. The old religious schemas can hardly carry conviction and without conviction their rituals are ineffective. It is interesting to see the need filled for some, first in beatnik form by the ritualization of the real trip, celebrated by Kerouac's *On the Road,* and next in hippie form by consecration of the spiritual trip induced not only by drugs but, more and more, by other spiritual exercises as well.

15

The Identity Struggle

(WITH RAYMOND D. FOGELSON)

In the fall of 1960, the writers were invited by Dr. Ivan Boszormenyi-Nagy and his associates to participate as anthropological observers in their family therapy program at the Eastern Pennsylvania Psychiatric Institute.[1] In the first meetings with Dr. Boszormenyi-Nagy, we were impressed by his group's interest in the styles of interpersonal conflict in which their treatment families were chronically engaged. These struggles seemed to center in obstinate, and verbally manifest, efforts by the participants to coerce each other into simple and culturally conventional, but mutually incompatible, nurturant roles, basically by the crude device of calling each other names; they often persisted for long periods of time, even in the face of resolute efforts by the therapeutic team to intervene on occasion and divert the several strivings into more healthy channels.

The label *identity struggle* seemed an appropriate one because in brief, we found that the manifest content of the verbal conflicts in family therapy often took the form of an argument over what kind of person each of the participants was. Each party alternately played the role of aggressor and defender, at times accusing the other of having one undesirable characteristic or another, and at times stoutly defending his own character from criticism. Such struggles appeared, once launched, to be more than simple, symptomatic expressions of libidinal needs (although certainly they depended on such needs for their origin) and to be, in fact, quasi-autonomous transactional processes with a "life" of their own.

This chapter is, therefore, a description of representative instances of identity struggle and a report of some theoretical formulations which, at the present time, we feel to be useful and even necessary, even if not all-sufficient, in any explanation of the phenomena we observed.

The chapter contains three sections. In the first, case materials are presented, for, at this stage of work, it is not possible to give controlled experimental data. Nevertheless, in order to communicate the concepts more clearly, to demonstrate that the identity struggle as a phenomenon does occur, and to illustrate some of the methods, and difficulties of observation, we shall present some "natural history" descriptions based on clinical observations of families in treatment. In the second section, theoretical formulations are presented. In the course of thinking over and discussing the family conflicts under our observation, we have gradually formulated a theoretical position which has, increasingly, determined the choice of phenomena to which we have paid attention. We shall state this formulation, and some of its social contexts beyond the family therapy situation, as precisely as we can.

And, finally, in the third section, we shall consider the identity struggle in family therapy of schizophrenia. Although we have made no special effort to relate our work to the literature on family therapy, we cannot avoid making certain inferences from our observations. These inferences concern the conditions under which either therapeutic or antitherapeutic processes may be promoted by identity struggle in the situation of psychotherapy, both individual and familial.

Throughout the chapter, we maintain (as well as one can in dealing with subject matter so highly charged with social, medical, and personal values) the role of *anthropological* investigators, impartially observing both patients and therapists in a system of interaction whose rules constitute just one more of the various ways in which human behavior can be structured. In so doing, we deliberately avoid the routine interpretation of behavior in psychiatric terms; thus, for instance, we only occasionally introduce the concept of unconscious psychodynamics, and we emphasize the manifest content of verbal communication rather than the sometimes more libidinally revealing nonverbal communication. We are well aware that by so restricting our attention, we leave out many important phenomena. On the other hand, various ego-controlled processes, conscious, cognitive, and verbal, are also important parts of human behavior, and are indeed the most characteristically human behavior of all. And in this work we are concerned with the manifest form of a type of interpersonal interaction which needs to be described first on the level of overt verbal behavior and of conscious cognitive process. Only after this description is reasonably complete can a meaningful explanation in terms of psychodynamics be essayed.

CASE MATERIALS

Our case materials are drawn from visual observations and tape recordings of family therapy sessions in Dr. Ivan Boszormenyi-Nagy's unit at the Eastern Pennsylvania Psychiatric Institute. The anthropologists observed the sessions through one-way windows, never entered the treatment situation, and, as far as we are aware, were personally unknown to the subjects (although the subjects were informed that research personnel might be observing and recording any session). During the course of about six months, from January to June, 1961, we observed four families in weekly treatment sessions over periods of several months each; one of these families, whom we shall call by the fictitious name of Smith, we followed throughout the six months' observation period. It is certain material from the Smith family sessions which we shall be discussing in some detail.

Initially, we devoted considerable effort to developing a system for coding the transcripts of the tapes and picking out the images of self and others presented by the participants. Our hope was to delineate the stochastic structure of the identity conflict characteristic of each individual family. Although in principle this approach has merit, the technical difficulties of establishing interobserver reliability in coding proved to be discouraging. An even more serious drawback of such an approach was the superficiality of the semantic interpretation of the participants' statements. Reducing each utterance, rich in imagery and illusion to a small number of symbols (twenty-seven), each signifying a category defining the type of image, its valence, and its vector, eliminated so much of its meaning from the analysis of what was happening in the communication that we abandoned the procedure and turned to a less rigorous, but more appreciative, method. This method placed reliance on the observers' abilities, as speakers of the same general language as the subjects, to "understand" a good deal of what they were saying to each other. This more intuitive procedure made it possible to recognize tactical gambits, to delineate the structure of conflict, and to relate interpersonal communication to psychodynamics not much less reliably, and a good deal more validly, than had the more austere coding procedure.

The Smith household consisted of the patient, a 17-year-old girl, and her father and mother. The parents faithfully attended the weekly sessions along with the patient's therapist (who was concurrently seeing her in individual therapy) and another therapist from Dr. Boszormenyi-Nagy's group.

The parents were a middle-class, middle-aged, middle-income couple, without college education but reasonably well aware of the purposes of modern dynamic psychiatry and accepting of the principle that they themselves might be harboring emotional difficulties whose resolution could contribute to their daughter's recovery and later successful adjustment to life on the "outside." The daughter, Mary, had entered treatment at the Institute after a nearly successful suicide attempt. When she first entered the hospital, some two months before the family treatment program began, she had been mute, withdrawn, disheveled, and prone to sit on the floor for hours staring at the wall. At the time of her initial involvement in the family treatment program, some improvement in her condition had occurred, presumably partly as a result of her work in individual therapy.

Throughout the series of sessions which we observed, despite manifest oscillations in the patient's condition, despite a change in her therapist midway through the process, and despite the variety of particular topics discussed, one feature of the interview remained virtually constant. This was the tendency for every conversation, whatever its subject, to spiral rapidly into an identity struggle. The therapists, of course, aided and abetted this process, since their standard tactic was to diagnose the identity implications of any utterance and then work to make implicit images explicit. Thus, if the father said he had felt uneasy about some specific event, one of the therapists would be apt to suggest that perhaps he was liable to be a little uneasy in a large class of situations of which that event was only a single instance; the mother would confirm this; a therapist would ask the patient what she thought; and the struggle was on, father on the defensive, the pack closing in, the father accusing the mother of having a characteristic which made him uneasy, mother defending herself, daughter defending mother, father accusing daughter of partiality, therapist generalizing this comment, and so on. The therapists, we believe, played this incendiary role deliberately in the interests, first, of making the conscious emotional issues among the family explicit and available for conversation, and, second, of bringing to conscious attention the internal conflicts of the individual participants, particularly the patient, who could then, both in the family session and in private sessions with her therapist, work out the dilemmas thus presented.

A recurrent dialogue in these sessions, particularly involving Mary and her mother, concerned their complementary images of themselves and each other as more or less understanding, and more or less friendly, persons. This struggle was apparently an old one, going back for several years. The mother wished Mary to be more friendly, outgoing, and confidential with her; the mother's tactic was to force Mary to act in a more friendly way by accusing her of being unfriendly, thus challenging her to prove that she was friendly. Mary would counter this by saying that her mother was not an understanding person and that she herself was not unfriendly in any hostile or antagonistic way but was simply honestly and actually cold, withdrawn, and indifferent. The mother would then say that Mary was basically not really indifferent, or cold, or withdrawn; if she would just behave in a more friendly way, as she could if she wished, then she would be rewarded by kindness, warmth, and release from the hospital. Mary would point out that this proved that her mother didn't understand; she really wasn't capable of warm interaction with people; she was too sick; this was her illness; and for anyone to say that she was "really" a lively person underneath was just a coy way of demanding that she display a warmth that wasn't there. Let us now allow the transcripts to speak for themselves.

First Excerpt

February, 1961. Present: Mary, father, mother, Dr. A (family therapist), and Dr. B (Mary's private therapist).

MOTHER: Well, I have tried to, I try to talk to Mary even if it is just about certain things. I do try to get some spark even if it is about everyday occurrences. I just can't sit there. I'm not that kind. I have to ask her questions and I . . . sometimes she shows a little interest, sometimes she doesn't. She's just like a piece of wood . . . sayin' words. But if . . . she . . . er . . . I sometimes see a little, little spark of response which I see, a little spark and I feel better. I'm happier and I'm glad for any sort of response that I get.

MARY: (laughs)

MOTHER: That's the way *I* feel.

DR. B: This puts your entire disposition, in a way, if she gives just a little spark, then you can be happy.

MARY: (laughs)

MOTHER: I feel I (unintelligible) but she doesn't; she has a lot of life, and she has a lot of feelin'.

DR. B: We just saw that now with the laughter. She thought a piece of wood was exciting, somehow.

MARY: No.

DR. B: No?

MARY: Struck me funny (low voice).

DR. B: Funny?

MARY: Not that . . . the whole thing . . .

FATHER: But don't you feel that . . . our visits could be a great deal more pleasant . . . if you'd, er, try to share them a little bit more? But you retreat . . . in other words, I feel that it doesn't really make too much difference to you whether we come or not, or when we go . . . or not. Of course, I may be wrong and I stand to be corrected, but that's what my impression is. Of course, like I said, you can comment on it.

MARY: This place is blooming . . . life . . . bubbling underneath me . . . (laughs) (pause). Ah, ah, I don't know really what, what you're requiring of me . . . (laughs) . . . to be frank.

FATHER: Very little. We haven't asked you for anything.

MARY: Oh. (laughs)

FATHER: Outside of a little bit of friendliness and I don't think that's a great deal. After all, if it was strangers that meet, they act friendly, and I assure you I don't believe that we're strangers.

MARY: (small laugh) I wouldn't be too sure.

FATHER: Why? Why do you say you wouldn't be too sure. Do ya mean that after all these years we're . . . I'm a stranger to you?

MARY: Well, (pause) you're overlooking something . . . I mean . . . I don't think that I communicated with you or for that matter anybody else for the past two years . . . and you seem to overlook that and that small matter, you know . . .

FATHER: Well, I admitted that I was negligent, but purely it was through . . . er . . .

MARY: (excited) I didn't say anything . . . about your neglect . . . un, ah . . . I didn't say that. I just said that I haven't communicated with you or other people . . . or on my part . . . I didn't say anything to do with you . . . so ah . . . I mean its not . . . ah . . . something I so abruptly, oh assumed, ya know, since I arrived here . . . or anything . . . and I didn't really, ah . . .

FATHER: But I feel that you retreated even further since you've been here . . .

MARY: I don't communicate with that many people or say that much to them that means very much. Ah . . . don't feel . . . ah . . . as if I . . . y'know . . . I just simply do this . . . when you, when you come to visit me . . . (laughs). Oh . . . and der I ah . . . don't really understand what you want me to talk about.

DR. B: I think that's true.

MARY: I don't know what you want me to say (laughs). I mean I don't have too . . . ah . . . too much to say.

FATHER: Well, possibly I don't want you to be bubbling over with enthusiasm, but I do expect you to show a little bit more feeling and joy at our coming.

MARY: I can't (high voice) you always . . . all you . . . want me to do something that I can't.

FATHER: Well, that at least is a little bit of explanation that I've never heard before.

MARY: You would like me to . . . oh, I, I suppose I could . . . play something there (laugh) which wouldn't be there. If you'd really like me to do that, I suppose I could manage (laugh) . . .

DR. A: I have somehow the feeling that Mary is in the position of someone who can give or withhold and, ah, both her parents are asking for something from her, Mary, that should give friendliness, and thereby make them feel happy.

FATHER: Well, let's put it this way: not only in our case — 'course we are possibly more personally involved than anybody else at the present time — but it's a theory that you must carry through with everybody. You expect friendliness, then you have to extend something. You cannot be cold, and expect friendliness. It's an impossibility. You wouldn't get that from anybody.

DR. A: It is very true — I am not disagreeing, I am not questioning that — all I'm saying is that this situation as it is now, you see her sickness, and your coming in visiting her as parents, creates, as it looks like, as though, the way you are talking, both of you, that, now, if you could be only a little nicer, you could make us happy, and this is the kind of thing . . .

FATHER: Well, na, er, uh, uh, possibly maybe you're right when you say that of course being so deeply concerned and coming as we do, it's very hard. After all, this is a three hour visit. In three hours, er uh, to try to hold interest in the conversation . . . with a someone who's very unfriendly . . .

MARY: I am not unfriendly

[at the same time]

FATHER: . . . seems to be unhappy

MARY: Wha' do I do? I argue with you occasionally.

FATHER: Well, that's something!

MARY: Twice I argued with you.

FATHER: Yes, I believe that an argument is better than nothing at all.

MARY: Twice I argued with you and ah . . . I don't really know what you want me to extend. I, ah, can't extend something that . . . that's simply not there. That would be difficult. And I really don't think it would make you so very much happier (laughs).

FATHER: Well, how do you know if you don't try?

MARY: There's nothing to try. You're . . . as far as I'm concerned, I ah, I can't instill something there that's not there. Ah, (laughs) I don't know what you want from me.

MOTHER: I have seen all sorts of interests . . . ah, Tuesday . . . I haven't been coming every Tuesday, but sometimes when I have, ah, can get out of the house, I do try, and this Tuesday I had a strong feeling that I wanted to see Mary, and my daughter-in-law helped me and we rushed and we got out of the house. And, ah, Mary shows some interests, sometimes. She asked her father if he had a brand new shirt and some days she asked me if I had a new bag. These are signs of some interest in her parents. I honestly don't expect the friendliness that my husband is talking about . . . knowing some of the things she feels right now.

MARY: I'm not unfriendly toward you. I don't see where you get the feeling that I'm, I mean I don't think that I'm unfriendly.

FATHER: Well, I said it could have been the wrong word. Let's say not overly friendly.

MARY: Well, I'm not especially an overly friendly person anyway, so its kind of hard to expect from me. I think sometimes you expect something to be there that isn't any longer there . . . might possibly have been there (laughs), but a, ah, I'm sorry but, but, not anymore. I can't help that.

DR. A: Do you also feel, Mary, that this is sort of a demand on you that sort of drains your energy, that you have to not only think of your own troubles, but you have to consider not to disappoint your parents?

MARY: I think sometimes that when my parents come, I have to be required to keep up a conversation and that a, to appear . . . I don't know . . .

DR. A: Cheerful, or . . . ?

MARY: Well, like when my sister comes, I mean, and knew my sister came a long way to see me, and I know well, ya know, if ah . . . she comes to see me and everything, and I don't say anything to her . . .

DR. A: You have to reward her?

MARY: Then she'll go back feeling perhaps bad, worried, I mean, I am her sister . . . and I don't think she'd come to see me unless she really wanted to, so I'm required to (sigh) huh, say something or two, be something which I'm not to . . . a certain extent.

DR. A: Do you ever feel that you have already went, gone to the end of your attempts to try to keep this good front even though you don't feel it, or that you just can't pretend any more when you don't feel it?

MARY: That I think would be very hard to do for me now. I mean, I can make conversation sometimes, but . . .

DR. B: In relation to Mary's own self and some connection that we know to be existing between you and her, ah, I want to point out that Mary has been neglecting her hair very much lately. Now, I don't know whether it was that way at the other hospital, but I have a feeling somehow that, ah, although I do not understand why, it started lately.

DR. A: Few days after she's been here. I do have the feeling it is connected with the incident we have talked about, not the incident itself as much as the importance of Mary's hair in relation with you.

MARY: (laughs)

DR. B: It, ah, it does impress me very much that Mary should neglect her hair that much, you know, Mary is not, ah, the type of patient who has really given up to the point where they are regressed, ah, even their body is not, ah, constantly present to themselves, and yet with the hair it is striking. There's also the lipstick which might have some connection with it all. I don't know, but I have, ah, asked Mary to consider this, and to comb herself, and this is something she wouldn't do at any cost, and I wonder what, whether you had noticed that yourself, and what had been your impression, how do you explain that?

MOTHER: I certainly do notice it.

Second Excerpt

March, 1961. Present: Mary, father, mother, Dr. A (family therapist), and Dr. B (Mary's private therapist).

MARY: I don't know. Anything you say practically. (laughs) You, you say that I never confided in you. Well, if you knew how . . .

MOTHER: I didn't say you *never* confided in me.

MARY: You said that I didn't *come* to you, or something like that, that I didn't come to you with much of anything. Well, if I didn't come to you, I didn't even think you'd be hardly aware of what, what I really was feeling or, or what my problems *were*, practically at all.

MOTHER: Well, you did come to me sometimes, Mary, but the day . . .

MARY: I came to you about the religion. About that, uh . . .

MOTHER: Well, you had also told me that you didn't *want* to feel.

MARY: I didn't!

MOTHER: That it hurt you too much to feel, that's why you didn't want to feel.

MARY: I didn't feel, that, that's just the point. You mean . . . the time you thought I was depressed? I'd long since passed that stage (laughs) where people get depressed (laughs). Oh, I don't know. It's not important.

DR. A: Yes, it is, because you feel that your mother is not seriously interested in you and she doesn't even know your problems.

MARY: She doesn't.

DR. A: But yet she feels that . . .

MARY: Well, I don't know you give me the feeling, ah, I don't know sometimes that, uh, you, the way you talk to me, you talk about the other people here and you say to me, Mary, when *she* came here, she was very sick and this one was very sick and that one was very sick, you know, as if sometimes you know, not that I say I'm very sick—I, I really, I couldn't estimate anymore at this point, I really couldn't estimate—but you, like what you said to me, Sunday, "Well, Mary," you know . . . I don't remember what you said to me. You said something about that I could be finished being, that you . . . All you said was, I remember now, all you said was, you didn't say anything about if I *tried* or anything like that. You said, that you'd been thinking about it and that you thought that, ah, yeah, you did say something about trying (laughs) that's right. You said that if I tried that I could be done being an out-patient [in-patient] by July.

MOTHER: No, I said it was not an impossibility.

MARY: Well, you said, well, I can't remember the exact word, that is all I remember what you said. I'm just telling you what I think you said.

MOTHER: Well, you remember some things I say to you, don't you?

MARY: Yes, well, I'm not, you know, I can't remember *everything* people say to me or, you know, *exactly* what they say to me.

DR. A: Now, and here your mother meant to tell you, you hope to get out in a few months and you took it as an underestimation of how sick you are?

MARY: Well, she does underestimate it because she doesn't know.

DR. A: Because you are sick enough not to get well in a few months?

MARY: No, I get the feeling, not that I say it's impossible, I simply get the feeling, you know, that my mother thinks that, well, if Mary puts just a little effort forward, everything will come out in some kind of a miracle, you know. In a couple of months, I'm, I get the feeling that I'm really supposed to bloom, you know, and I'll come out and I, you know, I mean really get the feeling that she expects something very great to happen and that I'll be so different and everything, and to me this is an impossibility, that I would be so very changed. I mean, it's not that it's a question of being *well* or anything I, I just get the feeling sometimes that she expects me with just very small little effort, you know, put forward that everything's going to be very fine, and you know and I, to me it's just that this is quite impossible.

DR. A: 'Cause you can't do it by yourself?

MARY: No, it's just impossible (laughs).

DR. A: Who should do it?

MARY: Well, it's not a question of people doing it. It's just a question that even if I did put a certain amount of effort into it, I don't think I'd be that so very, very changed as I get the feeling that she expects from me.

DR. A: Well, what could change you? What could change you and what *way* could it be done and what is the best plan for it? If your own effort is not enough, then what else will be needed?

MARY: Oh, I don't know.

DR. A: To change her attitude, is that it?

MARY: Well, I don't know. I, I don't even think I understand what she thinks. I think sometimes that she expects this something great from me and perhaps this gives me the feeling that she underestimates me and to the extent that she doesn't know really . . . Oh, I don't know. I can't explain it.

MOTHER: I don't understand, Mary, when you say *I* expect you to change. What do you mean by that?

MARY: Well, you do expect me to change, don't you?

MOTHER: Well, then do you know in what way?

MARY: Looking at the practical side of it, you know in order to get well I'd have to change. Wouldn't I to some extent?

MOTHER: Is that what you don't want to do?

MARY: You know people don't like change in other people and they don't like change in themselves, Mother. It's not something entirely personal to myself.

DR. A: What should be changed . . . we are talking about change . . . what should be changed?

MARY: Oh, I don't know . . .

DR. A: You must have an idea what changes should be . . .

MARY: What should be changed?

DR. A: Because you say you can't change in that length of time, so what would be the change that is expected of you? How would you know?

MARY: The change that *she* expects from me that I, I think . . . I think would be, I don't know. I, I just simply get the feeling she expects me to be very, with a very small amount, you know, just put this, put an effort forward and (laughs) you know and I'm, I'm simply going to blossom, which, uh, and just like she says, I'll be finished being an out-patient [in-patient] by July with really, ah, to me I don't know. I, ah, which seems like something really impossible for me to accomplish even if I really did want to accomplish, accomplish it . . . I, I think it would be impossible. It's not a question of my getting well or . . . anything like that.

DR. A: What's missing then that you possibly can't blossom, why not?

MARY: (laughs) Because I can't.

DR. A: What is missing?

MARY: I don't know (laughs).

DR. A: There on, see there's a very interesting thing because, on the one hand, many people would say that this is a very well-meaning support from your mother, but apparently it doesn't sound like this to you. A mother telling a sick daughter: you see, you put in all your best effort and maybe in a few months you will be out and come home and yet you find this as a . . .

MARY: She doesn't say get out and come home. She says, I'll be completely finished with all therapy, I'll have nothing to do, you know, I'll be finished, finished, finished, you know.

DR. A: I see.

MARY: Well, I don't think, I don't know . . .

MOTHER: Isn't that what you want, Mary?

MARY: I wanted, I, I don't want to go into it at all. I, I just said that before to you. We don't have to go through all this, I mean to begin with. But let's say that we were going to go through all this. If we did, I doubt very much if by July, we, er, I'd be blossoming all over the place so much.

Despite the absence of visual and a good deal of auditory material, the foregoing excerpts from family therapy sessions can be usefully evaluated from several standpoints. One can, for instance, say something about the libidinal wishes of several members of the group, particularly the demands on the part of each of the three principals that the others accept and love them for what they are, without placing impossible conditions of health, wisdom, or tolerance. And one can observe the aggressive and even self-destructive responses of the several family members to each other's fancied or actual refusal to play the nurturant role. But we wish to draw attention to another feature of these passages: their content of imagery. The argument about who is, or can, or should be doing what for whom is rapidly converted into *an argument over what kind of people they are.* This currency in which identity struggle is carried on is a set of adjectives, metaphors, comparisons, and other expressions which describe a person, either the speaker or the person spoken to.

Let us consider the first passage. It begins with the mother saying that when she visits Mary, although most of the time Mary is "just like a piece of wood," she sometimes shows "a little spark of response" that makes her mother feel better. Although the manifest content of the mother's utterance concerns Mary's withdrawal, the introduction of the mother's feelings (she is "happier" when Mary responds) implies that Mary is able to make her mother happy or sad. The father then accuses his daughter of being indifferent to her parents and of making the visits to the hospital unpleasant for them. This adds up to an explicit charge that Mary is hostile to her parents.

Mary in the meantime has been fending off these gambits with giggles; the father's charge forces her, however, to accuse them in turn of being demanding, of "requiring" some behavior from her which she claims she does not understand.

The father denies that they are demanding: all they want is "a little bit of friendliness," which isn't much to ask, not any more than he would expect from a stranger, and certainly the parents are not strangers to her. The father demands to know if she really thinks this. (If she were to agree, it would imply that she *was* hostile after all, since openly to accuse one's parents of failing to be closer to their child than strangers could only be done in anger; in this culture, at least, such a parental failure would not only justify, but would virtually require, anger in the neglected child.) Mary backs away, explaining that she meant that *she* has been too sick, too withdrawn to communicate with her parents for the past two years. The father, seeing that the daughter is on the defensive, presses his advantage, even admitting apologetically that he has been negligent.

Mary has now been worked into a corner: the parents have built up a case against her, in front of two psychiatrists (and perhaps, she may feel, in the presence of other observers), based on her indifference during visits and her supposed charge of negligence against them (although this was largely manufactured by the father), that she is hostile to her parents. But she tries to defend herself. She denies having said her parents were negligent and insists that her failures to communicate were and are not personal or purposive but are general aspects of her sickness; because of this sickness, she isn't able to communicate with anyone. The father and daughter now engage in brief face-to-face argument, father demanding that she abandon her hostility and show "feeling and joy" at their visits, and she retreating into the explanation that she is sick and withdrawn, and implying that the parents are demanding that she be hypocritical in pretending feelings which are not there.

The therapist now adds fuel to the fire by suggesting that Mary's parents are emotionally dependent on her and that she has the power to make them happy or unhappy. The statement implies a slightly sadistic quality in Mary's employment of the opportunity. The father, missing the point, interprets this as a criticism of himself and justifies *his* hostility by pointing to hers; finally, he states flatly that she is "very unfriendly."

Mary jumps to her own defense at this and says, equally flatly, "I am not unfriendly." She admits that sometimes she argues. Father says, "At least that is something." But she goes on to cite her illness as the reason for her emotional indifference, and asks him if he really wants her to be a hypocrite. He says she won't even try to be friendly. The mother now enters the argument, saying that Mary actually is capable of *some* emotional response, but that she has feelings now that make friendliness impossible for her.

Mary now repeats her claim that she is *not* unfriendly in the sense of being hostile; she is just not naturally a warm, outgoing kind of person, at least "not any more." She is sorry; she has nothing personal against her parents; she is just sick and "she can't help that."

The family therapist, who has been working on the premise that the parents actually depend on Mary for emotional support and that she resents this, especially now that she is sick, suggests this to her as an explanation for her hostility. Mary admits that her relatives, including her sister, *do* want to see her give signs of health, by chatting with them when they visit. She agrees with the doctor to the extent of admitting that keeping up a front of interested conversation is "very hard to do for me now."

The patient's therapist and the family therapist now break in, and temporarily divert the struggle by a long disquisition on Mary's disheveled hair.

The second episode largely concerns the degree of illness of the patient, Mary. It begins with a disagreement over the extent to which Mary confides in her mother. The implication here is that the mother sees her daughter as secretive and nonrelating, an image that both Mary and her mother soon come to repudiate. This leads to the mother's citation of a specific instance in which Mary confided that she didn't want to "feel" because it was too painful. The patient accuses the mother of misunderstanding this confidence, saying that she *didn't* feel, that she was well past the stage of depression at that point. The therapist intervenes and interprets the patient's reaction to mean that she feels her mother lacks interest in her and doesn't even know her problems. Mary accepts the latter part of this interpretation and launches into a description of her mother's image of her condition. She seems to accuse her mother of simplifying her sickness, of maximizing potential degrees of therapeutic progress, and of giving false hope that a little bit of effort is all that is required to improve her condition sufficiently to gain release from the hospital. Also in this passage, Mary claims to be unable to evaluate how sick she really is. After some qualifications of this image of both parties, the therapist again steps in and tries to summarize the structure of the dispute. He suggests that when the mother tries to offer encouragement, the daughter interprets it as an underestimation of the severity of her sickness. Mary agrees with the second part of the therapist's interpretation. She goes on to amplify what she takes to be her mother's naive view of her condition: that with a little effort miraculous change will occur. Mary considers this prediction improbable, if not impossible.

The therapist asks Mary about her ideas concerning the mechanisms of personality change. Mary seems to feel that such change as her mother expects of her would require something beyond mere effort. When the therapist suggests that perhaps the mother's attitude is the crucial element that has to be changed, Mary avoids the question and merely points again to the mother's underestimation of her illness. Next, the mother begins questioning her daughter about the nature of the change required. Mary admits that some change is a prerequisite to getting well (by which she seems to mean getting out of the hospital), but, on the other hand, she states incisively, " . . .

people don't like change in other people and they don't like change in themselves . . ."

The therapist then asks the patient for a clearer description of what this required change constitutes. Mary reiterates her contention that her mother expects a miraculous change with a small amount of effort but that such an expectation is unrealistic, even if she might be willing to expend such effort. The therapist tries to make the patient verbalize the essential ingredient necessary to make her well but Mary does not comply. The therapist again poses a seeming paradox to the patient: the mother appears to be offering her encouragement to get well, but the patient doesn't regard this offer as well-meaning support. Mary responds with her own rendering of her mother's attitude " . . . she (her mother) says I'll be completely finished with all therapy, I'll have nothing to do, you know I'll be finished, finished, finished . . ." The mother assumes that Mary is talking about the usually desirable goal of getting well and asks her daughter if that isn't what she wants. But Mary cuts off discussion of the topic with a final hypothetical example to the effect that even if she were willing to put forth maximum effort to get well, the magnitude of change expected by her mother would not be forthcoming in the specified time. As the patient so picturesquely describes the matter, " . . . I doubt very much if by July I'd be blossoming all over the place so much."

In sum, then, the manifest content of the sample of conversations which we have quoted (and which are, we believe, representative of the bulk of the interviews) is very largely devoted to *ad hominem* arguments. The purpose, initially, of these arguments presumably is manipulative: the libidinal needs of the speakers lead them to use this kind of harassment to force their kinsfolk to act in compliance with their own wishes. A functional consequence is no doubt also cathartic: the struggle affords an opportunity for ventilation of feelings of frustration and hostility. But we feel that there is another consequence of these arguments: the tendency for the participants to become preoccupied with the tactical problem of defending themselves against accusations of unworthiness. This latter tendency contributes heavily to the maintenance of the argument as an *identity* struggle. What begins, as it were, as an open forum for the declaration of mutual needs is transformed into an arena of identity combat wherein, if they do not protect themselves, unwary participants may find their self-esteem destroyed.

Let us now consider in more detail the concept of identity, which is crucial to the analysis of the phenomenon, and then proceed to formalize the structure of the identity struggle.

THEORETICAL FORMULATIONS

1. The Concept of Identity

By an *identity* we mean any image, or set of images, either conscious or un-conscious, which individuals have of themselves.[2] An image, in this sense, may be recognized introspectively as an internal "visual" or "verbal" represen-tation, but it is observed in others as an external assertion in words, deeds, or gesture which is assumed to reflect in some way an internal representation. The full set of images of self (or *total identity*) refers to many aspects of the person, on a number of levels of generality: his appetites, his strengths and capabilities, his fears, his vulnerabilities and weaknesses, his past experience, his moral qualities, his social status and role, his physical appearance, and so on. There is no requirement that the several images which compose this total identity be noncontradictory; thus, identity may, in some of its domains, be ambiguous or inconsistent. Not infrequently, and perhaps generally, the total identity, or full set of images, can be divided into two or more subsets, each more or less internally consistent and all more or less mutually interrelated in a complex pattern of conflicts and alliances. A minimal fourfold division, which is used throughout this study, recognizes *real identity, ideal identity, feared identity* and *claimed identity* as analytically separable aspects of one in-dividual's total identity. Real identity is a subset of images which the person believes, privately, to be a true present description of himself as he "really" is. Ideal identity is a subset of images which the person would like to be able to say was true but which he does not necessarily believe is true at present; the ideal subset of images often includes morally ideal components, but may also incorporate amoral or even, in relation to local conventions, immoral or "negative," in Erikson's sense, identities. (Ideal identity thus embraces both id-determined and superego-determined fantasies, and often is not internally consistent.) Feared identity is a subset of images which the person would not like to have to say was true of himself at present and which he does not neces-sarily believe is true; the feared subset of images may include socially disvalued components, but it may also include identities which are, by some public con-vention, positive in value. Claimed identity is a subset of images which the person would like another party to believe is his real identity. Sometimes, with respect to a given dimension of variation, the real, ideal, feared, and claimed identities can be construed as points on a linear continuum, such as a scale, or a discrete or continuous variable.

For example, a man's real identity might be an image of self as five feet five inches tall; his ideal identity, an image of self as six feet tall; his feared identity, an image of self as a midget of four feet; and his claimed identity (claimed by the use of specially built shoes, high-topped haircut, and militant posture) as five feet seven inches. Other dimensions, however, are nonordered except by affective value: a woman's real identity may be an image of self as a mental patient consigned by her family to the impersonal but potentially therapeutic care of a hospital staff; her ideal identity, an image of self as a beloved daughter at home with her family; her feared identity, an image of self as an evil, hostile, despised back-ward psychotic; and her claimed identity, the Queen of France. It may be useful to visualize the four aspects of identity as arranged, with respect to any given dimension of variation, on a scale of value, meaningful to the person himself, usually in the following order:

Feared Identity	*Real Identity*	*Claimed Identity*	*Ideal Identity*
Negative		*Positive*	

The location of real and claimed identity on the value continuum is especially subject to rapid change in response to personal experience, the communications of others, and the pressures of psychological forces on fantasies about the self. It may be noted that this scale implies a correspondence between similarity and value relationships among the components.

There is, of course, no reason for any observer to agree *a priori* that any component of identity is a valid description of its subject. Even "real" identity, in the sense used here, is not necessarily more valid than any other description of a subject. And commonly enough the individual himself may be uncertain about the validity of his real identity, seeing it now closer to the ideal, now farther away, on the value-ordered scale.

As we have suggested, an identity has value; that is to say, a particular set of images of self can be invested with positive or negative affect. The individual works to achieve a real identity that is positive in affective value and to avoid the experience of negative affect in connection with his real identity. Since he strives to keep his real identity reasonably close to the ideal, and reasonably far away from the feared identity, by definition the ideal identity is relatively more positive, and the feared identity more negative, in affective value than the real identity. Thus, there is generally a motivation, more or less pressing, to change the real identity into something closer in affective value to the ideal identity, or, if this is not successful, to change the ideal identity into something closer in affective value to the real identity,[3] and, *pari passu*, to increase the distance between the real and the feared identity. The process of identity change is, of course, closely, but not completely, dependent upon social interaction. To the extent that real, ideal, and feared identities are internalizations of the implicit or explicit commentaries and values of others, they are built upon, and require, repeated validation in social communication. But the individual also privately monitors and evaluates his own behavior and thus both refines his concept of ideal identity by the requirements of experience and also estimates for himself any discrepancy between real and ideal and between real and feared identity. Identity formation thus is dependent upon both self-evaluation and interpersonal communication.

We do not minimize the complexity and variety of the ways in which identity is formed and defended and in which it constantly changes. Hence, we avoid here touching upon the subjects of identity formation in childhood and adolescence, which depends upon the use of many processes (only some of which are the various forms of "identification" and the operation of the traditional mechanisms of defense in other phases of identity dynamics). We shall consider in detail, however, certain techniques of interpersonal communication which individuals employ to reduce the dissonance (what Erikson terms identity conflicts in an intrapsychic sense) between real and ideal identity and to maximize the dissonance between feared and real identity, because there is a certain social consequence of the employment of these techniques: the identity struggle.

2. The Identity Struggle

Two kinds of related personal motives, in varying combinations, may prompt a person to initiate an identity struggle.

First, there is the simple manipulative motive to persuade or influence another person to act in a certain way toward one's self by convincing him that one's identity, and his identity, make such a role on his part reasonable and in the mutual interest of both parties. Such a motive is, at least at the outset of the transaction, a simple and straightforward effort to satisfy a felt need and is to be observed in such everyday encounters as requests for favors (e.g., "Be a good fellow and lend me five bucks"); it can also, at the more extreme end of the continuum, be unashamedly exploitive ("Brother, can you spare a dime?"). This kind of simple maneuver does not generally set in motion an identity struggle because, on the part of the initiator, it is not so much an effort to resolve problems of personal identity as to satisfy needs, both practical and libidinal, which are already acceptable within his existing identity structure. But, occasionally, an identity struggle can be precipitated by a trivial challenge of this kind if the object of manipulation refuses to be "conned" and responds instead by attacking the other's identity (if, for instance, he refuses to make the loan and replies instead, "I can't afford to lend any more money to deadbeats").

Second, there is the psychodynamically more complex motive of maintaining or restoring a favorable identity in one's self. It is this second motive, arising from identity dynamics, that is of principal interest to us in this paper. Identity maintenance or restoration involves a minimizing of dissonance between the values associated with the real and ideal identities, and a maximizing of dissonance between real and feared identities. The problem of dissonance control can, of course, be met in many ways. One avenue of action is principally internal and consists of either exploiting certain mechanisms of defense, such as denial, repression, projection, rationalization, and so forth, or of "reforming" the self by means of a personality resynthesis achieved by such devices as religious conversion, prophetic inspiration, psychotherapy, or the seemingly perverse assumption of a "negative identity" (Erikson 1959). To the extent that neither inner defense mechanisms nor internal resyntheses are adequate (for any one of a number of reasons) to the task of maintaining the dissonance at a tolerable level, the individual must act outwardly to secure dissonance-reducing (or dissonance-increasing) communication from others. Rarely are the two types of dissonance-controlling tactics found in isolation, but one or the other may predominate in a given instance.

When the individual turns to another party for help to control identity dissonance, his fundamental strategy is typically twofold. First, A attempts to secure from B testimonials, overtly stated or implicit in the roles which B assumes toward A, that, in B's eyes, A's identity is what A wishes it to be; and, at the same time, A tries to avoid hearing, or even to prevent B from expressing, explicitly or implicitly, descriptions of A which are in A's identity structure unfavorable. Second, A attributes to B an identity which will be so negative in value that B will attempt to modify B's real identity in a direction less antagonizing to A. In effect, A says, "I want you to treat me as such-and-such kind of person; the reason why you won't do this for me is that you are a so-and-so." Furthermore, the wish is in these instances not for the treatment itself so much as for the identity-reinforcement which this treatment connotes. Typically, in self-defense, if not in response to his own identity needs, B will begin to apply the same strategy to the aggressor, A, and an identity struggle emerges. In time, such a struggle can involve a group, such as a family, in a complex net of mutual identity struggles, with various temporary coalitions arising in the course of combat.

In analysis of an identity struggle, we deal only with the *images* exchanged verbally in the communication network within the group. We must distinguish between these images and the affective states, and libidinal drives, which motivate both the struggle and also the other transactions simultaneously taking place. Thus, although the images in the previous excerpt concern love and affection, and the parties' demands for warm response from each other, we do not consider directly the communication of these wishes but only the exchange of images. The content of the images which constitute identity, when they are put into words, are most easily thought of as descriptive terms and phrases, sometimes simply adjectival, like "honest," "pretty," "oafish," "cruel," etc., and sometimes more complex, like, "He is always putting things off," or "She nags her husband." In verbal form they are easily conceived as attributes or predicates, denoting some more or less enduring characteristic of the object.

But images are, of course, not always communicated in clear and simple descriptive language. They may be conveyed by subtle, indirect, or elaborate verbal content, such as orders and instructions, questions, jokes, "double talk," parables and allegories, stories, abstract discussions, and even by the choice of topic; furthermore, images of self or others can be conveyed by tone of voice, dress, personal adornment, posture and stance, gesture, the gamut of kinesic communication, and even by relatively involuntary, but perceptible, physiologic responses, such as sweating, flushing, or pallor, respiratory pattern, etc. And, as Bateson et al. (1956) have pointed out, the images conveyed simultaneously or successively in these various modalities need not be consistent.

If the images are viewed more dynamically, however, they seem to imply an element of relevance to some class of plans or intentions and to express some evaluation of the competence of the object to succeed in enterprises of this kind. Thus, the images which a person has of himself generally have to do with some goal and his confidence in his ability to reach this goal. Viewed from this standpoint, then, the images which the person has of another are significant (at least in terms of interpersonal relations) in their promise, or lack of promise, of that other's performing some instrumental act, or class of acts, which are necessary to the success of ego's plan. Thus, for example, a young woman may have, as her libidinal goal, a clinging, childlike dependency relationship with her mother. Her ideal image of herself, and the image which she claims, is of a warm, friendly, lovable, and devoted daughter who is capable of eliciting the desired maternal behavior. The mother, however, has been behaving in a way which the daughter regards as rejecting, and although the mother denies that she is being cold to her daughter, she confesses to her friends that she *does* feel cold. The daughter wants the mother to accept her plea and give her motherly love, but she is unsure whether the rejection which she is now suffering is owing to a discrepancy between her own real and ideal identities (maybe, she thinks, she herself is not really warm, friendly, and lovable enough) or to her mother's coldness.

This leads to a consideration of the basic strategy of the game. Ego has intentions, a plan, and an identity (or rather, identities) related to that plan, which attest to his possession, or nonpossession of the qualities requisite to the completion of the plan. Other parties (either individuals or a group, such as the rest of the family) are important, partly in order to reinforce (by accepting a claimed identity) a real identity which is not too divergent from an ideal identity, and (sometimes) partly in order to play an instrumental role as well. Where the other party has an instrumental role to play, ego must endeavor to ensure that alter's identity is appropriate to that role, if alter's identity is not already appropriate; this he does by attempting to induce him to accept an attributed identity and to abandon his present (claimed) identity. Thus, to pursue the illustration given in the preceding paragraph, the daughter wants to secure two things from the mother: first, reassurance that she regards her daughter as being warm, lovable, and devoted; and, second, acceptance of the daughter's "request" that she once again play the role, and maintain the real identity, of the loving mother. In order to accomplish all this, the daughter schemes first to induce the mother to admit publicly that she now has a "cold" real identity; once such an admission has been secured, the daughter believes, the mother will be shamed or driven by guilt into redevelopment of the "motherly" real identity (because the daughter well knows, from past experience, that the mother's claimed identity is motherly).

The identity struggle, in a social sense, can be classified as a form of negotiation between parties (whether individuals or groups) whose interests and characteristics are mutually perceived as being in certain respects presently antithetical but potentially complementary. It has the form of conflict, but its proper outcome is an agreement or contract on mutual rights and duties (with their necessary identity concomitants) such that the two parties can interact to mutual satisfaction in an equivalence structure (see Wallace 1961). But an identity struggle is a hazardous negotiating procedure, partly because it invokes powerful and irrational internal motives and partly because of the unreliability of human communication. Other outcomes, less desirable than an equitable agreement leading to an equivalence structure, are possible: excessive stress, resulting in psychosomatic disorders, in one or both participants; cognitive and emotional damage, to one or both participants, in the form of an internalization of negatively valued images of self (see Searles 1959); mutual social withdrawal; violence leading to physical damage to, or destruction of, the participants and/or of material apparatus. Hence, a number of rules of behavior either emerge into consensus from the experience of the participants or are formally stated as expectations of the culture. The purpose of these rules or ethics is to prevent the conflict from becoming so bitter that the probability of a successful outcome is low. Indeed, overt identity struggles may in some cultural domains be regarded as so pernicious that they are proscribed in all but the most carefully regulated situations, such as the courtroom, the political arena, or the dueling ground. Too frequent participation even in these licit struggles, or participation outside the formally permitted contexts, may be regarded as a sign of personal inadequacy or of membership in a "lower" status group which permits such behavior; analogies to (if not homologies with) the mutual smelling and bristling behavior of dogs, and the mutual identity establishment procedures of other lower animals, may be pointed out with disdain. The nature of such rules varies, of course, from culture to culture and from subject matter to subject matter, but in general they would seem universally to involve a prohibition of open rage, physical violence, or excessive cruelty in nonphysical coercion; some confinement of allusion to matters both conventionally permissible and relevant to the subject of negotiation; the avoidance, if possible, of the involvement of others than the principal parties to the conflict; and the requirement that neither party ruthlessly seek a unilaterally acceptable solution.

It would take us too far afield in this preliminary paper to attempt to explore the range of logical complexities and special tactical maneuvers, involving such special problems as identity concealment, alliances, falsely claimed and attributed identities, ambivalent or even contradictory real identities, promises of mutual identity transformation, and the like, as well as the more straightforward assertions, counterassertions, and defenses (some of which, however, have been illustrated in the case materials earlier). Indeed, we are led to suspect that a full exploration of the internal dynamics and external tactics of identity struggles would contribute significantly to a truly social psychiatry, and to psychodynamic theory as well. But we move on now to examine some of the nonpathologic ways in which identity struggles have been institution-alized in various cultures.

3. Introductory Cross-Cultural Observations

We have suggested that a process as fundamental as the identity struggle, grow-ing as it does out of generic human (if not phyletic) characteristics, should not only be discoverable in any human society, but should also be institutionalized in various forms within different cultural traditions. There should be reflec-tions of the process in the myths and legends of nonliterate peoples and in the formal literature of civilizations; it should raise issues to be dealt with by codes of etiquette and ethics and law; it should generate sanctions intended to restrain and limit the ramifications of conflict in order to reduce damage both to the immediate participants and to the society more generally.

Let us consider first the simpler societies, the so-called "primitive" or "nonliterate" tribal peoples who have been of special interest to anthropol-ogists. In these simpler cultures, as in the advanced, minimum socially rele-vant aspects of an individual's identity, and the rights and duties pertaining thereto, are generally defined by the individual's status as a member of several publicly recognized groups: a kinship unit (such as a moiety, clan, or extended family), a community or band, an age grade, an occupational specialty, a se-cret religious society, etc. (see Goodenough 1961). But the prevailing concepts of identity in a society are more complex than a bundle of half a dozen sta-tuses and may more easily be regarded in anthropological jargon as aspects of the national character, modal personality structure, or ethos of that group. Primitive communities differ markedly in ethos, as well as in particular cus-toms, of course, and such variation implies variation in the forms and spirit of courtesy. In at least some primitive communities, however, and probably in most, the ethos opposes the sort of direct confrontation of opposing identities which we have been denoting as an identity struggle. Thus, among the Indi-ans of northeastern North America, identity struggles between individuals of any community, except in clearly sanctioned situations, often ceremonial, are avoided. If a person openly impugns the identity of a member of another com-munity, either by physical injury or insult, the offended party has available the resources of his community in a physical (and/or magical) assault on the other group to gain an appropriate revenge, and may proceed directly to retaliate in kind or, in many instances, to terminate the issue by killing the offender. Such retaliation would not be desirable within the small community, however; and perhaps in consequence tribal peoples of this area show noteworthy courtesy and discretion in their face-to-face interactions (even though there may be much malicious gossip, suspicion, and fear of witchcraft). In other culture areas, a preoccupation with reciprocal taboo and avoidance systems among members of different status positions in the same community—for instance, the taboos on male contacts with menstruating women—may work to the same end. In social structures of this kind, however, latent identity struggles may require ceremonial expression as a cathartic device to prevent the accumulation of hostility; this function is often performed through organized games, reinforcing ritual role reversal, and other devices. If a nonritualized intergroup struggle emerges within the society, the consequence is likely to be social disorganization or radical change.

Sometimes, however, and particularly among members of the same status group in a society, formalized identity struggles with a highly ritualized etiquette are permitted to occur over certain issues. For instance, formal struggles are apt to happen within elite groups where recognition of high rank by an individual must be earned by a demonstration of pre-eminence in some relevant characteristic. One familiar example of this is the potlatch of the Kwakiutl and other Indians of the Northwest Coast of North America. In the potlatch, leading men vie among themselves for dignity at public feasts at which vast quantities of goods are consumed or given away; the victor in a series of feasts is the man who can give away or destroy the most blankets, oil, slaves, and other items of worth in the society.

Another context in which identity struggles may be precipitated by intention is that of illness. Here, where the object is to remove the suspected supernatural cause of the affliction, the sufferer may be ritually harassed by accusations of taboo violation and be encouraged to confess, lest he, and perhaps others, suffer death or chronic illness in punishment. Somewhat similarly, adolescent males and sometimes females are often subjected to severe humiliation, deprivation, and even physical mutilation, in order to induce an abandonment of a childish identity in favor of an adult one.

Sometimes ritual is designed explicitly and consciously to resolve identity struggles. For example, among the Tangu, a Melanesian tribal group resident in New Guinea, the ideal in social relations is a state of neutral amity and moral (or, in our terms, identity) equivalence. But the circumstances of life, and the vagaries of impulse and opportunity, frequently bring about breaches in amity or equivalence, arousing anger and raising the ugly specter of sorcery or murder if someone suffers intolerable moral damage. For instance, as Burridge relates:

> An exchange which is not regarded as precisely equivalent, or which remains not honoured in full too long, is taken to indicate a lack of moral equivalence. A sense of grievance cannot imply either amity or equivalence. One or another party to the exchange is thought to be attempting a dominance or moral superiority. He who produces more is suspected of endeavouring to assume a loftier moral status in virtue of what may be a simple physical competence: which is deplorable. Brute strength may help towards attaining a higher social standing, but it can only reflect degrees of moral perfection when used in particular ways for certain ends. He who produces less may be suspected of contumely, of behavior which is essentially contemptuous and therefore not in conformity with amity. And either may be suspected by the other, or by members of the community, to be resorting to a technique which is meant to shroud the other in obloquy. The ideal is equivalence, neither more nor less, neither 'one-up' nor 'one-down.' To be 'one-up' is to offend and therefore to invite mystical retaliation. To be 'one-down' and remain content is almost unforgivable: it implies a complete retreat into sorcery, a resolve to maintain equivalence by doing evil only (Burridge 1960:82).

The proper way of handling such potentially explosive conflicts is to bring them to public forum where the contestants may engage in a delicate exchange of insults, so balanced that both can quit at some precise moment when neither is winning. The name for this ritual is *br'ngun'guni*. It begins with a redefining, if that is possible, of the issue into terms of food:

> All transgressions in Tangu may be seen as attacks on equivalence: and where possible the wrongdoing is related to an individual's potential for producing foodstuffs in an exchange. In this way public equivalence may be reached through *br'ngun'guni* and a series of feasting exchanges. Theft and trespass, the most frequent offences, are automatically regarded as attacks on food producing potential; those emotionally at odds can always take the opportunity to find fault with a food exchange; if adultery is not to slide into sorcery, or plain killing, it must be reduced to a matter of food production. Food is the conventional pretext for a quarrel; and *br'ngun'guni* is the accepted procedure for returning to amity. Just as a denial of equivalence can be for-

mulated in terms of behaviour relating to food, so is it re-established through activities directly connected with the production of foodstuffs: *br'ngun'guni* and a series of feasting and dancing exchanges. Moral relationships, therefore, are reflected in the way people behave over food; food is economic wealth; the amount produced and the way in which it is distributed yield political power; and each is geared to equivalence, the primary expression of amity. . . .

The *br'ngun'guni* is a talk between two antagonists in the dancing space of the village with other villagers as audience. Ideally, the debate is noisy but carefully kept within the bounds of possible return to amity. . . . The seemingly careless remark strikes home: and a riposte is immediate. Does the cap fit? One man probes to find a weakness; then thrusts, retreating for the parry. The language flickers to sting and annoy; it should not draw blood. There should be just enough room for one to advance, just enough room to fall back. To press an opponent into a corner leaves him with little alternative but to take refuge, later, in sorcery. If a man appears to be going 'one-up' by so hurting another he is only hurting himself. Sensibly, support falls away. By retiring a little, by parrying the consequent onslaught with a whoop and thump on the buttocks, the ball comes back into play. The victory is never to the dominant; it goes to the man who knows when to sit down, to the man who can look through his audience and know that nobody is certain who is 'one-up' (Burridge 1960:83).

In this type of combat, the winner of an identity struggle is, in a sense, the loser, since he has made it impossible for his opponent to return to amity or equivalence without resorting to sorcery.

In addition to establishing rules of superficial decorum which obviate manifest identity struggles, and in addition to providing a means for combatants in an identity struggle, once it has become manifest, to carry out the battle in a forum which permits a bounded resolution of the issue, societies generally recognize certain ethical principles which, however phrased and rationalized, have the function of inhibiting the proliferation of identity struggles. Nowhere is it desirable for a group to permit its own members to suffer identity damage; and those who, whether maliciously or self-righteously, wreak unnecessary and unprovoked damage upon the identity of their fellows are violating moral principle. The precise issues upon which identity depends are, of course, highly variable cross-culturally. But those who persistently treat sport or other forms of competition (in which the loser need not lose face or honor[4]) as identity conflicts; those who patronize; those who violate the identity of others by demanding that they assume roles incompatible with self-respect; such people are, we suspect, in all cultures regarded as dangerous, as committing the sin of pride, of risking the anger, not only of men, but of the gods (as the widely distributed trickster myths point out vividly and as is so well exemplified by the Greek notion of *hubris*). Sometimes this principle is applied even to the relations of men to animals; among the Algonkian and Iroquoian hunters of eastern North America, for instance, the good hunter was always careful to indicate, by ritual, his respect for the animals whom it was his duty to kill. And corresponding to the ethical commitment to respect one's fellows, there is the ethical commitment to an appropriate honesty (but not necessarily to modesty) in claiming only that identity which in its objective particulars is "true." Thus, if the society values bravery in war, the warrior must not boast unless his claim to valor has been confirmed by the test of battle; if it values chastity in women, the bride must not claim a virtue which is not hers. The possible intricacies of the interaction of respect and contempt, honesty and deceit, pride and shame are inherently interesting to human beings, it would seem; even the simplest peoples are entertained by tales, such as trickster stories (*vide* Radin 1956), which explore the many moral and emotional combinations of these stances, which are possible in any human culture.

4. Identity Struggles in American Society

The implications of the foregoing discussion are not only that identity struggles are well-nigh ubiquitous phenomena but also that they are regarded with some disfavor in most, if not all, societies, on the ground that they are potentially damaging to the relations of cooperation and mutual interdependency upon which any society is based. We have also seen, however, that identity struggles are often permitted in certain bounded situations in which the participants are restrained by formal or informal rules of decorum. It has been further suggested that in a few of these contexts, such as illness and status change, identity struggles are exploited in a rather formal way in order to force individuals to abandon socially inappropriate identities for appropriate ones and to negotiate amicable equivalence structures with their fellows.

In our society, there seem to be relatively few situations in which serious identity struggles are sanctioned by all segments of the community. In most circumstances they are regarded as unfortunate accidents, breaches of etiquette, or even violations of equity or law for which blame can be assessed and penalties assigned by the courts. Thus, for instance, a long-continued identity struggle between husband and wife can not only lead to unhappiness in marriage; it can also, for non-Catholics in many states, lead to divorce actions based on grounds of mental cruelty and humiliation. Three of the principal relationships in which serious identity struggles are explicitly licensed in our culture are: first, the relationship of ad-man and potential customer either in direct face-to-face interaction or through advertising media; second, the relation between contending parties, or their counsel, in adversarial proceedings in a court; and third (and in a special sense), the relation between psychotherapist and patient. It may be noted that the second and third situations may overlap or be connected in sequence. We shall, in the next section, discuss the psychiatric (and thus some aspects of the legal) identity struggle in connection with the psychotherapy of schizophrenia.

It has been suggested by Boszormenyi-Nagy and Framo (1965), that a fourth locus of sanctioned identity struggles is the nuclear family. We do not hesitate to agree that identity struggles do in fact occur at one time or another among the members of many, if not most, American families. We do hesitate, however, to accept the suggestion that serious identity struggles (as we have described them in this paper) are *culturally* defined as a *desirable* aspect of family living even though they may be accepted by many as inevitable. It seems more plausible to construe the prevailing cultural attitude as one of wary tolerance: spouses are advised to expect identity issues to develop as the marriage partners work out their relationship, and parents are warned that issues of identity occur among children and between children and their parents; but everyone is on notice that these matters should be resolved by friendly accommodation, and that if an outright struggle develops, it is to be regarded as "dirty linen," not to be aired in public, and to be resolved as quickly as possible, albeit as honestly as possible, within the family, lest it erupt in the courts or the doctor's office. The issue has a bearing on the strategy of family therapy in schizophrenia for, as we shall point out later, if the psychiatrist believes that such struggles are not only frequent but culturally sanctioned, then he may regard it as his responsibility to encourage latent struggles to find free and regular expression in his patient family as an aspect of normal family living; whereas, if he feels that open struggles are not culturally normal, then he may consider the struggles he observes in the patient family as symptoms, if not a cause, of illness, to be lanced when found but not nourished or cultivated.

Let us consider for a moment American popular fiction. In the works to which we refer, the identity struggle is conceived as a chronic, grinding war between two unhappy people who are bound together, like stags with locked horns, in a deadly embrace which even the death of one partner cannot end. This formulation is integral to some of the work of such popular writers as F. Scott Fitzgerald — *vide*, for instance, his novel *Tender is the Night* (1934), in which a recently psychotic heiress and a conscientious psychiatrist marry and drive each other to near-destruction with catatonic outbursts and adultery on the wife's part and professional abdication and alcoholism on the husband's. The only solution offered is the husband's leaving his wife in command of the field of battle (the Riviera) and retiring, alone, to the general practice of medicine in a small town. John O'Hara's *Appointment in Samarra* (1954) explores a similar type of cyclical identity struggle. An even more direct delineation of the theme is given in a recent popular movie, starring Alec Guiness, entitled *Tunes of Glory*. The story concerns a drunken, vulgar but heroic acting regimental commander, who rose from the ranks during the African desert campaigns of World War II, and an old-school-tie career officer, son of a former commanding officer, who is ordered to replace the acting commander in peacetime. The two men battle desperately to preserve their somewhat different conceptions of self-respect; in the end the tricked and shamed new man commits suicide, and the older man, humiliated by the circumstances of his own victory, disintegrates in a welter of hallucinations. These themes are presaged, in a limited way, by Hemingway's elegant exercises on the subject of manhood. In Hemingway's stories the opponent (whether man, woman, bull, lion, fish, or mountain) does not do much more than present a moral dilemma to the hero, who must work out for himself what it is to be a man under various trying circumstances (which, however contrived they may be for literary effect, are in a general sense types of situational traps into which any man may fall). The Hemingway story thus presents in sharp outline the identity struggle from one person's point of view. Hemingway, however, generally attempts to provide an ideal solution: a model of optimum fortitude, of doing the best one can under impossible circumstances, of failing nobly without destroying the identity of the opponent (for, in identity struggles, as the Tangu emphasized, sometimes the only way to win is not to win, especially if the opponent has the dignity of Hemingway's animals).

It must be pointed out, however, that in the United States not everyone reads Hemingway and F. Scott Fitzgerald and that some Americans did not see and enjoy *Tunes of Glory*. In other words, the ethos which we are attempting to delineate cannot be prescribed as valid for all citizens of the country, partly because of individual variability and partly because of differences among groups defined by ethnic, religious, occupational, regional, and other characteristics. Indeed, differences in attitude toward identity struggles probably constitute a profoundly important source of friction between groups who in many other respects share a common culture. Thus, one may suspect that some of the antagonism felt by Anglo-Saxon Protestants against Jews may grow out of differences in customary attitude toward identity struggles. The ideal-type Protestant, we suggest, has a lower threshold of tolerance for identity struggles, and perceives as unacceptable "pushing" and as ill-mannered squabbling patterns of interaction involving manifest commentary, however trivial the issue, on the partner's identity, which are tolerable and even desirable to the Jew. The Protestant in response tends to freeze and withdraw. The ideal-type Jew, in complementary fashion, regards mutual identity commentary as an acceptable and even necessary component of social interaction and regards the Protestant's manner as aloof, two-faced, and unfriendly. He responds at first by intensifying the commentary and then by a complementary withdrawal. Inasmuch as issues of identity, for the reasons which we have given earlier, involve self-esteem, such a cultural discordance, even with respect to "superficial" decorum in identity commentary, can be profoundly alienating.

In American society, identity struggles, or situations possessing the formal properties of the identity struggle, are frequently "denatured" by redefining them as "play" or "entertainment" and thereby rendering them less dangerous. Thus, hazing or initiation rituals, which in many simpler societies are taken as deadly serious mechanisms for status transformation, are publicly defined by Americans as tradition, as "innocent fun." Parlor games, friendly chit-chat, comedian's jokes, and public entertainments supervised by wisecracking masters of ceremony derive their spice in large part from the use of playful mutual insult; what is said in jest would be intolerable if said seriously: as the saying goes, "Smile when you say that."

Among American adolescents, especially lower-class Negro youth, a common game or verbal play involves mutual insults with semi-standardized responses which serve to neutralize the insult, transform the insult into a compliment, or turn the insult back upon the sender. The game goes under various names in different parts of the country. The oldest and most widely used name for the contest is "Dozens," although it is also sometimes referred to as "Sounding (down)," "Cuts" (or "Cutting each other up"), "Playing," "Slipping," "Screaming," or "Mocking."[5] The game has been described in the scholarly literature by Dollard (1939) and Abrahams (1962). The latter authority provides a concise description of the structure of the game:

> . . . One insults a member of another's family; others in the group make disapproving sounds to spur on the coming exchange. The one who has been insulted feels at this point that he must reply with a slur on the protagonist's family which is clever enough to defend his honor (and therefore that of his family). This, of course, leads the other (once again, due more to pressure from the crowd than actual insult) to make further jabs. This can proceed until everyone is bored with the whole affair, until one hits the other (fairly rare), or until some other subject comes up that interrupts the proceedings (the usual state of affairs) (Abrahams 1962:209–210).

Abrahams also notes that the game contains an implicit set of rules or ethics: "The rules seem to say, 'You can insult my family, but don't exceed the rules because we are dealing with something perilously close to real life' " (Abrahams 1962:211). In lower-class Negro culture the game is most appropriate to adolescent boys. Among pre-pubertal boys the game tends to be less intricate owing to incompletely developed verbal facility and an unfamiliarity with the semantic complexities of erotic slang, while later ages, between 16 and 26, the game becomes less acceptable and in those settings where it does occur, as in military service, poolrooms, or bars, it quite frequently results in physical violence (Abrahams 1962:210–211). This violence usually arises when one of the parties "goes too far" or oversteps the bounds of good form. If the game of "Dozens" is kept within reasonable bounds with no intent to do serious damage to the identity of the opponent, no violence is likely to occur, and the game may be enjoyed as a humorous interlude or innocent "letting off of steam" by both spectators and participants alike. From the example of "Dozens" and similar forms of verbal play, we can see that among adults, as well as children, one of the standard techniques of diverting an incipient identity struggle from erupting into an open feud is for one of the participants, or a third party, to twist the issues into a joke; thus what might have been an explosive conflict is by common consent transformed, by the fiction of humor, into "kidding around."

Many observers have remarked that contemporary society appears to contain an increasing number of persons who suffer from "character disorders," and particularly, in language closer to our own, "problems of identity." It can be argued that the incidence of persons suffering from identity problems is increasing in Western society as the technology makes human beings increasingly dispensable, and that our social problems are decreasingly the result of economic want and increasingly the result of efforts to resolve identity problems by means which lead to identity struggles between individuals and groups.

One of the semi-institutionalized mechanisms for resolving identity conflict (and in many ways the least threatening) is the assumption of a socially devalued identity. It is as if the person, after trying and failing to convince himself (with the help of others) that his "ideal" identity is his "real" identity, says, "To hell with it," and claims (and acts out) a "bad" identity with, literally, a vengeance. This process is, we believe, involved in those forms of deviation, delinquency, or criminality (as they are culturally defined, of course) which seem to be better explained as a revolt against society than as a means of securing needed goods and services, personal respect, or affection absolutely unavailable through other means. It is a kind of impulsive ritual of rebellion, highly social in character, in which a group of people agree to renounce "good" identities (as being "square" or "nowhere") and to accept fully the "bad" ones (as being "hip" or "cool"). It does not seem accidental that this value inversion is most common among precisely those groups (minority or majority) who happen, at any one time, to be classified as "inferior," or "immature," by those who operate the technology, control mass communication, or are otherwise influential in molding popular sentiment. The consequence of this process is, of course, an identity struggle between the rebellious person and his family, teachers, employers, or others whom he regards as his enemies.

Another kind of semi-institutionalized mechanism for resolving identity conflict is, in many ways, much more dangerous because it leads to massive intergroup identity struggles. This mechanism is the projection by an individual of his own feared identity onto another whole group. Inasmuch as many individuals in each group (e.g., whites and Negroes) may be employing this mechanism to resolve internal conflicts, the system of complementary negative projections can lead to extensive intergroup fear and hostility. This process is, we feel, in large part responsible for those extremes of racial prejudice, religious antagonism, and national chauvinism which seem to be particularly prevalent in technologic societies. It appears to us that these three phenomena, particularly racial prejudice, have not (despite the cross-cultural ubiquity of ethnocentrism) been in any degree as savagely and indiscriminately destructive in non-industrial societies as they have been in the technologic societies of the past four hundred years. The anti-Semitism of Nazi Germany, the ethnic conflicts of Algeria, the racism of the white South Africans and, to a somewhat lesser degree, of many white Americans, and of organized minorities of American Negroes (*vide* the Black Muslims), and similar phenomena elsewhere, are not really matched to our knowledge either among non-literate peoples or in the ancient classical civilizations. To be sure, slavery was a common feature in many of these earlier and non-Western societies, but it was generally maintained with impartiality toward the racial and ethnic characteristics of its victims. Wars were conducted with more obvious economic or cultural issues at stake than has been the case in modern times. Preoccupation with the idea of subordinating, segregating, or exterminating a racial or ethnic group *on the grounds of its alleged inherent and inborn inferiority in moral or intellectual spheres,* rather than simply on account of its perversity in refusing to behave properly or to follow orders, appears to be a unique product of technologic societies, and this idea arises, we suggest, precisely out of identity conflicts which this type of society induces to such a high degree in its members. If our suppositions concerning the nature of the identity conflict in technologic societies are correct, then it is no accident that the group against which prejudice is directed is always accused of having precisely the properties which the accuser fears may characterize himself: namely, worthlessness, infantilism, laziness, cupidity, dishonesty, incompetence for civilized living, and other "bad" qualities associated with the accuser's own sense of being expendable within the technologic society. The ruthless, bitter, vengeful nature of this kind of hostility, its frequent independence of actual experience with members of the hated group, and its immunity both to personal knowledge and to rational scientific thinking, are corroborative evidence of its origin in intrapersonal identity conflict rather than in any history of actual intergroup relations.

It is, of course, one of the tragedies of this type of situation that once many of the members of one group have begun to project their own feared identities onto another group, members of the second group, whether or not they had previously suffered from severe identity conflict, are likely to begin to experience complementary identity conflicts, and an identity struggle between the two groups will ensue. In the long run, at least in technologic societies, there are only three stable solutions for intergroup identity struggles: mutual withdrawal; the annihilation of one group by the other; or the abandonment of the struggle by both and the sanctioning of contractual relations, devoid of invidious distinctions, between individuals and institutions of both groups. Only the latter solution is conducive to the continued success of the technologic society, because intranationally it eliminates an important source of waste effort and psychological damage to the citizenry. Although it is hazardous to generalize a phenomenon discovered in dyadic relations between individuals to such complex entities as social classes, ethnic groups, nations, and coalitions of nations, it seems that some of the dynamics of the identity struggle may be applicable to events taking place on an international scale, as in the continued discussions between East and West over such matters as disarmament, colonialism, and the relative merits of "capitalist imperialism" and "communist totalitarianism."

THE IDENTITY STRUGGLE IN FAMILY THERAPY IN SCHIZOPHRENIA

In our discussion so far, we have illustrated and described the identity struggle as a phenomenon, and have shown how not only our own culture but also others attempt to prevent or to canalize by ritual such struggles in the interest of social stability. But we have avoided as much as possible introducing the familiar psychiatric concepts appropriate to the analysis of the individual motivations.

Our model of psychodynamics has principally utilized those conscious cognitive states, and their associated affects and verbalizations, which are directed toward identity maintenance. We have furthermore employed our own definitions of identity processes and have not explicitly discussed their relationship to the rich existing literature on identity or to the writings on family therapy. We took this position not because we felt that psychiatric concepts were of no explanatory value but because we believed that the first task was to describe the social phenomenon, and that psychiatric explanation and application had to be directed toward an accurately described type of event.

But now we turn to the psychodynamic and psychotherapeutic implications of the identity struggle, and the first order of business is to recognize that what we have described, under the rubric "identity struggle," is a manifest, overt, conscious process which presumably succeeds another phenomenon. This other phenomenon is less grossly manifest, and often less conscious, but it involves similar attitudes; we may refer to it as the latent identity struggle, in contrast to the manifest identity struggle which we have been describing. In the latent identity struggle, the participants do not overtly claim and challenge in an explicit, verbal way; rather, they cherish private claims for their own identities and nourish private contempts for their partners', and take considerable pains not to reveal their attitudes in a form sufficiently explicit to arouse manifest responses from one another. It is from a situation of latent struggle that manifest struggles undoubtedly arise.

Now what we have been calling the latent identity struggle is, in effect, a type of interpersonal and intrapersonal conflict that is presumed in psychiatric theory to be pathogenic if not pathologic, if it is permitted to continue indefinitely without resolution. It constitutes the setting of the double-bind; it is exemplified in the silent conflicts of transference and countertransference which the analyst endeavors, with his patient, to "work through." And the latent identity struggle is a form of family combat which, if it has not already developed into a manifest identity struggle, becomes manifest in the course of family therapy in schizophrenia, most conspicuously in the effort by members of a family to blame the family's problems on the sick member. The aim, in regard to treatment, is therefore the management of the latent identity struggle in such a manner that it is resolved; and the tactical question is the proper handling of the manifest identity struggle which seems inevitably to develop as soon as the latent struggle is probed.

Here we must reintroduce one of our cultural observations. It is difficult for the participants in an identity struggle to resolve their own conflict; hence many cultures surround such struggles with rituals designed to obviate or canalize them. Merely offering to a family a license for open conflict, in place of a silent struggle, will probably contribute nothing to the resolution of the latent struggle and may permit not only a rapid deterioration of morale but also irreparable damage to the structure of the group; it may well contribute to the progressive psychopathology of one or more members of the family. Yet, it is also probably impossible to deal with the real issues of the latent identity struggle without, in the process, transforming it into a manifest identity struggle. The tactical problem in family psychotherapy is thus to make the latent identity struggle manifest, and then, once it is manifest, to resolve it before the struggle itself destroys the family and damages one or more of its members.

Can we, in contemporary Western civilization, find models for this therapeutic process? I think we can in at least two settings: the conference method, and the method of psychoanalysis. In psychoanalysis, the patient is permitted, indeed he is encouraged, to enter into intimate communication with a doctor. He reveals to him, as well as he can, important thoughts and feelings, and depends heavily upon the doctor to relieve him of a burden of emotional, and sometimes physical, illness. As the relationship develops, the patient begins to look more and more to the doctor for the satisfaction of powerful and hitherto repressed needs, and because the doctor refuses to satisfy some of these needs, he also develops resentments. So a latent identity struggle develops between the two: the patient claims an identity (as child) which the doctor resolutely denies, and he attributes to the doctor an identity (as father) which the doctor refuses; the doctor, likewise, claims an identity (as doctor) which the patient denies, and attributes an identity (as mature and independent person) which the patient refuses. The explanatory concept for the origin of this process is the well known process of transference; it is the analysis of the transference, by making its elements and history conscious, which constitutes both the manifestation of the identity struggle and the means of its resolution in psychoanalysis. In our language, then, psychoanalysis is a technique for the resolution of the identity struggle between two people. But, it must be emphasized, the success of this technique depends upon surrounding it with restrictions which, however reasonable they may be, are comparable to the rituals which surround any culturally canalized identity struggle. The patient must remain upon the couch; the interview must be terminated at the end of the hour; the analysis must be performed in a specified place, in privacy; the analytic interaction between doctor and patient must be confined to the analytic situation, and therefore acting out the struggle in other contexts (such as job or social gathering) is prohibited; the patient should commit himself to the task of getting well.

Assuming that similar transference psychodynamics are responsible for the positions of the participants in a familial identity struggle, it is reasonable to suppose that analytic treatment (or analytically oriented psychotherapy) of all the family members would lead to a resolution of the identity struggle. In this sense, we can say that the hitherto unexplained intransigence of the struggle, its chronicity and immunity to rational intervention, is the result of the mutual transference (and fixation) problems of the family members and their lack of an analyst to resolve them.

But psychoanalysis is too expensive a procedure to permit its application to all of the members of a family simultaneously at the hands of the same, or different, therapists. Can family therapy, as a form of conjoint therapy, do the same work, and if so, under what conditions? Here we may look to the conference method for the resolution of manifest identity struggles. In various situations, such as labor-management conflict, racial strife, the cold war, etc., the participants, after a period of fruitless and frustrating confrontation of more or less rational demands according to the dictates of self-interest, fall into a phase of manifest identity struggle.[6] In this phase, names are called, characters are impugned, and progress toward settlement is nil. Only after representatives of the participants have come together (often under the chairmanship of a neutral moderator) with assigned and accepted responsibility to bargain continuously about the several needs of the contending parties, can a settlement be reached. Such a settlement has to take into account, not only the obvious economic and political needs of the parties, but also at least some of their emotional needs for such intangible, but important, values as "dignity," "self-respect," "honor," "good faith," and so on.

These considerations lead directly to the following propositions:

1. That in family therapy in schizophrenia (and in any other conjoint therapy process) it is necessary that the latent identity struggle be made manifest.

2. That the manifest identity struggle must be resolved as quickly as possible in order to minimize emotional damage to the participants and structural damage to the group.

3. That a principal role of the family (or group) therapist must be to interpret the identity struggle to the group: i.e., to point out the nature and structure of the conflicting claimed, real, feared, and ideal identities of the several participants. He should also set the rules which bound the conflict and define the permissible channels of expression.

4. That the group itself must consciously and openly accept the responsibility for achieving a settlement of the struggle which is agreeable to all parties. The therapist cannot prescribe a solution for a family any more than he can for an individual.

Theoretically, at least, in this culture such a procedure should permit the struggle to be resolved either by mutual agreement on identities or, if this is impossible, by an agreement to dissolve the group. This latter possibility should not be denied the group any more than the privilege of the patient in therapy to leave his family, or his job, or his therapist can be denied, provided the motives for the action have been brought to consciousness and analyzed and the "reality factors" have been faced.

If we were to evaluate the performance of the therapeutic group in the family therapy program which we have observed, it would seem to us that the therapeutic team was probably highly successful in making manifest struggles out of latent ones; at least we were struck, and sometimes shocked, by the directness with which the therapists, in the sessions we observed, brought such material into the verbal arena. Less activity, however, we felt, was shown in interpreting the manifest identity struggle to the family itself; and the level of family commitment to achieving a settlement appeared to be very low. One reason for this was a tendency, remarked on by the staff itself, to shift back and forth, on the part of both the therapists and the family (and of these observers too, for that matter), between primary concern for the patient's psychiatric status and primary concern for the emotional structure of the family. Another reason, of course, is that the identity struggle formulation was not developed until after the observations had been made, and, even if it had been, could not be communicated to the therapists without risk of changing the nature of the phenomenon being observed. A third reason, perhaps, may be a reluctance to concede that the motive of identity maintenance and enhancement can be regarded by itself as a "deep motivation," quite comparable, in its psychodynamic importance, to sexual and aggressive motives.

The patient's own identity problems have a dimension not shared by the other members of the family (although each of the individual members can and does have more or less severe identity problems). Not only does he bring with him the difficulties he experienced before he became a psychiatric patient, he has the additional burdens of being ill and of being publicly classified as incompetent. Considering that a schizophrenic illness means, for the victim, a painful decrement in self-esteem, we may assume that the schizophrenic's real identity is very sharply discrepant and highly negative in value in relation to his ideal identity. Inasmuch as we assume that the organism strives to achieve (although, no doubt, it never succeeds) a total identity in which the value of the real identity is no less than some optimal finite quantity in relation to the value of the ideal identity, we can expect the schizophrenic to work to reduce the dissonance. The kind of work he undertakes can be guided, fundamentally, by either of two strategies: first, to reduce the value of the ideal identity and increase the value of the feared identity; second, to increase the value of the real identity. The aim may, but need not, imply a congruence of content in the two identities. The two strategies may be labeled the withdrawal strategy and the paranoid strategy, respectively. In the withdrawal strategy, the victim says, in effect, "I give up, not only am I worthless, incompetent and crazy, but there is no point in aspiring to be anything better, all I want is to be left alone." His claimed identity is therefore his feared identity. In the paranoid strategy, the victim says, in effect, "It is not I, but someone else, who is worthless and incompetent, and perhaps even evil; I am good and pure and well able to take care of myself." His claimed identity is therefore his ideal identity; he attributes his real identity to others by the paranoid defensive process of projection. These strategies may, of course, be mingled by a single person, who will be withdrawn at one time with regard to a particular component of identity, and paranoid at another time with regard to another identity component. Inasmuch as the issue is of extreme importance to the schizophrenic, who will suffer from intolerable tension unless the dissonance is reduced, his efforts will be both desperate and stubborn and also more or less bizarre and crude because of the cognitive damage associated with the illness. Furthermore, there will, because of the intensity of the internal conflict, and because of the schizophrenic constriction of semantic range, be a tendency for the schizophrenic to feel that his total identity is at stake in issues which, to an observer, would seem to involve only one or a few components and relatively trivial plans.

It is too much to hope that the resolution of the identity struggle will, in the case of the psychiatric patient, bring about by itself a remission or cure of the psychosis. In addition to the possibility that the psychosis is dependent on a physiologic or biochemical disorder, the analysis of the struggle will not necessarily resolve all psychodynamic issues in either patient or family. But the resolution of the struggle should terminate the imputation of identities which the patient fears and, to the extent that this has been pathogenic, contribute to the patient's welfare. Furthermore, the resolution of the identity struggle should, theoretically, be accompanied by a minimizing of the "psychotic neurosis" (the neurosis *about* the psychosis; see Wallace 1960). These two changes in the patient's situation should facilitate the establishment of a milieu in which the program of individual therapy can proceed more efficiently, unimpeded by the patient's need to defend himself against multiple and chronic assaults upon an already damaged confidence in self, and not delayed by unnecessarily prolonged repetitions of a stalemated identity struggle.

NOTES

1. We wish to acknowledge our gratitude for the expert aid provided by the following members of the anthropology section, who served as secretaries, research assistants, and collaborators in various phase of the project: Dr. Robert Ackerman, Mrs. Nina Balis, Miss Connie Davidejt, Mrs. Josephine Dixon, Mrs. H. Pollard Dow, Miss Virginia Tovey.

2. The term "identity" (as well as the related term "self") has been used in a number of different senses in the psychological and psychiatric literature. Our definition does not correspond precisely to any of the several major usages but has been influenced primarily by Erikson (1959), Goffman (1959), and Rogers (1942, 1947, 1951, 1954, 1959), who have made distinguished contributions in, respectively, the psychoanalytic, the sociocultural, and the psychological tradition. Some of the bibliographic resources available in the literature are cited in the bibliography.

3. The process by which rapprochement between the real and ideal identity are achieved follow closely some of the postulates contained within Festinger's theory of cognitive dissonance (1957). The Q-sort studies reported by Rogers (1959) in which increased congruence between real and ideal self-concepts accompany positive therapeutic movement also have relevance to the statements made above.

4. The "good sportsmanship" ethic in American athletic contests would seem to be a device, *par excellence,* for minimizing the possible identity damage inflicted upon "losers."

5. We are indebted to Miss Pamela Dixon and Mr. Mark Davis for sharing with us some of their first-hand knowledge of the game.

6. R. R. Blake and J. S. Mouton (1961) have referred to this process in union-management disputes as the onset of Win-Lose dynamics and consider the process "pathologic" in intergroup relations.

References Cited

Aberle, David F., A. Cohen, A. Davis, M. Levy, and F. Sutton. 1950. The Functional Prerequisites of a Society. *Ethics* 60:100–111.

Abrahams, R. 1962. Playing the Dozens. *Journal of American Folklore* 75:209–220.

Allport, G. 1943. Ego in Contemporary Psychology. *Psychological Review* 50:451–478.

American Museum of Natural History, Photographic Division. 1914. Photographs of the Crockerland Expedition.

Ashmead, Henry G. 1884. *History of Delaware County, Pennsylvania.* Philadelphia: Everts.

Ashton, Thomas S. 1968. *The Industrial Revolution, 1760–1830.* London: Oxford University Press.

Austen, Ralph A., and Daniel Headrick. 1983. The Role of Technology in the African Past. *African Studies Review* 26:163–184.

Baashuus-Jensen, J. 1935. Arctic Nervous Diseases. *Veterinary Journal* (London) 91: 339–350, 379–390.

Barber, Bernard. 1941. Acculturation and Messianic Movements. *American Sociological Review* 6:663–669.

Barnett, Homer G. 1953. *Innovation: The Basis of Cultural Change.* New York: McGraw-Hill.

Barrett, Albert M. 1919–20. Psychosis Associated with Tetany. *American Journal of Insanity* 76:373–392.

Barron, Frank. 1958. The Psychology of Imagination. *Scientific American* 199:150–166.

Bateson, Gregory, D. D. Jackson, J. Haley, and J. Weakland. 1956. Toward a Theory of Schizophrenia. *Behavioral Science* 1:251–264.

Baxandall, Michael. 1972. *Painting and Experience in Fifteenth Century Italy.* Oxford: Clarendon Press.

Bellak, Leopold, ed. 1958. *Schizophrenia: A Review of the Syndrome.* New York: Logos Press.

Bergman, Paul. 1953. A Religious Conversion in the Course of Psychotherapy. *American Journal of Psychotherapy* 7:41–58.

Bertelesen, A. 1940. Grønlandsk medicinsk statistik og nosografi. *Meddelelser om Grønland,* Bd 117, Nr. 3. Copenhagen: C. A. Reitzels Forlag.

Bettelheim, Bruno. 1947. Individual and Mass Behavior in Extreme Situations. In

Readings in Social Psychology. Newcomb, Hartley, et al., eds. New York: Henry Holt.

Blake, R. R., and J. S. Mouton. 1961. *Group Dynamics: Key to Decision Making.* Houston: Gulf.

Boisen, Anton T. 1936. *The Exploration of the Inner World: A Study of Mental Disorder and Religious Experience.* New York: Harper & Brothers.

Boulding, Kenneth E. 1956. *The Image: Knowledge in Life and Society.* Ann Arbor: University of Michigan Press.

Brainerd, David. 1822. *Memoirs of the Rev. David Brainerd.* Sereno Edwards Dwight, ed. New Haven CT: S. Converse.

Brill, A. A. 1913. Pibloktoq or Hysteria among Peary's Eskimos. *Journal of Nervous and Mental Disease* 40:514–520.

Broehl, Wayne G. 1964. *The Molly Maguires.* Cambridge: Harvard University Press.

Buhler, C. 1962. Genetic Aspects of the Self. In *Fundamentals of Psychology: Psychology of the Self.* Earnest Harms, ed. *Annals of the New York Academy of Science* 96:730–764.

Bunyan, John. 1933 [1678]. *Pilgrim's Progress.* Philadelphia: Winston.

Burridge, Kenelm O. L. 1960. *Mambu, A Melanesian Millennium.* London: Methuen.

Burroughs, Betty, ed. 1946. *Vasari's Lives of the Artists: Biographies of the Most Eminent Architects, Painters, and Sculptors of Italy.* Abridged edition. New York: Simon and Schuster.

Callaway, Canon H. 1931. The Religion of the Amazulu of South Africa, As Told by Themselves. In *Source Book in Anthropology.* Alfred L. Kroeber and T. T. Waterman, eds. New York: Harcourt, Brace.

Cannon, Walter B. 1932. *The Wisdom of the Body.* New York: Norton.

———. 1942. Voodoo Death. *American Anthropologist* 44:169–181.

Cantril, Hadley. 1941. *The Psychology of Social Movements.* New York: J. Wiley and Sons.

Chance, H. M. 1883. Mining Methods and Appliances Used in the Anthracite Coal Fields. Harrisburg: Second Geological Survey of Pennsylvania.

Clausen, J. A., and M. R. Yarrow. 1955. The Impact of Mental Illness on the Family. *Journal of Social Issues* 11(4) (whole issue).

Cline, Walter. 1937. Mining and Metallurgy in Negro Africa. American Anthropological Association, *General Series in Anthropology no. 5.* Menasha WI: Banta.

Constantinides, P. C., and N. Carey. 1949. The Alarm Reaction. *Scientific American* 190:20–23.

Cook, Frederick A. 1894. Medical Observations among the Esquimaux. *Transactions of the New York Obstetrical Society, 1893–1894.* Pp. 171–174.

Cooley, Charles H. 1902. *Human Nature and the Social Order.* New York: C. Scribner's Sons.

Crane, Diana. 1972. *Invisible Colleges: Diffusion of Knowledge in Scientific Communities.* Chicago: University of Chicago Press.

Crozer, John P. c1862. Biographical Sketch of John P. Crozer Written by Himself. Philadelphia.

Curschmann, Hans. 1904. Tetanie, psuedotetanie und ihre mischformen bei hysterie. *Deutsche zeitschrift für nervenheilkunde* 27:article 12, 239–268.

Daddow, Samuel H., and Benjamin Bannan. 1866. *Coal, Iron, and Oil.* Pottsville PA: Benjamin Bannan.

Deardorff, Merle H. 1951. The Religion of Handsome Lake: Its Origin and Development. In *Symposium on Local Diversity in Iroquois Culture.* William N. Fenton, ed. *Bureau of American Ethnology Bulletin* 149:79–107. Washington, D.C.

Des Lauriers, A. 1960. The Psychological Experience of Reality in Schizophrenia: Therapeutic Implications. In *Chronic Schizophrenia.* Lawrence Appleby, J. M. Scher, and J. Cumming, eds. Glencoe IL: Free Press.

Dollard, J. 1939. The Dozens: The Dialect of Insult. *American Imago* 1:3–24.

Durkheim, Émile. 1915. *The Elementary Forms of the Religious Life: A Study in Religious Sociology.* London: Allen and Unwin.

Eggan, Fred. 1954. Social Anthropology and the Method of Controlled Comparison. *American Anthropologist* 56:743–763.

Erikson, Erik. 1950. *Childhood and Society.* New York: Norton.

———. 1959. Identity and the Life Cycle. *Psychological Issues* 1 (whole no.).

Fenton, William N. 1936. An Outline of Seneca Ceremonies at Coldspring Longhouse. *Yale University Publications in Anthropology* 9:1–23.

———. 1953. The Iroquois Eagle Dance: An Offshoot of the Calumet Ceremony. Washington, D.C. *Bureau of American Ethnology Bulletin* 156.

Ferguson, Eugene S. 1967. The Steam Engine before 1830. In *Technology in Western Civilization,* vol. 1. M. Kranzberg and C. W. Pursell, Jr., eds. Pp. 246–263. New York: Oxford University Press.

———. 1977. The Mind's Eye: Nonverbal Thought in Technology. *Science* 197:827–836.

Festinger, Leon. 1957. *A Theory of Cognitive Dissonance.* Evanston IL: Row, Peterson.

First, Ruth. 1983. *Black Gold: The Mozambican Miner, Proletarian and Peasant.* Sussex: Harvester Press.

Fisher, Allen S. 1935. *Lutheranism in Bucks County, 1734–1944.* Tinicum PA: Privately printed.

Fisher, Seymour, and Sidney F. Cleveland. 1958. *Body Image and Personality.* Princeton NJ: Van Nostrand.

Fitzgerald, F. Scott. 1934. *Tender is the Night.* New York: Scribner.

Fogg Art Museum. 1981. *A Masterpiece Close-Up: The Transfiguration by Raphael.* Cambridge, Mass.: Fogg Art Museum.

Foreman, Grant. 1946. *The Last Trek of the Indians*. Chicago: University of Chicago Press.

Foulks, Edward F. 1972. *The Arctic Hysteria of the North Alaskan Eskimo. Anthropological Studies*, no. 10. Washington, D.C.: American Anthropological Association.

Foulks, Edward F., and Russell Eisenman. n.d. A Spontaneous Therapeutic Process in Habitual Users of Psychedelic Drugs. In manuscript.

Freud, Anna. 1946 [1936]. *The Ego and the Mechanisms of Defense*. New York: International Universities Press.

Freud, Sigmund. 1959 [1914]. On Narcissism: An Introduction. In *Sigmund Freud, Collected Papers*, vol. 4. Ernest Jones, ed. Pp. 30–59. New York: Basic Books.

———. 1922. *Group Psychology and the Analysis of the Ego*. London.

Friedlander, J. N., R. Perrault, W. J. Turner, and S. P. Gottfried. 1950. Adreno-Cortical Response to Physiologic Stress in Schizophrenia. *Psychosomatic Medicine* 12:86–88.

Fromm, Erich. 1951. *Forgotten Language*. New York: Rinehart.

Frye, Northrop. 1957. *Anatomy of Criticism*. Princeton: Princeton University Press.

Garfinkel, Harold. 1967. *Studies in Ethnomethodology*. Englewood Cliffs NJ: Prentice-Hall.

Gersuny, Carl. 1981. *Work Hazards and Industrial Conflict*. Hanover NH: University Press of New England.

Gipson, Lawrence Henry. 1938. The Moravian Indian Mission on White River. *Indiana Historical Collections 23*. Indianapolis: Indiana Historical Bureau.

Glass, Albert J. 1953. Psychotherapy in the Combat Zone. In *Symposium on Stress*. Washington, D.C.: Army Medical Service Graduate School.

Goffman, Erving. 1959. *Presentation of Self in Everyday Life*. Garden City NY: Doubleday Anchor.

———. 1961a. *Asylums: Essays on the Social Situation of Mental Patients and Other Inmates*. Garden City NY: Doubleday Anchor.

———. 1961b. *Encounters: Two Studies in the Sociology of Interaction*. Indianapolis: Bobbs-Merrill.

Goldman, Irving. 1937. The Bathonga of South Africa. In *Cooperation and Competition among Primitive Peoples*. Margaret Mead, ed. Pp. 354–381. New York: McGraw-Hill.

Goldstein, Kurt. 1940. *Human Nature*. Cambridge: Harvard University Press.

Goldwater, Robert, and Marco Treves, eds. 1945. *Artists on Art from the XIV to the XX Century*. New York: Pantheon Books.

Goodenough, Ward H. 1961. Formal Properties of Status Relationships. Paper read at American Anthropological Association Annual Meeting, Philadelphia, November.

———. 1963. *Cooperation in Change*. New York: Russell Sage Foundation.

Gussow, Z. 1960. Pibloktoq (hysteria) among the Polar Eskimo: An Ethnopsychiatric Study. In *Psychoanalysis and the Social Sciences.* W. Muensterberger, ed. New York: International Universities Press.

Hallowell, A. Irving. 1955a. The Self and Its Behavioral Environment. In A. Irving Hallowell, *Culture and Experience.* Philadelphia.

————. 1955b. *Culture and Experience.* Philadelphia: University of Pennsylvania Press.

Hanning, Robert W., and David Rosand. 1983. *Castiglione: The Ideal and Real in Renaissance Culture.* New Haven: Yale University Press.

Harms, Earnest, ed. 1962. Fundamentals of Psychology: Psychology of the Self. *Annals of the New York Academy of Science* 96:681–894.

Harries, Patrick. 1981. The Anthropologist as Historian and Liberal: H. A. Junod and the Thonga. *Journal of Southern African Studies* 8:37–50.

Harrington, Mark Raymond. 1921. *Religion and Ceremonies of the Lenape.* Indian Notes and Monographs 19. New York: Museum of the American Indian, Heye Foundation.

Harris, Marvin. 1959. Labour Emigration and the Mozambique Thonga: Cultural and Political Factors. *Africa* 21:50–64.

————. 1968. *The Rise of Anthropological Theory.* New York: Crowell.

————. 1979. *Cultural Materialism: The Struggle for a Science of Culture.* New York: Random House.

Hays, John. 1760. Diary, May–June 1760. Genealogical Society of Pennsylvania Collection, Philadelphia.

Heckewelder, John. 1876. *History, Manners, and Customs of the Indian Nations.* Philadelphia: Historical Society of Pennsylvania.

Hewitt, J. N. B. 1917. Review of Arthur C. Parker, Constitution of the Five Nations, and Duncan C. Scott, Traditional History of the Confederacy of the Six Nations. *American Anthropologist* 19:429–438.

Hilgard, E. R. 1949. Human Motives and the Concept of the Self. *American Psychologist* 4:374–382.

Hindle, Brooke. 1981. *Emulation and Invention.* New York: New York University Press.

Hoaglund, Hudson. 1944. Schizophrenia and Stress. *Scientific American* 181:44–47.

————. 1950. Stress and the Adrenal Cortex with Special Reference to Potassium Metabolism. *Psychosomatic Medicine* 12:142–148.

Hoagland, Hudson, E. Callaway, F. Elmadjian, and G. Pincus. 1950. Adrenal Cortical Responsivity of Psychotic Patients in Relation to Electroshock Treatments. *Psychosomatic Medicine* 12:73–77.

Hoffer, A., H. Osmond, and J. Smythies. 1954. Schizophrenia: A New Approach. II. Result of a Year's Research. *Journal of Mental Science* 100:29–45.

Hollingshead, August B., and Fredrick C. Redlich. 1958. *Social Class and Mental Illness: A Community Study.* New York, Wiley.

Holm, Thomas C. 1834 [1702]. *A Short Description of the Province of New Sweden.* (Memoir 3) Philadelphia: Historical Society of Pennsylvania.

Honigmann, John J. 1954. *Culture and Personality.* New York: Harper.

Hoygaard, Arne. 1941. *Studies on the Nutrition and Physio-Pathology of Eskimos.* Oslo: Skrifter utgitt au Det Norske Videnskaps-Akademi i Oslo, 1. Mat.-Naturv. Klasse 1940 No. 9.

Hsu, Francis L. K. 1963. *Clan, Caste, and Club.* Princeton NJ: Van Nostrand.

———. 1965. The Effect of Dominant Kinship Relationships on Kin and Non-Kin Behavior: A Hypothesis. *American Anthropologist* 67:638–661.

Hunt, Joseph. M., ed. 1944. *Personality and the Behavior Disorders: A Handbook Based on Experimental and Clinical Research.* New York: Ronald Press.

Inspector of Mines, Annual Report. 1869–. Harrisburg: Pennsylvania State Printer.

Jackson, Halliday. 1830. *Sketch of the Manners, Customs, Religion and Government of the Seneca Indians in 1800.* Philadelphia.

James, William. 1902. *Varieties of Religious Experience.* New York: Longmans, Green.

———. 1890. *The Principles of Psychology.* 2 vols. New York: Holt.

Junod, Henri A. 1962 [1927]. *The Life of a South African Tribe,* 2nd edition. 2 vols. New Hyde Park NY: University Books.

Kallmann, Franz J. 1938. *The Genetics of Schizophrenia.* New York: J. J. Augustin.

———. 1948. The Genetic Theory of Schizophrenia. In *Personality in Nature, Society, and Culture.* Clyde Kluckhohn & H. Murray, eds. Pp. 60–79. New York: Knopf.

Kane, Elisha K. 1856. *Arctic Explorations: The Second Grinnell Expedition in Search of Sir John Franklin.* Philadelphia: Childs and Peterson.

Kasserman, David. 1971. Modernization through Conservative Entrepreneurs: The Establishment of the Cotton Industry in the United States. Unpublished dissertation proposal.

Katzenellenbogen, Simon E. 1982. *South Africa and Southern Mozambique.* Manchester: Manchester University Press.

Keesing, Felix M. 1953. *Culture Change: An Analysis and Bibliography of Anthropological Sources to 1952.* Stanford: Stanford University Press.

Kelsey, Rayner. 1917. *Friends and the Indians, 1655–1917.* Philadelphia.

Kenton, Edna, ed. 1927. *The Indians of North America.* 2 vols. New York: Harcourt, Brace, and Company.

Knox, Ronald A. 1950. *Enthusiasm: A Chapter in the History of Religion, with Special Reference to the XVII and XVIII Centuries.* New York: Oxford.

Kopytoff, Igor. 1964. The Mother's Brother in South Africa Revisited. *American Anthropologist* 66:625–628.

Kroeber, Alfred L. 1939. *Cultural and Natural Areas of Native North America.* Berkeley: University of California Press.

————. 1944. *The Configurations of Culture Growth.* Berkeley and Los Angeles: University of California Press.

————. 1947. *Cultural and Natural Areas of Native North America.* Berkeley and Los Angeles: University of California Press.

————. 1948. *Anthropology: Race, Language, Culture, Psychology, Pre-History.* New York: Harcourt, Brace and Company.

Kuhn, Thomas S. 1962. *The Structure of Scientific Revolutions.* Chicago: University of Chicago Press. (2nd edition, 1970).

Lecky, Prescott. 1945. *Self-Consistency: A Theory of Personality.* New York: Island Press.

Lee, D. 1950. Notes on the Conception of the Self among the Wintu Indians. *Journal of Abnormal and Social Psychology* 45:538–543.

Lenzen, Godehard. 1970. *The History of Diamond Production and the Diamond Trade.* New York: Praeger.

Letcher, Owen. 1974 [1936]. *The Gold Mines of Southern Africa.* New York: Arno Press.

LeVine, Robert A. 1984. Properties of Culture. In *Culture Theory: Essays on Mind, Self, and Emotion.* Richard A. Shweder and Robert A. Levine, eds. Pp. 67–87. New York: Cambridge University Press.

Levins, Michael. 1975. *High Renaissance.* Baltimore: Penguin.

Levy, Leonard W. 1957. *The Law of the Commonwealth and Chief Justice Shaw.* Cambridge: Harvard University Press.

Levy, Norman. 1982. *The Foundations of the South African Cheap Labour System.* London: Routledge & Kegan Paul.

Lewin, Kurt. 1936. *Principles of Topological Psychology.* New York: McGraw-Hill.

Lindestrom, Peter. 1925. *Geographia Americae* [1656]. Amandus Johnson, ed. Philadelphia: Swedish Colonial Society.

Linton, Ralph. 1943. Nativistic Movements. *American Anthropologist* 45:230–240.

Lowe, C. M. 1961. The Self-Concept: Fact or Artifact? *Psychological Bulletin* 58:325–336.

Lowe, Warner L. 1953. Psychodynamics in Religious Delusions and Hallucinations. *American Journal of Psychotherapy* 7:454–462.

Lynd, Helen M. 1958. *On Shame and the Search for Identity.* New York: Harcourt, Brace.

Macmillan, Donald B. 1918. Food Supply of the Smith Sound Eskimos. *American Museum Journal* 18:161–176.

————. 1934. *How Peary Reached the Pole.* Boston: Houghton.

Mandelbaum, David G. 1949. *Selected Writings of Edward Sapir.* Berkeley: University of California Press.

Mantoux, Paul. 1962. *The Industrial Revolution in the Eighteenth Century.* New York: Harper and Row.

Marabottini, Alessandro. 1969. Raphael's Collaborators. In *The Complete Work of Raphael*. Pp. 199–297. New York: Reynal and Co.

Maslow, Abraham H. 1954. *Motivation and Personality*. New York: Harper.

Maxwell, J. P. 1930. Further Studies in Ostcomalacia. *Proceedings of the Royal Society of Medicine* 23:639–640

Mayer, Philip, ed. 1980. *Black Villagers in an Industrial Society*. Cape Town: Oxford University Press.

Mead, George H. 1934. *Mind, Self, and Society from the Standpoint of a Social Behaviorist*. Chicago: University of Chicago Press.

Mead, Margaret. 1947. The Concept of Culture and the Psychosomatic Approach. *Psychiatry* 10:57–76.

———. 1954. Nativistic Cults as Laboratories for Studying Closed and Open Systems. Paper read at annual meeting of the American Anthropological Association.

———. 1955. How Fast Can Man Change? Address presented to Frankford Friends Forum, Philadelphia, December 4.

Merton, Robert K. 1949. Social Structure and Anomie. In *Social Theory and Social Structure*. Glencoe: Free Press.

Milbank Memorial Fund. 1952. *The Biology of Mental Health and Disease*. New York: Hoeber.

Miller, George A., Eugene Galanter, and Karl H. Pribram. 1960. *Plans and the Structure of Behavior*. London: Holt, Rinehart, and Winston.

Mooney, James. 1896. The Ghost-Dance Religion and the Sioux Outbreak of 1890. 14th Annual Report, *Bureau of American Ethnology*, 1892–93, part 2. Washington, D.C.

Moran, Bruce T. 1981. German Prince-Practitioners: Aspects in the Development of Courtly Science, Technology, and Procedures in the Renaissance. *Technology and Culture* 22:253–274.

Murdock, George P., et al., eds. 1950. *Outline of Cultural Materials*. 3rd edition. New Haven CT: Human Relations Area Files.

Murphy, Gardner. 1947. *Personality: A Biosocial Approach to Origins and Structure*. New York: Harper.

Murray, Colin. 1980. Migrant Labour and Changing Family Structure in the Rural Periphery of Southern Africa. *Journal of Southern African Studies* 6:139–156.

Nash, Manning. 1958. Machine Age Maya: The Industrialization of a Guatemalan Community. American Anthropological Association, *Memoir* 87.

Nash, Philleo. 1955. The Place of Religious Revivalism in the Formation of the Intercultural Community on Klamath Reservation. In *Social Anthropology of North American Tribes*. 2nd edition. Fred Eggan, ed. Chicago: University of Chicago Press.

Newcomb, Theodore M. 1954. *Social Psychology.* New York: Dryden Press.

O'Hara, John. 1954. *Appointment in Samarra.* New York: New American Library.

Papoonan's Revelation. n.d. Some Remarks made by a person who accompanied Papunahool . . . as far as Bethlehem. Indians, Box 9-A, Friends Historical Society Collection, Swarthmore College Library, Swarthmore PA.

Parker, Arthur C. 1913. The Code of Handsome Lake, the Seneca Prophet. *New York State Museum Bulletin 163.* Albany.

————. 1916. The Constitution of the Five Nations. *New York State Museum Bulletin 184.* Albany.

Parker, Ely S. n.d. Ms. on Medicine Men and Indian Dances. In Parker Collection, 1802–1846. Henry E. Huntington Library, San Marino CA.

Partridge, Loren, and Randolph Starn. 1980. *A Renaissance Likeness: Art and Culture in Raphael's Julius II.* Berkeley: University of California Press.

Passavant, Johann D. 1972 [1872]. *Raphael of Urbino and His Father Giovanni Santi.* New York: Garland Publishers.

Peary, Robert E. 1907. *Nearest the Pole.* New York: Doubleday, Page.

Peckham, Howard H. 1947. *Pontiac and the Indian Uprising.* Princeton NJ: Princeton University Press.

Peterson, Donald B., et al. 1950. Role of Hypnosis in Differentiation of Epileptic from Convulsive-Like Seizures. *American Journal of Psychiatry* 107:428–443.

Petrie, W. M. Flinders. 1911. *The Revolutions of Civilisation.* New York: Harper and Brothers.

Petrullo, Vincenzo. 1934. *The Diabolic Root.* Philadelphia: University of Pennsylvania Press.

Piaget, Jean. 1926. *Language and Thought of the Child.* London: Kegan Paul.

Polanyi, Karl. 1944. *The Great Transformation.* New York: Farrar and Rinehart.

Pope-Hennessy, John. 1970. *Raphael.* New York: New York University Press.

Post, Christian Frederick. 1942. Journal . . . to the Great Council of the Different Indian Nations, 1760. Friends Historical Society collection, Swarthmore College Library: copy made by the Pennsylvania Historical Commission, Harrisburg.

Radcliffe-Brown, Alfred R. 1965 [1925]. The Mother's Brother in South Africa. In *Structure and Function in Primitive Society.* A. R. Radcliffe-Brown, ed. Pp. 15–31. New York: Free Press.

Radin, Paul. 1927. *Primitive Man as Philosopher.* New York: D. Appleton.

————. 1956. *The Trickster: A Study in American Indian Mythology.* New York: Philosophical Library.

Rasmussen, Knud, and Niels Rasmussen. 1915. *Foran Dagens Ooje: Liv I Grønland.* Copenhagen.

Redfield, Robert. 1953. *The Primitive World and Its Transformations.* Ithaca NY: Cornell University Press.

Rodahl, K. 1957. Human Acclimatization to Cold. Arctic Aeromedical Laboratory, Technical Report 57–21.

Rogers, Carl R. 1942. *Counseling and Psychotherapy: Newer Concepts in Practice.* Boston: Houghton Mifflin.

———. 1951. *Client-Centered Therapy: Its Current Practice, Implications, and Theory.* Boston: Houghton Mifflin.

———. 1959. A Theory of Therapy, Personality, and Interpersonal Relationships, as Developed in the Client-Centered Framework. In *Psychology: A Study of a Science,* vol. 3. Sigmund Koch, ed. Pp. 184–256. New York: McGraw-Hill.

Rogers, Carl R., and Rosalind F. Dymond, eds. 1954. *Psychotherapy and Personality Change: Co-Ordinated Studies in the Client-Centered Approach.* Chicago: University of Chicago Press.

Sarbin, T. R. 1954. Role Theory. In *Handbook of Social Psychology,* vol. 1. Gardner Lindzey, ed. Pp. 223–258. Cambridge, Mass.: Addison-Wesley.

Sargant, S. Stansfield, and Marian W. Smith, eds. 1949. *Culture and Personality.* New York: Viking Fund.

Sargant, William. 1949. Some Cultural Group Abreactive Techniques and Their Relation to Modern Treatments. *Proceedings of the Royal Society of Medicine* 42:367–374.

———. 1951. The Mechanism of Conversion. *British Medical Journal* 2:311 et seq.

Schilder, Paul. 1935. *The Image and Appearance of the Human Body.* London: K. Paul, Trench, Trubner.

Schneider, David M. 1957. Typhoons on Yap. *Human Organization* 16:10–15.

Schneider, David M., and Lauriston Sharp. 1969. The Dream Life of a Primitive People: The Dreams of the Yir Yoront of Australia. American Anthropological Association, *Anthropological Studies* no. 1.

Schoolcraft, Henry R. 1839. *Algic Researches.* New York.

Schwartz, Theodore. 1954. The Changing Structure of the Manus Nativistic Movement. Paper read at annual meeting of the American Anthropological Association.

Scott, Duncan C. 1912. Traditional History of the Confederacy of the Six Nations. *Transactions of the Royal Society of Canada* 5:195–246.

Searles, H. F. 1959. The Effort to Drive the Other Person Crazy—An Element in the Aetiology and Psychotherapy of Schizophrenia. *British Journal of Medical Psychology* 32:1–18.

Selye, Hans. 1956. *The Stress of Life.* New York: McGraw-Hill.

Selye, Hans, and C. Fortier. 1950. Adaptive Reactions to Stress. *Psychosomatic Medicine* 12:149–157.

Sharp, Lauriston. 1952. Steel Axes for Stone Age Australians. In *Human Problems in*

Technological Change: A Casebook. Edward H. Spicer, ed.. Pp. 69–90. New York: Russell Sage Foundation.

Shelling, David H. 1935. *The Parathyroids in Health and Disease.* St. Louis: Mosby.

Sherif, Muzafer, and Hadley Cantril. 1947. *The Psychology of Ego-Involvements, Social Attitudes, and Identifications.* New York: Wiley.

Singer, Charles, E. J. Holmyard, A. R. Hall, and Trevor I. Williams, eds. 1958. *A History of Technology: Vol. 4, The Industrial Revolution, c1750–c1850.* Oxford: Clarendon Press.

Skinner, Dorothy. n.d. Seneca notes. Ms., Pennsylvania Historical and Museum Commission, Harrisburg, Pa. (copy loaned to the author by Merle H. Deardorff).

Smelser, Neil J. 1959. *Social Change in the Industrial Revolution.* Chicago: University of Chicago Press.

Smith, Alan K. 1973. The Peoples of Southern Mozambique: An Historical Survey. *Journal of African History* 14:565–580.

Smith, Marian W. 1952. Different Cultural Concepts of Past, Present, and Future: A Study of Ego Extension. *Psychiatry* 15:395–400.

———. 1954. Shamanism in the Shaker Religion of Northwest America. *Man* 54: 119–122.

Snygg, Donald, and Arthur W. Combs. 1949. *Individual Behavior.* New York: Harper.

Speck, Frank G. 1933. Notes on the Life of John Wilson, the Revealer of Peyote. *The General Magazine and Historical Chronicle.* Philadelphia: General Alumni Society, University of Pennsylvania 35:539–556.

———. 1941. *A Study of the Delaware Indian Big House Ceremony.* Harrisburg: Pennsylvania Historical Commission.

———. 1949. *Midwinter Rites of the Cayuga Longhouse.* Philadelphia: University of Pennsylvania Press.

Steward, Julian N. 1953. Evolution and Process. In *Anthropology Today.* Alfred. L. Kroeber, ed. Chicago: University of Chicago Press.

———. 1961. Alfred Louis Kroeber, 1876–1960. *American Anthropologist* 63:1038–1087

Symonds, Percival M. 1951. *The Ego and the Self.* New York: Appleton-Century-Crofts.

Tolman, E. D. 1948. Cognitive Maps in Rats and Men. *Psychological Review* 55:189–208.

———. 1949. The Psychology of Social Learning. *Journal of Social Issues.* Suppl. No. 3.

Tooth, Geoffrey. 1950. *Studies in Mental Illness in the Gold Coast.* London: H. M. Stationery Office.

Tylor, Edward B. 1874. *Primitive Culture.* New York: H. Holt and Company.

Underhill, Evelyn. 1955. *Mysticism: A Study in the Nature and Development of Man's Spiritual Consciousness.* New York: Noonday Press.

Van Onselen, Charles. 1982. *Studies in the Social and Economic History of the Witwatersrand, 1886–1914,* vols. 1 and 2. London: Longman.

Voget, Fred W. 1954. Reformative Tendencies in American Indian Nativistic Cults. Paper read at annual meeting of the American Anthropological Association.

Wallace, Anthony F. C. 1947. Political Organization and Land Tenure among the Northeastern Indians, 1600–1830. *Southwestern Journal of Anthropology* 13:301–321.

———. 1949. *King of the Delawares: Teedyuscung, 1700–1763.* Philadelphia: University of Pennsylvania Press.

———. 1952a. Handsome Lake and the Great Revival in the West. *American Quarterly* 4(2):149–165.

———. 1952b. Halliday Jackson's Journal to the Seneca Indians, 1798–1800. *Pennsylvania History* 19(2):117–147, (3):325–347.

———. 1953. A Science of Human Behavior. *Explorations* 3:127–136.

———. 1955. The Disruption of the Individual's Identification with his Culture in Disasters and Other Extreme Situations. Paper read at National Research Council, Committee on Disaster Studies, Conference on Theories of Human Behavior in Extreme Situations, Vassar College, Poughkeepsie NY.

———. 1956a. The Mazeway. *Explorations* (6).

———. 1956b. Revitalization Movements. *American Anthropologist* 58(2):264–281.

———. 1956c. Tornado in Worcester: An Exploratory Study of Individual and Community Behavior in an Extreme Situation. Washington, D.C.: National Academy of Sciences-National Research Council, Publication 392, Disaster Study No. 3.

———. 1956d. Mazeway Resynthesis: A Biocultural Theory of Religious Inspiration. *Transactions of the New York Academy of Sciences* 18: 626–638.

———. 1958. Dreams and the Wishes of the Soul: A Type of Psychoanalytic Theory among the Seventeenth Century Iroquois. *American Anthropologist* 60(2):234–248.

———. 1959a. Cultural Determinants of Response to Hallucinatory Experience. *A.M.A. Archives of General Psychiatry* 1:58–69.

———. 1959b. The Institutionalization of Cathartic and Control Strategies in Iroquois Religious Psychotherapy. In *Culture and Mental Health.* Marvin K. Opler, ed., Pp. 63–96. New York: MacMillan.

———. 1960. The Biocultural Theory of Schizophrenia. *International Record of Medicine* 173(11):700–714.

———. 1961. *Culture and Personality.* New York: Random House.

———. 1970a. *Culture and Personality.* 2nd edition. New York: Random House.

———. 1970b. *The Death and Rebirth of the Seneca.* New York: Alfred A. Knopf.

————. 1972. Paradigmatic Processes in Culture Change. *American Anthropologist* 74:467–478.

————. 1978. *Rockdale: The Growth of an American Village in the Early Industrial Revolution.* New York: Alfred A. Knopf.

————. 1982. *The Social Context of Innovation: Bureaucrats, Families, and Heroes in the Early Industrial Revolution, as Foreseen in Bacon's New Atlantis.* Princeton: Princeton University Press.

————. 1983. The Perception of Risk in Nineteenth-Century Anthracite Mining Operations. *Proceedings of the American Philosophical Society* 127:99–106.

————. 1987. *St. Clair: A Nineteenth-Century Coal Town's Experience with a Disaster-Prone Industry.* New York: Knopf.

Wallace, Paul A. W. 1946. *The White Roots of Peace.* Philadelphia: University of Pennsylvania Press.

Wallis, Wilson D. 1918. *Messiahs: Christian and Pagan.* Boston: R. G. Badger.

————. 1943. *Messiahs: Their Role in Civilization.* Washington, D.C.: American Council on Public Affairs.

Weber, Max. 1930. *The Protestant Ethic and the Spirit of Capitalism.* Translated by Talcott Parsons. London: Allen and Unwin.

————. 1946. *From Max Weber: Essays in Sociology.* Translated and edited by H. Gerth and C. W. Mills. New York: Oxford University Press.

————. 1947. *The Theory of Social and Economic Organization.* Translated and edited by A. M. Henderson and Talcott Parsons. New York: Oxford University Press.

Wenkart, A. 1962. The Self in Existentialism. In *Fundamentals of Psychology: Psychology of the Self.* Earnest Harms, ed. *Annals of the New York Academy of Science* 96:814–822.

Wheelis, Alan. 1958. *The Quest for Identity.* New York: Norton.

White, Leslie. 1959. The Concept of Culture. *American Anthropologist* 61:227–251.

Whitney, Harry. 1911. *Hunting with the Eskimos.* New York: Century.

Williams, F. E. 1923. The Vailala Madness and the Destruction of Native Ceremonies in the Gulf Division. Port Moresby: Territory of Papua, Anthropology Report (No. 4).

————. 1934. The Vailala Madness in Retrospect. In *Essays Presented to C. G. Seligman.* E. E. Evans-Pritchard, Raymond Firth, Bronislaw Malinowski, and Isaac Schapera, eds. London: K. Paul, Trench, Trubner, and Co.

Williams, Gardner. 1905. *The Diamond Mines of South Africa,* 2 vols. New York: Buck.

Wilson, Francis. 1972. *Labour in the South African Gold Mines, 1911–1969.* Cambridge: Cambridge University Press.

Winters, Clyde. 1977. The Importance of Mine Workers in Southern Africa. *Journal of African Studies* 4:452–473.

Witthoft, John. 1949. *Green Corn Ceremonialism in the Eastern Woodlands*. Ann Arbor: University of Michigan Press.

World Federation for Mental Health. 1957. Identity. Introductory study no. 1.

Wright, Muriel. 1951. *A Guide to the Indians of Oklahoma*. Norman: University of Oklahoma Press.

Wylie, Ruth C. 1961. *The Self Concept: A Critical Survey of Pertinent Research Literature*. Lincoln: University of Nebraska Press.

Young, Sherilynn. 1977. Fertility and Famine: Women's Agricultural History in Southern Mozambique. In *The Roots of Rural Poverty in Central and Southern Africa*. Robin Palmer and Neil Parsons, eds. Pp. 66–81. Berkeley: University of California Press.

Zeisberger, David. 1910. History of the Northern American Indians. *Ohio Archaeological and Historical Quarterly* 19:1–189.

Source Acknowledgments

Chapter 1: "Revitalization Movements." *American Anthropologist* 58(2):264–281 (1956). Reprinted by permission of the American Anthropological Association. Not for further reproduction.

Chapter 2: "The Dekanawideh Myth Analyzed as the Record of a Revitalization Movement." *Ethnohistory* 5(2):118–130 (1958).

Chapter 3: "New Religions among the Delaware Indians, 1600–1900." *Southwestern Journal of Anthropology* 12(1):1–21 (1956).

Chapter 4: "Handsome Lake and the Decline of the Iroquois Matriarchate." In *Kinship and Culture*. Francis L. K. Hsu, ed. Pp. 367–376. Chicago: Aldine, 1971.

Chapter 5: "Paradigmatic Processes in Culture Change." *American Anthropologist* 74(3):467–478 (1972). Reprinted by permission of the American Anthropological Association. Not for further reproduction.

Chapter 6: "Technology in Culture: The Meaning of Cultural Fit." *Science in Context* 8(2):293–324 (1995). Reprinted with the permission of Cambridge University Press.

Chapter 7: Paradigms and Revolutions in the Arts. Unpublished paper presented at the Raphael Symposium, University of Notre Dame, South Bend, Indiana (1983).

Chapter 8: "The Disaster Syndrome." In *Tornado in Worcester: An Exploratory Study of Individual and Community Behavior in Extreme Situations*. Washington, D.C.: National Academy of Sciences-National Research Council, Publication 392. Pp. 109–111, 116–118, 123–129, 140–146, 151–159 (1956).

Chapter 9: "Mazeway Resynthesis: A Biocultural Theory of Religious Inspiration." *Transactions of the New York Academy of Sciences* 18:626–638 (1956).

Chapter 10: "Mazeway Disintegration: The Individual's Perception of Socio-Cultural Disorganization." *Human Organization* 16(2):23–27 (1957).

Chapter 11: "Dreams and the Wishes of the Soul: A Type of Psychoanalytic Theory among the Seventeenth Century Iroquois." *American Anthropologist* 60(2):234–248 (1958). Reprinted by permission of the American Anthropological Association. Not for further reproduction.

Chapter 12: "The Psychic Unity of Human Groups." Excerpt from the Introduction to Anthony F. C. Wallace, *Culture and Personality*, 2nd Edition. Pp. 15–37. New York: Random House, 1970.

Chapter 13: "Mental Illness, Biology, and Culture." In Francis L. K. Hsu, editor, *Psychological Anthropology.* Pp. 255–295. Homewood, Illinois: Dorsey Press, 1961.

Chapter 14: "The Trip." In Richard E. Hicks and Paul Jay Fink, editors, *Psychedelic Drugs: Proceedings of a Hahnemann Medical College and Hospital Symposium.* Pp. 151–156. New York and London: Grune and Stratton, 1969.

Chapter 15: "The Identity Struggle." Raymond D. Fogelson, co-author. In Ivan Boszormenyi-Nagy and James L. Framo, editors, *Intensive Family Therapy: Theoretical and Practical Perspectives.* Pp. 365–406. New York: Harper and Row, 1965.

Index